ITALY'S GREAT CHEFS
AND THEIR SECRETS

WHITE STAR PUBLISHERS

TEXT
DEVELOPED BY ACADEMIA BARILLA
WITH THE SUPPORT OF
GIANCARLO GONIZZI AND MARIA GRAZIA VILLA

INTRODUCTIONS
GUIDO, LUCA AND PAOLO BARILLA
GIANLUIGI ZENTI
MARIO BATALI
PAUL BARTOLOTTA

PHOTOGRAPHS
LUCIO ROSSI

PROJECT EDITOR
VALERIA MANFERTO DE FABIANIS

EDITORIAL COORDINATION
LAURA ACCOMAZZO

GRAPHIC DESIGN
MARINELLA DEBERNARDI

PHOTOGRAPHY ASSISTANT
ALESSANDRO DELCANALE

CONTENTS

A THOUSAND ITALIAN CUISINES

There's no such thing as one national gastronomy in Italy. However, there's a food and wine scene that is so vast, in terms of its infinite variations and local abundance, that it can proudly represent this unique situation around the world.

There are different reasons for this, which are essentially of an historical and geographical nature.

History paints a picture of a country that, after the decline of the Roman Empire, was divided into courts, principalities, and small states for centuries, which were often influenced by foreign rulers.

Due to an absence of unitary guidelines, each city and territory therefore laid down its own independent paths in the kitchen, often working and adapting exotic influences into its own culture which still remain and are preserved today, after the country's unification in the nineteenth century.

However, the real reasons for our gastronomic good fortune are based on an even more deep-seated reality. Cuisine in Italy is created using genuine and delicious products, proffered by the generosity of nature in its many forms and enhanced by one hundred percent innate Italian creativity and ingenuity, which motivated our peoples to identify ways in which to "salvage" every foodstuff that was available (even the less noble parts) through suitable, varied, and complicated recipes, capable of turning even the simplest of fare into a unique gastronomic experience.

Our cooking is therefore based on a myriad of products determined by the climate and terrain of the land. The seas and mountains, market gardens and forests, lakes and plains have all marked the birth of unique ingredients, as unique as our land. This gives rise to a cuisine that is deeply anchored to tradition and the characteristics of the regions. The Italy of a thousand bell towers is also the Italy of a thousand cuisines and just as many products, once the offspring of instinctive knowledge, handed down by generations and in harmony with the culture of the place, now envied – and copied – all over the world. This is the reason why Barilla, which has distributed one of our country's most characteristic products – pasta – all over the world, decided to found the *Academia Barilla* to enhance the Italian gastronomic tradition.

Academia Barilla promotes courses to spread the knowledge of our gastronomy, distributes the best of Italy's products, and spreads our culture of flavors through publications such as this, which recounts the wealth of food and wine in our country through the voices of thirty of the most valued Italian chefs and the extraordinary heritage of products par excellence which past generations left us as an heirloom. *Academia Barilla* is situated in Parma, the heart of the Food Valley, a city much appreciated for its food products – from Parmigiano-Reggiano cheese to Prosciutto

DI PARMA, PASTA, AND NUMEROUS SPECIALTIES – A STONE'S THROW AWAY FROM THE CITY CENTER, WITH THE STONEWORK OF THE BAPTISTERY BY BENEDETTO ANTELAMI AND THE DOMES FRESCOED BY DA CORREGGIO, THE TEATRO REGIO, THE TEMPLE TO OPERA, WHICH HAS CONSECRATED THE GENIUS OF VERDI AND TOSCANINI OVER TIME.

CROSSING THE THRESHOLD OF *ACADEMIA BARILLA* MEANS ENTERING A STATE-OF-THE-ART ESTABLISHMENT IN TERMS OF ITS EQUIPMENT AND MATERIALS USED: FROM THE 90-SEAT AUDITORIUM TO THE SENSORY ANALYSIS LABORATORY, FROM THE HALL USED FOR PRACTICAL TRAINING TO THE MULTIPURPOSE SPACES, AND FINALLY THE GASTRONOMIC LIBRARY, AN EXCEPTIONAL TOOL OF KNOWLEDGE ON THE EVOLUTION OF GASTRONOMY AND TASTE, WITH A PATRIMONY OF OVER 8,500 VOLUMES AND PERIODICALS (FROM THE SIXTEENTH CENTURY TO THE PRESENT DAY), THOUSANDS OF HISTORICAL MENUS (FROM THE NINETEENTH CENTURY ONWARDS) AND HUNDREDS OF GASTRONOMY-RELATED PUBLICATIONS (FROM THE SIXTEENTH CENTURY ONWARDS).

NEVERTHELESS, *ACADEMIA BARILLA* REACHES OUT TO THE WORLD ESPECIALLY THROUGH ITS PRODUCTS, PUBLICATIONS, AND CULTURAL INITIATIVES, AN UNTIRING AMBASSADOR OF THIS COUNTRY WHERE THE BEST INGREDIENTS MAKE SURE THAT EVERY FLAVOR IS TRANSFORMED INTO A MEMORABLE EXPERIENCE. IT'S UNIQUE, JUST LIKE ITALY.

GUIDO, LUCA, AND PAOLO BARILLA

A JOURNEY TO ITALY:
WHERE BEAUTY MEETS GOODNESS

Italy is a truly unique country: a long strip of land that stretches out of the European continent for over 800 miles (1,300 kilometers) into the waters the Mediterranean Sea. In this sea-kissed land, many populations have left their mark over the centuries. So much so that today Italy is considered – and rightly so – a true open-air museum: monuments and works of art, architecture and sculpture, landscape and nature all blend into one complete and totally fascinating entity.

But the mark left by the various populations – Etruscans, Greeks, Romans, Longobards, Byzantines, Spanish, French, Austrians, just to name the most famous – is evident not only in aesthetic tastes but also, and above all, in culinary tastes. There are more than 170 "typical" products that are linked to a specific geographical area and to certain ingredients, and dozens of food "regions" characterize the country, making it a real trove of traditions and flavors. Thus the "journey to Italy" - that Grand Tour which, for the European aristocracy, was considered since the 17th century an indispensable part of a young person's education – became an unrepeatable experience in which beauty and goodness merged, making the ancient Greek ideal of perfection a reality.

Since Medieval times the journey to the mild Mediterranean climate represented a fundamental experience; artists in search of work, merchants looking for new merchandise and new markets and pilgrims searching for their own spirituality or for forgiveness on the tomb of Peter the Apostle, traveled all over the country. Over the centuries, the motives varied and, beginning in the 17th century, the journey acquired added value due to its own intrinsic qualities. A trip to Italy was longer made for specific ends, but as a unique and sole objective in itself, to satisfy a bold curiosity. It was not just a journey taken in the name of knowledge and awareness, but also for diversion and pure delight. Thus, the sons and daughters of the European aristocracy embarked for Italy, intent on maturing an education that derived from that lost classicism of which Italy held the last vestige and memory. They found, along with other young tourists, colors so rare in their cold native lands--warm hues and unexpected

TASTES IN A PALETTE OF EMOTIONS, EXPERIENCES THAT WOULD ALWAYS REMAIN IN THE MEMORY AND THE EDUCATION OF THE TRAVELER.

THE CENTURIES OLD STRATIFICATION OF TRADITIONS AND CUSTOMS AND THE CREATIVITY OF THE ITALIAN PEOPLE HAVE GIVEN RISE TO AN EXTREMELY VARIED CULINARY HERITAGE, SO DIFFERENT FROM THE UNIFIED CUISINE OF THE EUROPEAN NOBILITY WHICH WAS INFLUENCED VERY LITTLE BY LOCAL CUSTOM AND CHARACTERIZED BY AN ABUNDANCE OF MEAT AND FISH AND COMPLEX PREPARATION IN WHICH DECORATION TOOK PRECEDENCE OVER TASTE.

THIS BOOK, TAKING UP THE *"GRAND TOUR"* TRADITION ONCE AGAIN, SEEKS TO PROPOSE A LONG JOURNEY THROUGH THE VARIOUS CUISINES OF THE ITALIAN PENINSULA. A JOURNEY, FROM NORTH TO SOUTH, FROM THE MOUNTAINS TO THE SEA, DIVIDED INTO THIRTY SECTIONS, WHICH IS THE NUMBER OF "CUISINES" OF A STRONG CHARACTER THAT CAN STILL BE IDENTIFIED TODAY IN ITALY AND WHICH DO NOT ALWAYS COINCIDE WITH THE ADMINISTRATIVE REGIONS (OF WHICH THERE ARE ONLY TWENTY) INTO WHICH THE TERRITORY IS DIVIDED.

YOUNG COOKS WERE CHOSEN TO MAKE THESE TRADITIONS COME TO LIFE THROUGH STORIES AND RECIPES, BECAUSE THEY ARE PASSIONATE ABOUT THEIR MISSION AND VERY MUCH IN LOVE WITH THEIR OWN LAND. THEY ARE CAPABLE OF TRANSMITTING ANCIENT FLAVORS WITH FRESH EYES AND A SENSITIVITY TOWARDS TODAY. THE RESULT IS A BOOK THAT IS FILLED WITH SPECIFIC AND UNIQUE INGREDIENTS AND PRODUCTS, BUT ALSO DEMONSTRATES HOW THE COLORS, HISTORY AND MONUMENTS OF EVERY ITALIAN REGION "PLAY THEIR PART" IN THE KITCHEN, BLENDING VISION AND FLAVOR IN A CREATIVE, INTENSELY EMOTIONAL EXPERIENCE THAT HIGHLIGHTS THE TASTE OF QUALITY.

ACCORDING TO THE STYLE AND THE *MISSION* OF THE "ACADEMIA BARILLA".

THE ACADEMIA BARILLA WAS FOUNDED IN PARMA IN 2004 WITH THE OBJECTIVE OF BEING AN INTERNATIONAL CENTER DEDICATED TO ITALIAN GASTRONOMIC CULTURE, WITH THE CAPABILITY OF PROVIDING TRAINING, SERVICES AND PRODUCTS THAT HAVE BEEN SELECTED WITH GREAT CARE FROM THE ITALIAN GASTRONOMIC HERITAGE.

GIANLUIGI ZENTI
DIRECTOR ACADEMIA BARILLA

THE LOVE OF CREATION

There is a common misperception around the world that there is something called Italian cooking. In reality, 60 million people who live to shop and cook and hunt and fish and cook and forage and cook have all agreed to be called Italian even though they really feel more attached to a more specific piece of earth--the one they were born on. The variations from town to town in Emilia-Romagna in what we perceive to be a classic Italian recipe like Ragu Bolognese may seem minor to the casual observer, but can, in fact, divide a family completely in an all-out culinary point-of-view battle. To me, this captures the idea that there is nothing in the world more constantly delicious and endlessly fascinating than the regional cooking of Italia. The name Barilla is synonymous in the world with Italian food and the love and creation of it. This book is the one single book all cooks will need on a deserted island and even on a crowded one like the one I live on.

Mario Batali

MUCH MORE THAN JUST
A COLLECTION OF RECIPES

The book in front of you is more than a collection of recipes. It's a journey – a surprising journey, for it even took me back in time.

As I turned the pages, I couldn't help but stop and recall my first meal in Italy. I was just 18 years old – a kid from Milwaukee landing in Rome. An apprentice position was waiting for me the following day in a restaurant far to the North. I took a bus from the airport to the train station and stared at a giant board listing arrivals and departures. I'd never seen anything like it. I tried to make sense of the numbers. It didn't help that they were furiously spinning to announce the next arrivals and departures.

I figured out how to translate the board just in time to discover that the last train had departed and I couldn't get a train until the next day. I asked about an inexpensive hotel at the information booth. A kind receptionist told me to go to the Hotel Rafaello. At the hotel, I asked about an inexpensive restaurant and was directed to a small trattoria two doors down. Seated by the window, I studied the menu. There was a dish I recognized from back home, *Saltimbocca di Vitello alla Romana*. It felt good to order something familiar. It's a textbook dish. But the food that arrived in front of me was a revelation. The veal tasted different, so delicate, the incredible perfume of fresh tiny sage leaves, the sweetness of the prosciutto, the grassiness of the butter--in fact, there was absolutely nothing familiar any longer. The tastes in that single meal transformed a six-month restaurant apprenticeship into eight years of study of the highest order as I worked my way through more than a dozen restaurants from Sicily to the Alps. The chefs and their recipes, on these pages, not only took me back to that first meal, but nearly thirty years later they're inviting me to take new journeys. Each day as I step into my kitchen I am in search of these "taste memories" and find myself so often chasing the past, so to speak, to evoke the memories of my life there. It is those smells and flavors that are the most heartfelt memories to me. Paging through this book made me relive these intense emotions. I see myself as a student of Italian culinary history and culture and I am reminded by this book, that as well versed as I may feel on

THE SUBJECT OF ITALIAN COOKING, THE BEST CHEFS IN ITALY HAVE TRACED AN UNPARALLELED JOURNEY OF "SAPERI E SAPORI" OR "KNOWLEDGE OF TRADITION AND TASTE" THAT I CAN ONLY LEARN FROM. IN THIS EXTRAORDINARY GASTRONOMIC PAINTING OF CONTEMPORARY REGIONAL ITALIAN COOKING, BORN OUT OF THEIR GREAT RESPECT FOR CENTURY OLD CULINARY TRADITIONS AND THE RIGOROUS SELECTION OF INDIGENOUS REGIONAL INGREDIENTS OF THE HIGHEST QUALITY, EMERGES A SEARCH FOR AUTHENTIC TRADI-

TIONAL FLAVORS THAT ARE ADAPTED TO TODAY'S MODERN CULTURE WITHOUT BETRAYING IT'S FOUNDATION. TO ME "SAPERI E SAPORI" IS THE WISDOM TO SEARCH FOR CONTEMPORARY TASTES WITHIN THE FRAMEWORK OF TRADITION.

THE FUTURE OF THE ITALIAN KITCHEN IS WITHIN THESE PAGES. IT IS A PLACE WHERE TECHNICALLY PROFICIENT CHEFS USE AS INSPIRATION THE REGIONAL HOME COOKING AND ITS INGREDIENTS; THROUGH TECHNIQUE THEY ELEVATE A DISH TO A MORE SOPHISTICATED LEVEL WITHOUT LOSING ITS SOUL, WHICH IS ROOTED IN REGIONAL TRADITION. THIS VOLUME IS THAT STORY, A STORY OF ART AND CULTURE AND HOW IT PLAYS A PROMINENT ROLE IN THE FLAVORS THAT BLEND TO FORM THIS MEMORABLE LANDSCAPE. HOW THE PERFUMES OF COASTAL ITALY AND THOSE OF THE RICH COUNTRYSIDE CREATE THIS EXTRAORDINARY MARRIAGE. TODAY, THANKS TO THESE PRECIOUS PAGES, MANY OF THE CULINARY SECRETS OF THE ITALIAN KITCHEN MAY NOW FIND THEIR WAY INTO KITCHENS ALL AROUND THE WORLD AND ALLOW ALL TO TASTE THE FLAVORS AND FEEL THE EMOTIONS OF THIS MOST UNIQUE PLACE ON EARTH - MY BELOVED ITALY.

PAUL BARTOLOTTA

ACADEMIA BARILLA

AN AMBASSADOR OF ITALIAN GASTRONOMY AROUND THE WORLD

ACADEMIA BARILLA IS THE INTERNATIONAL CENTER DEDICATED TO THE DEVELOPMENT AND PROMOTION OF ITALIAN GASTRONOMIC CULTURE OFFERING TRAINING, SERVICES, AND RIGOROUSLY SELECTED PRODUCTS, WHICH HAVE BEEN CHOSEN AS PART OF THE ITALIAN GASTRONOMIC HERITAGE. ACADEMIA BARILLA WAS FOUNDED IN 2004 WITH ITS HEADQUARTERS IN PARMA, THE CAPITAL OF ITALIAN CUISINE FAMOUS WORLDWIDE FOR THE QUALITY OF ITS LOCAL PRODUCTS AND ITS PRESTIGIOUS FOOD INDUSTRY, AND IS THE IDEAL MEETING POINT BETWEEN THE LEADING REPRESENTATIVES OF FOOD AND WINE AND LOVERS OF THE ITALIAN FOOD CULTURE.

ACADEMIA BARILLA WAS SET UP WITH THE MISSION OF DEFENDING AND SAFEGUARDING ITALIAN FOOD PRODUCTS FROM FORGERIES AND IMPROPER USES OF ORIGINAL TRADE NAMES AND BRANDS, PROMOTING AND SPREADING THE UNDERSTANDING OF THESE PRODUCTS AND ITALIAN COOKING WITH SPECIAL EVENTS ORGANIZED IN PARTNERSHIP WITH LEADING INSTITUTIONS AND ENDORSERS, AS WELL AS DEVELOPING AND SUPPORTING ITALIAN GASTRONOMY BY INVESTING IN THE RESTAURANT INDUSTRY AND THE IMPLEMENTATION OF SPECIAL SERVICES FOR ITS OPERATORS.

THE HEADQUARTERS OF ACADEMIA BARILLA ARE LOCATED IN THE OLD BARILLA PASTA-MAKING FACTORY AREA, RE-DESIGNED BY RENZO PIANO, AND UNITES THE SAFEGUARDING OF TRADITION WITH THE UTMOST IN MODERN INNOVATION. IT IS EQUIPPED WITH AN AUDITORIUM, A SENSORY ANALYSIS LABORATORY, A HALL USED FOR PRACTICAL TRAINING, MULTIPURPOSE SPACES, AND AN EXTREMELY COMPREHENSIVE GASTRONOMIC LIBRARY.

ACADEMIA BARILLA ALSO HOLDS A RANGE OF TRAINING COURSES

THAT IS VAST ENOUGH TO SATISFY A WHOLE ARRAY OF DIFFERENT NEEDS: FROM GASTRONOMIC EXPERTS TO SIMPLE FOOD LOVERS, FROM PROFESSIONAL CHEFS TO AMATEUR COOKS. THE TEACHING STAFF OF *ACADEMIA BARILLA* IS MADE UP OF A TEAM OF INTERNATIONALLY RENOWNED CHEFS AND WITH THE CONTRIBUTION OF LEADING VISITING CHEFS, INCLUDING MORENO CEDRONI, SCOTT CONANT, GIANCARLO PERBELLINI, CARLO CRACCO, ETTORE BOCCHIA, ALFONSO IACCARINO, VALENTINO MERCATILLII, GIADA DE LAURENTIIS, ANDREA ZANIN, IGINIO MASSARI, AND MANY OTHERS.

ACADEMIA BARILLA IS ALSO WELL-POSITIONED IN THE FIELD OF CORPORATE SERVICES, OFFERING SOLUTIONS FOR SALES MEETINGS, PRESS CONFERENCES, AND PRODUCT PRESENTATIONS, INCENTIVE PROGRAMS, MEETINGS AND CONVENTIONS, THEMED SEMINARS AND CONVENTIONS, CULINARY-RELATED MANAGEMENT TRAINING COURSES, TEAM BUILDING, AND MUCH MORE.

ACADEMIA BARILLA ALSO OFFERS GOURMET TOURS: PERSONALIZED FOOD AND WINE EXPERIENCES LASTING FROM ONE TO SEVEN DAYS. THE FOOD AND WINE TOURS ALLOW ONE TO EXPERIENCE THE BEST OF ITALIAN CULTURE AND GASTRONOMY: FROM THE TRADITIONAL ACETAIE (VINEGAR AGEING ESTABLISH-MENTS) OF MODENA AND REGGIO EMILIA TO THE RENOWNED WINE AND SALAMI CELLARS, FROM OPERA CONCERTS TO SHOPPING IN STORES AND OUTLETS SELLING QUALITY ITALIAN PRODUCTS, FROM DINNERS ORGANIZED IN CASTLES AND HISTORIC HOMES TO TOTAL RELAXATION AND FITNESS IN OUR DAY SPAS.

ACADEMIA BARILLA DISTRIBUTES AND APPENDS ITS SIGNATURE TO A RANGE OF HIGH-QUALITY ITALIAN SPECIALTIES, SELECTED BY LEADING CHEFS AND CATERING EXPERTS, PRODUCED BY SMALL ITALIAN ARTISAN COMPANIES.

THE SELECTION INCLUDES MATURE CHEESES (PARMIGIANO REGGIANO PDO, PECORINO TOSCANO PDO, PECORINO GRAN CRU SARDO, AND PECORINO DOLCE), PROSCIUTTO DI PARMA, SALAME DI PARMA, PDO EXTRA-VIRGIN OLIVE OILS FROM A RANGE OF ORIGINS, ACETO BALSAMICO TRADIZIONALE DI MODENA, COMPOTES AND PRESERVES (GOURMET CHIANTI WINE JELLY; SPICY FIG COMPOTE; AND FRESH PEARS WITH BALSAMIC VINEGAR OF MODENA) AND SICILIAN SEA SALT FLAVORED WITH BLACK OLIVES OR WITH FRESH ORANGE ZEST.

ACADEMIA BARILLA WAS AWARDED WITH THE IMPRESA–CULTURA AWARD IN 2007 FOR THE PROMO-TION OF ITALIAN GASTRONOMIC CULTURE AND CREATIVITY AROUND THE WORLD.

THE CUISINE OF VALLE D'AOSTA

Here the Alps are sharp peaks, which are white-capped even in summer. The summits are mirrored in the clear lakes that rest silently along the mountain slopes. The winding course of the river Dora Baltea is the main feature of the landscape, which descends twisting from the roof of Europe to the Padan plain.

The *Parco Nazionale del Gran Paradiso* extends amid all this natural beauty. Founded in 1922 to protect the old hunting reserves of the House of Savoy, it is the forefather of Italian national parks. Its symbol is the steinbeck and it is home to larches, firs, pines, chamois, marmots, and golden eagles. Valle d'Aosta is not only about scenery. Heir to the proud civilization of the Salassi people, it has always maintained its own identity. This little boundary region, despite the smallness of the territory, is rich in external influences, with a linear yet important history and a varied and interesting culture.

Formerly inhabited by populations of Gallic origin, after the Roman domination and savage people that caused it to become a territory of the Franks again, it was part of the kingdom of Bourgogne and then the Savoy duchy until the Kingdom of Italy was created. The transalpine influence is therefore the most significant in the region's culture. It remains in the dialect, of French origin, and also in the gastronomic traditions, albeit often revisited from a more local perspective. In the Valdostan area, there is also an independent culture that has kept its original customs and costumes over time, the Walser population, a group that originally settled in the Valle del Lys long ago.

The Medieval and Renaissance periods also left important marks here. More than 100 castles and mansions perch on rocks, precipices, and high summits, creating a seductive continuity between art and nature.

In Aosta, Romanism and Medievalism interweave, evidence of a remarkably interesting era. The city is entered through Porta Pretoria, one of the four gates that originally provided access to the city, protected by a defensive wall with high towers. One can admire many churches, the cathedral, the arch of Augustus, and the Roman theater and amphitheater. Close by are the ski resorts of Courmayeur under Mont Blanc, La Thuile, Cogne and, at the foot of the superb Matterhorn, Breuil-Cervinia connected by a cable car to the glaciers of Zermatt. All year round, the clean, crisp air is mixed with the aromas of the greenery, wood and good home cooking.

Apart from the era of the savages, agriculture and hunting have always flourished in the area.

The almost total absence of dried pasta and rice dishes stands out in the culinary traditions of Valle d'Aosta, with the exception of some dishes that combine wheat flour with other flours that are more commonly used in mountain areas, such as fettuccine pasta made with chestnut flour. So-called *"alla bava,"* or potato gnocchi, are served with the area's most typical cheese, Fontina.

In terms of the pasta course, the region offers a wide range of alternative offerings, from a soup based on day-old rye bread to polenta cooked in copper pots to the delicious aromas of the region's famous fondue. Soups are often made with bread and vegetables gathered in fields and constitute the basic diet of farmers; they usually combine with meat, stock, and cheeses and are present even in the richest of restaurants. Fondue is also typical of Valle d'Aosta, despite its clearly French origins. The Valdostan cheese fondue uses Fontina as its base, which is ideal for this dish due to its creaminess, but it is rich in ingredients like eggs, which do not feature in the versions of the bordering countries.

In Walser gastronomy, *"chnéf-fléne"* feature, a dish consisting of gnocchetti made from milk and flour, then served with melted butter or cheese fondue.

The meat courses are similar to other Italian recipes or dishes from the neighboring countries: cutlets, game stew, *Carbonade* (meat preserved in salt and cooked in red wine), and trout in red wine.

When you think of the tables set up in one of the many welcoming *baite* (chalets) in Valle d'Aosta, your mind turns to Fontina PDO (see box). A regional product, fontinia is famous not only for its quality, but also for the image that it conjures, of flowering meadows and clear skies that seem to go on forever.

Created in the same mountains, other products accompany Fontina in terms of quality and tradition: *Fromazdo* PDO, with its compact white, semi-sweet cheese when it is fresh and yellow, spicy and slightly salty flavor when left to age; *Reblec*, the toma cheeses of the Gressoney valleys and Bassa Valle; and *Séras*, ricotta ripened in straw. All share the intense flavor of milk and herbs from the aromatic mountain pastures.

In terms of charcuterie, there are some unique products like *Mocetta*, which was originally made from steinbeck leg meat and is now mostly produced from chamois or beef; *Boudin*, black pudding that mixes potatoes or turnips with meat and blood; *Teuteun*, dried meat from cow udders that have been salted and flavored with herbs; and some hams aged in special microclimates that are particularly aromatic, such as *Jambon de Brosses* or *Saint-Marcel*. There are also excellent sausages.

Typical of the Valle d'Arnad is the lard with a protected designation of origin, flavored with herbs, sweet and delicate, delicious served on slices on black bread as a sublime starter. It can sometimes be served with a thin layer of floral honey. Rhododendron honey is one of the most esteemed, which comes from meadows 1,200 meters above sea level. The aroma of this honey is intense and recalls the woods and meadows.

Apples are also grown in the region, especially the Renetta variety, perhaps imported from France, whose ideal habitat is the fresh alpine valleys. Both local apples and honey are widely used in desserts, as are the locally grown Martin pears.

Despite the region's modest area, grape vines are cultivated and about twenty Valdostan wines are clustered in the protected designation of origin of Valle d'Aosta, such as Donnas, Enfer d'Arvier, Blanc de Morgex et de la Salle, and Torrette.

FONTINA PDO

This is one of the first mountain cheeses to have received the PDO recognition. Full-fat Fontina is produced all over the region. The deep flavor of the grass, especially if from the summer pastures, lies at the heart of its quality. Ageing takes place from four to five months, in natural caves or controlled environments. As soon as it is cut, fontina offers the palate a compact and elastic cheese that is soft and easy to melt. Combined with milk, butter, and egg yolks, it is the main ingredient of fondue, one of the area's most famous and nourishing dishes. It is eaten with croutons, polenta, and *vol-au-vents*. It should be served with red wine that is young, fresh, and aromatic, like Petit Rouge or Bonarda dell'Oltrepo Pavese.

ALFIO FASCENDINI

RESTAURANT VECCHIO RISTORO DA ALFIO E KATIA - AOSTA

It seems like a fairytale, but it's a true story with a happy ending. When 15 year-old Alfio Fascendini left his home in Val Chiavenna to go and wash pots and pans at a restaurant, he had no possessions and just one dream: to become a chef. He came from a humble farming family and was the second of seven children. It was difficult for him to surrender his dearest attachments knowing that so many sacrifices would be in front of him, but his ambition could not wait. Strong-willed, lively and positive, he took on the challenge. *"It's exactly 30 years since I left home,"* he tells us, *"and the idea that I am now a famous chef, to whose restaurant customers come from all over the world, gives me great satisfaction, like being able to provide my parents with priceless emotions through my cooking. Mine and Katia's sacrifices, the truly special person to whom I have been married for twenty years, have mostly been repaid."*

The source of his pride is the restaurant *Vecchio Ristoro*, which he runs with his wife, the *maître d'hôtel*. It is situated in Aosta's historic center: *"a place that I like as it has all the conveniences of a city with the benefits of a town."* It is the small capital of Valle d'Aosta, the most mountainous region in Italy, characterized by a landscape of rare beauty between Gran Paradiso and Monte Rosa, surpassing even Mont Blanc and the Matterhorn. It is the best of the European mountains and outlines bewitchingly charming landscapes: woods, meadows, vineyards, and orchards, all marked with peace and silence, among the Roman remains of old churches, and castles.

The restaurant is a welcoming treasure with a thousand-year history, where you can refresh your soul as well as your palate, as the name states. *"It's very small – only ten tables in two rooms – and set in an old watermill that has been superbly restored. You can still use the grinders and wheel. According to the oldest documents, it appears to date back to 1100."*

It is a rustic yet elegant environment that is intimate and refined without being affected, which Alfio calls *"nicely pampering."* It is also a stone's throw away from the ancient Roman forum, and, most strikingly, near one of the most valuable testimonies of Valdostan sacred art: the striking collegiate church buildings of Sant'Orso, a Late-Gothic jewel box, which still shows the influence of Carolingian and even Early-Christian architecture and contains important works of art, including the famous Romanesque cloister.

"There were no chefs in my family and I was the only one of my seven siblings who chose this job. Ever since I was a child I was overwhelmed with interest for hotel work. I often daydreamed about an uncle who worked in a hotel in Germany. And that's not all. I have always loved the products, been curious to understand them and to constantly discover new ones," he explains.

After attending the hotel institute in Sondrio, in Valtellina, in 1978 he began his career in Valmalenco, followed by a few seasons at seaside resorts, working in Sardinia, Calabria, and Puglia. In 1985 he went to Hotel Gallia in Milan, then to the Grand Hotel Brun, before reaching Aosta with his wife, who is also from Valtellina, in the spring of 1989. There he obtained work at the renowned *Cavallo Bianco*, run by the brothers Paolo and Franco Vai, with its two Michelin stars. This is where he began his professional transformation in a kitchen that came to represent a milestone for Italian catering. He worked there until 1991 when the restaurant closed for a variety of reasons. *"I was given the chance to focus on what I had learned in the years before and to understand that I could express my personality."* After a few years at Hotel Europe in the heart of Aosta, in 1995 he took over *Vecchio Ristoro* and decided to remain in the Valle d'Aosta where Fate had led him. It took only two years until his skilled traditional cuisine allowed him to pick up a Michelin star.

From that point on, the restaurant has continued to serve some historic dishes, including the distinguished *marbré* of mixed boiled meats with an exquisite green *bagnetta* and the succulent Saint Pierre kid – a beautiful medieval village dominated by the icy pyramid of the magical summit of Grivola – in roasted suckling pig, flavored with thyme. *"My cooking is closely linked to tradition,*

but I revamp it slightly, or rather I personalize it, without being too creative." In short, the regional cuisine prevails, but it isn't a dogma. For example, he prefers to use Fassone Piemontese meat, maybe because the indigenous breeds of beef, such as Valdostana Pezzata Rossa, Pezzata Nera and Castana, which feed on summer pasture straw that is rich in aromatic essences, are almost completely used for their excellent milk, which is used to produce high-quality cheeses.

Among the typical regional products that Alfio uses most frequently, Fontina cheese is undoubtedly at the top of his list. *"Valle d'Aosta is a land that has strong bonds with sheep-farming. Cheeses are at the center of Valdostan cuisine, especially Fontina, which is essential. In the valleys, the people are still very attached to the land and therefore to food traditions of the past. For example, in Valpelline, a festival of* seupa valpellinentze *is held, a well-known typical dish that is offered by many of the area's restaurants during the winter. It is halfway between soup and lasagne, consisting of layers of rye bread, Fontina, and Savoy cabbage cooked in stock, with cinnamon and nutmeg, covered with Fontina and baked in the oven."* In his cooking, the chef also includes *"Valdostan salumis, such as* mocetta, *which is more often salted beef rather than deer, that slightly resembles bresaola from Valtellina, even though it is made with more herbs, and local kid in April and May, which comes from an* agriturismo *that also supplies us with milk and fresh goat's cheese."* There is also the aromatic lard d'Arnad, produced in a village in the low-lying Valle d'Aosta, which is also known for the exclusive Arnad-Montjovet wine, situated on the banks of Dora Baltea, the river that winds through the entire region.

He respects the area's dishes: *"Being a mountain man, I'm quite strict, so I never change the ingredients. I think that's dangerous."* Sometimes he revises the tradition, breaking the typical dishes into their component parts. For example, in Valle d'Aosta, *Carbonade, which is often served with polenta,* is the king of the meat courses. It's beef marinated in red wine for 24 hours with onion and spices, juniper, bay leaf, cloves, and pepper, and tastes like a cross between a beef stew and a game stew. "*In our restaurant, we make carbonade to order; otherwise we offer a dish inspired by it: a beef fillet served on polenta toast with carbonade sauce and onion cream.*"

For Alfio, "*We always treat tradition with respect. I only feel free and unrestricted by limits if I'm preparing a creative dish. Tradition means history and continuity; it means looking back to move forward.*" Like the Neoclassical façade of the Aosta cathedral, the dry austerity of its triumphal arch, which recalls the city's prestigious Roman past, ushers you into an early Renaissance portico beautifully decorated with frescoes and stucco, the cuisine takes all the colors, flavors, and aromas of the past combining them in a solid and loyal contemporary structure. "*It is fundamental for a chef to have an in-depth knowledge of traditional cooking. I often start with tried and tested traditional dishes because you can't go wrong with them. Then I add a little of my professional experience and imagination to make something new.*"

His working day begins at 8:00 am when he goes to the restaurant to make the bread, a foundation of the sober Valdostan culinary tradition. There are seven different types, a mark of refinement and devotion. Then he starts to plan the day when the other staff arrive. "*As we only have twenty covers, we buy the ingredients we need every day, we don't store them, and this allows us to always have them fresh.*" There are a few small stores close to the restaurant where Alfio goes to do the shopping every day. The fruit and vegetables are local, such as potatoes, zucchini, and apples, especially the delicious *Renetta*, typical of the flood plain, whereas "*some products come from Piedmont, such as fresh mushrooms and truffles, and we have suppliers that bring them directly to us. We can find mushrooms in Valle d'Aosta, but only for a very limited time of the year, so I can't guarantee the continuity of the product.*"

He usually manages to have a couple of hours' rest before going back into the kitchen for the dinner service. "*I love to cycle and I go for a ride when I can. We have some beautiful valleys here, such as Gran San Bernardo, which is spectacular."* It's 35 kilometers uphill, you feel like you've won a battle with yourself when you reach the top. From the pass you can enjoy the view of a small lake, which is frozen until spring, and breathtaking panoramas over the surrounding mountains. *"When I reach the Passo del Gran San Bernardo, at approximately 2,500 meters above sea level, looking at the valley affects me every time. I stand in a place where I'm alone and enjoy this indescribable moment."* For Alfio, cycling is also a time for reflection about life and work. *"The solitude of pedaling helps me to create new dishes."*

The entire menu created for this book is territorial. The starter is a leek timbale with lard d'Arnad mousse and rye bread sauce flavored with honey. *"In Valle d'Aosta it is traditional to make black bread crostini spread with butter on top – which I have removed in this recipe – and honey, which is collected at various altitudes in all of the region's valleys, with slices of lard on top. I haven't altered this traditional dish much. I've added a leek timbale and have held firm to the principle of lard with rye bread and honey."*

The first course is a Fontina Bavarian cream, served with a warm creamy pearl barley risotto and carrot cream. *"Barley or spelt soup is often eaten here in the winter months."* On the other hand, the meat course is a beef fillet that alludes to the traditional *Carbonade*. Finally, for dessert, a frozen yarrow semifreddo with chestnut honey and mountain juniper sauce. *"Yarrow is a mountain herb, slightly bitter yet enjoyable, that is often used here to prepare herbal tea in the summer evenings."* A dessert not to be missed, like those made by Alfio. It's enough to consider the fact that a couple from New York, who allow themselves a trip to Europe every year, always make a trek to Aosta just to eat his peach zuccotto filled with amaretto pastry cream, served with a raspberry sauce. *"For me, this is the focus of a chef's success that goes way beyond money."*

LEEK TIMBALE WITH LARD D'ARNAD MOUSSE

Ingredients for 4 people
Preparation time: 50' – Resting time: 20'

SHORTCRUST PASTRY
1¾ cups (250 g) all-purpose flour
4 tablespoons (60 g) butter
1 egg
Salt to taste
Water, as needed

LARD MOUSSE
7 oz (200 g) lard d'Arnad, or other
good-quality lard
Scant ¼ cup (50 g) whipped cream
Scant ¼ cup (50 g) stiffly beaten
egg white

TIMBALE
7 oz (200 g) shortcrust pastry
5 oz (150 g) stewed leeks
2 eggs
2 Scant ½ cup (100 g) cream
Salt, pepper and nutmeg

RYE BREAD SAUCE
Generous ¾ cup (200 g) water
Scant ¼ cup (50 g) milk
Scant ¼ cup (50 g) flower-scented
honey
3½ oz (100 g) rye bread

Method

SHORTCRUST PASTRY
Knead together all the ingredients listed above on a wooden surface and
let the pastry rest for a few hours in a cool place.

TIMBALE
Roll out the shortcrust pastry to ¼ inch (½ cm) thick and cut out four discs
with a pastry cutter. Use the discs to line 4 timbale molds. Arrange the
stewed leeks in the molds, dividing them evenly.
Meanwhile, beat the eggs with a whisk. Add the cream and season with
salt, pepper, and nutmeg. Pour the mixture into the molds and bake in the
oven for 15 minutes at 425°F (220°C/gas mark 7).

MOUSSE
Dice the lard and blend it in a food processor until a smooth, thick puree
is obtained. Mix together the whipped cream and stiffly beaten egg white
and add the lard puree. Chill for 20 minutes.

RYE BREAD SAUCE
Place a saucepan over medium heat and bring the water, milk, and honey
to a boil. Add the bread, cut into cubes, and blend with a hand-held
immersion blender. Strain through a sieve and keep warm.

Serving

Turn out the timbales and arrange them in the center of each serving plate.
Use a pastry bag to pipe a rosette of the mousse on the top of each
timbale. Garnish with fried leek and serve with the rye bread sauce.

Wine pairing

"Rayon" Blanc de Morgex 2006 – White
Winery: Cave du Vin Blanc de Morgex et de La Salle, La Ruine – Morgex (AO)

CREAMY PEARL BARLEY RISOTTO IN CARROT SAUCE, SERVED WITH FONTINA BAVARIAN CREAM

Ingredients for 4 people
Preparation time: 45' – Soaking: 12 h – Resting time: 2 h

STOCK
1½ lb (700 g) beef
1 lb (500 g) veal
Salt
1 onion
1 carrot
1 celery stalk
1 bay leaf

FONDUE
5 oz (150 g) fontina cheese
1 cup milk, plus additional for soaking cheese
1½ oz (40 g) butter
⅓ cup (40 g) all-purpose flour

BAVARIAN CREAM
Generous ¾ cup (200 ml) fondue
2 sheets of gelatin

Scant ¼ cup (50 ml) cream, whipped
1½ oz (50 g) egg whites, beaten to stiff peaks

CARROT SAUCE
10 oz (300 g) carrots
1 potato, approximately 3½ oz (100 g)
Salted water
Generous 1 tablespoon (20 ml) extra-virgin olive oil

BARLEY
2 cups (500 ml) vegetable stock
12½ oz (360 g) dried barley, soaked in cold water for 12 hours
Raw, julienned carrots, for serving
½ cup (80 g) toasted hazelnuts, for serving

Method

STOCK

Put the meat in a large saucepan and cover with cold water.
Bring the water to a boil over medium heat, covered.
When the water comes to a boil, skim the froth, season with salt, and add the whole vegetables and the bay leaf.
Lower the heat, cover again, and simmer for about 2½ hours.
Let cool and chill for at least 3 hours.
Before using the stock, remove the layer of fat that will have solidified on the surface.

FONDUE

Cut the Fontina into small cubes and soak in a little milk.
Melt the butter in a small saucepan and add the flour to make a roux. In a separate saucepan, bring the milk to a boil; slowly pour it into the roux and bring mixture to a boil. Add the Fontina and stir until melted (You can add a drop of white wine, which will help you to dilute the cheese.). Remove from heat and cover with plastic wrap once fully melted.

FONTINA BAVARIAN CREAM

Pour the fondue into the top of a double boiler and let melt. Add the gelatin, which has been softened beforehand in cold water, drained, and squeezed out. Dissolve the gelatin and lower the temperature of the fondue to 105°F (40°C). Fold in the whipped cream and egg whites until well combined. Pour the mixture into individual molds. Chill for at least two hours before serving. (You can also prepare these the day before.)

CARROT SAUCE

Peel the carrots and potato, cut them into large pieces, and cook in salted water until tender. Transfer the vegetables to a food processor with one-part of the cooking water. Add the extra-virgin olive oil and blend until a smooth, even cream forms. Pour into a saucepan and keep warm.

BARLEY

Bring the vegetable stock to a boil; add the barley. Cook until tender and drain. Add the barley to the carrot sauce and boil for 4 minutes, stirring with a wooden spoon (like a risotto). When the carrot sauce and barley are thick and there is plenty of liquid, cover the saucepan for 1 minute before serving.

Serving

Place each Bavarian cream mold in the center of a deep, chilled plate. Garnish with raw carrot sticks and pour the barley mixture around the cream. Sprinkle with hazelnuts and serve.

Wine pairing

Chardonnay DOC 2006 – White
Winery: Maison Anselmet, La Crête – Villeneuve (AO)

FILLET OF BEEF SERVED ON POLENTA TOASTS WITH CARBONADE SAUCE

Ingredients for 4 people
Preparation time: 2 h 30' – Marinating: 1 day

SAUCE
4 cups red wine
1 lb (500 g) beef cuttings
½ cup (50 g) smoked pancetta
2 medium onions, finely chopped
1 celery stalk, finely chopped
15 black peppercorns
10 whole cloves
¾ teaspoon (2 g) ground cinnamon
10 juniper berries
1 bay leaf
2 tablespoons all-purpose flour
2 cups water

BEEF
3 beef fillets, each weighing 4 oz (120 g)
Extra-virgin olive oil, for frying

Method

SAUCE
Place all the ingredients in a stainless steel or other nonreactive bowl and chill for 24 hours to marinate.
Drain the marinade, reserving the liquid. Sauté the drained vegetables and beef cuttings in a deep frying pan. Sprinkle with 2 tablespoons of flour and add the wine from the marinade. Add 2 cups (500 ml) of water and simmer for 2 hours.
Strain mixture into a bowl; you should have a sauce that is fairly thick and shiny. Keep warm while you prepare the beef.

BEEF
Fry the 4 fillets in extra-virgin olive oil in a frying pan until cooked. Remove from heat and let rest in warm pan for 5 minutes.

Serving

Arrange 4 round polenta toasts, which have been sautéed in butter, in the center of the plates. Place the fillets on top and drizzle with the sauce. Serve at once.

Wine pairing

"Vin du Prevot" 2005, Cabernet Sauvignon and Franc with Merlot – Red
Winery: Institute Agricole Régional – Aosta (AO)

YARROW SEMIFREDDO WITH CHESTNUT HONEY AND MOUNTAIN JUNIPER SAUCE

Ingredients for 4 people
Preparation time: 40' – Cooling: 8 h

YARROW SYRUP
½ cup (125 g) water
Scant ⅔ cup (125 g) sugar
2 teaspoons (10 g) lemon juice
2 tablespoons (30 g) dried yarrow

PARFAIT
12 egg yolks
⅓ cup (50 g) confectioners' sugar
2 cups (500 g) cream, whipped
2 teaspoons (10 g) glucose

CHESTNUT HONEY AND MOUNTAIN JUNIPER SAUCE
Generous ¾ cup (200 ml) chestnut honey
10 juniper berries, crushed
Scant 1 teaspoon (4 g) gelatin

Method

YARROW SYRUP
Boil all the ingredients together for several minutes; strain syrup into a pot.

PARFAIT
Beat the egg yolks with the confectioners' sugar. Slowly beat in the the syrup, which has been heated to 230°F (112°C), and mix until the mixture has cooked. Fold in the whipped cream and pour the mixture into individual molds. Freeze for at least 8 hours before serving.

HONEY SAUCE
Boil the chestnut honey; whisk in juniper berries and gelatin until gelatin is completely dissolved. Let cool.

Serving

Remove the semifreddo from the mold and arrange in the center of the plate.
Decorate with yarrow, fresh mint, and caramelized sugar. Glaze with the honey sauce.

Wine pairing

"Chambave Muscat" DOC Passito 2004 – Dessert wine
Winery: La Crotta di Vegneron – Chambave (AO)

THE CUISINE OF PIEDMONT

Stretched out between the Valdostan Alps and the gentle outline of the Langhe, Piedmont is beautiful all year round, but shrouded in autumn mists it embraces and charms. When the fog descends silently over the lands of Piedmont, the atmosphere is a party for the foodie who pursues the aroma of truffle amid the white shroud, a dominant note in the symphony of Piedmontese flavors. The white Alba and Mondovi truffles, whose gathering is traditionally handed down from father to son, is one of the most valuable. They have a delicate flavor yet intense aroma, with a velvety pulp. They emit the best of themselves in a plate of *Tajarin*, thin egg tagliatelle that are often homemade. The precious tuber plays a princely role in the gastronomy of Piedmont, washed down by soft, aromatic wines. If the dish is egg-based, the perfect wine is a well-structured white. A big white or a red made from Nebbiolo grapes is preferable with fondue. Barbera is ideal with agnolotti, and Barolo is best with game. Autumn is the season of Nebbiolo, game, and *cardo gobbo* (cardoons), which, with garlic and anchovies, is the main ingredient in *bagna caôda*. A delicious sauce that is served in a heated earthenware pot in the center of the table, bagna caoda is one of the sociable dishes of Piedmontese cooking. The Langhe in particular offers spectacular charm when it emerges from the autumnal mists. It is an ancient land situated between the Tanaro River and the valley of Bormida di Spigo, the provinces of Asti, Cuneo, and Alessandria, which surfaced out of the sea in the Miocene Age, a pleated contour of hundreds of hills. *"A vineyard that rises on the crest of a hill until it is etched on the sky is a familiar view, and yet the screens of simple, deep rows appear like a magical door. Beneath the vines, there is dark, tilled land, the leaves hide treasures, and the sky is there beyond the leaves,"* wrote Cesare Pavese (1908-50), who was born and lived in Alessandria. The Langhe is also important for its cheese production, such as Monferrato. *Formaggette*, or *tome*, are produced here that are eaten simply or preserved in various preparations of oil, spices, and flavorings. Other well-known cheeses include varieties of *tome* left to marinate for several months in terrines and processed until a creamy consistency is obtained, and *Brus, a fermented cheese usually* spread on bread or eaten by the spoonful. Its strong, lingering flavor is suitable for the palates of connoisseurs. Just beyond the Langhe rise the beautiful mountain peaks of Monviso and Monte Rosa. From here to the banks of the Po, Piedmont is a region of striking features, from its wide valleys, hills, and vineyards, to the springs and pools of water that spill into the rice fields, where the herons take to the sky. Then there's Turin, the nineteenth-century capital of the House of Savoy. The heart of the historic center, rich with monuments and buildings, is Piazza Castello, where you can start to explore the city's classic attractions: the Royal Palace, Palazzo Madama, the Egyptian Museum (one of the wealthiest in the world), Mole Antonelliana, now an outstanding film museum, the Lingotto, the Parco del Valentino along the river, and the Basilica di Superga. When hunger calls, it is worth taking the time to sit at one of the many tables set out by the city's restaurants and trattorias. Piedmontese cuisine is based on simple dishes washed down by great wines. It values the products from the different geographical areas that make up the region, and meld them with French-inspired meat dishes and Ligurian-influenced fish and seafood dishes. Among the pasta dishes, agnolotti is always featured. A stuffed, fresh egg pasta, agnolotti has a different filling for each province. Common fillings include cheese fondue, roasted beef, pork, or rabbit, with the addition of sausage, eggs, and spices. They are served with butter and sage or with juices from roasted meats. The risottos are also something special, thanks to the expanses of rice fields in Novarese and Vercellese. They are often garnished with excellent truffle that has been thinly sliced, as well as with many other ingredients, such as mushrooms, melted cheese, eel, frogs, game, roasted larks, and thrushes. The French influence in meat dishes comes from the geographical vicinity and the historical relations between the Italian and French courts and makes a prime appearance in Barolo stew, or *finanziera*. Probably a Torinese abbreviation of *"ragout de abates de volailles à la financière,"* finanziera is a jewel of traditional Italian (and French) peasant cooking destined for the tables of gentlemen. The boiled meat options of Piedmont are triumphant, with an explosion of pork, beef, veal, and turkey, often served with vegetables, sauces (including the famous *salsa verde* made from vinegar-soaked breadcrumbs, parsley, garlic, hard-boiled egg, oil, and pepper), and pickles. As well as the main courses, the classic *grissini torinesi*, crunchy and delicious Italian breadsticks, are always on offer. Longer and thinner than the classic version, *grissini torinesi* were invented by the baker Antonio Brunero, at the request of the doctor of Vittorio Amedeo II of Savoy in 1668. Brunero created *Ghersìn* (modern grissini) by pulling and stretching out the *Ghersa*, the traditional bread of the time, to a thin thickness. The city of Turin with its coffees - *Bonèt*, a type of amaretto and chocolate flan, should not be missed - and its cake shops is the appointed home of Italian desserts. Some of the most famous chocolate-making companies in Italy such as Peyrano, Giroldi e Giuliano, and Baratti e Milano are based here, heirs of the first Valdese artisans who moved here from France to escape the religious persecutions at the end of the eighteenth century. At the beginning of the nineteenth century, crafts-men came to Turin from all over Europe to perfect and learn more about this art. Among these were Pierre Paul Caffarel, Michele Prochet, and Michele Talmone, who can be regarded as the first generation of Italian confec-tionery industrialists, founders of a tradition that is still alive today. It is said that Philippe Suchard did an intern-ship in Turin before founding a chocolate company, Chocolat Suchard, in Switzerland in 1826 that would become one of the most famous of its kind worldwide. In Pinerolo, Caffarel still produces *gianduiotti* (typical Piedmontese hazelnut chocolates) today according to a formula that dates back to 1865. It is important to explain that this typical chocolate consists of gianduja paste, which is created by mixing cocoa into hazelnut paste from the Langhe. Another forest-derived product, the *marron*, or chestnut, is also turned into a delicacy. From these are created *marrons glacés*, candied chestnuts, and a dessert made from marron paste and cream, delicious and dedicated simply to the highest mountain in Europe: Mont Blanc. The particularly sweet nougat torrone d'Asti can be washed down with a glass of Piemonte Moscato Passito. In the province of Novara, where lakes, rivers, and rice fields depict the landscape, Taleggio is a constant feature, a soft and full-flavored cheese. With Ossolano d'Alpe (or Bettelmatt) and Robiola di Roccaverano, it represents the typical products of the Piedmontese dairy industry. Piedmont offers over 50 illustrious wines that are important, universally known (both DOCG and DOC) and able to satisfy the many flavors of the region's stimulating cuisine, including Asti, Barbaresco, Barbera, Barolo, Brachetto d'Acqui, Gattinara, Gavi, Ghemme, Grignolino, and Nebbiolo. These wines pair perfectly with risotto, roasted and boiled meats, game, cheeses, and truffles.

PIEDMONTESE HAZELNUTS

PIEDMONTESE HAZELNUTS ARE MUCH SOUGHT-AFTER BY THE CONFECTIONERY INDUSTRY, ESPECIALLY FOR MAKING COOKIES AND CAKES. THE AREA WHERE THE HAZELNUTS ARE FOUND IS VAST, BUT THE MAIN CONCENTRATION IS IN THE ALTA LANGA CUNEESE REGION. SPECIAL CARE IS TAKEN WHEN GATHERING AND PRESERVING THE HAZELNUTS, TO HELP PROTECT THEIR EXCELLENT SCENT, FLAVOR, AND COLOR. THESE HAZELNUTS ARE USED IN MAKING *GIANDUIOTTI* AND WELL-KNOWN SPREADABLE CREAMS.

THE "NOCCIOLA DEL PIEDMONT" (TONDA GENTILE DELLE LANGHE QUALITY) IS OFTEN FOUND IN BAKING MIXTURES AND PAIRS WELL WITH AMIABLE, SWEET, WELL-STRUCTURED WHITE WINES, LIKE ERBALUCE DI CALUSO PASSITO.

GIUSEPPE (BEPPE) BOLOGNA

TRATTORIA I BOLOGNA - ROCCHETTA TANARO (ASTI)

If you could take a photograph of Piedmontese cuisine today, it wouldn't resemble a robust and austere lady who's getting older, but rather the cordial and genuine face of the young chef Beppe Bologna, the owner of Trattoria I Bologna in Rocchetta Tanaro, in the province of Asti, and his family. He wouldn't just be wearing just autumnal clothing, in accordance with the crowning season of the region's food and wine, consisting of big reds, game, and truffles, but he'd be also smiling all year round, showing off the sumptuous stuff of a rich and complete land, from the Alps to the rice fields, a true paradise for food lovers.

Rocchetta Tanaro, home of the white truffle and Barbera wine, is a small town immersed in the seductive countryside of Monferrato. Arranged in a horseshoe shape, surrounded by a gentle amphitheater of hills cultivated with vines and overlooking the flowing Tanaro river, it is historically linked to the Marchesi Incisa della Rocchetta, internationally known for having created the famous wine Sassicaia at his family estate of Bolgheri, in Tuscany, and for having bred the great horse, Ribot, the English thoroughbred European flat champion. The family's chivalric and feudal history marks the town from the year 1,000 to the eighteenth century.

The atmosphere of the trattoria (it would be wrong to call it a restaurant and Beppe would be upset if we did) is rustic, but with an elegance that is completely Piedmontese, reserved and suited to those who can truly appreciate it. Filled with wooden flooring, tables, chairs, and other early twentieth-century furniture, such as chests and china cabinets, it has a country atmosphere, yet one that is professional and passionate, lively and jovial. It is a warm place, full of great energy, where people talk, toast, joke, relax and enjoy the pleasure of the dishes prepared by the chef. *"I am moved by the way of life in my town,"* he tells us, *"as we don't follow trends. We eat simply and enjoy a drink among friends. My goal is to offer my guests cooking that always leaves a happy memory."* It's a sign of a generous temperament that Beppe would never relinquish the chance to give something to those who come into his trattoria: a smile, attention, a flavor, a feeling, a heartfelt gesture.

The trattoria, set in an old farmhouse in the countryside of Asti that was completely restored a couple of years ago, has about 50 seats that turn into 80 with the patio in the summer and consists of two rooms: One, the old stable with the feeding trough still on show, and the other, larger, room that looks onto the cellar. The kitchen is visible and you can visit the cellar. *"I don't have a wine list. Customers can go and choose the wine themselves,"* he explains. The business, which also offers accommodation, was founded from a long family tradition. *"My grandmother Caterina had a trattoria in a different place. It was passed down to her son Carlo, or rather my father, who in turn handed it down to me. I took it over in 1992, but my parents still work here. My mother Mariuccia works with me in the kitchen and takes care of the fresh pasta. My father and my wife Cristina work in the dining room."*

Beppe offers excellent regional food, washed down with wines of the first order, especially the Barbera from the associated Braida winery, which belongs to his family. *"I cook typical Piedmontese food, which is characterized by making fresh pasta,"* he explains. There are also historic dishes that always feature on his menu. The typically Piedmontese *vitello tonnato* (cold veal in tuna sauce) is one of the starters, made from thin slices of veal round and covered with a tuna, anchovy, and caper sauce. Piedmontese-style agnolotti always features on the menu as a pasta dish, so-called *"del plin"* because of the pinching that is given to the pasta during preparation. These are sweet-shaped ravioli, filled with veal, pork, and rabbit and served with butter, sage, and Parmesan. Another timeless dish is *bagna caôda*, medieval in origin and a delicious dip for raw vegetables, made from olive oil, anchovies, the *cardo gobbo* (cardoons) from the neighboring Nizza Monferrato, and Monferrino garlic. The horse cheeks cooked for four hours in the ubiquitous Barbera wine and served with apple puree is also one of his signature dishes, like the goat *formaggetta* with grape *mostarda,* which is actually produced by the Bologna family.

In regards to traditional dishes, Beppe has a heavy, yet kind, Padan hand, a little like Gandolfino da Roreto, the fifteenth-century painter from Asti, whose works are still largely on

show there, especially in the great *Cattedrale di Santa Maria Assunta*, the most important expression of Gothic architecture in Piedmont. *"I often make the dishes lighter as they're all a bit heavy and I don't want my guests to leave the table with a stomachache [...].*" For example, I serve lasagnette della Vigilia, *a customary Christmas dish, with a* bagna caôda *and some beets. I've added the beets to sweeten it a little and to make the* bagna caôda *more digestible,*" Beppe says. In some cases, he changes or removes some ingredients from a traditional dish or makes it using more innovative techniques.

For example, *Finanziera*, a classic Piedmontese dish, which takes its name from the jacket worn in Turin in the nineteenth century by Piedmontese financiers who loved the dish, is made from veal sweetbreads, brain, cock's combs, and chicken livers. Beppe removed the vegetable base from the dish and added porcini mushrooms, flour, and butter. In his Piedmontese-style sauté, consisting of various types of meat and vegetables, he has removed the liver and carrots and replaced them with small sausages and the famous soft amaretti cookies from the nearby town of Mombaruzzo, to which the almond-scented kernels contained in the pit of apricots are added with the usual ingredients – sweet and bitter almonds, egg white, and sugar – to give it a slight bitterness. *"I trust my taste when I'm making these changes, but above all my mother who, having worked with my grandmother, has 'stolen' the secrets of old Piedmontese cooking. In turn, my grandmother swiped them from a cook at the castle [...]"*

In Rocchetta Tanaro, which has just over 1,000 inhabitants, Beppe was one of the last babies to have been born at home. You could say that he was actually born in the kitchen. He has always been intrigued by cooking. When the time came to decide between going to an accountancy college or a hotel institute, he had no doubts whatsoever; he chose the same love as his grandmother and mother. *"As soon as I had finished studying, I started my internship. I spent seven years doing work experience in great restaurants in my area and also in other regions, like San Domenico in Imola, as well as abroad. To be honest, I was then cornered by my father who had bought this restaurant [...] I would have preferred to have carried on gaining experience for a bit longer [...],"* he admits. This was how Beppe started at the bottom and, assisted by his mother, *"who is the pillar holding up the family, the person who understands the subtlety of details, the female touch,"* he created his trattoria. Beppe works 12 to 14 hours a day. He isn't a chef angel, like the builder angels who, tradition has it, built the Chiesetta di Santa Maria de Flesco at the gateway into Rocchetta Tanaro, but he certainly works hard. *"At 9 a.m. I go into the kitchen and have a chat with the staff, deciding how the day will pan out, then I take care of the shopping."* He usually goes straight into the countryside and the surrounding area. *"Living in the countryside, I have the good fortune of being able to choose seasonal products, allowing for better quality and flavor in the dishes. My suppliers are my peers who have continued the business of their fathers and who live in the same area"* – or in Asti, the nearby town known all over the world for its Spumante and as being one of Piedmont's artistic treasure chests, with its fourteenth-century cathedral, Romanesque, Renaissance and Baroque churches, ancient medieval towers and noble homes, including the house where the eighteenth-century poet and dramatist Vittorio Alfieri was born. Beppe goes into Asti for the products that he cannot find close to home, such as horse meat or certain vegetables, such as the *peperone quadrato d'Asti* (square bell pepper from Asti), with its delicate, fleshy, and highly aromatic pulp. On Friday, he visits the farmers' market at Nizza Monferrato instead, the hometown of *cardo gobbo* and truffle. *"I work with the land. Depending on the time of year, I use mushrooms, truffles, our fruit and vegetables."* In the afternoon, when the lunch service has ended, he devotes himself to gardening. He tends to the restaurant's garden, where the herbs used in the kitchen are also grown. The garden is situated beneath the Parco Naturale di Rocchetta Tanaro, which starts from the castle of the Marchesi Incisa and extends along a hilly area covering about 247 acres through an uninterrupted expanse of age-old trees, such as beech, oak, and chestnut. Here, you are likely to come across many species of protected animals, including badgers, foxes, wild boar, different species of birds, such as herons, and red crayfish in the river (an important biological indicator of the health of the water).

In the province of Asti, food traditions are still alive, especially in the small towns. This is one of the reasons why Beppe wouldn't want to live anywhere else. At Asti there's the *Douja d'or* food festival during the Palio period (September), one of the oldest festivals in Italy, which takes place in September and culminates with a bareback horse race, an event where all the villages offer two dishes that are typical of their area. There is also *Città del tartufo*, from October to November, which has a vibrant, aromatic food and shopping market. Various events dedicated to Fassone also take place in the province, also called *bue grasso*, which is the beef of the Bianca Piedmontese breed that has the so-called "double thighs." The menu that Beppe has chosen for this book is indeed an anthem to this territory that is still, in many ways, untouched with its old-world charm. The starter is a classic Asti dish: veal tartare, served here as a salad with celery hearts and thinly sliced Parmesan. For the pasta course, he has chosen the typical Piedmontese agnolotti, even though the *tajarin*, or thin egg tagliatelline stretched by hand, would also have been representative of traditional cooking, especially tagliatelline from Monferrino, served with a basil cream. *"We are close to Liguria and Acqui Terme and produce high-quality basil,"* Beppe explains. For the meat dish, he opted for horse cheeks, *"even though I'm also serving another three regional dishes at the moment to my guests: stewed veal tripe with potatoes, locally sourced roasted rabbit with thyme and crunchy suckling pig with glazed green onions."* Last but not least, is the traditional Asti-style *bonet*, a forefather of the *budino*, which was once extremely popular in Monferrato, and that owes its name to the tinned copper mold shaped like a beret in which it was cooked. A delicious dessert, it is a worthy tribute to a region that truly loves patisserie.

RAW VEAL SALAD

Ingredients for 4 people
Preparation time: 20'

14 oz (400 g) lean veal (fillet)
2 tablespoons (30 ml) extra-virgin olive oil
Salt and pepper to taste
1 lemon
2 celery hearts
3½ oz (100 g) Parmesan (preferably Parmigiano-Reggiano)

Method

Prepare the veal: lean the veal, removing any nerves and connective tissues using a sharp knife. Finely chop it with a knife, then season it with the oil, salt, pepper, and lemon juice.
Clean the celery, only keeping the hearts. Wash and cut them finely.

Serving

Arrange the meat on the plate. Garnish with 2 hearts from 2 heads of celery and shaved Parmesan.

Wine pairing

Grignolino d'Asti DOC – Red
Winery: Braida – Rocchetta Tanaro (AT)

AGNOLOTTI

Ingredients for 4 people
Preparation time: 45' – Resting time: 20'

FILLING
7 oz (200 g) roasted veal
7 oz (200 g) pork
1 onion
1 clove red garlic
1 carrot
1 celery stalk
Extra-virgin olive oil
Rosemary
Generous ⅓ cup (100 ml) red wine
3½ oz (100 g) sausage
7 oz (200 g) rabbit (loin meat, if possible)

3½ oz (100 g) spinach
2 tablespoons Parmesan
Nutmeg
4 eggs
Salt and pepper

PASTA
1⅓ cups (200 g) flour
2 whole eggs
2 tablespoons (30 ml) water
Melted butter, for serving
Fresh sage, for serving
Grated Parmesan cheese, for serving

Method

FILLING
Cut up the veal, pork, and vegetables into small pieces. Sauté it all in a saucepan in the oil with the rosemary. Add the wine and let it evaporate. Add the sausage and cook for 30 minutes.
In a separate pan, sauté the rabbit over medium heat. When all the meat is well cooked, mince it using a meat grinder. Add the boiled and chopped spinach, Parmesan, and nutmeg and mix it all with the eggs. Season with salt and pepper to taste.

PASTA
Sift the flour onto a wooden surface and shape into a mound. Make a well in the center. Pour the eggs with the water into the hollow and knead until the dough is smooth and even. Let rest for 20 minutes. Roll out a very thin sheet of pasta using a pasta machine.
Arrange small mounds of filling at ⅓ inch (1 cm) intervals about ⅓ inch from the edge of the pasta.
Fold the edge of the pasta over the filling, sealing it by pressing down slightly with your finger.
Use a ravioli cutter to cut the row of agnolotti and seal them one at a time pressing down slightly with your fingers (pinching them). Separate the agnolotti using the ravioli cutter. Cook the agnolotti in plenty of salted water for 3–4 minutes. Drain, then and serve with melted butter, sage, and Parmesan cheese. Serve hot.

Wine pairing
"Bacialè" Monferrato Rosso DOC – Red
Winery: Braida – Rocchetta Tanaro (AT)

HORSE CHEEKS BRAISED IN RED WINE

Ingredients for 4 people
Preparation time: 3 h

1 tablespoon (20 g) extra-virgin olive oil
5 or 6 horse cheeks
Salt and pepper to taste
2 cloves garlic
3 bay leaves
750 ml bottle of red wine
Flour, as much as needed
Water, as needed

Method

Place a saucepan over medium heat. Add the oil and sauté the cheeks. Season with salt and pepper.
After a few minutes, add the garlic and bay leaves and sauté for 1 minute.
Pour in the red wine and let it evaporate.
Sprinkle with a little flour and add water to cover. Cover with a lid and simmer over low heat for 3 hours. If necessary, add more water during the cooking time.

Wine pairing

"Bricco dell'Uccellone" Barbera d'Asti DOC, barrel-aged 2005 – Red
Winery: Braida – Rocchetta Tanaro (AT)

BUNET

Ingredients for 4 people
Preparation time: 40'

5 whole eggs
Generous ½ cup (120 g) sugar
2 tablespoons (30 g) cocoa
1⅔ cups (400 g) milk
3 tablespoons (50 g) light cream
5 Mombaruzzo amaretti cookies, crumbled
Rum

Method

Beat the eggs, sugar, and cocoa together in a bowl. Whisk in the milk, cream, and amaretti.
Prepare the caramel for the mold. Place the sugar in a copper pan over low heat. When the sugar melts and turns amber brown, pour it into a mold, followed by the amaretti mixture.
Place the mold in a roasting pan filled halfway with hot water and cook in a uncovered bain-marie at 285°F (140°C) for about 30 minutes.

Wine pairing

Moscato d'Asti DOCG – Dessert wine
Winery: Braida – Rocchetta Tanaro (AT)

MANOLO ALLOCHIS

RESTAURANT IL VIGNETO - RAVINALI, RODDI (CUNEO)

Manolo Allochis, the talented chef of the restaurant *Il Vigneto* in Ravinali located in the heart of the Piedmontese Langhe, didn't spend his cash going out for pizza with friends or nights out clubbing since he attended the culinary institute-- instead he used all the money he earned during the summer and winter seasons to go and eat at the best restaurants. He even traveled 100 to 150 kilometers just to sit down at a refined table. *"My parents regarded it as a waste of money and we often squabbled about it,"* he tells us. *"Coming from another world – I wasn't following in their footsteps; my mother and father both worked in a hospital – they weren't able to understand me."* Yet it was an excellent investment for the future.

He has always been passionate about cooking. *"When I finished junior high school, I immediately went to wash plates in a restaurant close to home. To become a chef, I think that you have to understand all the stages that come before. To command and respect someone else's work, you need to have done it yourself."* After three years of study and having passed the final examination, he went to work in various restaurants. Between one season and another, he did some internships. He was an intern at *Enoteca Pinchiorri* in Florence *"where I actually paid to be able to work there,"* and a series of courses at *Istituto Superiore di Arti Culinarie Etoile* in Sottomarina di Chioggia. He then started to be employed in hotels and restaurants, initially in Valle d'Aosta, then in Liguria, followed by in Lyon, France, by Jean-Paul Lacombe, the second finest chef in the city after Bocuse. Finally, he ended up in a restaurant in the Langhe with a Michelin star, where he stayed for five years. *"It was my dream to work there and to become the chef. When I had achieved my goal, I wanted to work towards another objective: to open a restaurant of my own."*

And that's what happened. On a cold evening in January three years ago, he happened upon the restaurant *Il Vigneto* and, as a stroke of luck, discovered he knew the owner. It was love at first sight. *"It was dark and snowing, but I liked the farmhouse very much, even though back then it still hadn't been restored and there was no summer patio area."* He had the foresight to see the potential that the distinctive atmosphere had to offer. A few months later, in April, he decided to take over the restaurant, proposing the idea of managing it together with his brother Rossano, who had been working on a private yacht as hotel manager. They restored the farmhouse, respecting the original style, in record time and it opened officially on September 19, 2005, and kept the name.

Il Vigneto, a stone's throw away from Alba, the delightful walled town known as the capital of the celebrated white truffle, is a farmhouse immersed in a uniquely peaceful and serene setting. From the restaurant's summer patio you can admire the small villages and bewitching medieval castles, like Verduno, the vineyards of Dolcetto, Nebbiolo, and Barbera on one side, and on the other side, the gentle hazelnut groves that clamber up the hills. It is located in the municipality of Roddi, in the province of Cuneo, in the first town where the Registered and Protected Designation of Origin begins for the prized wine, Barolo. That's not all; this is also one of the production areas of the *Nocciola Tonda Gentile delle Langhe*, one of the most vaunted hazelnuts of the region. *"It is beautiful to live in a place where you can still see the stars. I am lucky to live here in the quiet of the countryside."* He also enjoys the traditional customs of the Langhe. During the first week of Easter, for example, he joins the rest of the village to do the *Canté jeuv*, the ancient Easter egg hunt from farmyard to farmyard under the first spring moon.

The old stable was renovated to create the restaurant, with its vaulted brick ceiling, typical of rural Piedmontese architecture kept intact. The hayloft upstairs, where rooms have been created, offers comfortable accommodation to its guests. The cellar is a real pearl, where there is the *crutin*, the tuff-carved alcove, typical of the Langhe, which was once filled with snow to preserve products. Here you can now enjoy a pre-dinner drink, trying the Piedmontese starters made by Manolo.

The decor of the restaurant is spartan, without going overboard, able to render an atmosphere that isn't too elegant to the surroundings while not being too rustic either. *"We have found a good combination, creating modern spaces, for example, the steel chandeliers that contrast with the bricks of the ceiling."* There is a young staff to make the restaurant work. *"We are the oldest; I'm 30 and my brother Rossano, sommelier and maître d'hôtel, is nearly 32."* It's a close-knit team, *"When we've finished the evening service, we all have a drink together. The kitchen can be likened to a clock; a commis is like a second and a second is nothing, like time, but only many seconds put together make a minute, the chef de partie, and many minutes make an hour, or rather the chef."*

Above all, Manolo enlivens *"a kitchen where we have fun while we're cooking. As our job is demanding work, we try to create dishes that stimulate us while remaining bound to tradition."* On the one hand, if he is enjoyably bound to traditional dishes *"it's because we're located in a nice place. Those who come to the Langhe are there for food and wine tourism."* On the other hand, he makes sure that he doesn't fall into letting flavors drop off, *"by discovering combinations that are a bit particular, without making mistakes."* In short, a cuisine inspired by this generous land, a true gold mine of flavors, which painstakingly revamps and personalizes the relationship with tradition.

A new, albeit old, dish that has now become a historic offering on his menu is the *vitello tonnato* that Manolo has dedicated to the "new generation." Almost a spell of the *masche*, the peasant witches of the Langhe who, according to popular legend, know how to take on an appearance that makes them more congenial from time to time: a fruit, a cat, a leaf, or something entirely unrecognizable. This dish also isn't what it seems. *"It looks like the traditional dish, but it isn't just made of meat. Inside there's a fillet of marinated tuna. I chose tuna, because there's tuna in oil in the tuna sauce and also as there's no coastline in Piedmont there are many dishes made with canned fish, which is inserted in a pocket made with lean veal."* The outer meat is browned; while the fish inside remains uncooked and, therefore, red in color. The slices are served as if it were veal round. In the traditional recipe, this is cooked in such a way that the inside becomes pink. It is then combined with a tuna sauce made with extra-virgin olive oil *"because the flavor stays stronger and allows a contrast with the flavor of the tuna."*

Manolo has also modernized another traditional dish: raw meat. *"I offer it in two versions: raw meat of the past broken down with today's knife. The traditional version was prepared as follows. The meat is cut very finely and seasoned with salt, pepper, oil, garlic, and lemon juice. Nowadays, the meat is pounded with a knife, so that the raw meat maintains its quality, and it is only seasoned with salt, pepper, and oil. I have removed the garlic, as many people dislike it, and the lemon juice, which ruins the palate to go on to drink wine as well as cooking the meat."* Up until last year, he also offered raw meat of the past marinated in red wine, which was called "the raw meat of yore." *"I served it on the stave of a barrique, from the violet side where the Barolo has been, and I accompanied it with a glass of the same wine with a slice of lemon inside, just as my grandfather did."*

Another interpretation are the classic *agnolotti del plin* ("plin" in Piedmontese dialect means a "small pinch" and this seals the pasta between one ravioli and another), which are usually made with meat. *"My parents use chocolate pasta and a Gorgonzola Dolce fondue filling. They toss them in butter with crumbled amaretti cookies. Ingredients which therefore bring back memories of the stuffed Piedmontese-style peaches where there's amaretto, cocoa, etc. During the truffle season, I remove the amaretto crumbs and replace them with grated white truffle, a strange yet winning combination."*

Despite what he has achieved, Manolo still enjoys going to eat at his colleague's restaurants. *"I do it to see how I measure up to them."* And he doesn't do it with an air of presumption, but humbly, as if he were going on a pilgrimage. *"I always think that others work better than me!"* Other chef's recipes have often been the stimulus of his new dishes. *"I once had ground coffee that was too fine and I didn't know how to use it. So I decided to make a shrimp and curry risotto with a powdering of coffee over the top, having been inspired by the saffron rice with powdered licorice from the restaurant Le Calandre in Sarmeola di Rubano, but the coffee didn't really go. Then I removed the curry and added ginger. The end risotto was better, but an ingredient was still missing."* Thinking about it – and his mind honed in on the objective like the historic center of Roddi develops in concentric circles around the thirteenth-century bell towers and in the style built in the year 1000 – Manolo added star anise, giving a central core to the dish.

Typical regional products are needed for the cuisine of *Il Vigneto*, despite its new interpretations. *"It is a contradiction in terms to buy ingredients that come from outside the area. I procure them from small producers that are located within a radius of 15 kilometers from the restaurant."* Above all, he uses the excellent meat of Piedmontese Fassone and hazelnuts, the *Tonda Gentile*, which he combined with shrimp, for example, that he fries, breaded in finely chopped hazelnuts and breadcrumbs. He uses mushrooms and truffles when they are in season, as well as seasonal fruit and vegetables. Throughout the year, he also offers the best catches from nearby Liguria and freshwater fish; the restaurant is located a few kilometers from where the Po begins and next to the course of the river Tanaro (the Celtic name of Roddi, *raud* or *rod*, means river).

In the menu chosen for the book, the starter is *"veal with tuna for the new generation, which offers a new way of understanding and following tradition."* This is followed by potato gnocchi, a typical pasta dish from the Cuneo region, made with potatoes from the Alta Langa. *"I make them big in size like ping-pong balls. Inside I put a liquid quail's egg and toss them in a pan with butter and white truffle, one of the products of excellence from our land."* For the meat course, there is a *"Fassone veal cheek braised in Barolo, combined with the sweet part of the Piedmontese-style mixed fried dish, which also contains pieces of meat, fish, and vegetables: amaretto, semolina, and apple."* For dessert, a *"gianduja mousse, which is made from our Piedmontese chocolate and Tonda Gentile delle Langhe hazelnuts,"* a worthy and delicious seal of a chef's beautiful friendship with the land.

VEAL WITH TUNA FOR THE NEW GENERATION

Ingredients for 4 people
Preparation time: 2 h 30' – Marinating: 2 h

14 oz (400 g) fresh tuna fillet
1⅓ lb (600 g) lean veal
Extra-virgin olive oil, for sauteing

TUNA MARINADE
⅔ cup (100 g) coarse sea salt
⅓ cup (50 g) table sea salt
Scant 3 tablespoons (40 g) brown sugar
Zest of 1 lemon
Zest of 1 organic orange
¾ oz (20 g) parsley leaves
5 juniper berries
5 cloves
4 lemongrass leaves
Small bunch of herbs (such as dill, rosemary, thyme, sage, marjoram, and tarragon)

TUNA SAUCE
2 fresh egg yolks
Generous ¾ cup (200 ml) extra-virgin olive oil
1 teaspoon (5 ml) lemon juice
1 hard-cooked egg yolk
2 salt-cured anchovy fillets
1 tablespoon (15 g) salt-cured capers
¼ cup (40 g) tuna in oil
Salt and pepper

GARNISH
10 oz (300 g) mixed salad greens
4 quail's eggs, hard-boiled
4 capers
¼ cup (50 g) mullet roe

Method

Trim the tuna to obtain a cylinder-shaped fillet that is about 7 inches (18 cm) long with a diameter of approximately 1½ inches (4 cm).

Place all the marinade ingredients in a food processor and blend for about 1 minute.

Spread a layer of marinade to make one square on a sheet of parchment that is doubled up. Arrange the tuna on top and wrap it in the paper. Chill for 2 hours.

By doing this, the water that comes out of the tuna is absorbed by the paper and it is marinated dry.

Meanwhile, prepare a mayonnaise by emulsifying the egg yolks with the oil drizzled in very slowly and whisking energetically; add the lemon juice a little at a time. Separately chop the hard-cooked egg yolk, anchovies, capers (which have been rinsed well in cold water), and tuna in oil, drained and oil discarded. Add the chopped mixture to the mayonnaise and season with salt and pepper.

Wash the tuna fillet well under cold running water and dry with kitchen paper.

Cut a 1-inch (3-cm) thick slice from the widest side of the lean veal. Trim to make an evenly sized 8-inch (20 cm) log. Use a knife to cut a slit inside the veal, making a pocket. Insert the tuna fillet into the meat and secure tightly with kitchen string. Sauté in a non-stick frying pan, let rest and then remove the string.

Cut four slices of cold veal with tuna crosswise about ¾-inch (2-cm) thick. Arrange a slice in the center of a plate and garnish with a little mixed greens, a caper, hard-boiled quail's egg, sliced in half, and a little roe. Finish the dish with a quenelle of tuna sauce in front of the veal with tuna.

Wine pairing

Chardonnay "Costa di Bussia" 2006 – White
Winery: Costa di Bussia, Bussia – Monforte d'Alba (CN)

ALTA LANGA POTATO GNOCCHI FILLED WITH RUNNY QUAIL'S EGG AND SERVED WITH BUTTER AND WHITE ALBA TRUFFLE

Ingredients for 4 people
Preparation time: 45'

FILLING
16 quail's eggs

GNOCCHI
2.5 lb (1.2 kg) potatoes from Alta Langa
2 cups (300 g) all-purpose flour
2 whole eggs
2 tablespoons (30 g) butter, softened
⅓ cup (40 g) grated Parmesan
Salt
Nutmeg

SERVING
2 tablespoons (50 g) butter
2 tablespoons (50 g) beef stock
2 oz (60 g) white Alba truffle (Tuber Magnatum Pico)

Method

FILLING
Break the quail's eggs and beat well. Pour the beaten eggs into the plastic trays they came in (so that they form half-spheres of egg). Freeze for a couple of hours.

GNOCCHI
Boil the potatoes in their skins in plenty of salted water. Peel and mash them with a potato masher or fork on a wooden surface, mixing them with the remaining ingredients to make the gnocchi.
Divide the mixture into shapes that are slightly smaller than ping pong balls. Insert half a ball of frozen egg in each gnocco and smooth over with the mixture so that the egg isn't on the outside.
Cook the gnocchi in plenty of salted water until they rise to the surface. Wait a couple of minutes before draining them.

Serving

Toss the gnocchi in the pan with the butter and beef stock.
Serve four gnocchi per portion, keeping them soft with some of the cooking juices.
Finish the dish by grating with plenty of white truffle.

Wine pairing

Barbera d'Alba 2006 – Red
Winery: Ermanno Costa, Cascina Spagnolo, San Defendente – Canale d'Alba (CN)

FASSONE CHEEKS BRAISED IN BAROLO WINE
WITH SWEET FRIED MORSELS

Ingredients for 4 people
Preparation time: 1 h – Cooking time: 2 h – Marinating: 24 h

4 Piedmontese veal cheeks

MARINADE
3½ oz (100 g) carrots
3½ oz (100 g) celery
3½ oz (100 g) onions
5 cloves
1 teaspoon (5 g) juniper
cinnamon stick
1 small bunch of herbs, consisting of bay
leaves, rosemary, and sage
2 quarts (2 liters) Barolo wine

BATTER
⅔ cup (100 g) flour
3 tablespoons (45 g) water
2 tablespoons (45 g) Maraschino
2 egg yolks

2 teaspoons (10 g) melted butter
2 teaspoons (10 g) sugar
Pinch of brewer's yeast for desserts
Vanilla

SWEET FRIED MORSELS
8 dry amaretti cookies
1⅔ cups (250 g) all-purpose flour
6 whole eggs
4 cups (500 g) breadcrumbs
4 Golden Delicious apples

SEMOLINA
Generous 2¾ cups (700 g) milk
½ cup (100 g) sugar
Generous 1 tablespoon (20 g) salt
⅔ cup (100 g) semolina
1 egg yolk

Method

Coarsely chop the marinade vegetables. Arrange the veal cheeks in a large container and add the marinade spices, herbs, and vegetables. Cover with the wine and let infuse for at least 24 hours.

BATTER
Place all the ingredients in a food processor and blend until smooth. Let rest in the refrigerator.
Meanwhile, dip the amaretti first in the flour and then in the egg. So sandwich them together, then dip in egg, then breadcrumbs, then egg, then breadcrumbs. Reserve any leftover flour, egg, and breadcrumb for dipping the semolina cubes.

SEMOLINA
Bring the milk to a boil with the sugar and salt. Sift in the flour and beat with a hand-held blender to make sure that no lumps form. Let simmer for a couple of minutes, remove from the heat, and beat in the egg yolk. Pour the semolina in a deep baking pan and spread the mixture out to about 1-inch (3-cm) thick. Let cool. Once it has cooled, cut into small cubes. Dip them into the flour, egg, and breadcrumbs. Reserve any leftover flour, egg, and breadcrumb for battering the apples.

CHEEKS
Drain the meat from the marinade and dry it well. Place the cheeks in a saucepan with a little oil over medium heat and sear. Add all the ingredients needed for cooking, reserving some stock.
As soon as the wine comes to a boil, ignite it with a match so that the alcohol in the wine does not remain during cooking. Continue cooking over low heat for a couple of hours, adding stock if needed. Blend the cooking juices in a food processor with the herbs and vegetables to obtain a smooth sauce.

SWEET FRIED MORSELS
Remove the core and peel from the apples and cut them into ¾-inch (2-cm) thick slices. Dip the apples in the batter and deep fry them. Also fry the amaretti and semolina.

Serving

Arrange the cheek in the center of the plate, cover with the sauce, and serve with a couple of pieces of the fried apple, amaretto, and semolina.
Garnish with the bunch of the same herbs (fresh) used for cooking.

Wine pairing

Barbaresco Lorens 2005 – Red
Winery: Eredi Lodali – Tréiso (CN)

GIANDUJA MOUSSE WITH LANGHE HAZELNUTS

Ingredients for 4 people
Preparation time: 30' – Cooking time: 30' – Resting: 6 h

TORTE
Generous ¼ cup (70 g) egg whites
Generous 1 tablespoon (20 g) sugar
Generous ⅓ cup (40 g) toasted ground
Langhe hazelnuts
Generous ⅓ cup (40 g) toasted ground
almonds
Scant ¼ cup (40 g) chopped semisweet
chocolate

MOUSSE
1 cup (250 g) milk

1 cup (250 g) cream
Scant ½ cup (100 g) Langhe hazelnut paste
⅔ cup (150 g) egg yolks
1 teaspoon (5 g) potato starch
3¼ cups (800 g) chocolate gianduja
3¼ cups (800 g) lightly whipped cream
½ cup (100 g) sugar

DECORATION
4 white chocolate and gianduja cigarette
Custard, for serving
4 physalis, for garnish

Method

TORTE
Whip the egg whites with the sugar until stiff peaks. Meanwhile, sift together all the remaining ingredients and gradually fold them into the beaten whites. Spoon into the individual cylindrical silicon molds. Bake in the oven at 275°F (140°C/gas mark 1) for about 30 minutes.

MOUSSE
Boil the milk, cream, sugar and hazelnut paste. Slowly beat in the egg yolks and starch. Cook in the top of a double boiler for a couple of minutes without letting mixture come to a boil. Add the chocolate gianduja and let all the chocolate melt. Let cool slightly. Fold in the whipped cream to lighten. Let rest in the refrigerator for at least 6 hours.

Serving

Position the torte in the center of the plate. Spread with a thin layer of chocolate and arrange a quenelle of gianduja mousse on top. Decorate the plate with a little custard, a physalis, and a white chocolate and gianduja cigarette.

Wine pairing

Moscato Passito: Sol
Winery: Cerruti – Castiglione Tinella (CN)

PIER GIUSEPPE VIAZZI

RESTAURANT ARIANNA - CAVAGLIETTO (NOVARA)

There's no romantic reason for the origin of the name "Arianna" that was given to the restaurant, but there is an entertaining anecdote. When the father of chef Pier Giuseppe Viazzi, who currently owns the restaurant with his wife Caterina, decided to undertake his business in 1965 in Cavaglietto, a small village in the Novarese countryside made up of a handful of houses in a wet landscape of lakes, rivers, and rice fields, everyone thought he was mad. *"One day,"* Pier Giuseppe tells us, *"when we were going somewhere, I no longer remember where, my father saw an advertising board for a mental health nursing home that was called Villa Arianna. This is where he took the idea of the name from, saying 'it means that if the restaurant doesn't work, we'll turn it into an annex of the clinic!'"*

At the beginning, the restaurant was a bar more than anything else boasting a billiards table, a television and a few tables for card playing. Then it was gradually turned into an inn with a few rooms and a restaurant with good food in abundant portions, as was the custom back then. *"My mother Maria was in the kitchen and she was a good cook, offering typical Novarese dishes. During the week, it was above all the laborers who worked in the area and employees at the nearby factories who came to eat here; whereas at the weekend we organized wedding banquets or lunches and dinners for groups and parties."*

Pier Giuseppe continued in his parents' footsteps right from the start, attending a hotel institute, followed by a range of work experience from 1975 to 1979. *"When I finished studying, my aim was to become a chef in a large hotel, not to work in a restaurant, as I wanted to manage an enormous kitchen staff."* This is why he worked his first two seasons at the *Grand Hotel des Iles Borromées* in Stresa, followed by the *Hilton* in Milan, the international hotel chain with whom he also went to England, specifically, to the town of Stratford-upon-Avon, Shakespeare's birthplace. Then he went to France to the *Hotel Royal La Baule* in the region of Brittany, followed by the old *Auberge de Condé* in La Ferté-sous -Jouarre in the region of Vallée de la Marne. This is where he began to see how the job functions in a large restaurant that specializes in traditional cuisine.

"I tried to put what I had learned into practice, taking into account my possibilities and the customers we already had." For a couple of years, he worked with his parents, with his mother in the kitchen and his father and brother in the dining room, offering a fusion cuisine of traditional and new dishes. *"Then I found myself at a crossroads between traditional food or the more modern take that the region's products favor, cooking, combining, and presenting them in a new way; and where this can't offer what I needed, being able to serve other ingredients, always of the utmost quality."* In the end, he opted for this cuisine, which starts with the regional delicacies, but which isn't so rigidly restrictive. It doesn't topple the Romanesque establishment built up by the family, like the Novarese architect Alessandro Antonelli did when he built the neoclassical cathedral of Novara in the second half of the nineteenth century, but he embraces it with open arms. *"A cuisine that, now like then, I would define as simple. It doesn't tend to mix too many ingredients in the same dish and its main aim is to enhance the ingredient."*

Up until 1985, the entire Viazzi family ran the restaurant. Then when his brother Francesco decided to take over a bakery at *Lago d'Orta* and his parents retired from the business, Giuseppe and his wife remained at the helm. The restaurant began to transform into the elegant and refined place that it is today, with lovely table settings, stylish, comfortable armchairs and soft lighting. It's a place where customers can feel at home in a tranquil atmosphere. During the first year of his management, the young chef had already earned a Michelin star, an important accomplishment that allowed him to become known outside the Novara area. In the early '90's, he was one of the founding members of the Italian branch of the *Jeunes Restaurateurs d'Europe* association (he is now an honorary member as he's exceeded the age limit), which brings together young chefs and restaurateurs who share the motto of "talent and passion," as well as respecting, interpreting, and spreading the culinary traditions of their own region.

"Ours is a small farming village with less than 400 residents, but I like it here; I'm friends with everyone. It is an attractive, sunny village. We have three churches, a couple of squares, and a

wide main avenue. Of course, given that we are situated in such an isolated place, those who come to our restaurant deliberately make the journey. Nobody comes by accident." In terms of natural beauty, its fortunate position cannot be denied. It is set between maize fields, a short distance away from an island of the so-called *prateria d'Italia*, the *Riserva Naturale delle Baragge*. It is a unique environment, with a rare combination of oak, birch, hornbeam, and Scots pines, all magnificently showcased in stunning nature trails. The village is not insignificant in a geographical sense either. Novara, with the imposing Antonelli dome of the *Basilica di San Gaudenzio* that stands out over the placid horizons of the surrounding countryside, can be seen 20 kilometers away; whereas the largest town in the area is just 10 kilometers away, Borgomanero, a town founded in ancient times, with the beautiful Romanesque church of San Leonardo. Borgomanero is famous in the food world for its *tapulon*, the curious donkey meat stew that is chopped up and cooked in wine.

Pier Giuseppe offers an à la carte and tasting menu that changes with the seasons, while keeping the dishes that have been enjoyed the most from year to year. Among the starters, a carpaccio of foie gras with fig preserves and a cardoon flan with a garlic-flavored sauce are always on the menu. The same applies to the risottos, which are a constant feature throughout the year, although they vary from season to season. In the summer they are served with frogs' legs and zucchini flowers, whereas in the winter he includes sausage and radicchio risottos. *"We use Carnaroli rice, which is the best variety for risottos."* The poetic scenery of the rice fields, dotted with herons, actually begins a few kilometers away from Cavaglietto before then continuing towards southern Piedmont and Lombardy. The area's gastronomy has been based on rice for at least five centuries, like in the traditional Novarese *paniscia*, where this cereal is cooked in vegetable stock with beans and sausage and seasoned with plenty of black pepper.

One of the restaurant's specialty dishes is the slice of Piedmontese Fassone fillet, the excellent locally bred beef, combined with a potato tart in the winter or with beans cooked with shallots in the summer, and served with a wine sauce. Pier Giuseppe usually uses the prized Ghemme, a full-bodied, quality red wine, produced from Nebbiolo grapes in the town with the same time. Nebbiolo is practically a stone's throw away from Cavaglietto, in the morainic hilly area, and its wine pairs up well with recipes that are full of character. *"Here there are also cheeses that are typical regional products, as well as meat, rice, frogs, and snails."* From alpine cheeses, such as Bettelmatt from the Val Formazza, to cheeses from the plain, the most famous of which is Gorgonzola, a dairy product of Lombard origin, yet the province of Novara is its most important production area. *"We have an excellent Gorgonzola produced on site, which we use in many dishes in our restaurant, from the classic gnocchetti served with Gorgonzola to the veal kidneys with Gorgonzola sauce."* This is also a freshwater fish area, crossed as it is by the rivers Sesia and Ticino, marked with torrents and canals, and embellished by Lake Maggiore, one of the main alpine lakes and the second largest lake in Italy, and the small *Lago d'Orta* (Lake Orta) so "delicious and coquettish," as described by Honoré de Balzac, that it has bewitched and inspired some of the greatest philosophers and artists of the world.

On Wednesday morning, making the most of the restaurant's day off, Pier Giuseppe does the rounds of his trusted suppliers to choose the best ingredients. *"We purchase fruit and vegetables from a greengrocer in the area as cultivation here is directed towards breeding and dairy, and no vegetables are grown. Yes, we have a garden where we grow a few vegetables and herbs that we need in the restaurant, but there's not much. The butcher and fishmonger are also within a radius of 30 kilometers and are the same ones that supplied my father."*

We can't say that the chef proposes a new interpretation of traditional dishes; he tends to offer them in a fairly faithful way. *"For example, in the winter, we serve a braised beef cheek. We start off* with the classic braised dish, but we also do it with this piece of meat." However, he often makes them lighter. "In our area, the typical recipe for stewed cabbage for a goose breast involves the use of lard as a condiment. If we were to use it today, not only may it cause digestive problems, but many people wouldn't like it as we're no longer used to its flavor; therefore I replace the lard with olive oil." Unlike other regions, there aren't that many characteristic dishes from the Novara area. "Our area has never been a rich region, so the traditional dishes are very poor." The most common dish was the fritura, pork loin cooked with onions. "There's still someone who makes it during the village fair at the end of July for Santa Aurelia." Another typical dish is salam d'la duja, preserved under pork fat in a terracotta jar. "In such a wet area, it was the only way to prevent the fresh salami from growing mold and to preserve it until the summer."

The menu chosen for the book has a strong personality while also being intimately linked to the land, "with some dishes that you'll either love or hate." As a starter, "herb-crusted frogs' legs, baked in the oven rather than frying them to make them lighter." As this is a land of rice fields and irrigated canals, frogs are naturally a typical food. Once considered peasant food, they are now a rare delicacy. For the pasta course, "stewed veal tortelli served with roasted juices. Here in Piedmont we have the tradition of agnolotti pasta, which this dish refers to, even though it's different in terms of its shape and filling, and use just braised beef instead of the usual mix of meats." For the main course, there is a dish based on the favorite mollusks in Piedmontese cooking: "snails with garlic butter sauce, cooked in a base of vegetables and Ghemme wine." To conclude, as dessert, "zabaglione ice-cream with Moscato d'Asti passito, instead of Marsala, served with a pureed melon sauce." Zabaglione, too, is typical. A hot cream of eggs, sugar, and wine, it is found all over Italy and considered to be Piedmontese in origin. Its name comes from San Giovanni Baylon, the patron saint of pastry chefs, venerated in Turin in the church of San Tommaso.

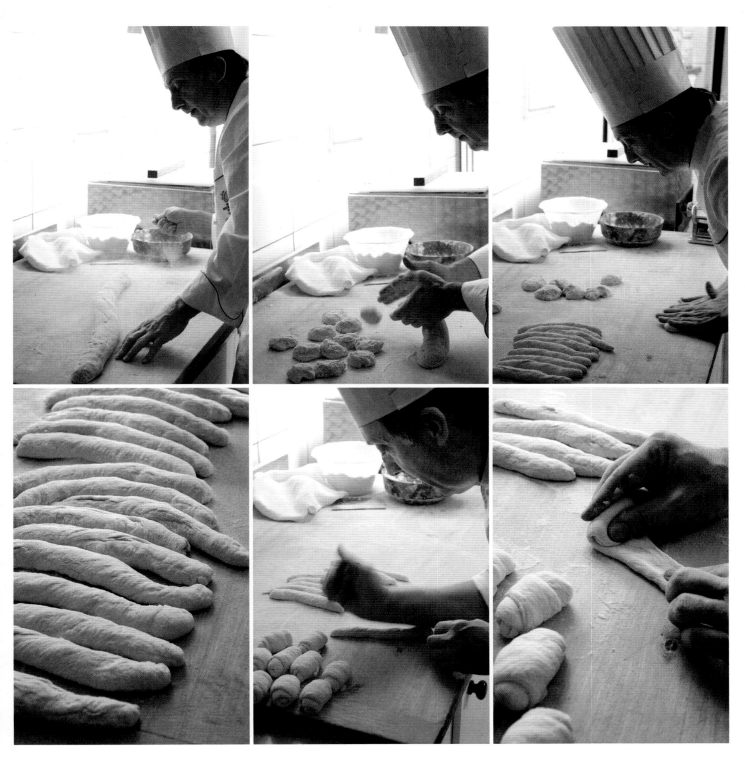

The chef is preparing bread with different shapes, like little rolls
or twisted bread which are leavened and then baked.

HERB-BREADED FROGS' LEGS

Ingredients for 4 people
Preparation time: 20'

5 oz (150 g) sliced white bread
⅔ oz (20 g) herbs (such as chervil, chives, calamint or mint, parsley)
1 clove garlic
1 lb (500 g) frogs' legs
Salt and pepper
Extra-virgin olive oil

Method

Break up the bread in a bowl and process with the herbs and garlic. Season the frogs' legs with salt and pepper and brush with a little extra-virgin olive oil. Dip them into the herb breadcrumbs. Arrange the frogs' legs on a baking sheet lined with parchment paper. Bake in a preheated oven at 475°F (240°C/gas mark 9) for 7 minutes. Remove from the oven and arrange on serving plates.

Wine pairing

Roero Arneis DOCG – White
Winery: Ceretto – Alba (CN)

STEWED VEAL TORTELLI WITH ROASTED JUICES

Ingredients for 4 people
Preparation time: 2 h 30'

PASTA
1⅓ cups (200 g) all-purpose flour
2 eggs
2 teaspoons (10 g) extra-virgin olive oil
1 teaspoon (6 g) salt

FILLING
3½ oz (100 g) onion, chopped
1¾ oz (50 g) carrot, chopped
1¾ oz (50 g) celery, chopped
1 clove garlic, chopped
1 bay leaf
1 sprig of rosemary
Salt and pepper
2 tablespoons (30 g) extra-virgin olive oil
10 oz (300 g) veal shoulder
Scant ½ cup (100 g) red wine
1 egg
Scant ½ cup (50 g) grated Parmesan

Method

PASTA
Sift the flour onto a cutting board and shape into a mound. Make a well in the center. Add the eggs, oil, and salt into the hollow and knead until the dough is smooth and even. Let rest for about 1 hour in a cool place.

FILLING
Sauté the vegetables, garlic, and herbs in the oil. Add the meat, cut into large pieces. Add salt and pepper. Pour in the red wine and simmer for 2 hours. Reserve the cooking juices and chop the meat and vegetables in a meat grinder.
Mix the ground meat with the egg and cheese. Roll out the pasta into thin sheets using a pasta machine. Cut it into rounds with a 2½-inch (6-cm) diameter pastry cutter. Fill with the filling and seal the tortelli. Cook the tortelli in plenty of salted water for 4 minutes. Drain and serve with ¼ cup (60 ml) of the roasted cooking juices.

Wine pairing

Gattinara DOCG – Red
Winery: Antoniolo – Gattinara (VC)

SNAILS COOKED IN GHEMME WINE WITH GARLIC SAUCE

Ingredients for 4 people
Preparation time: 2 h

48 prepared snails
2¾ oz (80 g) shallots
2¾ oz (80 g) carrots
2¾ oz (80 g) celery
⅓ cup (80 g) extra-virgin olive oil
3 cloves garlic
1 bay leaf
Salt and pepper
Generous ¾ cup (200 ml) Ghemme wine
3 tablespoons (50 g) butter
1 egg

Method

Boil the snails in salted water for 30 minutes. Let cool, remove from the shell, and clean, removing them from the black end part.
Finely dice the vegetables and sauté them in the oil with 1 clove of garlic and the bay leaf. Add the snails and season with salt and pepper.
Let them brown for a few minutes. Pour in the wine and let it evaporate. Cover with a lid and cook over low heat for about 1 hour.
Prepare the sauce by emulsifying the butter, cut into cubes, with 1 tablespoon of water and the remaining finely chopped garlic in a saucepan.
Serve the snails with the garlic sauce.

Wine pairing

Ghemme DOCG 2003 – Red
Winery: Antichi Vigneti di Cantalupo – Ghemme (NO)

ZABAGLIONE ICE-CREAM FLAVORED WITH MOSCATO D'ASTI PASSITO ON PUREED MELON

Ingredients for 4 people
Preparation time: 2 h

ZABAGLIONE
6 egg yolks
1 cup (200 g) sugar
Generous ¾ cup (200 ml) Moscato
2 cups (500 ml) whipped cream

PUREE
1 melon (cantaloupe), peeled, seeded, and cut into chunks
¼ cup (50 g) sugar

Method

ZABAGLIONE
Place the egg yolks in a bowl and add the sugar. Use a whisk to beat the mixture until frothy and increased in volume. Slowly whisk in the Moscato. Whisking constantly, over moderate low heat, bring the zabaglione to 175°F (80°C) in the top of a double boiler filled of water. When the zabaglione starts to thicken, remove from heat and let cool. Then fold in the whipped cream. Pour mixture into a terrine and freeze.

PUREE
Puree the melon chunks with the sugar.

Serving

Remove ice cream from the terrine. Spoon a ladle of the puree in the bottom of the dish and arrange thin slices of the ice cream on top.

Wine pairing

Moscato d'Asti passito – Dessert wine
Winery: La Spinetta – Castagnole Lanze (AT)

THE CUISINE OF LOMBARDY

Viewing the region from north to south, Lombardy gently slopes from the mountains of Valtellina and Valcamonica to the valleys with their great lakes, from Maggiore to Como and Garda, whose shores are edged with olive and lemon groves, to the hills and lakes of Brianza, down to the south of Cremona and Oltrepo Pavese. Such a varied landscape is home to a wide range of quality food products.

In terms of cured meats, we should mention Bresaola della Valtellina. It's made from lean beef and aged like a ham, hard and dark while whole, yet pink and soft when finely sliced. Then there's the typical Violino from Val San Giacomo, a unique sheep or goat cured meat, which takes its name from the size and type of cut. It's a pleasure to try it in the traditional *crotti*, natural caves used as cellars and restaurants. On the other hand, typical of Lomellina, there's the uniquely flask-shaped *Salame d'oca*, salami stuffed in goose's skin and boiled; whereas *Prosciutto d'oca* actually comes from Mortara, in the Pavese. Not forgetting *Salame di Varzi* and *Salame Milan.*, They take their name from their respective city and are made from pork and beef, salt, cracked pepper, and an optional infusion of garlic and white wine.

The cows reared on the fertile Lombard plain provide excellent milk, which is used to make world-class cheeses: Gorgonzola PDO (see box), with its creamy texture, marbled by the wholesome green streaks from the mold that grows during the ageing and lends it that unmistakable piquant flavor and strong aroma; Taleggio PDO, with its typical square shape, soft texture and signature aroma, created around the tenth and eleven centuries in Val Taleggio, in the area to the north of Bergamo, but now produced all over the Lombard Pre-Alps and on the plain; Bitto della Valtellina, a full-fat cheese made in the summer in alpine huts from cow and sheep's milk, dry-salted and stored at altitude until it is brought down into the valleys in the autumn, with ageing that varies from 70 days to a few years; Quartirolo, a white or straw-yellow colored cheese and an aromatic and slightly sour flavor, made all over the region; Mascarpone, originally from the Lodi area, made from triple-cream cheese, refined and buttery, once upon a time only made in the winter and sold in small gauze bags, to be eaten very fresh; Grana Padano PDO, invented in around the year 1,000 by the Cistercian monks of Abbazia di Chiaravalle, with a coarse grain and straw-yellow color, aged for up to four years (Granone or Stravecchione), and weeps drops of liquid that have been captured in the cheese when cut. The birth of the "Milkyway" is owed to the Medieval age, the endless expanse of white Romanesque churches dotted all over Lombardy – Sant'Ambrogio in Milan, Sant'Abbondio in Como, and San Michele Maggiore in Pavia, just to recall the most famous examples – rich in artistic treasures and with simple yet striking architectural lines, whose charming name calls to mind the world of food.

Lombardy's lakes and rivers provide many fish, which are prepared in a style particular to the area. Just consider the perch fillets that you can taste on the shores of Lake Maggiore or shad cooked with sage butter, a specialty of Lake Como. In Lecco, *Missultitt* are prepared by drying shad, which are eaten with buttered black bread or polenta and red wine from Valtellina.

Traditional Lombard cooking, which uses butter as a fundamental condiment, rivaled only by the lard – needed to give minestrone its unique flavor – gives ample opportunity to cook rice in a thousand different ways: Milanese risotto gilded with saffron; the version from Monza with the addition of sausage; with mushrooms; or in Lomellina and Pavese, with frogs or *al salto* (the name means "jump"), made from yesterday's leftover saffron risotto; rice and parsley in stock, or minestrone with seasonal vegetables thickened with rice, all of which are served with butter and Grana cheese. In addition to rice, pride of place is given to polenta: *Polenta taragna* from Valtellina, served with slices of cheese; *Polenta e osei,* with small game birds, a specialty from Bergamo and typical of those early cold autumn days; and *Polenta unta* from Lake Como, typical of Gravedona and Dongo, cut into slices and baked with plenty of Semuda, the local spicy cheese. Pizzoccheri, prepared in Valtellina, is a flat ribbon pasta made with buckwheat flour, a cereal that is believed to have come from the East and which highlanders grow in their fields, cooked in water with potatoes and greens and served with sage butter and Bitto cheese. In Mantua and all over southern Lombardy, pumpkin tortelli are widespread, descendants of the Renaissance cuisine of the court of Gonzaga.

Among the main courses on offer are the omnipresent Milanese veal chops, which are breaded and fried; veal shank osso buco, cooked slowly and eaten with saffron risotto; and pig's temple with garbanzo beans, the traditional dish for All Souls' Day. *Cassoeüla,* a typical pork-based winter dish, could be called the Italian version of the Alsatian dish *sauerkraut.* The secret of its tremendous flavor lies in the quality of the cabbage used to make it, in the pork ribs which must have the correct amount of fat, and in the lard rinds that are added with the trotter, head, and sausage. In Valcuvia one of the most famous specialties is guinea fowl cooked in clay, according to one method, which keeps the flavor of the meat intact. The local say this recipe was tested by the soldiers of fortune, who would cover a stolen bird in the wet clay and cooked it over a campfire. The famous Mostarda di Cremona – *"mosto ardente"* – is always served with boiled meats, made from fruit and available in both sweet and spicy versions. In terms of vegetables, there are the Cilavegna asparagus, perfect with uova in cereghìn, eggs cooked in butter in a pot, and the aromatic Sèrmide onion. Those with a sweet tooth will be spoilt for choice: the now famous Panettone – Pan de Toni – from Milan, rich in butter, sultanas, and candied fruits, with its long and complicated leavening; the Easter Colomba, flavored with candied orange; Cremona nougat, made from almonds and honey and a constant on the Christmas table; Torta Paradiso from Pavia; Amaretti cookies from Saronno, also inspired by the liqueur of the same name; Tortionata from Lodi, made from almonds and sultanas and flavored with lemon; Bussolano from Mantua, a large ring of leavened dough to be dipped in wine; Persicata from Brescia, a dense sweetmeat made from peaches cut into pieces; and Mascarpone served with honey (or sugar) and flavored with a sweet liqueur.

BRESAOLA DELLA VALTELLINA IGP

BRESAOLA DELLA VALTELLINA IGP, A TYPICAL PRODUCT OF THE PROVINCE OF SONDRIO, IS MADE FROM THE MOST VALUABLE CUTS OF LEG OF BEEF, SALTED, CURED, AND AGED. IT IS SERVED IN SLICES, WITH GRANA CHEESE AND EXTRA-VIRGIN OLIVE OIL.

GORGONZOLA PDO

LEGEND HAS IT THAT IN THE TOWN OF GORGONZOLA, IN THE OUTSKIRTS OF MILAN, THE METHOD TO PREPARE THIS FAMOUS AND EXQUISITE CHEESE WAS DISCOVERED IN THE TWELFTH CENTURY. AN UNKNOWN CHEESE-MAKER WORKED THE CURDS LEFT-OVER FROM THE NIGHT BEFORE WITH THOSE IN THE MORNING, THEREBY CREATING A PRODUCT WITH THE UNIQUE APPEARANCE AND FLAVOR OF GORGONZOLA.
IN PRESENT-DAY PRODUCTION, WHICH CONCERNS BOTH THE DOLCE AND PICCANTE TYPES, THE SPORES OF THESE MICROSCOPIC FUNGI ARE ADDED TO THE MILK AND THEY ARE GIVEN A WAY TO GROW ONLY DURING THE AGEING WHEN THE FORMS ARE DRILLED WITH AN APPROPRIATE TOOL, LENDING THE TYPICAL AND DELICIOUS STREAKS TO THE CHEESE.

DAVIDE BROVELLI

RESTAURANT IL SOLE - RANCO (VARESE)

"If it should befall that you possess a heart and a shirt, then sell the shirt and visit the shores of Lago Maggiore," wrote the French writer Stendhal. If you would like to try some creative cuisine with old-fashioned flavors, there's a relais et chateaux of unspeakable beauty. It's *Il Sole* in Ranco, in the province of Varese, whose class and excellence has been recognized by leading Italian and foreign gastronomic associations, including *Le Soste, Traditions et Qualité – Les Grandes Tables du Monde,* and *Les Jeunes Restaurateurs d'Europe.*

The Lombard shore of the second largest lake in Italy is immersed in a beautiful landscape, in its succession of lakes and wooded valleys, with amazing panoramic views and embellished with luxury villas and nineteenth-century hotels, with silent parks and lush gardens. The area has been one of the favorite destinations of the Milanese rich since the nineteenth century for its superb natural scenery and hunting and fishing trails, but also due to Sacro Monte, a place of devotion and art with its fourteen seventeenth-century chapels that line the walk to the Marian sanctuary.

"It was my great-great-grandmother Emilia who opened an inn here in 1850," Davide tells us, the current chef and co-owner of *Il Sole* in Ranco with his family members. At the time, the village consisted of a handful of houses and a small church. Guests arrived from the city on horse-drawn carriages to find accommodation and refreshment in this restful and welcoming environment, along the romantic lakeside road which runs between the imposing Rocca Borromea di Angera, one of the best-kept medieval castles in Lombardy, and the fourteenth-century retreat of Santa Caterina del Sasso overlooking the lake. Even back then, the cooking was first class, made using free-range products, from fresh eggs to fresh milk. *"There was a farm manager a few kilometers away, who fed goats and farmyard animals with the restaurant's leftovers, and cultivated a vegetable plot; therefore there was the chance to cook for customers using excellent ingredients."*

The restaurant was then called *Locanda del Sole* due to its fortunate situation, immersed in a luxuriant garden and peaceful with a view of the lake, it was and still is bathed in sun all day long.

"My grandmother Marina continued the inn's business with my grandfather Augusto. In the summer, beneath the cool arbor, trippers and families could eat the area's specialties." In the 1950's, Davide's father, their son Carlo, started in the kitchen, backed by his considerable training and experiences abroad, with his wife Itala. *"When I was young, I remember that my parents cranked out cover after cover in the summer season and at the weekends, but this was a seasonal success, limited to just three months in the summer."* This was the reason why Davide's mother and father felt the need to take a chance on haute cuisine in the Seventies. There wasn't a clear-cut turning point, but a different approach to cooking gradually took shape, an approach which paid attention to the refinement and care taken in presenting dishes and the aesthetic appearance of the courses, as well as the professionalism of the restaurant service. *"After some initial difficulties, new customers started coming from beyond Varese and Milan and throughout the year."* With Carlo Brovelli, the restaurant gained its two Michelin stars, customers from all over the world and the business was established. This quality has now been re-confirmed after the restaurant passed into expert hands of son Davide.

The restaurant's atmosphere is extremely elegant with a touch of retro style that enhances its charm and is perfected down to the last detail. *"We have a beautiful arbor with a lake view, perhaps the only one left, where we serve in the summer, as well as an indoor room. In the last few years, my idea has been to move this room outdoors so that the view, which is moreover striking, can also be admired in the winter.*

This was a privately owned house that has been altered over the years to make it into a hotel and restaurant." However, its strength lies in the fact that it was formerly a house. *"I think that the guests of Il Sole breathe in a family spirit. At the end of the day, there are only five of us who work here. My father works in the kitchen with me and gives me a hand; my mother helps my wife Cristina in the dining room; and my brother Andrea manages the hotel. It is a fairly big business, but which has been family-run for over a century, and you can feel it; it gives it personality."*

Davide started working in the kitchen at Il Sole at the age of 16, but he has been managing it by himself for about 10 years. *"My training as a chef was on the job. I didn't attend a hotel institute. Instead I chose to go and work immediately and gain some experience in different places."* In the mid-1980's, he worked for Vergé in France at *Moulin de Mougin*, which was at the peak of catering back then, followed by Los Angeles, in the USA, where he worked at some of the leading restaurants there at the time, such as *Citrus* and *Valentino*, before returning home. *"I have my own idea of cooking, with dishes that are a bit original, perhaps because I haven't been influenced that much by other chefs. I didn't struggle to discover my identity."* Also because it was already prepared for him in the family scrapbook. *"I believe that the history of one's cuisine should be respected, otherwise we'll all end up offering the same meals."* His pledge is to honor the land in which he was born and has lived for 40 years. *"Without a doubt, I would call my cooking regional. First of all, I try to use and enhance the fish from the lake, as well as all the products of the area, including the great cheeses and excellent meat."* The typical food of Lombardy effectively comes from animal husbandry and the dairy industry.

In terms of the legacy of freshwater fish, still abundant in the larger lakes, Davide enjoys cooking black bass, pike, tench, carp, eel, perch, and whitefish. There's also a product that he makes himself: pike caviar. *"I use pike roe and leave them in brine for a couple of weeks. Then I clean them all again, leave them in small trays, and cook then at 60 degrees for three hours. The unique detail is that they stay a beautiful golden color."* He also prepares sea fish, which comes twice a week from Sicily, but he prefers to recommend fish from the lake to his customers. *"It is caught during the day and often has a tastier meat that is hard to find on the market."*

He uses the famous goat cheeses from Valcuvia in particular, the luxuriant pre-alpine valley whose sides are clad in beech and chestnut trees, and Bettelmatt from the nearby Val Formazza, produced on the border with Switzerland, around the summer pasture with the same name. In terms of meat, *"here in Ranco there's a small farm that has an excellent selection of products: locally bred beef, but also other local animals such as ducks and pigeons."* As regards the area's typical products, there's one in particular that the chef uses happily: peaches from Lago di Monate, which are grown 20 kilometers from Ranco. *"These are white peaches that have been peeled and preserved in syrup, whose particularity is that they always stay crunchy as if they were fresh."*

At the moment, the restaurant has a special menu, whereby everything served is produced within a radius of 30 kilometers from Ranco. *"My supplies always come from small-scale local producers, carrying on the tradition of my great-great-grandmother, using high-quality, local ingredients."* He doesn't go and do the shopping himself. He orders the products and they are delivered straight to the restaurant. *"At the beginning of the year, I visit our suppliers, explain to them my style of cooking and, knowing what I want, they bring me their produce."*

There are timeless dishes on the restaurant's menu, or which have never been changed, like the untouchable scampi lasagne with Sauternes sauce, created by Carlo Brovelli, or dishes whose inspiring idea has been maintained yet modified in terms of the main ingredient, such as a ball of fois gras wrapped in potato threads and then fried, in which Davide has revised the salmon version made by his father. There's also great excitement in discovering dishes that date back to the second half of the nineteenth century, such as fried breaded perch, a classic recipe of this area. *"I've changed it in terms of presentation and combination of flavors, for example, I serve it as a skewer, with mixed herbs, marinated cherry toma-*

toes, a very finely chopped Tropea red onion, lemon gelatin, and mayonnaise flavored with lemon and shallot; but the basic recipe is still the same in the end." There's also whitefish *in carpione*, or rather steamed and then pickled in vinegar and white wine with a variety of vegetables and herbs. *"This is my great-great-grandmother's recipe, although I serve it with a raspberry mousse."* In short, like the main historical dwellings of Varese, whose outward appearances remain unchanged, but whose interiors have been renovated to include new functions, such as Palazzo Estense, surrounded by gardens inspired by those at the Austrian castle of Schönbrunn, now home to the town hall, or Villa Recalcati, also bedecked with a lovely park, which is home to the provincial government, Davide's meals echo the language of past times, yet serve to transmit thoughts in the present. In his recipes, *"always with a base of renewed tradition,"* Davide also tries to *"bring new techniques to traditional dishes, or rather old yet revalued techniques, such as cooking at a low temperature, which have always been used."* For example, in the Easter period, he serves Val Formazza kid *"by cooking it for 19 hours in a vacuum pack at a low temperature, followed by sautéing them in a pan just before serving. The meat remains extremely tender and pink, and the crispy crust gives it extra flavor on the outside."* Davide feels close to his village. *"During the afternoon break, I like to go for a run to get rid of some of the stress of the kitchen. I almost always go to the San Quirico hills to the chapel of the same name."* He also goes to see a natural monument that has an air of mystery about it, a couple of kilometers from the restaurant: Sasso Cavallaccio, called *"sass cavalàsc"* in local dialect. *"It is a gigantic rock planted in the middle of the lake that seems to bear witness to geological events of the distant past."* In fact, Ranco has many of these rocks, so-called erratics, moranic materials that perhaps date back to the fourth glaciation of the Quaternary period. The lake is the thread that runs through the dishes selected for the book. For starters, lake carpaccio with sea urchins and caviar. For the pasta course, green tagliolini with smoked whitefish and basil. For the main course, pistachio, hazelnut, and almond-breaded black bass with mustard ice-cream. For dessert, peaches from the nearby Lago di Monate, one of the few glacial lakes where you can go swimming, the ugly-but-good cookie soufflé, the famous hazelnut amaretti cookies that are typical of two towns further inland, Cittiglio and Gavirate, and Vin Santo ice-cream. A menu in which each ingredient whisks you away on a journey, making you think of the *Museo Europeo dei Trasporti "Ogliari"* in Ranco, whose outdoor exhibition shows all the public and private means of transport in use and in their heyday from the start of the nineteenth century to the present day.

LAKE CARPACCIO WITH SEA URCHINS AND CAVIAR

Ingredients for 4 people
Preparation time: 25'

1¾ oz (50 g) cherry tomatoes
1¾ oz (50 g) small zucchini
1¾ oz (50 g) green beans
1¾ oz (50 g) green asparagus
1¾ oz (50 g) shelled peas
1¾ oz (50 g) eggplant
1 pike fillet
3½ oz (100 g) mixed greens
Extra-virgin olive oil
Salt
Pepper
12 sea urchins
Soy sauce
3 tablespoons (40 g) Beluga caviar

Method

Blanch the cherry tomatoes. Remove the skin and seeds and dice the flesh.
Dice the remaining vegetables, then blanch them, one type of vegetable at a time, keeping them crunchy. Set them aside.
The simplest thing to do is to ask for a pike fillet from your fishmonger, originally at least 15–22 lb (7–10 kg). The larger the pike, the more tender and sweeter the meat. You can remove the annoying and fine fishbone that's usually among the fish meat.
Arrange the salad greens on individual plates, dressing them with oil and salt.
Cut the raw white pike meat very finely to make a carpaccio. Arrange it on the salad and season with salt and pepper.
Arrange the sea urchin flesh and all the blanched vegetables on top. Process the oil with the soy sauce using a handheld immersion blender. Drizzle the soy oil over the dish. Garnish with caviar in the center and serve.

Wine pairing

"Greco di Tufo" DOCG 2005 – White
Winery: Benito Ferrara, Fraz. San Paolo – Tufo (Av)

Wine obtained from Greco grapes selected from the Vigna Cicogna, owned by a small producer that has the peculiarity of being located above a former sulfur mine. This ground gives rise to highly concentrated grapes. The resultant wine is rich in personality, with a great freshness that is tangy and high in minerals.

GREEN TAGLIOLINI PASTA
WITH SMOKED WHITEFISH AND BASIL

Ingredients for 4 people
Preparation time: 20' – 1 h – Marinating time: 1 h

PASTA
3¼ cups (500 g) all-purpose flour
2 whole eggs
2 egg yolks
1 tablespoon extra-virgin olive oil
7 oz (200 g) spinach leaves
Salt

BASIL MOUSSE
2 sheets of gelatin
fish fumet
16 basil leaves
cream
Salt
Pepper

SERVING
200 Pachino or cherry tomatoes
Salt
Pepper
3½ oz (100 g) wild arugula
1¾oz (50 g) shallots
Parsley
1 clove garlic
2 smoked whitefish, each weighing 7 oz (200 g)
4 tablespoons extra-virgin olive oil
Generous 1 tablespoon (20 g) Belgian caviar (20 g)

Method

PASTA
Sift the flour onto a cutting board and shape into a mound. Make a well in the center. Pour the eggs and egg yolks and oil into the hollow. Add the spinach, which has been blanched, squeezed dry, and finely chopped, and salt. Knead until the dough is smooth and even. Let rest for about 1 hour in a cool place.

MOUSSE
Soak the gelatin in cold water. Drain and squeeze out. Blend the fish fumet with the gelatin, basil leaves, and cream in a food processor. Let rest and set in a bowl in the refrigerator.

PASTA SAUCE
Blanch and peel the cherry tomatoes. Put them in a bowl and season with salt and pepper, crushed in a mortar. Add the arugula and finely chopped shallot. Let marinate for about 1 hour. Finely chop a large handful of parsley with the garlic and put this in the bowl.

Serving

In a saucepan, cook the ingredients for the pasta sauce over low heat with a little oil, keeping them slightly crunchy.
Cook the pasta in salted water. Drain and toss in the prepared sauce in the pan.
Arrange the pasta in the center of a deep plate with a fairly large brim. Garnish with the fillets of smoked whitefish that have been broken up roughly and a dollop of caviar. Serve with the basil mousse.

Wine pairing

"Picol – Sauvignon" IGT 2006
Winery: Lis Neris – San Lorenzo (UD)

PISTACHIO, HAZELNUT, AND ALMOND-CRUSTED BLACK BASS WITH MUSTARD ICE-CREAM

Ingredients for 4 people
Preparation time: 1 h

BLACK BASS
⅔ cup (100 g) hazelnuts
⅔ cup (100 g) pistachios
⅔ cup (100 g) blanched almonds
1 black bass, weighing about 2½ lb (1.2 kg)
1 egg

JERUSALEM ARTICHOKES PUREE
2 shallots, finely chopped
Generous ⅓ cup (100 ml) extra-virgin olive oil
10 oz (300 g) Jerusalem artichokes
5 oz (150 g) firm, ripe pumpkin
Generous ¾ cup (200 ml) white wine
Water
Salt and Pepper

CELERY ROOT PUREE
1 lb (500 g) celery root
1 quart (1 liter) whole milk
Water
Salt
Pepper

MUSTARD ICE-CREAM
5 egg yolks
2 cups (500 ml) whole milk
Scant 2 tablespoons (25 g) wine vinegar
Generous 3 tablespoons (50 g) Pommery
Whole Grain Mustard de Meux
Fleur de sel, for serving
Toasted bread slices, for serving

Method

BLACK BASS

Spread the hazelnuts, pistachios, and almonds on a parchment-lined baking sheet. Toast at 400°F (200°C/gas 6) for about 10 minutes.

Place the nuts on a marble surface and let cool. Transfer to a food processor and grind well.

Scale and gut the black bass, removing the backbone and skin. Remove the stomach from the fillets and cut the fish at the back into 2⅓ x 1-inch (6 x 3-cm) fingers (or ask your fishmonger to do this for you).

Dip the fish fingers in the ground nut mixture, followed by the beaten egg.

Heat the oil in a saucepan and fry the black bass fingers until golden brown all over.

JERUSALEM ARTICHOKE PUREE

Brown the shallots in the oil in a frying pan. Add the Jerusalem artichokes and pumpkin, cut into cubes. Add the white wine and let it evaporate. Pour in the water and season with salt and pepper.

When the vegetables are tender, remove them with a slotted spoon, reserving the cooking water. Blend the vegetables in a food processor to obtain a smooth puree. Gradually add the cooking water, until you reach the desired consistency. Keep warm.

CELERY ROOT PUREE

Clean and peel the celery root, dicing it. Place the celeriac in a large pot and cover with the milk and water. Cook over medium heat until tender. Repeat the method used above to make the Jerusalem artichoke puree, blending the vegetable until pureed. Keep warm.

MUSTARD ICE-CREAM

Use a whisk to beat the egg yolks in a bowl, adding the cold milk.

In a saucepan, gently heat the mixture to 180°F (82°C).

Remove from the heat and let cool. Use a whisk to carefully add the vinegar and mustard. Pour into an ice-cream machine and churn according to the manufacturer's instructions.

Serving

Arrange the Jerusalem artichoke puree and celery root puree on warm plates, using a spoon to draw a line of squid ink. Arrange a whole fish finger on top, as well as another one cut at three-quarters, so you can see the white of the fish. Sprinkle with *fleur de sel* and place a quenelle of mustard ice-cream on a slice of toasted bread.

Wine pairing

Alto Adige Bianco DOC 2005 – Bianco
Winery: Mondevinum Weingut Niklaserhof – Kaltern – Caldaro (BZ)

PEACHES FROM LAGO DI MONATE, UGLY-BUT-GOOD COOKIE SOUFFLÈ AND VIN SANTO ICE-CREAM

Ingredients for 4 people
Preparation time: 30' – Resting: 3 h

PEACH PUREE
4 Peaches, pitted
Generous 3 tablespoons (50 ml) lemon juice
Generous 3 tablespoons (50 ml) sugar syrup

UGLY-BUT-GOOD COOKIE SOUFFLÈ
5 sheets of gelatin
¼ cup (60 ml) water
¾ cup (150 g) sugar
6 egg yolks
2 cups (500 g) Lago di Monate peach puree
2 cups (260 g) Tuscan ugly-but-good cookies (brutti e buoni), crumbled
Generous 2¾ cups (700 g) cream, whipped

VIN SANTO ICE-CREAM
4 egg yolks
Generous ¼ cup (60 g) sugar
1⅔ cups (400 ml) Vin Santo
Scant ¼ cup (50 ml) whipping cream, whipped

Method

PEACH PUREE
In a blender, puree the fresh Lago di Monate peaches and add the lemon juice and syrup.

UGLY-BUT-GOOD COOKIE SOUFFLÈ
Soak the gelatin in water. Drain and squeeze out.
Bring the water and sugar to a boil in a copper pot, heating it to 248°F (120°C). Beat the egg yolks in a small electric mixer beat in the hot syrup, a little at a time.
Warm the peach puree in the microwave and mix in the gelatin.
Mix the beaten egg mixture into the peach puree and add the crumbled ugly-but-good cookies. Fold in the whipped cream.
Pour the mixture into a mold and freeze.

VIN SANTO ICE-CREAM
Place the egg yolks, sugar, and Vin Santo in a metal bowl. Use a whisk to beat the mixture in a bain-marie (in the top of a double boiler) until heated to 158–167°F (70–75°C). When it has cooled, fold in the whipped cream. Pour the mixture into an ice-cream machine and churn according to the manufacturer's instructions.

Wine pairing

"Moscato Passito" IGT 2006 – Dessert wine
Winery: Cantine Viola – Saracena (CS)

LUCA BRASI

RESTAURANT LA LUCANDA - CAVENAGO BRIANZA (MILANO)

The restaurateur has traveled a distance of 20 kilometers, and what change this distance has made: from thinking on his own to thinking big. It's a successful conclusion to the entrepreneurial adventure that the chef Luca Brasi tried in 1997. Now he's attempted another adventure: from restaurateur to manager. His journey is not only symbolic, but a literal one because his restaurant *La Lucanda* has moved from Osio Sotto, in the central Bergamasco plain, restaurant and kitchen staff included, to Cavenago di Brianza, a few kilometers from Milan, in the brand new, prestigious structure of *Devero Hotel 4 Stelle Executive*.

Michelin-starred and a member of *Jeunes Restaurateurs d'Europe*, Luca has been entrusted with the catering for the entire hotel. In addition to La Lucanda, only open in the evenings, where he continues to offer new interpretations of traditional Lombard recipes with inspired and refined creativity, he also manages the grill bar *Dodici24*, a dynamic and informal space where he proposes faster and simpler food from midday to midnight, non-stop, seven days a week. There also follows the matter of the hotel's banquet hall, which with over 400 covers is the largest business in greater Milan for receptions and banquets. He also manages the lounge bar for breakfasts, pre-dinner drinks, and happy hour. *"It has been a great stimulus for me. Above all, being able to design the environments and the kitchen of such an important business without having any limitations or conditions; then there is the fact of being able to manage the restaurant independently as if it were my own,"* Luca tells us, with his calm nature and his feet firmly on the ground, the ideal personality to manage such a complicated structure without batting an eyelash. *"I sold La Lucanda, as a name, to the hotel's parent company which purchased it, but it is tied up with my being here. That's how I left all my problems behind as a small businessman so I could devote myself exclusively to my work."*

Perhaps not everyone would make the same decision, but it's had an excellent outcome for him. *"I believe that being able to be an all-round chef, covering all the catering bases, is a growth, if not a completion, from a professional point of view. Haute cuisine struggles to exist if it isn't supported by a large company. You need to look at the substance, not just at the poetics. Here I have the chance to cater for many covers, always paying attention to quality, as well as continuing my project with* La Lucanda, *actually being able to put more into it as I have the backing of a high-level business."*

The new restaurant is situated in the heart of Brianza, a region with a high urbanization rate, but strikingly dotted with clear stretches of water, placid cultivated fields, and gentle pre-alpine valleys, and looks like its former version in Osio Sotto. *"It was designed by the same architect and it plays on the materials. There's lots of wood, visible bricks, and natural materials, from Indian silk to raw cottons."* It is a tall, extremely light environment, with light hazelnut color tones; fairly modern, yet very warm and welcoming. It is made up of a main room with the kitchen on view and two smaller rooms separated by glass walls that are four meters high, on which panels of ecru colored Indian silk have been placed. There's a large, spectacular outdoor area with a swimming pool – it's not suitable for swimming and is purely aesthetic – surrounded by about 40 tables. *"In the evening, when it's lit up, it's very striking."*

Like Monza cathedral, the capital of Brianza, where the Iron Crown of Lombardy is kept, which was used to crown the kings of Italy from the Medieval era to Napoleon, Luca has also preserved his own in moving Bergamasco food to Brianza and arranging it on each plate, prepared by his expert and inventive hands. There are two *La Lucanda* classics that have remained on the menu: the sweet almond tortelli with Bergamasco black truffle, which has been a feature for 11 years, and the elegant creamy risotto with oysters, Franciacorta, and Beluga caviar, cooked in a gold-plated pot, *"a copper pot plated in gold that allows the rice to cook evenly."* Above all, however, the aim of his cuisine has remained the same: to be deeply rooted in the land where he cooks. A project

of immense value, especially in areas like the province of Milan, which is one of the most heavily industrialized in Italy, as well as welcoming a mass of Italians and foreigners and offering the widest possible catering. "Here local food traditions tend to disappear." Therefore, defending Lombard flavors that would otherwise be forgotten isn't just a noble purpose, but a cultural effort.

"If up until a short time ago, our cuisine was based on revisiting traditional Bergamasco food, now we tend to look at foods typical of Milan and Brianza." Obviously the quality of the ingredients remains the same, "which represents 99 percent of my cooking." The products always come from selected suppliers, which Luca trusts implicitly. "From time to time, I go and visit suppliers, of fish, meat, and vegetables, also because after all these years they know how we work and what we want. As I have the new business to manage, I don't have the time to go and personally do the shopping. However, they are mostly suppliers in the area, even though some, which work with the same spirit as us, are outside the region."

The chef intends to keep a few Bergamasco dishes, "although the food of my homeland isn't extremely rich in ingredients," based above all on cheeses, from the Taleggio produced in the valley of the same name in the Alto Bergamasco to Branzi and Formai de mut (mountain cheese) of the Alta Val Brembana, to the formaggelle of the Val di Scalve, as well as polenta, mushrooms, pork-based salamis, farmyard animals and small birds, such as thrushes and starlings. "The typical dishes are very rustic, based on bread or leftovers, such as minestra di latte, of which I offer a new version with lobster and black truffle." From now on, the centerpieces of his menu will however rely on the Brianza gastronomic tradition, which is also based on the countryside, rustic in terms of its ingredients, yet rich in flavor. Dairy products are some of its main produce, from Gorgonzola to Grana Padano, from Provolone Valpadana to Quartirolo, and the charcuterie, like the salami and prosciutto of Brianza, but also polenta, served in many ways, and freshwater fish, of which there

are many due to the numerous lakes and networks of canals and navigable channels that were set out around the year 1000 by the monks of the grand monasteries, which still continue to render the fertile and farm-dotted countryside fertile today.

In autumn and winter, Luca almost always includes cassoeula on the menu, a Milanese dish par excellence, prepared traditionally for the festival of St. Anthony on January 17th. He has revamped it as a small timbale of pork rind with cabbage and a rib, also pork, first steamed and then roasted, brushed with a citrus fruit reduction, slightly sweet and sour. "The idea of offering traditional cassoeula, or rather a stew made from cabbage and pork meats – ribs, trotters, rind, skin, etc. – in our restaurant would be unthinkable; it's a dish that just too heavy, which needs to be made lighter." He applies the same philosophy to other recipes from the area, such as ossi buco, a specialty of Milan that is often served with the classic saffron risotto, Milanese veal cutlets, or lake fish that is cooked in various ways. Luca thinks back to the delicate cultural tradition like the great eighteenth-century allegorical fresco that decorates the ceiling of the Salone di Apollo of Palazzo Rasini in Cavenago, the country home of the noble Lombard family.

"Offering new interpretations of traditional dishes is dictated by many factors: new food trends, different preparation and serving methods, as well as innovative cooking techniques." For example, the osèi scápac (runaway birds), an historic Lombard dish consisting of veal rolled and stuffed with prosciutto and sage, rolled up and cooked in butter, Luca offers them anew like this: veal fillet rolls stuffed with prosciutto and black truffle, rolled up and cooked, then served with morels, black truffle, wafers of Culatello, the exquisite cured meat from the Parma area, and crispy potatoes. Here a classic is revised with a respectful memory of the past, while being vibrantly modern, adding new ingredients, although not strictly from the area, and embellishing it with an extra touch of flavor.

"I have always been passionate about cooking since I was a child to the point at which I decided not to follow in my parents' footsteps who have a family business. To follow my calling, I decided to attend a hotel institute and was already working in a kitchen during the summer. After college, I gained experience working in some of the leading Italian kitchens, from Don Alfonso to

Sant'Agata sui Due Golfi to the kitchen of the Vai brothers in Courmayeur, then I went to Switzerland, to Lugano and Gstaad, and onto the Côte d'Azur. Even to Bermuda and the Maldives, where I was the kitchen manager at a holiday village of an Italian tour operator. At the age of 28, I decided to stop traveling to open a restaurant of my own." Originally from Clusone, a historical town of standing in the Val Seriana, in the Bergamo Alps, he would have based his establishment there, but "despite it being a tourist resort, there was no room for a high-class restaurant." That's why he went to the city, to Osio Sotto, an industrious town in a strategic position between Milan, Bergamo, and Brescia. "I started my experience as a restaurateur in a very simple building. At the beginning, I only had two young people who helped me in the kitchen and my wife Cinzia worked in the restaurant; then we grew slowly but surely. In 1999 I bought the property and it was renovated in 2001, also adding eight guest rooms."

The courses chosen for the book uphold the name of Paneròpoli (from "panera", cream in Lodigian dialect) that the Italian writer Ugo Foscolo gave to the city of Milan and the surrounding areas at the end of the eighteenth century, in light of the fact that a little butter, milk, cream, or a grating of cheese is always given to each dish. As a starter, a memory of Bergamo is served, or rather polenta with cave-aged Taleggio fondue and crispy polenta toasts. For the rice course, Cold Milanese-style rice, where the rice is cooked with saffron as in the traditional recipe and then combined with Parmesan ice-cream added in the center, and a crispy sausage that is placed on top. For the main course, there are common shrimp sausages with white polenta discs and black-eyed peas. For dessert, a melted dip of 70 percent chocolate is served with ice cream and, as decoration, saffron strands and puffed rice.

It is a Lombard menu that also looks toward Bergamo and Brianza. Like the eighteenth-century Villa Reale of Monza, designed by the imperial architect Giuseppe Piermarini, which embraces the space with the two wings that part from the building's central nucleus, this is how Luca combines his Bergamasco origins and his future in Brianza, bringing them together in a unique, captivating gastronomic experience.

A MEMORY OF BERGAMO

Ingredients for 4 people
Preparation time: 1 h 30'

2 quarts (2 liters) water
Pinch of salt
3 cups (450 g) stone-ground polenta flour
8 oz (250 g) raw milk, cave-aged Taleggio

Method

POLENTA
Bring the salted water to a boil. Add the flour and simmer the polenta for about 1½ hours, stirring it often.

CRUSTS
Spread out half the polenta to a thickness of ¾ inch (2 mm) on a sheet of parchment paper. Dry in the oven at 300°F (150°C/gas mark 2) for about 2 hours.

FONDUE
Melt the Taleggio in the top of a double boiler for about 30 minutes, stirring often.

Serving

Reheat the fresh polenta gently over low heat; arrange on plates covered with the fondue and garnish with the toasted polenta crusts.

Wine pairing

"Donna Marta" IGT 2004 – Red
Winery: Tenuta Le Mojole – Tagliuno di Castelli Calepio (BG)

COLD MILANESE-STYLE RICE

Ingredients for 4 people
Preparation time: 2 h

PARMESAN ICE-CREAM
1 cup (250 g) milk
⅔ cup (150 g) cream
3 egg yolks
Scant 2 tablespoons (25 g) sugar
Scant ¼ cup (25 g) Parmesan
Scant 2 tablespoons (25 g) isomalt

RICE
1¼ cups (250 g) Carnaroli rice
5-6 saffron strands
2 quarts (2 liters) water
Table salt
3½ oz (100 g) sausages
Coarse salt
5 oz (150 g) Parmesan ice-cream*

Method

ICE-CREAM
Mix the milk with the cream and bring to a boil. Mix all the remaining ingredients together separately in a bowl. Slowly whisk the milk mixture into the egg mixture. Transfer to the top of a double boiler and cook to 180°F (82°C). Let cool and churn in an ice-cream machine according to the manufacturer's instructions.

RICE
Cook the rice with the saffron in a saucepan with plenty of salted water. Drain and let it cool. Brown the sliced sausages in a separate nonstick pan until crispy.

Serving

Layer the ingredients using a mold, starting with the rice, then the ice-cream, rice again, and the sausage.

Wine pairing

Chardonnay 2005 – Terre di Franciacorta Bianco DOC – White
Winery: Ca' del Bosco – Erbusco (BS)

SHRIMP SAUSAGES WITH WHITE POLENTA DISCS AND BLACK-EYED PEAS

Ingredients for 4 people
Preparation time: 2 h

BLACK-EYED PEAS
Generous 1 cup (140 g) dried black-eyed peas
1 quart (1 liter) water
3½ oz (100 g) prosciutto rind
2 tablespoons (30 g) chopped onion
2 teaspoons (10 g) chopped garlic
Generous 3 tablespoons (50 g) extra-virgin olive oil
2⅔ cups (700 g) vegetable stock
¾ teaspoon (3 g) salt
½ teaspoon (2 g) pepper

SAUSAGES
14 oz (400 g) brown shrimp

Generous ¾ cup (100 g) breadcrumbs
1 oz (30 g) egg whites
¾ teaspoon (3 g) salt
½ teaspoon (2 g) white pepper
19½ inches (50 cm) sausage casings, either made from pig's intenstines or synthetic
27½ nches (70 cm) kitchen string
Extra-virgin olive oil

POLENTA
1⅔ cups (250 g) white cornmeal
1 quart (1 liter) water
Salt

Method

BLACK-EYED PEAS
Soak the black-eyed peas in a preferably copper container for 12 hours. Rinse and drain them. Sauté the garlic, onion, and rind in the oil in a saucepan over medium heat until golden. Add the peas and stock. Season with salt and pepper. Simmer over low heat until the stock has been absorbed.

SAUSAGES
Clean and devein the shrimp and remove the shells. Blend the shrimp tails with the breadcrumbs, egg whites, salt, and pepper in a food processor. Place the filling in a pastry bag and fill the casing, sealing the end with the kitchen string to form four small sausages.

POLENTA
Bring the salted water to a boil in a copper pot. Sprinkle in the cornmeal, stirring it with a wooden spoon. Cook over low heat, stirring constantly, for 30 minutes. Spread out the polenta on a baking sheet to a thickness of ½-inch (1.5 cm). Let cool and cut out four discs the same diameter as a cocktail glass.

Serving

Brown the sausages in a drop of extra-virgin olive oil in a very hot iron pan. Heat the polenta in a nonstick pan. Place two tablespoons of peas in the bottom of each glass, cover with a polenta disc and top with a sausage. Serve hot.

Wine pairing

"Incrocio Manzoni" IGT 2006 – Red
Winery: Cantina Sociale Bergamasca – Pontida (BG)

MILANESE-STYLE CHOCOLATE DIP

Ingredients for 4 people
Preparation time: 2 h

10 oz (300 g) 70% dark chocolate
Generous 1 cup (200 g) cream
Generous ¾ cup (200 g) egg yolks
Generous 1¼ cups (267 g) sugar
1 quart (1 liter) milk
Saffron strands
10 oz (300 g) puffed rice

Method

Melt the chocolate with scant ½ cup (100 g) cream in the top of a double boiler.
Whip the egg yolks and sugar in an electric stand mixer or hand mixer.
Meanwhile, mix the milk with scant ½ cup (100 g) of cream and the saffron
in a saucepan and bring to a boil. Slowly whisk the hot milk into the egg
yolk mixture (to avoid curdling the eggs). Return to the heat and heat to
160–175°F (70–80°C). Churn mixture in an ice-cream machine according
to the manufacturer's instructions.

Serving

Gently reheat the chocolate in the double boiler. Pour one part of the hot
chocolate into a deep dish and arrange a soup spoonful of saffron ice-cream
on top. Sprinkle with the puffed rice.

Wine pairing

Moscato passito – Dessert wine
Winery: Cantina Viola – Saracena (CS)

GIULIANA GERMINIANI

RESTAURANT CAPRICCIO - MANERBA DEL GARDA (BRESCIA)

Giuliana Germiniani, chef and co-owner with husband Giancarlo Tassi, *maître d'hôtel* and refined sommelier, of the restaurant *Capriccio* in Montinelle, municipality of Manerba, on the Brescian shores of Lake Garda, started off her renovation with the dessert menu; and she achieved her success with a great sense of humility and mastery. Galeotti made the desserts at the beginning, but then they also conquered the main and pasta courses and the starters. It has been a reciprocal, joyful and faithful love that has blossomed in a state-of-the-art kitchen.

The Michelin-starred establishment is an elegant house surrounded by greenery, with a lovely, large summer conservatory and a refined interior with many windows, where you can enjoy an extraordinary view, with a myriad of flowers tended to by Giuliana that frame the panorama; the gentle shape of the hills with their olive groves and vineyards among green pastures and the blue, tranquil waters of the lake. A stone's throw away from Capriccio, there's the beautiful *Parco della Rocca di Manerba-Sasso*, a truly natural botanical garden, one of the last untouched habitats around Lake Garda, which boasts 400 types of vegetation, including 21 wild and rare species of orchids. A showcase of natural environments, from woods of black hornbeam and downy oak to dry golden beard grasslands and many Mediterranean trees and shrubs, such as holm oak, which bears witness to the pleasing climate that embraces this land. Also famous for its scenery is the pretty *Isola di San Biagio*, commonly known as *Isola dei Conigli*, a frequent destination for those who love scuba diving. The island can also be reached on foot when the lake's water is low. Nearby is the even more majestic *Isola del Garda*, private property of the counts Borghese-Cavazza, with their Venetian neo-gothic style villa and its amazing park, characterized by species from all over the world.

"It is a classy establishment, tastefully and elegantly furnished down to the last detail, but I feel that the customers experience a homey atmosphere. We do everything possible to make them feel comfortable, giving them a warm welcome," declares Giuliana, beautiful and graceful like the Madonna and Child in the Late Gothic frescoes of the *Chiesa di Santa Lucia* in Manerba. "*The service is professional, but without being intrusive. The waiting staff stay close to the table, attentive to the client's every need, but they remain discreet.*" At this restaurant, everything from the bread that is freshly baked every day and offered in different versions to the desserts which always made with enthusiasm and originality and even the fanciful petits fours "*demonstrate the specific wish to think of the customer above all as a guest, to be cosseted and given a serene experience that they can look back on with pleasure.*"

Il Capriccio was founded in 1967 by Maria Veggio and Martino Germiniani, Giuliana's parents, who decided to commit themselves to a restaurant – she managed the kitchen, he took care of the dining room – open from Easter to the end of September. It was originally situated along the road between Manerba and Moniga, a few kilometers away from its current location. "*My mother was self-taught, but very good at her job. Although it was a much simpler establishment than this, it has always been well-known in the area.*" As often happens in these cases, Giuliana and her future husband, who worked at a car dealership at the time, helped out in the restaurant. "*Given that Giancarlo had a gift for working in the dining room, my father proposed that he went in search of another place to which to move once the restaurant's rental contract expired, this time with the intention of buying. That's how he became part of the business with us. The new Capriccio opened in 1985, when we got married, and this marked the beginning of the work of a close-knit team.*"

As a girl, Giuliana never considered becoming a chef. "*After having finished the high school leaving certificate, specializing in languages, I had to go abroad to improve my languages, but my mother said to me, 'Help us out for this season and leave in October,' I accepted, and ended up never leaving the restaurant again!*" At the new *Capriccio*, Giuliana worked in the dining

room with her husband for eight years until she realized that the desserts weren't on a par with the restaurant. *"At that point, a young guy in the kitchen said to me, very politely, 'If you don't like them, why don't you make them?' I took on the challenge and then started to attend courses and call high-level pastry cooks to learn how to make better desserts. In the end, I enjoyed patisserie so much that I went into the kitchen halfway through the service to make the desserts. That's how my mother offered me the chance to work on a permanent basis in the kitchen and to learn everything that she could teach me, so that I could, one day, take her place. I accepted and, slowly but surely, I also learnt to love savory dishes. Now cooking is my life!"* Her love for cooking has revealed a talent: her dishes are well thought-out, coherent, balanced, and never boring. They are able to marry flavor and lightness. Her culinary career has been a date with destiny, deferred, but not ignored. It's no surprise then that the pleasure of food is her only clear childhood memory. *"In the small hotel ran by my maternal grandparents, my grandmother brought me a cappuccino with a warm, freshly-baked brioche in the mornings or she cooked me osso buco or cold veal with tuna sauce. In the summer, she made me thirst-quenching elderflower herbal tea."*

There are certain dishes that have shaped the history of *Il Capriccio*. *"Many of these belong to the past and we don't make them anymore; on the other hand, some have been revised in line with current insight and a touch of inspiration."* The classics are Parmesan eggplant, pennette or pasta rags with salt-cured *aoline* (a type of sardine) from the lake – *"a recipe from the past as nowadays hardly anyone cooks aoline anymore. The fish are salted and left in the sun for a couple of days to dry, then they're pickled"* – as well as ravioli filled with polenta cream and Bagoss cheese, made from the gem of the Brescian dairy industry, typical of the nearby town of Bagolino, capital of the Valle del Caffaro, with Valtenesi truffle, where at least seven species of the valuable tuber have been ascertained, which ripen at different times of the year – *"we have now revamped this pasta course, adding a poached egg and marjoram butter"* – and perch browned with thyme served, for example, with tiger shrimp, a shellfish reduction, and chanterelles, some of which are sautéed in a frying pan with parsley and other fried in a polenta crumb.

"Although I would call my cuisine Mediterranean because I offer sea fish, we like to finish off our menu with traditional local dishes either based on meat or lake fish."

Garda's typical cuisine takes advantage of the many types of fish found in the lake, *"even though our lake unfortunately offers less and less."* Giuliana often cooks perch *"because trout, for example, can hardly ever be found anymore, only if it's farmed."* In terms of the regional products that she uses on a regular basis, there's Garda PDO extra-virgin olive oil, which adds flavor to almost every recipe, truffles from Valtenesi, the farming area that extends to the southwest of Garda, alpine cheeses like Bagoss, traditional polenta, which she uses to fill ravioli, and lamb from the valleys of Brescia, which is only featured on the menu at certain times of the year, making dishes such as *agnello castrato*, or castrated mutton chops, in an almond and hazelnut crumb with sautéed chanterelles.

"Families here follow culinary traditions less and less. Perhaps this is the reason why people want to return to the food of the past because they hardly know it anymore." When cooking traditional dishes, innovation should never be lacking and cooking techniques, like sous vide and low temperature, and the presentation always should be put into play on the recipes. *"I care a lot about the latter aspect as I believe that people see a dish first and then they taste it and see if it's good."* After all, the poetics of the two souls of sixteenth-century Brescia co-exist in her kitchen. Giuliana uses simple ingredients to make her dishes, but manages to create an architecture of flavors of great effect, rather like Girolamo Romani who created the so-called Sistine Chapel of the Poor with the Passion of Christ fresco cycle in the *Chiesa di Santa Maria della Neve* in Pisogne, in the province of Brescia. He achieved an intense poetic force by taking the literal image of the people and making it into a figurative expression. On the other hand, in presenting her creations the chef demonstrates a rare pictorial precision. She pays so much attention to detail and does this in such a delicate and composed way that it brings to mind Moretto da Brescia, looking at the plen-

tiful Flemish painting, in the background of the scene with Tobias and the angel in the *Cappella del Sacramento* in San Giovanni Evangelista in Brescia.

"During my working day, I try to have an hour off in the afternoon. Usually I go into the garden and have a look at the vegetable plot where I grow the herbs I use in the kitchen, as well as peaches, cherries, apricots or elderflowers, and the flowers which I use to decorate the tables in the restaurant." Giuliana's day is long, especially in the summer months when Manerba becomes one of the preferred holiday destinations for Italians and foreigners alike. Like Minerva, the Roman goddess who gave her name to the village and had a thousand jobs to do, not just as the patron saint of war, but also of wisdom, medicine, poetry, trade, and the arts, as well as being a composer of music, so has Giuliana, who starts work in the kitchen at 9:00 am and leaves at 1: am the next morning. *"I don't go and do the shopping myself. My father and husband do it for me. There's a long-standing relationship based on trust with our suppliers – all of which are local, as regards the fruit, vegetables, meat, and lake fish – and they guarantee us products of proven freshness and excellent quality: fresh fish, selected meats, alpine cheeses and wild or organic purpose-grown vegetables."*

The menu chosen for this publication is completely local. The starter is a variety of lake fish, a true harmony of flavors: whitefish and vegetable terrine, couscous with carp tartare (a fish with an exquisite meat that lives in Lake Garda), crayfish marinated in passion fruit with fennel sorbet, and fried bleak. For the pasta course, fresh ravioli pasta filled with polenta cream and Bagoss cheese and Valtenesi black truffle with a poached egg. For the main course, browned perch fillet in a light thyme breadcrumb with crispy tiger shrimp and two types of chanterelles and their reduction. And for dessert, a mixed grain tart with elderflower cream and marinated peaches and their sauce. These are dishes whereby you can breathe in the fresh, sun-kissed perfumed air of the Garda Riviera. Like in the much-loved *Piazza della Loggia* in Brescia, a splendid example of a closed Renaissance square, everything happens within the valuable facades of the surrounding buildings, here the whole of Garda lies in the skilled hands of Giuliana.

A VARIETY OF LAKE FISH: WHITEFISH AND VEGETABLE TERRINE, COUSCOUS WITH CARP TARTARE, CRAYFISH MARINATED IN PASSION FRUIT WITH FENNEL SORBET, AND FRIED BLEAK

Ingredients for 4 people
Preparation time: 2 h – Cooking time for couscous: 2h 30'

WHITEFISH TERRINE
3⅓ lb (1.5 kg) whitefish
2¼ lb (1 kg) perch and pike
2 cups (500 g) butter
Scant ½ cup (100 g) Lugana white wine
2 cups (500 g) cream
1 carrot
1 zucchini
1 freshly squeezed orange
2 small bunches of mixed herbs, chopped
5 oz (150 g) tomato confit*

COUSCOUS WITH CARP
5 cups (500 g) couscous
Scant ½ cup (100 ml) oil
Generous ¾ cup (200 ml) Garda extra-virgin olive oil
Pinch of salt
2 carp, each weighing 1 lb (500 g)
shallot
Pinch of pepper nad few capers
1 small bunch of marjoram

FRIED BLEAK
2¼ lb (1 kg) bleak
1⅔ cups (250 g) all-purpose flour
1¼ cups (300 ml) extra-virgin olive oil
Pinch of salt

FENNEL SORBET
1¼ cups (300 ml) water
¾ cup (150 g) sugar
¼ cup (50 g) glucose
2 cups (500 ml) pureed fennel
1 tablespoon extra-virgin olive oil
Pinch of pepper
Pinch of salt

CRAYFISH
12 crayfish
1 small bunch of herbs
1¼ cups (300 ml) passion fruit juice
Pinch of pepper
Pinch of salt

Method

WHITEFISH TERRINE

Clean and fillet the whitefish, perch, and pike (or ask your fishmonger to do it for you. Brown the fish in the butter in a large pan over medium heat. Add the white wine and cook, letting it evaporate for a few minutes. Lower the heat and add the cream. Cook until thickened and it has reduced by one-third.

Clean the carrot and zucchini. Only keep the green part of the zucchini and dice both vegetables. Sauté the vegetables in oil over high heat. Let cool to room temperature.

Meanwhile, mix the fish mixture in a bowl with the cold butter (2 cups) and orange juice. Puree in a blender until a smooth cream has been obtained. Divide mixture into three parts: one part flavored with the herbs, the second part with the sautéed carrot and zucchini, and leave the remaining part plain.

Layer the different mixtures in a terrine mold, starting with the plain cream, alternating with the tomato confit and then the herb and vegetable mixtures to finish. Let rest in the refrigerator for at least 1 hour.

*Tomato confit: bring a pot of water to a boil. Cut a cross in the bottom of the tomato, so that the skin can be removed easily afterwards. Blanch the ripe tomatoes for a few seconds in the water.

Remove and let cool in ice water. Drain and remove the skin. Cut tomatoes into quarters, removing the seeds. Arrange on a baking sheet and season with table salt, sugar, and julienned lemon zest. Bake in the oven at 225°F (100°C) for about 2 hours.

COUSCOUS WITH CARP

Cook the couscous.: fill a pot with water and bring to a boil. Place the couscous in a sieve over the pot, steaming it for about 45 minutes. Remove and mix in 3 tablespoons of water and oil. Return to the steam and cook for about 45 minutes. Remove from the steam, adding 2 more tablespoons of oil and break up the grains rubbing it through your hands so that the grains have separated completely. Return to the steam for 30 minutes and add the remaining 2 tablespoons of oil. Add a few chopped capers, if desired, or season with salt. Let cool. Drizzle with a little Garda extra-virgin olive oil and mix well. Mold the couscous in a pastry cutter, filling it halfway.

Clean the carp and fillet it (or ask your fishmonger to do this for you). Dice it with a sharp knife, making a tartare. Finely chop the shallot. Drizzle the fish tartare with extra-virgin olive oil, a pinch of salt and pepper, and a little shallot. Fill the rest of the pastry cutter with the fish mixture.

Garnish with a few marjoram leaves.

FRIED BLEAK

Leave the bleak whole without removing anything.

Dry with kitchen paper. Place the flour on a plate and dip the bleak in it, covering them completely, shaking off the excess.

Heat the extra-virgin olive oil into a deep frying pan. Add the bleak, a few at a time, into the boiling oil. Let them brown, turning them carefully, for 3 minutes. (The cooking time varies according to their size.) For them to be cooked well, the flour must be browned and crispy. Make sure you don't cook them too long, or the flavor will alter.

Drain with a slotted spoon on several layers of kitchen paper. Season with salt and repeat the method to cook the remaining fish.

FENNEL SORBET

Combine the water, sugar, and glucose over the heat until the sugar has dissolved. Add the pureed fennel and strain through a fine-mesh sieve. Add the sorbet powder. Let rest for 1 hour, before churning in an ice cream maker according to the manufacturer's instructions. If you don't own an ice-cream machine, place sorbet in the freezer in a metal container. Season with salt and pepper. Mix the sorbet well every 30 minutes, 5 or 6 times.

CRAYFISH

Clean the crayfish, removing the black vein along the back (or ask your fishmonger to do this for you). Steam the crayfish with the herbs in a pan or a pressure cooker. Remove the shells and marinate in the passion fruit juice.

Serve with the fennel sorbet.

Wine pairing

"Livina" Garda Chardonnay – White
Winery: La Meridiana – Puegnago sul Garda (BS)

RAVIOLI FILLED WITH POLENTA CREAM AND BAGOSS CHEESE, SERVED WITH VALTENESI BLACK TRUFFLE

Ingredients for 4 people
Preparation time: 2 h

POLENTA CREAM
2 cups (500 g) water and a pinch of salt
⅔ cup (100 g) *farina di Storo* (or polenta flour)

PASTA
1⅓ cups (200 g) flour
2 whole eggs
Pinch of salt

FILLING
1¾ oz (50 g) summer Bagoss cheese, aged for 36 months
4 eggs

SERVING
Scant ¼ cup (50 g) butter, melted
1 sprig of marjoram
4 whole eggs
Shavings of Bagoss
Valtenesi black truffle

Method

POLENTA CREAM
Bring 2 cups (500 ml) of water and salt to a boil in a pot. Sift in the polenta and cook for 30 minutes, stirring constantly.

PASTA
Sift the flour onto a wooden surface and shape into a mound. Make a well in the center. Pour the eggs into the hollow, add the salt, and knead until the dough is smooth and even. Wrap in plastic wrap and let rest for 30 minutes.
Use a long rolling pin to roll out the pasta into very thin sheets. Lay out the pasta on a baking sheet and cover with a cloth. Cut it into rounds with a 3-inch (8-cm) diameter pastry cutter. Fill with the polenta cream and grated Bagoss and close with another round.
Cook the pasta in salted boiling water for a few minutes.

Serving

Arrange 4 ravioli per portion on plates. Drizzle with the butter flavored with the marjoram. Arrange a poached egg yolk in the center, which has been cooked in boiling water for 2–3 minutes.
Garnish with the shavings of Bagoss and plenty of truffle.

Wine pairing

Groppello "Zephiro" – Red
Winery: Cominciali – Puegnago sul Garda (BS)

BROWNED PERCH FILLETS IN A LIGHT THYME BREADCRUMB WITH CRISPY TIGER SHRIMP AND TWO TYPES OF CHANTERELLES AND THEIR REDUCTION

Ingredients for 4 people
Preparation time: 40' + 12 hours for the reduction

REDUCTION
1 clove garlic, central green part removed
1 Tropea red onion, coarsely chopped
1 bay leaf
Chanterelles
Basil
12 tiger shrimp
1¾ lb (800 g) perch
Salt, pepper

Majoram and thyme leaves
Scant ½ cup (100 g) butter, melted
bread crumbs

MUSHROOMS
10 oz (300 g) chanterelles
3 tablespoons polenta flour
1¼ cups (300 ml) extra-virgin olive oil
pine nuts

Method

REDUCTION
Cook all the ingredients for the reduction over low heat. Add 8 shrimp heads and let them stew.
Add 3 cups (750 ml) of water and cook over low heat for about 30 minutes. Pass through a vegetable mill and strain well.
Cook strained mixture for about 15 minutes over medium heat, adding water if needed. Strain through a fine-mesh sieve and let rest overnight in the refrigerator. Gently reheat in a saucepan before serving.

PERCH
Clean the perch, scaling and filleting it, and removing the central bones (or ask your fishmonger to do this for you). Cut the perch into fillets. Season the perch with salt and pepper and add a few marjoram leaves. Pair them up, coating with the thyme and bread crumbs, after having brushed the fish with the melted butter.
Place the buttered fish in a very hot frying pan to cook.

MUSHROOMS
Clean the mushrooms and remove the caps. Sauté half of them in a little oil with the thyme and marjoram. Add the chopped parsley and pine nuts at the end. Dip the remaining mushrooms in the polenta flour and sauté them in a frying pan.
Remove the mushrooms and set aside. Change the oil and sauté the shrimp until opaque.

Serving

Spoon the warm reduction into the bottom of the plate. Arrange two perch fillets in the center of each plate with the shrimp on one side and the mushrooms on the opposite side. Drizzle with extra-virgin olive oil.

Wine pairing

"Lugana" DOC Arilica – White
Winery: Pilandro – Desenzano del Garda (BS)

MIXED GRAIN TART WITH ELDERFLOWER CREAM AND PEACH PUREE

Ingredients for 4 people
Preparation time: 1 h – Sorbet infusion: 1 h

SWEET SHORTCRUST PASTRY
1²⁄₃ cups (250 g) bread flour
¾ cup (125 g) mixed grain flour
1 cup (250 g) butter
Generous ½ cup (125 g) sugar
3 egg yolks
Pinch of salt
vanilla pod, seeds scraped

ELDERFLOWER CREAM
7 oz (200 g) dried elderflowers*
vanilla pod, split and scraped
2 cups (500 g) milk
Scant 2½ cups (600 g) cream

6 egg yolks
½ cup (100 g) sugar
1 sheet of gelatin
white chocolate

PEACH PUREE
1¼ cups (300 g) peach puree
Generous ¼ cup (60 g) brown sugar
1 teaspoon (5 g) pectin

ELDERFLOWER SORBET
Dried elderflowers*
2 cups (500 g) water at 90°F (32°C)
Syrup for sorbets

*Available from herbalist's shops

Method

SWEET SHORTCRUST PASTRY
Sift the flours onto a wooden surface and make a hollow. Place all the ingredients in the center and knead together quickly. Let rest for 30 minutes in the refrigerator. Roll the pastry out and use it to line tart molds. Bake at 300°F (150°C/gas mark 2) until golden all over.

ELDERFLOWER CREAM
Add the elderflowers and vanilla to the milk. Let infuse overnight. Strain and add the cream, egg yolks, and sugar. Simmer over low heat, stirring constantly, until the mixture forms a custard.
Add the gelatin, which has previously been softened in cold water. Add the white chocolate and mix well.

PEACH SAUCE
Cook all the ingredients together over low heat.

ELDERFLOWER SORBET
Add the elderflowers to the water and let infuse for 1 hour.
Prepare the sorbet by churning it in an ice cream maker according to the manufacturer's instructions. If you don't own an ice-cream machine, pour the liquid into a wide, shallow metal pan and place in the freezer. Stir again after 30 minutes. Return to the freezer and repeat the operation twice more. Just before serving, break up the sorbet, puree briefly in a blender and return the mixture to the freezer for 10 minutes. Serve.

Wine pairing

Passito – Dessert wine
Winery: Cantina della Valtenesi e della Lugana – Moniga del Garda (BS)

THE CUISINE
OF TRENTINO-ALTO ADIGE

Water, valleys, rocky peaks, and glaciers — Trentino-Alto Adige is a region of untamed natural beauty, of shadows in the gorges, silence in the forests, and gurgling waterfalls that unexpectedly appear amid mountains and rocks. It's in these almost fairytale-like scenes that small churches, fortresses, chapels, and castles--masterpieces of past architecture--are wedged. Fragments of the history of the region, from Bolzano to Merano and the Tyrol, these castles tell of the strenuous defense of yore from enemy invasions.

The high mountains stand out over all these surroundings, acting as a perpetual background for travelers. The Val Pusteria, the Sella group, and the Brenta are among the most famous mountains of this region that offer ski slopes in the winter and trekking trails in the summer. Famous architect Le Corbusier (1887–1965) once called the area's Dolomites, *"the most beautiful architecture in the world."* It is the mountain group that has fascinated humans for millennia, with imposing massifs and bizarre walls and pinnacles that trace a dreamlike landscape that has inspired myths and legends handed down to the present day.

That's not all. The winemaking tradition in Alto Adige is ancient in origin. Wine, culture, and art are inextricably linked. The vineyard-clad hills act as a backdrop to castles, villages and stately homes in a magical landscape. The series of little villages are striking due to their typical Überetsch style, with stone and marble framed doors and windows, stylized doorways and internal courtyards. This is where top-class wines are made, such as Merlot, Cabernet, and Sauvignon, all of which are enjoyed all over the world. Traditional dishes which have different flavors from one area to another are served with wines.

The border between the provinces also marks a landscape of clear, decisive flavors. The cultivation of Trentino's vineyards, orchards, and olive groves extend from Verona to Brennero. On the other side, in Alto Adige, one is thrown back in time, to the old farmhouses in the Dolomites and the House of Habsburg. On one side, there are the flavors of Trentino, strong and still Venetian and Padan; on the other side, there are the delicate flavors of South Tyrol, Überetsch in origin. Typical of the alpine area, the two cuisines share the need to preserve foods for long periods, hence the hearty breads, the smoked meats, such as speck, beef, and *mortandela della Val di Non*, cheeses, and pickled cabbage (or *crauti*).

In terms of the typical products of this region, there are forest fruits, such as berries and currants, and apples—the vast orchards of the Golden Delicious, Morgenduft, Granny Smith, Jonagold, and Royal Gala apples extend from the Val Ventosa to the Bassa Atesina and in Valle Isarco. However, the Renetta apple is the oldest variety in the apple-growing tradition, introduced in the nineteenth century from the French Loire Valley. This leader in Trentino fruit cultivation found its ideal growing environment in the Val di Non.

The region owes its culinary heritage to the land, and the traditions that live upon it, despite the sprawl of customs across the different provinces of the area. For example, in nearby Veneto, Trentino cuisine is based on polenta. In the different valleys, maize flour is often added to grain flours that are easier to grow in the mountains such as buckwheat. Using grain flour gives the polenta a darker color and more intense flavor. Starting from polenta, countless combinations are made: potatoes, cheese, beans, mushrooms, greens, etc.

Various desserts are made using the Val di Non apples, like fritters, preserves, and tarts. The desserts also come from the Venetian tradition and have even kept their names, like *Grostoli*, *Torta fregolotta*.

On the other hand, Southern Tyrolean cuisine almost completely imitates Austrian and central European traditions. The flavor combinations are practically unheard of in the rest of Italy.

Speck, the unique smoked cured meat made from pork leg, is the main product of Southern Tyrolean gastronomy, and is eaten often, even at breakfast. The best speck is homemade, having been prepared according to the farmers' tradition: The meat, boned and cut into regular square pieces, is soaked in brine containing salt, garlic, bay, juniper, pepper, and herbs in various amounts and qualities depending on the recipe. Once the speck has been removed from the brine and dried, it is hung in a cold, dry environment to be smoked. Aromatic wood is used to do this, as well as fresh juniper branches. The speck is smoked for only for a few hours a day until it is gradually imbued with smoky flavor.

The typical dish of Southern Tyrolean cuisine are the *Canederli* (or *Knodel*), balls of yesterday's bread mixed with milk, eggs, and flour, and flavored with speck, pancetta, salami, offal, or vegetables. They are served in stock or, after having been cooked in the stock, dried and served with various sauces or with *goulash*.

Game is a constant feature in main courses, served with a range of honey, blueberry, or currant-based sauces, as is the norm in Austria.

Apples also continue to be the main ingredient in the most famous dessert of Alto Adige, the strudel. Dessert recipes involve an abundance of cream, cocoa, berries, and dried fruit, like in panettone-like *Zelten*, a dessert typically prepared by mountain-dwelling communities of the region.

SPECK DELL'ALTO ADIGE
SÜDTIROLER SPECK IGP

FROM THE FLOODPLAIN TO THE MOUNTAINS, THE DAIRY AND CATTLE INDUSTRY CHARACTERIZE THE FARMING LIFESTYLE.

THE UNDISPUTED KING OF ALTO ADIGE IS SPECK, WHICH HAS ACHIEVED THE STATUS OF PROTECTED GEOGRAPHICAL INDICATION. IT IS A PORK PRODUCT THAT GOES WAY BACK IN TERMS OF TRADITION. IT IS MADE FROM BONED, SALTED, AND FLAVORED LEG OF PORK. ACCORDING TO LOCAL CUSTOMS, IT IS THEN DRY-SMOKED AND AGED. WHEN IT IS SLICED, IT SMELLS HEAVILY OF SMOKE AND SPICES: FROM BLACK PEPPER AND ALLSPICE TO GARLIC AND JUNIPER BERRIES. FULL-FLAVORED AND AROMATIC, IT GOES WELL WITH WHITE, RED AND ROSE WINES THAT ARE SOFT AND PERFUMED, LIKE MALVASIA DELL'ALTO ADIGE AND PINOT NERO DELL'ALTO ADIGE.

PAOLO DONEI

RESTAURANT MALGA PANNA - MOENA (TRENTO)

On the veranda of the restaurant *Malga Panna* in Moena, a famous skiing destination in Trentino, you can experience the perfect silence of a breathtaking view. The "Dolomites' Fairy," as the first town in the Val di Fassa is known due to its spectacular beauty, the valley rests in the calm stream of peace of a narrow basin embraced by the striking Latemar, Valacia, and Costalunga mountain ranges. Depending on the season, on a few special days at sunset, the setting is a stage for the fantastic natural phenomenon of *Alpenglow*, when the summits are tinged with a warm red color, as if a magical rose garden blossoms all around, giving the environment a fairy tale-like feel.

The same easygoing pace and charming, timeless hospitality is also felt in this restaurant, set in an old alpine hut that has been completely renovated, on the slopes of enchanting wooded scenery. *"Where there was the family hut, the alpine retreat where fresh cream was made from cows' milk of the high mountain pastures, now there's a restaurant that has kept the name of that cream, as well as its goodness and genuine flavors,"* the chef Paolo Donei explains. Donei co-owns *Malga Panna* with his brother Massimo, maître d'hôtel and a wine connoisseur.

The establishment, which is characterized by welcoming rooms covered in wood, typical of the mountain *baite*, with various rooms that are still heated by the traditional stone *musa*, and furnished with an elegance inspired by nature, has belonged to the Donei family since the 1950s. At this family restaurant where hikers from the surrounding mountains once came to eat polenta and mushrooms, haute cuisine is now on offer.

With tradition as its starting point, the restaurant's cuisine reflects both the local traditions of the Ladin people, a protected ethnic enclave that has been present in the Dolomites for a thousand years, and the historical traditions of Trentino. That surrounding region ranges from—and embodies—the bishop's principality of Bernardo Clesio to the subsequent Southern Tirol and central European influences. Since Trent is an old junction town on the road to Brennero, it combines elements of the creative and research-driven culture, balanced with local pride in mastery of technique and knowledge of ingredients. *"For me the relationship with the land is extremely strong, also because our restaurant is historical – it's been passed down for four generations. We would like our customers to experience a journey back in time into the flavor of our farming, of what we were like before tourism arrived. But we don't want to offer dishes that are typical of the past. We try to bring out the flavors of yore from tradition."*

In Paolo's original and thoughtfully conceived dishes, every detail is processed and filtered through an inspiration that bridges history and innovation. For example, the composition consisting of rye bread, Puzzone di Moena (the famous cheese produced in the region), eggs, and onions, was created by reinterpreting a farmer's snack. *"In fact, it's got very little to do with what our farmers could eat in the fields. We have interpreted the flavors in a modern sense, using a Pacojet—the siphon used to make hot zabaglione—to make a Puzzone ice-cream."*

Another specialty of Valligian cuisine is the wild herb soup, typically prepared during the winter months. Paolo serves it with beet-filled cappelletti pasta and potato millefeuilles with blue-veined cheese. *"The aim of the dish is for the customer to feel as though he were in a meadow. All the wild herbs that we grow or gather in the woods give the soup a very herbaceous flavor. The beet tastes undoubtedly of the earth and the blue-veined cheese adds the aroma of mold."*

The warm kid salad with a raspberry vinaigrette and crisp greens, pumpkin and sunflower seeds, crisp pancetta, and walnuts is a dish that, on the other hand, *"has been created to relive the environment where the kid graze, kid which I see even now right in front of my restaurant."*

Situated on the hill that overlooks Moena, the restaurant is the perfect place to immerse oneself in nature and be pampered by Paolo's vibrant inspiration, which recreates the spirit of this thriving and seductive mountain. *"Our dishes are all made using local products that are absolutely genuine as the chain is short."* They are based above all on cheeses, such as Puzzone, Grana Trentino PDO, and the goat cheeses of the nearby town of Cavalese, a popular tourist resort that comes to life in the winter with its ski slopes and in the summer with its bewitching mountain scenery. Paolo's dishes also rely on furred game, mushrooms, and truffles

from Val Lagarina, the last stretch between the mountains of the valley through which the river Adige flows. The area, characterized by the many forts built to defend the Austro-Hungarian Empire at the end of the nineteenth century, boasts an abundance of wild herbs, such as stream watercress, *"which has a strong flavor, almost of mustard, and gives a slight sensation of rust on our plates."* His creations also use the organic lamb of Val di Fiemme (which, with Val di Fassa and Val di Cembra, forms the watershed of the torrent Avisio) and fish from Alpine water courses, such as pike, perch, and char. The chef possesses a deep knowledge of the quality and origin of other regional goods, such as the broccoli from Santa Massenza. Legend has it that Massenza, the mother of San Vigilio, died in this village in 5 AD – the Golden Delicious apple of Val di Non – one of the main valleys in Trentino, which became home to important judicial and administrative centers such as Cles and Coredo in the Medieval era, where death penalty sentences were handed down during the time of witch-hunts – and the Dro plum, a small town in the northern part of Garda. Here, where the river Sarca meets the lake, marking a change in perspective towards the perfumes and light of the Mediterranean, the oil that Paolo prefers is produced: the Garda Trentino extra-virgin olive oil.

His cuisine, which honors the territory, is created with precision and love. Like the parish church of San Vigilio in Moena, the lowly grey stone exterior emphasizes the light, solid serenity of the system of volume, while inside the works of the Moenese Valentino Rovisi speak the language of one of the most ingenious protagonists of the Italian Settecento, Giambattista Tiepolo; Paolo utilizes the same sophisticated, perceptive, and bright style in his interpretation of tradition without losing sight of the region's constraints, advantages, and most importantly, essence. After all, his ancestors were able to cultivate land through perseverance, hard labor, and faith; over the centuries, they were tested by long winters, floods, landslides, and plagues. It follows that *"the local gastronomic culture was based on the preservation of food above all else: the smoking of meats, pickling vegetables, making long-lasting bread, and fruit preserves."*

The menu at *Malga Panna* varies, as it adheres to the seasonality of the ingredients. *"To create high-class cuisine, you definitely need quality products. When these can't be found on the market, we change the shopping list and therefore the dishes included on the menu."* Paolo does the shopping himself. His typical day starts at 7:30 a.m., going to breeders and producers in the area. *"We source from some individuals who breed free-range rabbits and chickens, or who make their own cheeses and age them in cellars like in the past, without the haste demanded by the large-scale market. The ingredients are fundamental; it's 80 percent of a dish."*

Paolo has achieved important professional recognition. He has a Michelin star and is a member of the *Jeunes Restaurateurs d'Europe* association, but it wasn't at all easy to convince his grandparents and parents to offer their blessing and approval to a new culinary approach at the restaurant. It is his trademark to offer the recipes of the past in a modern, lighter guise. After initially learning the basics of food preparation and cooking from the women in the family, Paolo attended a culinary institute for a year, *"but the thought of carrying on studying didn't exactly excite me."* That's why he left the college to learn the ropes on the job. *"From the age of 15 until I turned 30, I did internships in leading restaurants in order to learn and improve my style, finding out the best-kept secrets in top class catering. Initially I worked in restaurants in Alto Adige, then in other regions, such as at Trigabolo di Argenta, in the province of Ferrara, where Igles Corelli worked, but also abroad in Switzerland and Germany. Meanwhile, between one internship and another, I always continued to work in the family restaurant."* At the beginning, he wanted to import the cuisine he had seen on his travels into his town, from when he had worked with preeminent and famous chefs, and he experimented with this for a brief period. But it didn't work. The hypothesis on which it was based was depersonalized and detached. *"I realized almost immediately that it was a mistake. My own personal signature was missing. And that's what you need to find to be able to communicate feelings with your cuisine."* There's no shadow of doubt that he loves his roots. *"I have a deep attachment to the whole of my land. Above all, I'm most attached to our forests and everything that they have to offer, as well as our mountain air."*

It is indeed the landscape where he was born—and the sensory experience it evokes—that charms us in the dishes chosen for the menu in this book. As a starter, pink leg of kid with mixed green salad with dried fruit and mustard ice-cream, features the classic meat of Trentino and other flavors of its natural habitat, including the Golden Delicious apple. Following that, the first course: barley risotto with hop sprouts, crayfish, and smoked garlic cream. Barley is one of the most widespread grains in the area; indeed barley soup was a traditional dish in farming families. *"Hop sprouts, which we call* bruscandoli, *are found in our meadows in the spring. The garlic is smoked with juniper and helps to recreate that flavor of smoke, which was given by smoked pork in the old barley soup."* Next, the meat course: leg of jack rabbit with smoked potatoes, sprout salad (from radish to onion sprouts), and crispy speck. *"The jack rabbit found in our woods is of top quality and is combined with smoked potatoes, typical of our land like speck, and sprouts that give it an herbaceous flavor."*

The dessert is an arrangement of fruit and flowers, with an *"elderflower mousse, served on a strawberry sauce; a violet petal granita, served with fresh raspberries; a little dog rose parfait placed on top of a rhododendron honey gelatin, served with blackberry puree; a lavender and calendula crème brûlée, served with fresh currants."* It is a miniature kaleidoscope of flavors, aromas, and colors of the woods of Moena. This is what surrounds the restaurant: shades of bronze in the autumn, a silvery peace under the snow, fragrant joy in the spring, and a gentle green at the start of summer.

PINK LEG OF KID WITH MIXED LEAF SALAD, DRIED FRUIT AND MUSTARD ICE-CREAM

Ingredients for 4 people
Preparation time: 50'

LEG OF KID
1⅓ lb (600 g) leg of kid, cleaned (ask
your butcher to do this for you)
Salt, pepper
10 oz (300 g) whole dried spices, such
as cumin, juniper, pepper, mustard grains
Extra-virgin olive oil, for drizzling

MUSTARD ICE CREAM
Scant ½ cup (100 g) extra-virgin olive oil
Scant 1 cup (225 g) mascarpone
1 tablespoon (15 g) plain yogurt
Scant 1 tablespoon (8 g) fresh chopped
chives
⅓ cup (80 g) tomato paste
Grainy mustard, such as *Moutarde de
Meaux*

MIXED LEAF SALAD
2 Golden Delicious apples
2 bell peppers, 1 red, 1 yellow
3 oz (90 g) rye bread
2 tablespoons (30 g) veal demi-glace
1¼ cups (300 g) pumpkin seed oil
¼ cup (60 g) apple vinegar
Extra-virgin olive oil, for sautéing
3½ oz (100 g) mixed greens, such as beet
leaves, lovage, or sprouts
Plain yogurt, for serving
Olive oil, for serving

Method

LEG OF KID
Divide the leg of kid into parts weighing about 2¾–3½ oz (80–100 g) each. Marinate it in salt, pepper, the dried spices, and a drizzle of olive oil for about 10 minutes.
Place the meat in a vacuum pack and cook in a steam oven at a temperature of 140°F for 17–20 minutes.

MUSTARD ICE CREAM
Meanwhile, mix the olive oil, sugar syrup, mascarpone, yogurt, chives, tomato paste, and mustard (all of which are cold). Season with salt to taste and churn in an ice-cream machine according to the manufacturer's instructions.

MIXED LEAF SALAD
Dice the apples. Sauté the apples for a few minutes with the white wine and pepper. Cut the rye bread into cubes and toast in the oven. To dress the bell peppers, beat the reduced veal cooking juices with the pumpkin oil and apple vinegar. Sauté the bell peppers in a little oil in a frying pan. Add them to the dressing.

Serving

Arrange the mixed salad on the plate with the apples, croutons, and dressing. Add a few drizzles of plain yogurt over the salad and place the kid on top, after having browned it all over. Add the mustard ice-cream and drizzle with a little olive oil.

Wine pairing

"Pinot nero", IGT 2004 – Red
Winery: Vallarom – Avio (TN)

BARLEY RISOTTO WITH HOP SPROUTS, CRAYFISH, AND SMOKED GARLIC CREAM

Ingredients for 4 people
Preparation time: 40'

*STOCK
1½ lb (700 g) beef
1 lb (500 g) veal
Salt
1 onion
1 carrot
1 celery stalk
1 bay leaf

SAUCE
1¾ lb (800 g) meat stock*
Generous ¾ cup (200 g) mascarpone
2 oz (60 g) smoked garlic, unpeeled
Salt, pepper

BARLEY
1¾ oz (50 g) shallots, chopped
1½ cups (300 g) pearl barley
Scant ¼ cup (50 g) white wine
1 lb (500 g) hop sprouts
Generous ¾ cup (200 g) extra-virgin olive oil
Salt, pepper
Scant ¼ cup (50 g) butter
2 oz (60 g) Parmesan
14 oz (400 g) crayfish
3½ oz (100 g) rolled pancetta
4 hop sprouts
1 clove of garlic

Method

STOCK

Put the meat in a large saucepan and cover with cold water.

Bring the water to a boil over medium heat, covered.

When the water comes to a boil, skim the froth, season with salt, and add the whole vegetables and the bay leaf.

Lower the heat, cover again, and simmer for about 2½ hours.

Let cool and chill for at least 3 hours.

Before using the stock, remove the layer of fat that will have solidified on the surface.

SAUCE

Bring a little stock to a boil with the mascarpone. Make small cuts in the unpeeled garlic and add to the stock. Let infuse. Season to taste and emulsify the sauce with the extra-virgin olive oil.

BARLEY

Sweat the chopped shallot in a saucepan. Toast the barley for a few minutes. Add the white wine and let it evaporate. Continue cooking, adding the hot stock, mixing constantly. Meanwhile, blanch the hop sprouts. Sauté the sprouts in oil with the garlic and shallot. After the barley has been cooking for 40 minutes, add the prepared hop sprouts. Season to taste and add the butter and Parmesan at the end, like a risotto.

Serving

Spoon the barley risotto into the center of a deep plate. Drizzle the foaming sauce around the barley and arrange the crayfish on top in the center, having just cooked them in a pan. Garnish with the pancetta, which has been dried in the oven, and the hop sprouts.

Wine pairing

Lagrein "Capor" 2003 – Red
Winery: Arcangelo Sandri – Faedo (TN)

LEG OF JACK RABBIT WITH SMOKED POTATOES, SPROUT SALAD, AND CRISPY SPECK

Ingredients for 4 people
Preparation time: 1 h 10'

1 lb (500 g) potatoes
Salted water
1¾ oz (50 g) larch shavings, or other aromatic smoking chips
14 oz (400 g) leg of jack rabbit
Extra-virgin olive oil
Fresh thyme branches
Fresh rosemary branches
Fresh sage leaves
Unpeeled garlic cloves
5 oz (150 g) speck (aged for 6 months)
3½ oz (100 g) mixed sprouts, such as onion, radish, spelt, peas
Apple vinegar, to taste
Pumpkin oil, to taste
2½ oz (100 g) game cooking juices
⅓ cup (80 g) butter
Wild thyme, or fresh thyme leaves, for serving

Method

Cook the potatoes, skin on, in plenty of salted water. Meanwhile, toast the wood shavings dry in a pot. Once the potatoes have cooked, drain them and place them over the smoking shavings. Cover with a lid. Leave the potatoes to smoke for a few hours. If the aroma of the wood isn't sufficient, toast the shavings again.
Remove the fat and bone from the rabbit leg; clean the meat. Let marinate in olive oil, thyme, rosemary, sage, and garlic for 20 minutes. Brown the jack rabbit in very hot oil. Bake in the oven at 350°F (180°C/gas mark 4) for 5-6 minutes and let rest at 140°F (60°C) for 12 minutes.
While the meat is resting, cut the speck into thin sticks and brown in very hot oil. Drain on straw paper so that it stays crispy. Dress the sprout salad with apple vinegar, extra-virgin olive oil, pumpkin oil, salt, and pepper.

Serving

Sauté the smoked potatoes in a pan with a pat of butter. Season with salt and pepper to taste. Arrange them on a plate. Cut the jack rabbit into four medallions and place on top of the potatoes. Drizzle the meat with the game cooking juices, whisk in butter and thyme (if possible, wild thyme that grows in the woods). Finish with the sprout salad and crispy speck.

Wine pairing

"Granato" 2004 IGT – Red
Winery: Foradori – Mezzolombardo (TN)

AN ARRANGEMENT OF FRUIT AND FLOWERS

Ingredients for 4 people
Preparation time: 4 h

MLDERFLOWER MOUSSE
Generous ½ cup (125 g) sugar
Scant ¼ cup (50 g) water
Scant 3 tablespoons (40 g) lemon juice
4 sheets of gelatin
Generous 1 tablespoon (20 g) soy lecithin
Generous 1¾ cups (450 g) elderflower syrup
2 cups (500 g) whipped cream
1 tablespoon (15 g) candied lemon
1 egg white

DOG ROSE PARFAIT
¼ cup (60 g) egg whites
2 tablespoons (30 g) confectioners' sugar
4 egg yolks
½ cup (100 g) sugar
Scant 1 cup (140 g) dog rose puree
2 cups (500 g) whipped cream

LAVENDER FLOWER CRÈME BRÛLÉE
1¼ cups (300 g) fresh cream
2 teaspoons (10 g) dried lavender flowers
3 egg yolks
⅓ cup (70 g) sugar

VIOLET GRANITA
1¼ cups (300 g) water
Scant ½ cup (90 g) sugar
Scant 3 tablespoons (40 g) violet petal syrup

ELDERFLOWER SYRUP
1 cup (250 g) water
Generous ¾ cup (160 g) sugar
1 organic lemon
15 elderflowers

SERVING
Scant ¼ cup (40 g) brown sugar
Assortment of forest fruit, such as strawberries, raspberries or gooseberries

Method

ELDERFLOWER MOUSSE
To make a meringue, cook the sugar and water to a temperature of 250°F (121°C). Mix the sugar syrup into the beaten egg white; beat until it has cooled completely. Warm the lemon juice and add the gelatin, which has been soaked beforehand in water. Mix in the lecithin and elderflower syrup. Let the mixture cool. Mix it into the cream. Use a rubber spatula to spread out the meringue and chill in the refrigerator.

DOG ROSE PARFAIT
Beat the egg whites with the confectioners' sugar until stiff peaks form. Beat the egg yolks with the sugar in the top of a double boiler. Mix in the rose puree and the whipped cream. Fold in the beaten whites. Divide the mixture into small molds and freeze for a few hours.

LAVENDER FLOWER CRÈME BRÛLÉE
Bring the cream to a boil with the lavender flowers. Beat the egg yolks with the sugar and mix in the boiling cream. Strain the mixture and pour the cream into small ceramic molds. Cook in a steam oven at 195°F (90°C) for 30 minutes or in a static oven in a bain-marie for 25 minutes at 255°F (125°C).

VIOLET GRANITA
Mix together the water, sugar, and violet syrup, all of which are cold. Pour the mixture into a wide, shallow container and place in the freezer. Use a whisk to break up the ice crystals every hour at least three times.

ELDERFLOWER SYRUP
Boil the water with the sugar. Add the lemon, juiced and cut into tiny pieces, and the elderflowers and let marinate, in an airtight container, for 1 week.

Serving

Sprinkle a small teaspoon of brown sugar over each crème brûlée and burn with a brûlée blowtorch. Decorate with currants and small lavender flowers. Spoon the granita into a small glass and decorate with fresh raspberries. Use a tablespoon to shape the elderflower mousse into quenelles and arrange them on a strawberry sauce. Remove the rose parfait from the freezer and decorate with a blackberry puree and small fresh fruits.

Wine pairing

"Mandolaia," Late Vintage 2006 – Dessert wine
Winery: Cantina La Vis – Lavis (TN)

HERBERT HINTNER

RESTAURANT ZUR ROSE - S. MICHELE APPIANO (BOLZANO)

CENTRAL EUROPE CONVERSES WITH THE MEDITERRANEAN IN THE KITCHEN OF HERBERT HINTNER, CHEF AND CO-OWNER WITH HIS WIFE MARGOT OF THE RESTAURANT *ZUR ROSE* IN SAN MICHELE APPIANO, IN THE PROVINCE OF BOLZANO. ALTHOUGH BORN 51 YEARS AGO IN VALLE DI CASIES, IN THE HEART OF THE DOLOMITES, AND OF GERMAN MOTHER TONGUE, HE FORGED HIS CREATIVE NATURE IN AUSTRIA, AT *HOTEL KLOSTERBRÄU* IN SEEFELD, AND WORKED IN THE BEAUTIFUL PARKLAND OF SOUTH TYROL, ALONG THE CHARMING WINE TRAIL THAT REACHES NALS FROM SALORNO. HERBERT FIRMLY BELIEVES THAT THE MOUNTAINS ARE PERFECT IN TERMS OF CUISINE, IF COMBINED WITH THE HILLS, PLAINS, AND SEA.

IT MAY SEEM STRANGE, THIS CHEF TRYING TO FIND THE MEETING POINT BETWEEN WORLDS THAT SEEM FAR APART, BUT THE DISHES OF *ZUR ROSE*, LIKE THE VALLE DI CASIES OX TARTARE WITH A GREEN SAUCE OF PARSLEY, CUCUMBERS, AND CAPERS, ARE, IN FACT, THE GASTRONOMIC EXEMPLIFICATION OF THE SPIRIT OF BOLZANO. THE SCENERY: THRIVING, TYPICALLY MEDITERRANEAN VEGETATION PROSPERS ON THE SUN-KISSED SLOPES, WHILE THE MASSIFS OF THE DOLOMITES DISPLAY THEIR WHITE BLANKETS OF SNOW. AND, FROM AN ARTISTIC AND ARCHITECTURAL PERSPECTIVE, THE SPLENDID FRESCOES OF THE SCHOOL OF GIOTTO IN THE CHIESA DEI DOMENICANI IN BOLZANO HARMONIZE WITH THE AUSTERE NORDIC DESIGN OF ITS BUILDING. DESPITE ATTEMPTS TO FOSTER A DIALOGUE, OR MAYBE THANKS TO THIS, HERBERT IS DEEPLY ATTACHED TO SOUTH TYROL. THE RESTAURANT, LOCATED IN ÜBERETSCH, IN A BEWITCHING LAND-SCAPE THAT IS RICH IN INTERESTING CASTLES (LIKE CASTEL RONCOLO, PERCHED ON A PEAK AT THE ENTRANCE OF VAL SARENTINA AND KNOWN AS THE 'ILLUSTRATED CASTLE' BECAUSE OF THE VALUABLE AND PERFECTLY PRESERVED FOURTEENTH-CENTURY FRESCO CYCLE), GENTLE HILLS OF VINEYARDS AND ORCHARDS, AND PEACEFUL LAKES SURROUNDED BY GREENERY, IS COPIOUSLY IN LINE WITH TRADITION, STARTING WITH ITS APPEARANCE. *"WHEN WE RENOVATED THE RESTAURANT, WE RESPECTED THE BUILDING'S ORIGINAL ARCHITECTURAL CHARACTER. THE ENVIRONMENT IS TYPICAL OF MOUNTAIN HOMES: VAULTED CEIL-INGS, WOOD ON THE WALLS, AND A 'STUBE,' THE OLD TYROLEAN MAJOLICA STOVE. AT THE SAME TIME, IT HAS EVERYTHING IT NEEDS TO BE A TOP-CLASS RESTAURANT: SILVER CUTLERY, QUALITY GLASSWARE, FRESH FLOWERS, PRIZED FABRICS, ET CETERA."*

The restaurant is situated in a twelfth-century building, where the first evidence of a restaurant establishment dates back to 1773. It was purchased and completely renovated by the Margot family 60 years ago. *"My in-laws had a trattoria here and they had many covers,"* says Herbert. In 1982, Herbert married the young daughter of the Rabensteiner family, a love that blossomed in the lecture halls of the hotel institute in Bolzano. Slowly but surely, supported by his wife, who manages the hospitality in the dinner room and recommends wines, he started to change the philosophy of cuisine held by his in-laws. After all, he wasn't short on experience. He made his debut in the kitchen at the age of 14 as an apprentice cook at Hotel Centrale in Alta Badia. Once he finished his studies, he started to learn the ropes in Alto Adige and abroad. In 1985, the Hintners took over the restaurant and bravely made the decision to revolutionize all the dishes on offer. *"Those were three very difficult years as we lost all the old customers. Then all it took was that the food and wine critic Luigi Veronelli listed the restaurant in one of his guides, as well as a short review in a local newspaper, something like 'you eat well here' and we were able to make the qualitative leap and to position ourselves in this band of haute cuisine where we still are today."* In 1995, the restaurant was awarded with a Michelin star, as well as a whole set of hat, fork, and spoon symbols in other food and wine guides, which contributed towards giving it a certain visibility outside of the region's boundaries. From 1997 to 2003 Herbert was president of the *Jeunes Restaurateurs d'Europe* association, of which he is now an honorary member, and perhaps by virtue of this international experience he says of himself that he's *"not a closed-minded traditionalist, but on the contrary, open to other cultures,"* a little like the towering sandstone open-work spire of the bell tower of Bolzano cathedral, which affords 360° views of the water basin, lake, hills, and perpetually windy alpine landscapes. And yet, he believes that *"other gastronomic traditions can be respected just by pampering my own."* His future is right here. *"People will increasingly always want to try the typical products that come from a place and, by offering them the food of the land, they will think about what they're eating – that's the pièce de résistance for a chef! Furthermore, if you make this kind of*

food, you're also communicating. People become curious about why certain flavors taste the way they do and their history." Herbert's bold statement is *"to make globalization a thing of the past, keeping our products to ourselves and using them. If we just eat the foods that grow where we live and when the land makes it available to us, we live better."* This discussion therefore also leads us to another topic that is close to his heart. *"The ethical aspect of food means a lot to me. If the soul of a connoisseur truly touches the intelligence and simplicity of nature, it includes the art of cooking."* In line with his thoughts, he offers a *"cuisine that is very attached to the land*

and aimed at freshness, using local and seasonal products." He's a minimalist. *"Just a few ingredients in the dish, but bound together with a correct concept that is always thought-out."* Many are the products of his land that Herbert uses regularly, always trying to demonstrate a commitment to what is, *"not only more modern and quicker, but also lighter,"* given that Southern Tyrolean cuisine is rather robust and therefore traditionally served with rustic rye bread, the grain cultivated most intensively in the Valle dell'Adige. On the chef's list of local products, there are vegetables, from July to mid-October, the winter root produce of Valle Aurina (blue, white, and yellow carrots, Jerusalem artichokes, parsnips, land-grown almonds, etc.) and apples, produced from Val Venosta to Bassa Atesina and in Valle Isarco. There are also other regional flagship food products, such as the soft and piquant *Graukäse*, the so-called *formaggio grigio*, typical of the eastern part of Alto Adige, and the aromatic *speck*, the unique smoked cured meat in South Tyrol. Then there are all the dairy products – breeding and the dairy industry still regulate the rhythms of farming life in South Tyrol. There are also potatoes, mushrooms, and the ground dried pears, the *Kloaznmehl*, an old traditional product, originally created because *"in Alto Adige almost all the masi, or rather the typical rural dwellings, have a fruit tree in front of them. Up to 100 years ago, these trees provided the sugar needed for home economics. The pears were dried and then ground to form a powder."* And when it comes to meat, says Herbert, *"I always use 100 per cent local game, lamb, and kid; indigenous beef 60 per cent and local veal 40 per cent of the time. The rest comes from outside of the* region." He does the shopping for the restaurant himself. "*Locally I'm only supplied by farmers and small producers that have a livestock license, therefore those that are authorized to sell their products. Buying from a farmer that you've seen breed an animal or how he cultivates his land is great, but I have to have healthy and controlled products in my restaurant.*" Herbert's days are demanding – he sometimes works from seven in the morning to one at night. When he can, however, he allows himself an afternoon break for a few hours. To unwind and recharge his batteries, he either reads or goes for a bike ride. "*The fresh air and movement allow me to work out any problems that I have on my mind. On the way back, I'm more motivated, physically and mentally.*" Pedaling from his restaurant you can reach the Brenner Pass "*along a fantastic bike path*" or follow other paths in the wonderful woodland. "*When I go up here into our mountains to 2,000 or 3,000 meters (6500 to 9800 feet), I go back in time to when I traveled to the alpine huts as a child.*" These same peaks, which aroused the sentiment of the sublime in the romantic poets of the nineteenth century, elicit a profound gratitude for life in Herbert. "*Only mountains give me this nostalgia of a beautiful and nice time where I was able to grow up without worries.*" The relationship with the gastronomic memories of the area is fundamental in his cuisine. "*I always offer new interpretations of typical dishes. For example, in Schlutzkrapfen, which are the classic ricotta and spinach-based Southern Tyrolean ravioli, I remove the spinach from the filling and I make a soup in which the* Schlutzkrapfen *are served. By doing this I'm able to heighten the flavor, while not losing the originality of the tradition at the same time.*" Alternatively, he plays on the mixture between established alpine structures and Mediterranean ardors, such as in the natural phenomena of the *buche di ghiaccio*, or ice holes, at the foot of Monte Ganda at Appiano, where plants burgeon at 1600 feet (500 meters) (about 1600 feet) above sea level that would usually grow at 3900 feet (1,200 meters), on an aromatic plateau with the sun and sea you can catch a glimpse of aspects of the Dolomites. Also in terms of his restaurant's historic dishes, Herbert is well aware of the fact that "*a classic only remains as such if it is revamped over time*". For example, calf's head has been on the menu for many years, combined with mustard ice-cream or served baked in foil with boiled potatoes, fried in a herb crust with horseradish, or with a fresh tomato vinaigrette of the local tomato variety, *paradise*. In terms of the pasta course, the classics vary from the soufflè of *canederli* with cheeses, the typical Tyrolean gnocchi, and ricotta-filled *cannellone*, rolled in a spiral shape. On the sweets cart, there's always *Schmarren*, the traditional Southern Tyrolean dessert of Austrian origin, which the chef offers in various ways, with cherries, apples, ricotta, quinces, or chestnuts. The menu designed for this book truly expresses the chef's love for his roots. The starter is Valle di Casies oxtail tartare with potatoes and thyme vinaigrette—it contains the potato, queen of mountain cuisine, a typical Southern Tyrolean meat, and an aromatic herb with a Mediterranean charm, that manages to grow up to 4900 feet (1,500 meters) above sea level. Then there's dried pear ravioli with *formaggio grigio*. "*I like to be able to taste the origin of true flavor in my dishes and this can only be done if I can use a product in both its cooked and uncooked form together. In this case, the ground dried pears and the Graukäse are used in the ravioli and in the sauce.*" For the meat course, there's roasted veal shank with vegetable ratatouille, a simple dish, yet rich in flavors, in which lovage or mountain celery is used in addition to other herbs. To finish, a *Schmarren* with caramelized apples and ice-cream, "*a puffed-up version of the traditional dessert.*" These dishes are like a postcard from Alto Adige, the image is old-fashioned, but the handwriting on the back is contemporary.

OXTAIL TARTARE WITH POTATOES AND THYME VINAIGRETTE

Ingredients for 4 people
Preparation time: 1 h 30' - Resting: 1 day

PASTA
14 oz (400 g) oxtail braised in red wine
14 oz (400 g) potatoes, diced
5 tablespoons (50 g) shallots, finely chopped
5 sprigs of thyme
¼ cup (50 g) balsamic vinegar
¾ cup (150 g) extra-virgin olive oil
¼ cup (50 g) olive oil for frying
2 teaspoons (10 g) butter
salt and pepper

BRAISED OXTAIL
1 lb (2 kg) oxtail
½ cup (60 g) carrots, coarsely chopped
½ cup (60 g) onions, coarsely chopped
½ cup (60 g) celery, coarsely chopped
2 shallots, chopped
2 cloves garlic
5 juniper berries
salt and pepper
2 tablespoons tomato paste
3½ oz (100 ml) Madeira wine
2 quarts (2 liters) red wine
Herbs (2 bay leaves, 2 sprigs of thyme, a small bunch of parsley)

GARNISH
3½ oz (100 g) mixed salad (lollo, corn salad, lamb's lettuce, curly endives)

Method

Clean and wash the oxtail. Season with salt and pepper. Brown the oxtail in the oil in a large pot over high heat. Drain any fat from the pan. Add the carrots, onions, and celery, chopped coarsely, and sweat for a few minutes. Add the peppercorns, juniper berries, garlic, chopped shallots, and tomato paste. Add the Madeira wine and let it evaporate. Pour in the red wine.
Bake the meat, covered, in a preheated oven at 350°F (180°C/gas mark 4) for 2-3 hours. Halfway through cooking, add the herbs and season with salt. When the meat is very tender, remove meat from the bones (discard bones) and pick out any cartilage. Place the meat in a nonstick mold, pressing it down as much as possible, using a weight if needed. Let cool completely.
Brown the shallots in a small saucepan. Make a vinaigrette by beating the vinegar with the thyme, salt, and pepper. Slowly whisk in the extra-virgin olive oil until a sauce forms. Add the browned shallots before serving.
Sauté the potatoes in the oil in a frying pan for 7 minutes. Season with freshly ground salt and pepper. Add the oxtail tartare, made by cutting half the meat into small cubes the same size as the potatoes, a pat of butter, and toss to combine. Continue sautéing for 3 minutes more.

Serving

Cut the other half of the meat very thinly. Arrange the slices like petals on a plate. Place round molds 2 inches (5 cm) in diameter on top and fill with a mixture of oxtail and potatoes. Carefully remove the molds and garnish with a little mixed salad. Drizzle with the vinaigrette.

Wine pairing

Pinot bianco "Schulthauser" DOC 2007 – White
Winery: Cantina Produttori San Michele Appiano-Eppan – Appiano (BZ)

DRIED PEAR RAVIOLI WITH *FORMAGGIO GRIGIO*

Ingredients for 4 people
Preparation time: 30' - Resting: 1 h

PASTA
½ cup (50 g) all-purpose flour
2 ½ tablespoons (30 g) durum wheat semolina
1 ¾ oz (50 g) ground dried pears (kloaznmehl)
1 whole egg

FILLING
7 oz (200 g) boiled and peeled potatoes
3 ½ oz (100 g) *formaggio grigio*
salt and pepper
1 ¾ oz (50 g) butter
chopped chives

Method

PASTA
Sift the flour and semolina onto a wooden surface and mix in the ground dried pears.
Shape into a mound. Make a well in the center. Break the egg into the hollow and
knead until the dough is smooth and even. Let rest for 1 hour in a cool place.

FILLING
Press potatoes through a strainer or food mill. Season with salt and pepper.
Add half of the formaggio grigio and mix well.

Serving

Roll out the pasta using a pasta machine to a thickness of ¼ inch (2 mm). Cut into
rounds 2 ½ to 3-inch (7 cm) in diameter, add the filling, and fold over rounds and press
edegs to seal, making half-moon shapes. Cook the ravioli in plenty of salted water for
about 3–4 minutes. Melt the butter in a small frying pan. Shape the remaining
formaggio grigio into 4 small balls and cover them in chopped chives.
Arrange some ravioli on each plate and drizzle with the melted butter. Place a
formaggio grigio ball in the center of each dish.

Wine pairing

Gewürztraminer "Cornell" 2007 – Aromatic white
Winery: Produttori Colterenzio Soc. Agr. Coop. – Cornaiano (BZ)

ROASTED VEAL SHANK WITH RATATOUILLE

Ingredients for 4 people
Preparation time: 4 h

SHANK
1 boned veal shank
1 carrot, diced
1 medium onion, diced
5 cloves garlic, diced
1 sprig of rosemary
3 sprigs of thyme
20 bay leaves
5 sprigs of marjoram
1 sprig of lovage
5 bay leaves

1 celery stalk, diced
2 quarts (2 liters) vegetable stock
salt and pepper
extra-virgin olive oil

RATATOUILLE
3 ½ oz (100 g) zucchini
3 ½ oz (100 g) peeled tomatoes
3 ½ oz (100 g) eggplant
3 ½ oz (100 g) peeled bell peppers
1 tablespoon herbs (thyme, basil, parsley), finely chopped

Method

SHANK
Bone the veal shank and separate the large part from the small part (or ask your butcher to do this for you). Season with salt and pepper.
Brown the meat on both sides in extra-virgin olive oil. Dice the carrot, onion, garlic, and celery. Spread them out in a roasting pan and place the meat on top.
Bake in a preheated oven at 325°F (160°C) for about 30 minutes.
Add the herbs, pour in the vegetable stock, and continue to bake at 250°F (120°C) for another 3 hours, basting the meat with the cooking juices from time to time.
Remove from the pan and transfer to a bowl, keeping it hot.
Strain the cooking juices through a fine-mesh sieve (removing the fat) and return to the heat. Let it reduce until a fairly thick consistency forms.

RATATOUILLE
Dice all the vegetables. Sauté them in the olive oil in a frying pan over medium heat for about 10 minutes. Season with salt and pepper and add the chopped herbs.

Serving

Arrange the ratatouille in the center of the plate using a metal mold.
Slice the shank and arrange on top of the ratatouille, drizzling with the cooking juices.

Wine pairing

Pinot nero Riserva 2005 – Red
Winery: Haderburg Buchholz – Salorno-Salurn (BZ)

SCHMARREN WITH CARAMELIZED APPLES AND ICE-CREAM

Ingredients for 4 people
Preparation time: 40'

ICE-CREAM
2 cups (500 g) sour cream
¾ cup (100 g) confectioners' sugar
2 tablespoons (15 g) powdered milk
3 tablespoons (50 g) lemon juice

SCHMARREN
1 ¼ cups (300 g) milk
2 tablespoons (30 g) butter
¼ cup (70 g) Ricotta cheese
2 egg yolks
1 ½ tablespoons (20 g) vanilla sugar
¾ cup (100 g) flour
½ lb. (200 g) apples
5 ½ tablespoons (70 g) sugar
1 tablespoon (15 g) butter
1 tablespoon (10 g) golden raisins
3 egg whites
pinch salt

Method

ICE-CREAM
Mix all the ingredients together in a bowl. Churn in an ice-cream maker according to the manufacturer's instructions.

SCHMARREN
Bring the milk to a boil with the butter. Transfer to a food processor, gradually adding the Ricotta, egg yolks, vanilla sugar, and flour.
Continue blending for 5 minutes (if necessary, strain the mixture through a fine-mesh sieve); refrigerate.
Peel the apples and slice them thinly. Mix them with the sugar and cook in the butter in a pan over medium heat for 4 minutes. Remove from the heat and add the raisins.
Beat the egg whites with the salt until stiff peaks form. Fold one-third into the batter (prepared in the food processor), mixing well. Add the remaining two-thirds, folding them in carefully.
Arrange the apples and sultanas evenly in a nonstick pan. Pour the batter over the top. Bake in a preheated oven at 300–325°F (150–160°C) for 10–15 minutes.

Wine pairing

"Anthos" 2005, Passito DOC – Dessert wine
Winery: Erste & Neue - Prima & Nuova Cantina Sociale di Caldano – Caldaro (BZ)

THE CUISINE OF VENETO

From the Dolomites to the Adriatic Sea, from the lagoon to Lake Garda, Veneto is one of the most varied and spectacular regions in Italy, with a wealth of truly unique treasures. Venice, the maritime republic and queen of the trade routes to the East (which reflects centuries of art and matchless beauty on the waters of the Grand Canal), is found here, bathed in its lagoon. Along the River Brenta, the villas of Palladio rise up, jewels of sixteenth-century architecture desired by the Venetian rich looking for a place to spend time away from the merchant business. On the River Adige, The ancient Roman city of Verona sits comfortably, with its majestic arena that is still home to music performances today, as well as to theater performances of the opposed love of Romeo and Juliet, handed down by the pen of William Shakespeare. The Ampezzo plain opens up along the alpine archway with Cortina, the pearl of mountain tourism, surrounded by the *Tre Cime di Lavaredo* (the three peaks of Lavaredo) in a breathtaking landscape.

A view of Padua arises out of the marshy valleys, where aquaculture is carried out, cultivated in maize and rice fields and embellished with vegetable plots and orchards. It is followed by the hills thick in vineyards, olive and cherry trees, and chestnuts, pastures and wooded plateaus as you climb up towards the mountains. Such a variety of climates and landscapes is mirrored in Venetian cuisine, a melting pot of products and flavors.

In terms of the grains grown on the plain, the *Riso Vialone Nano Veronese IGP* stands out, the only Italian rice to have received European protection so far. It is grown on the low-lying land of the Verona area, where the sources of water give a special quality to the product.

The main dishes typical to Venetian cooking are rice-based, made with vegetables, fish, and seafood. *Risotto alla bechera* is famous, and is made by adding vegetables, cow's brain, chicken giblets, and *secole*, small pieces of meat that are wedged between cow's vertebra, to the rice. *Riso in cavroman* (a rice dish) is also excellent with *castrato* (castrated ewe), as well as *Risotto coi bisati,* an eel-based dish, typical of Murano, the island in the lagoon where blown glass has been worked for centuries. The island also boasts *bisato sull'ara* as its specialty, char-grilled eel. *Risi e bisi,* a rice-based soup with peas, is also a famous dish that was served to the Doge of Venice on special occasions. Pumpkin and grape risottos are equally delicious, although not as common.

Less room is given to pasta in traditional cooking, but the Venetian *pasta e fasoi* (pasta with beans) is one of the best-loved regional soups.

In the mountainous areas, polenta dishes are widespread, served with rich condiments, such as Venetian liver, the *pastissada,* a type of beef or horse stew, and salt cod from Vicenza.

It makes sense that seafood lies at the basis of good cooking in Veneto, where there's room for shellfish alongside saltwater and freshwater fish. In terms of freshwater fish, the lake trout, lagoon eels, and the famous *marsoni,* fish found under the stones of mountain streams, are of note. In a recipe book dedicated to the Veneto, there are many fish stews, called *brodetti;* easily found in this region just like all over the Adriatic. The one handed down by the fishermen of Chioggia, the small town with of multicolored houses that lies at the southern end of the lagoon, is particularly delicious.

In terms of the fish recipes, the various fried dishes, golden and crispy, take first place, among which are the award-winning scampi, particularly large and tasty in this region. There's also fish *in saor,* soaked in a sauce made from vinegar, white wine, herbs, and flavorings, which is a well-known Venetian specialty. The salt cod-based dishes are also famous, cooked here with particularly refined recipes that create delicate offerings, primarily because of the addition of milk, such as in the well-known Vicenza-style salt cod cooked in milk and onions, or in dishes of creamed salt cod.

The roasted meats of this region are well-known and chicken, turkey, pigeon, and duck are mainly used. Pigeon is also the main ingredient in *Sopa coada,* the typical broiled soup from Treviso.

In the region's overflowing food hamper, typical cheeses play an important role; most are produced in the mountain range. Among these, one of the champions of Italian cheese-making cannot be overlooked, Asiago PDO (see box). Another important cheese is the soft and creamy Casatella Trevigiana, a fresh cheese that's white in color, with a sweet flavor that errs on the slightly sour side. Rare and made according to an old tradition, there's also *Schiz*, produced in the province of Belluno, a compact and elastic cheese that possesses a marked flavor of milk. It is usually eaten heated in a pan with butter.

The salamis are renowned, from Sopressa Vicentina, a sausage made from prized cuts of pork, to Prosciutto Veneto Berico-Euganeo PDO, guaranteed by the consortium brand of the lion of St. Mark and produced in the town of Montagnana, one of the most famous intact walled towns in Europe.

There are many vegetables with protected geographical indications, from the white Bassano asparagus to Lamon beans and the famous red radicchio of Treviso, with their characteristic spade-like elongated shape and purple, white-ribbed color. Treviso has a strong, rather bitter flavor, and is perfect grilled, while Radicchio Variegato di Castelfranco, is a rose-like vegetable with speckled, open petals and sweeter flavor. Fruit here is a pure joy: From the peaches of Verona to the Marostica cherries (which hail from the lovely turreted town, the setting of a striking game of chess with real-life figures, held once every two years), the entire hilly area of the region produces an abundance of fruit.

Desserts are rather simple, but they take advantage of old traditions. Some are still made according to the traditional recipes of the *Scaletari*, the name given to Venetian pastry cooks of the past, which derived from the *Scalete*, desserts documented at the beginning of the fifteenth century. Also of note are the *Pàndolo*, are usually dipped in hot chocolate, *Bàicoli*, thin, crunchy cookies, taken in the past by seafarers on their long voyages at sea, and fried Venetian custard. The exquisite Pandòro is made in Verona; it is a product that is also still made industrially and is widely distributed for special occasions. Despite being a yeasted cake, it is mixed using the technique for puff pastry. It has a delicate flavor and a unique shape, tall and grooved, and is covered with a thick coating of confectioners' sugar. Delicious *Marrons glacés* are made with the famous marron chestnuts of Treviso and Verona.

Venetian winemaking is certainly one of the Italian champions. Not only does it offer high-quality wines (Cabernet, Merlot, Colli Berici, Colli Euganei, Refosco, Recioto di Soave, just to name a few), but pairing the wines with traditional products is always a winning combination. Some of the oldest coffee bars in Italy are found in Veneto: *Caffè Florian* in Piazza San Marco in Venice, which opened on 29 December 1720, and *Caffè Pedrocchi* in Padua, designed by the famous Venetian architect Giuseppe Jappelli (1783–1852), which opened in 1831.

ASIAGO PDO

ORIGINALLY FROM THE ASIAGO PLATEAU, THIS IS A COW'S MILK CHEESE WITH A SEMI-COOKED MIXTURE THAT IS AVAILABLE IN TWO DIFFERENT TYPES: *D'ALLEVO*, OR RATHER AGED (*MEZZANO*, IF THE AGEING RANGES FROM 3 TO 5 MONTHS; *VECCHIO* IF MORE THAN 9 MONTHS), OR *PRESSATO*, FRESH WITH A DECIDEDLY LESS ACCENTUATED FLAVOR. IT IS DELICIOUS SERVED WITH YOUNG RED WINES, SUCH AS COLLI EUGANEI CABERNET OR PIAVE PINOT NERO.

GIANCARLO PERBELLINI

RESTAURANT PERBELLINI - ISOLA RIZZA (VERONA)

It's not true that *"there is no world without Verona's walls,"* as the protagonist of Shakespeare's *Romeo and Juliet* maintained in the celebrated play set in the bewitching city where the River Adige flows. South of Verona, there's a place where great Venetian cuisine, both aristocratic and plebian, has found its full expression: *Ristorante* Perbellini.

The restaurant is situated 24 kilometers from Verona, in Isola Rizza, an industrial and farming area with few charms, and stands next to the family's production plant. On the surface, it doesn't appear to be an extraordinary location that would attract patrons. But the name on the sign is enough: "Perbellini, premiata offelleria" (award-winning bakery). The Italian name *offelleria* comes from *offella*, the dessert invented by the Perbellini family in 1891 and which is still the flagship product of their bakery today, tempting those who arrive in front of the establishment. *"The restaurant was undoubtedly born out of madness,"* the chef and owner Giancarlo Perbellini confesses. *"Despite its location, inside I was able to make it into what I wanted and after 20 years it now works perfectly. I have no regrets or any other requirements."* Furnished with a touch of class, the restaurant is stylish, without being overly formal. *"I'd like our customers to experience a convivial atmosphere, as if they were at home; they should all feel at ease."* Customer relations are friendly and warm. The chef, his wife Paola, the maître d'hôtel, and the serving staff often stop to converse with the guests.

Giancarlo resumed the family business because catering had been in the Perbellini blood since 1952. *"My grandfather and his brother had a bar and restaurant with a hotel and bakery. In 1989, when I decided to do this job, I carried on along the path set out by my grandfather, who worked as a chef for his entire life."* He is truly following in his grandfather's footsteps, he admits. *"Yes, because my father has always been (primarily) a baker. However, he was the one who chose the places where I should train when I was still at the hotel institute, and he showed me how to open my own restaurant."*

His training first took him to his hometown of Verona, to *Dodici Apostoli*, then one of the most famous restaurants in Italy, and to *Marconi*, which no longer exists. When he finished his studies, he moved on to *San Domenico* in Imola, then one of the top restaurants with a new approach to haute cuisine. From quality to even more quality, he went to France, working at *Taillevent*, *Ambroisie*, *Terrasse* of Juan les Pins, and *Château d'Esclimont*, then on to England with a chef from the school of Angelo Paracucchi, *"one of the greatest Italian chefs who was using high-quality ingredients 30 years ago."* On returning to Italy, he did a spell as sous chef at *Concorde* of Villa Poma, in the province of Mantua. Then he decided to open his own restaurant, which earned its first Michelin star in 1996, followed by a second one in 2002.

Although the restaurant has a menu that changes frequently, there are some dishes which tend to remain. Two of these belong to the Perbellini family tradition: *pasta reale*, a mixture of flour, Parmesan cheese, and eggs, which is used to make gnocchetti served in stock. *"On special occasions and certain Sundays, it was my grandfather who made them and it's still the men of the family who make them today."* Another is a traditional Perbellini dessert: Alchermes, vanilla, and chocolate pudding. There are also three of the chef's own creations: *"Colors and Flavors of the Sea, my first course has a certain effect, perhaps it's not very current anymore, but it's particularly enjoyed by our customers; braised veal cheek, part of the Venetian and Veronese tradition of braising, which I currently serve with a slice of fois gras on mashed potato with fried leeks. To finish, there's a sesame wafer with sea bass tartare, goat's cheese with chives, and a licorice sensation, which I believe is my masterpiece; a second stroke of luck in my life as a chef will be difficult to find."*

Giancarlo defines his cuisine as *"modern classic."* The same philosophy as the great Venetian architect Palladio, who understood in the mid-sixteenth century how the classic ideal, the supreme image of a perfect social life, would have been uninspired without being flexible enough to change with modern situations. That explains how the dishes of restaurant Perbellini are not some olympic abstraction, but are born from the intelligent research of a comparison with the reality of history

and nature. *"My cuisine relates to the seasons and, at certain times, also has a bond with traditional recipes."* For example, in the winter, the menu offers a contemporary reworking of *pastissàda de caval*, a typical stew from the Verona area made with horse meat marinated in red wine with herbs and spices. *Risoto col tastasal* is a constant feature, the traditional risotto of farming families in the area. *"It's made with fresh salami meat, flavored with garlic, salt, and coarsely crushed pepper, which is left to marinate for a couple of days."* In this part of Veneto, the resurgent waters ensure that top class rice is produced: the Vialone Nano Veronese variety. It's only natural then that risottos are the mainstay of regional food: risotto with eel, traditional on Christmas Eve; with peas, the so-called *risi e bisi;* with Lamon beans from the area of Belluno; as well as with *luganega*, the traditional Treviso sausage.

Polenta, another standard of Venetian cuisine, is also typical in the area. *"We offer it in many different combinations, with fish or meat. In some cases, we use it to make first courses, for example, ravioli filled with polenta and turnip greens flavored with garlic, served with rabbit ragù."* However, the king of culinary tradition in Isola Rizza is undoubtedly the pig. A sow with rice in her mouth still appears on the municipal coat-of-arms today, capturing the old community symbol, depicted at the bottom of the bell tower of the parish church in 1535. *"At the moment,"* the chef explained, *"we have a creamy cinnamon and Parmesan risotto on the menu with a spit-roasted suckling pig ragù."* Giancarlo tends to use many Venetian products, not just from the Verona area. *"Although we're about 100 kilometers from the Adriatic coast, we have a strong relationship with the sea."* Where *castraure* of Sant'Erasmo in Venice, the fleshy violet artichokes that constitute the apex fruit of the artichoke plant, or *schie*, the typical grey prawns of the Venice lagoon and Po Delta, or *moeche*, the extremely tender sea crabs in the soft-shell stage are available, he uses them in his dishes. He is recreating the sea on the plain.

Innovation, as regards tradition, may be in terms of taste, but also in the preparation and cooking techniques. *"We always try to offer dishes which aren't flights of fancy, but based on reason, or creative dishes, such as smoked caviar and frozen zabaglione, or typical dishes which have been slightly revamped. However, there are some aspects where I don't compromise. For example, I cook pork cheek in the oven, with the same cooking method as 20 years ago.*" The history of food is anchored in the present and should be tied down to prevent it from dispersing or vanishing. As Andrea Mantegna taught in the splendid Basilica of San Zeno in Verona, the ancient should be carved as in the semi-precious stone, rendered in a minute, multifaceted, and slow manner.

"*Here food traditions are still strong, not only in the province where every village has its own, but also in town.*" In Verona, there's not only the custom of eating Pandoro, the typical Christmas cake. On Carnival Friday, potato gnocchi are made in honor of the city's typical character, the *Papà del Gnoco*, an old and ruddy man, with a long, white beard, who holds an enormous fork on which a gnocco is pierced. On Sundays the tradition of boiled meats is still close to their hearts, served with *pearà*, a creamy sauce made from day-old breadcrumbs, meat stock, ox marrow, butter, and plenty of pepper, which appears to have come about from the idea of a Veronese chef of the Longobard queen Rosmunda to encourage her appetite.

A typical day in the life of Giancarlo is demanding. "*I'm always there on the five days of the week when the restaurant is open. I couldn't abandon ship, not even for one evening.*" He never gets to bed before 1:30 a.m. and starts work in the kitchen at 8:30 a.m., making the bread, fresh pasta, and desserts. "*This is the area of cooking where I help out the most. We have a sweet trolley consisting of 28 desserts, which is put together everyday.*" He's always there in person to receive goods and to check them. "*For the vegetables, we have two suppliers, which we alternate according to them providing us with either ordinary or less common products, like the wild herbs which are still hand-picked.*" For example, he uses the *bruscandoli*, wild hop sprouts, in a shrimp risotto; ravioli with red shrimp with *carletti*, the delicate Silene herb; and a poached egg with *brusaoci*, or common dandelion. He has more than one supplier for fish, in particular one is based at Chioggia market, the vibrant sea port that seals the Venice lagoon to the south, who procures what Giancarlo needs. Although it's more of a fish restaurant, he has a butcher he trusts in the town from whom he buys the meat.

Although his birth town of Verona moves him with its special charisma and he loves to go up to the *Torricelle*, the foothills of the Lessinia Prealps, which rise to the north of the province of Verona, where he can admire the city from on high and its most famous monument, the arena, the best-preserved Roman amphitheater in Italy and now home to an important opera festival, the dishes chosen for this book pay tribute to the Veneto. For starters, salt cod and potato millefeuille on a bed of salad, made with Venetian-style salt cod puree. *"This is dedicated to the long history that the Venetian plain has with a fish that, while not coming from the area, has become an integral part of it. Every province has its own version of salt cod, which is also combined with fresh or toasted polenta."*

For the rice course, squid ink and basil risotto with tomato confit, *"a Venetian classic with a modern take"* and for the main course, one of the region's most traditional dishes, *polenta and birds*, which he makes two ways, *"in yesterday's version, with small birds wrapped in pancetta and flavored with sage, cooked in the oven at a low temperature for 1½ hours, and today's version, where the polenta, which is very soft, is served with spit-roasted birds."*

For dessert, there's polenta *fogazzin*, a cake taken from the Venetian farming tradition, based on polenta left over from the day before and flavored with sultanas, and anisette. *"A dish made from leftovers, which is delicious nevertheless and can be eaten hot or cold."* It's therefore a regional menu that also widely satisfies the *anguane*, the siren-witches that dance on wires suspended in a void according to Venetian tradition. Here the culinary flavors stretch from the Adriatic to Lake Garda, from the Po to the Dolomites.

SALT COD AND POTATO MILLEFEUILLE ON A BED OF SALAD

Ingredients for 4 people
Preparation time: 1 h

3 medium potatoes
Scant ½ cup (100 ml) extra-virgin olive oil
Scant ½ cup (100 ml) milk
1 bay leaf
1 clove garlic
Salt, to taste
Pepper, to taste
10 oz (300 g) fresh salt cod (gabilo)
Scant 2 tablespoons (25 g) butter
½ lemon, squeezed
Chives, as many as needed
2 tomatoes
Scant ½ cup (100 ml) balsamic vinegar
1½ oz (40 g) salad greens
Chervil, as much as needed

Method

Peel the potatoes and cut them very thinly on a mandolin. Arrange them on an oiled baking sheet in a rose-shaped pattern. Drizzle with oil. Bake in the oven at 250°F (110°C) until golden and crisp.
Bring the milk to a boil in a pot with the bay leaf and garlic. Season with salt and pepper to taste.
Add the salt cod, having removed the skin and bones. Let cook at 200°F (90°C).
Drain cod and beat with a whisk, gradually adding the olive oil, butter, lemon juice, and finely chopped chives.
Cut a cross in the bottom of each tomato; blanch the tomatoes, remove the seeds and skins. Cut into evenly sized cubes.
Dissolve a pinch of salt in the vinegar in a small bowl. Gradually pour in the oil and emulsify to make a vinaigrette.
Clean and wash the salad greens, drying it well.

Serving

Layer the potatoes with the salt cod, forming three layers. Warm in the oven and serve on a little salad dressed with the balsamic vinaigrette. Garnish with the diced tomatoes and a sprig of chervil.

Wine pairing

"Agnobianco" 2005 – White
Winery: Masari – Valdagno (VI)

SQUID INK AND BASIL RISOTTO
WITH TOMATO CONFIT

Ingredients for 4 people
Preparation time: 55'

STOCK
1½ lb (700 g) beef
1 lb (500 g) veal
1 onion
1 carrot
1 celery stalk
1 bay leaf
Salt

*SHELLFISH BISQUE OR FISH SOUP
1½ lb (700 g) shellfish
⅓ cup (50 g) flour
1 tablespoon extra-virgin olive oil
Generous ¾ cup (200 ml) brandy
2 tablespoons tomato paste
2 tablespoons water
Salt, to taste
Pepper to taste
⅔ cup (150 g) butter
1 oz (30 g) mixed herbs (sage, rosemary, etc)
3 quarts (3 liters) water

RISOTTO
7 oz (200 g) black squid
4 shallots
1 clove garlic
White wine
1 quart (1 liter) fish soup or shellfish bisque*
Scant ¼ cup (50 g) tomato passata
2 quarts (2 liters) stock
2½ cups (300 g) Carnaroli rice
Butter
Grated Parmesan
Salt
Tomato confit
1 basil leaf
Basil-infused oil
Extra-virgin olive oil
1 lemon

Method

STOCK

Put the meat in a large saucepan and cover with cold water.

Bring the water to a boil over medium heat, covering it with a lid.

When the water comes to a boil, skim the froth, season with salt, and add the whole vegetables and the bay leaf.

Lower the heat, cover again, and simmer for about 2½ hours.

Strain, let cool and chill for at least 3 hours.

Before using the stock, remove the layer of fat that will have solidified on the surface.

SHELLFISH BISQUE

Toast the flour in a frying pan over high heat for about 3 minutes so that it loses its humidity and becomes slightly brown. Set aside.

Brown the vegetables in the oil in a large pot over high heat. Add the shellfish and mix well. Break them up with a spoon and continue mixing for 5 minutes. Add the toasted flour, mixing well.

Pour in half the brandy, add the tomato paste and water, and season with salt and pepper.

Mix well and let the liquid reduce to half the original volume over high heat. This will take 1 hour. When reduced, add the remaining brandy, mix for 1 minute, and remove from the heat. Add the butter, melting it, and continue mixing.

Place a strainer in the pot and pour the bisque, breaking up and mashing the contents up well so that all of it is strained.

RISOTTO

Clean the squid, removing the quill and taking care to keep the ink sacs intact.

Sauté the chopped shallots and garlic until pale gold. Let it braise.

Add 3½ oz (100 g) of squid and let them brown. Drizzle with the white wine. Pour in the fish soup or fumet, the squid ink, and tomato passata. Season with salt and pepper. Cook and puree in a blender when ready.

Toast the rice without any oil in a large skillet. Drizzle with the white wine and then add the squid ink mixture. Continue cooking, slowly adding the fish soup or shellfish bisque and the stock. Stir constantly.

Add the butter at the end and a sprinkling of grated Parmesan. Season with salt to taste.

Serve the risotto, garnishing it with the tomato confit, a basil leaf, basil-infused oil, the remaining squid (finely cut into a julienne and lightly cooked in the fumet, drizzled with extra-virgin olive oil and chives) and the grated lemon zest (optional).

TOMATO CONFIT

Bring a pot of water to a boil. Cut a cross in the bottom of each tomato (this will make it easier to remove the skin afterwards) and blanch the ripe tomatoes in the water for a few seconds.

Remove and let cool in ice water. Drain and remove the skin, cut tomatoes into four, removing the seeds. Arrange on a baking tray and sprinkle with table salt, sugar, and very finely cut lemon zest. Bake in the oven at 225°F (100°C) for about 2 hours.

Wine pairing

"Staforte," Soave 2004 – White
Winery: Azienda Agricola Prà – Monteforte d'Alpone (VR)

POLENTA AND BIRDS, TODAY

Ingredients for 4 people
Preparation time: 1 h 30'

1 tablespoon coarse salt
1²⁄₃ cups (250 g) polenta flour
10 oz (300 g) pork
2 carrots
2 onions
2 celery stalk
7 oz (200 g) smoked bacon

4 egg whites
4 warblers or larks, cleaned
Salt, to taste
Pepper, to taste
1 pat of butter
1 oz (30 g) foie gras
2 teaspoons (10 g) hazelnut paste

Method

Bring a liter of water to a boil. Dissolve a tablespoon of coarse salt in it and sift in the polenta flour, mixing with a whisk to make a smooth polenta. Continue cooking for about 45 minutes, stirring constantly. Meanwhile, cut the pork into pieces, as well as 1 carrot, 1 onion, and 1 stalk of celery. Cover with water and bring to a boil, keeping the surface free from impurities using a slotted spoon and making sure that the liquid remains at a simmer. Blend the polenta and keep it in a whipped cream siphon properly charged. Strain the pork stock through a fine-mesh sieve and wait until it cools. Clarify: pass the bacon through a meat grinder with 1 carrot, 1 onion, and 1 stalk of celery. Mix it all together with the egg whites, which have been beaten to stiff peaks. Pour the mixture into the stock, letting it simmer for 3 hours. It will collect any impurities from the stock. When the clarification has been completed, you will be able to pour the consommé through a fine-mesh strainer covered with gauze. Clean the birds, setting the internal parts, such as the liver, heart, and lungs, aside. Cook the birds on a spit arranged horizontally on the cooking axle. Season with salt and pepper and let them turn until cooked. Let the consommé reduce in a large pot and bind it together with a pat of butter.
Pass the interiors of the birds and the fois gras through a strainer. Mix together with the hazelnut paste to form a puree. Plate, arranging the polenta mousse in the center with the fois gras puree on top. Drizzle with the hot bacon consommé and arrange the roasted birds on top.

AND YESTERYEAR

Ingredients for 4 people
Preparation time: 1 h 30'

8 warblers (or larks or thrushes), cleaned
8 slices of marinated pancetta
8 sage leaves
¼ cup (60 g) butter
1 cup (150 g) polenta flour
Salt
1 clove garlic

Method

Clean the birds on the outside, removing the feathers, but leaving the interiors intact. Wrap in the slices of pancetta with the sage leaves. Bake at a low temperature of about 200°F (90–95°C), for 1½ hours.
Meanwhile, make the polenta, bringing the salted water to a boil and mixing in the flour. Cook for 45–50 minutes.
Serve the birds on the soft polenta with their cooking juices.

Wine pairing

"Valpolicella Superiore" DOC 2004 – Red
Winery: Azienda Agricola Marion – San Martino Buon Albergo (VR)

POLENTA FOGAZZIN

Ingredients for 4 people
Preparation time: 1 h 20'

Generous 2 cups (250 g) polenta flour
1 tablespoon coarse salt
Scant ⅓ cup (70 g) melted butter
5 oz (150 g) eggs
Generous ⅓ cup (80 g) sugar
1 teaspoon (5 g) all-purpose flour
10 oz (300 g) sultanas, soaked
1 tablespoon (15 g) anisette
Pinch of vanilla
breadcrumbs

Method

POLENTA
Bring 1 liter of water to a boil. Add a tablespoon of coarse salt and sift in the polenta flour, mixing with a whisk to make a smooth polenta. Continue cooking for about 45 minutes.

FOGAZZIN
Pass the polenta through a vegetable mill. Add the melted butter, followed by the eggs and sugar mixed with the flour and the remaining ingredients.
Butter the mold and sprinkle with breadcrumbs. Bake in the oven at 325°F (160°C) for 18 minutes.

Wine pairing

Comtess "San Valentin" 2002 – Dessert wine/Passito
Winery: Cantina Produttori di S. Michele Appiano – San Michele Appiano (BZ)

THE CUISINE OF FRIULI-VENEZIA GIULIA

The region begins with the untouched and spectacular beauty of the Carnia mountains, with the small lake basins set into them, like Lake Verzegnis. It drops down into the landscape of the Prealps and the hilly cover in the shape of an amphitheater, which accompanies the course of the rivers Tagliamento and Isonzo, down to the plain. This sparse and restless course is followed by *magredi,* immense river shores colonized by vineyards and orchards, and slips into the southern part of the region, green with irrigated cultivation among poplars and maize. And there's the sea, with the beach of Lignano Sabbiadoro and the lagoons of Marano and Grado. There's also the striking and scraggy landscape of Il Carso, the setting of the moving poetry of Giuseppe Ungaretti (1888–1970) during World War I. A land of hard workers of few words, but with cultured charms, especially in Trieste, the preferred destination of many ex-pat writers and poets, including James Joyce (1882–1941), Rainer Maria Rilke (1875–1926), and the homeland of Italo Svevo (1861–1928) and Umberto Saba (1883–1957). Friuli-Venezia Giulia has a subtly foreign charm due to its being a frontier region between Austria, Slovenia, and Croatia.

From a culture that has varied so much over the course of time and such a diversified terrain across the territory, food and wine has been created that often has few points in common with the rest of Italy. The cuisine of Friuli has in fact known how to treasure the flavors which have come from the other side of its borders: Austrian, Slavic, and those having an oriental influence, with an abundance of spices and sweet-and-sour flavors, expertly blending them with its own Veneto-based traditions.

If polenta associates the region with the Veneto, in recipes like *zuf,* hot polenta and cold milk; *mesta* also made from milk and flavored with beans; *paparot* with spinach and sausage, the almost total absence of pasta-based first courses reveals the Central European influences, where soups prevail and sweet flavors are combined with salty, smoked, and sour ones. The *cialson* of Il Carnia are an example of this, tortelli filled with day-old rye bread, spinach, candied fruits, sultanas, chocolate, sugar, and cinnamon. They are eaten served with smoked Ricotta, sweetened melted butter, and *stravecchio* cheese (see box). Then there's *pistum,* gnocchi made from bread, eggs, sugar, sultanas, and herbs, which are served cooked in a special stock made from pork. Another typical recipe, this time from Trieste, are *gnocchi con le prugne,* potato gnocchi containing a pitted prune, cooked and then served with sweetened melted butter and poppy seeds. Other close relations to gnocchi, and also of *Knödel,* are those made with liver and day-old bread. Among the noteworthy soups are those consisting of barley, *jota,* made from polenta flour, milk, and beans, *brovada,* or as made in Trieste, with potatoes, sauerkraut, and smoked pancetta. Though Hungarian in origin, goulash is made in Friuli. Cooked salamis like *muset,* a type of *cotechino* sausage flavored with cinnamon and vanilla, are served with *brovada,* a sliced turnip fermented with marc. This is a recipe that's very similar to Tyrolean sauerkraut. The sauce, served with boiled meats, is made from horseradish and apple and cooked in a mixture of wine and stock.

The fish dishes almost totally abandon foreign influences to reunite with the maritime traditions of the Adriatic. There are the excellent *brodetti,* with an abundance of different types of fish, cooked simply or with the addition of tomatoes, with fish cut into pieces, but also pureed to make a dense soup.

The specialty of Trieste is *granseola,* crab from the Adriatic with its prized and delicate meat, delicious steamed and served simply, or accompanied with subtly flavored sauces. Then there's a whole range of recipes of stuffed baby cuttlefish, which are stewed or baked in the oven. Trout and freshwater fish based recipes are also featured, especially in the mountainous area.

Friulian charcuterie boasts products such as Prosciutto di San Daniele PDO, similar to Parma ham, from which it is distinguished by its shape with a whole little trotter, and well-known as far back as the Celtic Roman era. It involves an ageing of 12 months and has a sweet flavor with a more accented aftertaste. Other cured meats include the rare Prosciutto di Sauris smoked and aged in the mountains in the lovely German-speaking village in the Carnic Alps from which it takes its name; Carsolino, the characteristic prosciutto of the Monrupino area, on the border with Slovenia; and Peta della Val Cellina, in the Giulian Prealps, a roundish shaped sausage made from ground beef, pork, goat, and game, especially chamois and kid, with the dominant aroma of fennel.

Among the sausages, the most remarkable is *muset* (made from snout meat, rind, and shank flavored with salt, pepper, cloves, cinnamon, nutmeg, white wine, and vanilla), we should mention *cevàpcici*, pork, beef, and lamb sausages flavored with salt, pepper, and chile pepper. The name gives away its Slavic origin and it's eaten fresh, cooked on a grill. In addition to the pork charcuterie, there's a whole range of products made from goose meat on offer in Friuli: smoked goose breast, prosciutto, and salami, stuffed into the animal's neck skin, also called *salame giudeo* due to its popularity among those who couldn't eat pork because of their religious beliefs. The cheese production is also interesting, among which Montasio PDO (see box) stands out, used in various stages of ripening like those served on a cheeseboard, used in cooking, or grated. This cheese is used to make *frico*, an extremely delicious and crispy cheese fritter.

There are many other typical cheeses, which have been brought back from the brink of extinction and are still produced by hand. Examples include the salted cheese from Il Carnia, whose production is flourishing in particular in the Valle d'Arzino, or *Tabor* from Il Carso, a local version with a more outstanding character from the community dairy.

The prized Carnia beans shouldn't be forgotten among the region's typical vegetables.

Among the dessert specialties, we find sweets which are evidently Austrian in origin due to their complicated preparation: *gubana*, a large leavened pastry snail filled with dried fruit, chocolate, and candied fruit which goes well with the dessert wine Collio Goriziano Picolit. Similar in terms of ingredients, there's also *presnitz*, a type of filled salami. Finally, there's *strucolo*, a strudel with its classic apple filling, although there's also a plum version. A region with a strong winemaking tradition, Friuli-Venezia Giulia isn't just the cradle of great and famous wines, such as the white Tocai, red Refosco, made from indigenous vines, Chardonnay made from naturalized vines, Cabernet Sauvignon, and Merlot, but also prized, preferably single-variety grappas, which certainly don't disappoint spirit enthusiasts.

MONTASIO PDO

Already known in the thirteenth century, this full-fat cow's milk cheese with its compact pasta riddled with small eyes takes its name from the relief of the same name in the Giulian Alps.

It is called a fresh cheese and has a soft and delicate flavor if the ripening ranges from 60 days to 5 months. It's called *mezzano* if aged up to 12 months and has a full flavor and more crumbly cheese. It's stravecchio if aged for more than one year and becomes fairly spicy and suitable for grating. Aged in wine barrels, the so-called *ubriaco* (drunk) Montasio should be noted for its particular aftertaste.

EMANUELE SCARELLO

RESTAURANT TRATTORIA AGLI AMICI - GODIA (UDINE)

THE CUISINE OF EMANUELE SCARELLO, CHEF AND OWNER WITH SISTER MICHELA OF THE RESTAURANT AND TRATTORIA *AGLI AMICI* IN GODIA, A SMALL MUNICIPALITY JUST OUTSIDE OF UDINE IN THE HEART OF FRIULI-VENEZIA GIULIA, RESEMBLES THE FRIEZE OF THE *ORATORIO DI SANTA MARIA IN VALLE* IN THE NEARBY CIVIDALE. THERE, IN ONE OF THE MOST IMPORTANT ARCHITECTURAL TESTIMONIES TO THE LONGOBARD ERA, THE PROCESSION OF THE SAINTS STANDS OUT STRONGLY IN THE CLASSICAL MANNER, WHILE DEMONSTRATING A KNOWLEDGE OF THE DECORATIVE FORMULAE OF THE BYZANTINE CULTURE, WHEREAS HERE IN ONE OF THE BEST RESTAURANTS IN THE REGION, THE DISHES NEVER SURRENDER THEMSELVES TO MONUMENTAL AND HONEST TRADITIONAL FLAVORS, BUT THEY ARE ALWAYS IMBUED WITH A FRUITFUL, MOTIVATED, AND ELEGANT CREATIVITY.

A CULINARY PHILOSOPHY THAT PAYS TRIBUTE TO THE RESTAURANT'S LONG HISTORY, ESTABLISHED BY HIS FAMILY IN 1887. *"YOU CAN'T SEE THAT IT'S 120 YEARS OLD, BUT YOU CAN FEEL IT,"* EMANUELE ASSERTS. *"MY SISTER AND I HAVE BEEN AT THE HELM SINCE 1999. WE MAY BE THE YOUNGEST, BUT WE HAVE AN AWARENESS OF WHAT THE FOUR GENERATIONS THAT PRECEDED US DID."* SET UP AS A RETAILER OF GENERAL AND COLONIAL FOODSTUFFS MANAGED BY HIS GREAT-GREAT GRANDFATHER UMBERTO, IT STOOD 50 METERS FROM THE CURRENT SITE. WHEN IT WAS LATER TRANSFORMED INTO A LARGER VENUE ON TWO FLOORS, WITH A BAR AND A TV ROOM, IT ADVANCED BY 20 METERS. FINALLY, THE LAST 30 METERS WERE COVERED IN ITS BECOMING A TRATTORIA, MANAGED BY HIS GREAT-GRANDMOTHER EMILIA. FROM THAT POINT IT REACHED ITS CURRENT SIZE AND APPEARANCE, INITIALLY WITH EMANUELE'S GRANDFATHER AND GRANDMOTHER, AND THEN HIS PARENTS, WHO RENOVATED THE ENTIRE BUILDING IN 1993.

HIS FATHER TINO AND MOTHER IVONNE STILL WORK IN THE RESTAURANT; SHE WORKS IN THE KITCHEN WITH HER SON AND HE'S IN THE DINING ROOM WITH HIS DAUGHTER MICHELA, THE SOMMELIER. *"MY MOTHER GIVES ME A HAND, NOT SO MUCH DUE TO THE PARENTAL BOND THAT CONNECTS US, BUT BECAUSE SHE'S A COMPETENT PERSON WHO HAS FREQUENTED SOME OF THE LEADING KITCHENS IN FRANCE AND ITALY."* HE'S ALSO SURROUNDED BY EXCELLENT COLLEAGUES. *"I ALWAYS THINK THAT WE'RE LIKE A FOOTBALL TEAM. I'M THE STRIKER AND HAVE TO SCORE THE GOALS, BUT THERE HAS TO BE A GOALKEEPER, A DEFENDER, AND MIDFIELDER, AND SO ON. EVERYONE HAS TO PERFORM THEIR ROLE WELL AND THEY'RE ALL IMPORTANT."*

At the beginning, his parents had discouraged him and Michela, steering them towards doing other jobs. *"We listened to them for a bit, but then we realized that the desire for catering was in our blood, so much so that we followed in the family business and, after gaining experience elsewhere, we came back home."* Indeed, to them it isn't a restaurant, but *"our home, which we open to guests."* Located on the village square, a small farming village in a suburb that's miraculously been spared from factories and chimneys, it is an elegant house that is lacking in pomp. It is furnished in a minimalist style without being plain, with just a few precious objects. *"We have seven tables indoors and five outside. Outside of the restaurant, there's a small garden, in the shadow of ancient oak trees, where we have also set up two lounges for pre-dinner drinks or as somewhere to sit after dinner."*

Emanuele is very attached to Godia, where he is fortunate to live a privileged life. Instead of the noise of cars flashing past, he can hear the sound of time beaten by the tolling of the bell of the parish church. This is the reason why he happily came back here after his apprenticeship. *"Having finished the hotel institute and gained the diploma, I was convinced that I'd be able to start working in the restaurant straightaway. Instead this wasn't the case. My parents sent me off to experience the world and to learn. It was a stroke of luck. I received many of the right stimuli to continue to have the desire to put my foot down on the accelerator."* He worked in the best places in Europe and Italy, but he found his two maestros just around the corner, *"obviously after my parents,"* the people who made him understand what haute cuisine was: Giorgio Trentin and Vinicio Dovier, owner and chef of the restaurant *Boschetti* respectively in Tricesimo. *"At the time I was 16 years old and the restaurant, with its two Michelin stars."* Anyway, Emanuele doesn't feel as though he's anyone's disciple. *"I have my own clear identity, which is linked to my land. If you ride a wave that isn't your own, you don't go far."*

He calls his cuisine contemporary and it has been bejeweled with a Michelin star. *"Although I always keep my feet firmly anchored to the ground where I was born, I like to look beyond."*

Member of the *Jeunes Restaurateurs d'Europe* association, he is open to dialogue and comparison with other chefs and new frontiers in terms of flavor. In this regard, he is the perfect image of Friuli-Venezia Giulia, which has as many cuisines as it has landscapes, from the striking Carnia mountains to the abundant scenery of the pre-alpine and hilly area, from the plain colonized with vineyards and orchards to the verdant south with its irrigated cultivations that stretch to the sea, the calm of the Adriatic lagoons and the harsher landscape of Il Carso. *"I think of myself as very lucky as the sea is 45 kilometers away, the mountains are the same*

distance, and I live in the middle of the countryside. I can actually tap into whatever I like!" He is very attached to his land and to those who work on it. *"Beppino, for example, is the man who makes my salamis. He's someone who's known me since I was born, he's my dad's friend and before then he was my grandfather's pal. I know how he rears his pigs and how he feeds them. I can touch the quality of his meat. Just 200 meters from my restaurant, there's an artificial canal where one of the oldest mills in Friuli is located, where grinding take place with stone. When the farmers take their maize, the miller proudly calls me to let me feel the flours and breathe in their aromas. Isn't that amazing?"*

He uses everything that the territory has to offer, but also everything he grew up with. *"When I was 15, the kiwi fruit only came from New Zealand. Now Friuli is one of the leading European producers of this fruit. However, the kiwi isn't in my blood; perhaps it will be in my son or grandson's DNA. It will become part of the Friulian tradition. We will have lost our Seuka apple, but gained the kiwi. I, however, will never cook chicken with kiwi.]"* His cuisine radiates out into the territory, but retains the local characteristics at its core. It's a little like the nearby fortress town of Palmanova, with its well-preserved town walls in the shape of a nine-pointed star that wedges itself into the surrounding landscape. On one hand, his knowledge of food allows him to treasure everything which the horizons of his land offer; on the other hand, his outstanding personality doesn't allow him to be invaded by other flavors.

Emanuele personally checks every ingredient that enters his kitchen. *"We have trusted suppliers, which are all shown on the bottom of the menu, as our work would not be possible without them. I don't care if I have to pay more for a product, as long as those who are getting them for me know what I want and they don't waste my time."* He has people who buy fish for him on the markets at Chioggia, Grado, and Marano; and the local butcher provides his meat. He goes to the community dairy in Godo, in the municipality of Gemona del Friuli, to get fresh milk, cheeses, and Ricotta, *"because I know those who make the milk as well as the dairyman."* For fruit and vegetables, *"I use the village farmers of whom I'm very fond."*

He uses typical products in his dishes, such as the two kings of the cuisine of Friuli, Montasio cheese and Prosciutto di San Daniele. For example, he serves *sanganel*, a smoked black pudding that is typical of Il Carnia, with his ravioli filled with runny pumpkin. However, he never offers any old-fashioned dishes. *"I don't make musetto e brovada or barley and bean soup, which are the standard regional dishes. In the restaurant I try things which I find appetizing and fun to make, allowing me to taste the flavor of the traditional dish, but without letting me see the same form. I love and believe in tradition, but I look at it from a new perspective."* He revises *musetto e brovada*, cotechino sausage served with white turnips fermented on marc, by offering a warm *musetto* and sea bass tartare flavored with horseradish, which is called *cren* in Friuli-Venezia Giulia. *"I created this dish for a reason: the fat of the* musetto *preserves the flavor of the sea in my mouth from the sea bass and the grating of* cren, *by cleansing my palate, makes me want another mouthful."*

An exemplary dish and a model of his way of understanding his territorial roots is the Friulian Tocai soup, one of the wines that made the region famous, which Emanuele serves with potato gnocchi and sea urchins. *"The extremely bitter edge of the wine and the iodine of the raw sea urchins are mediated by the gnocchi, and a great combination is created."* Godia is famous for its potatoes. There's actually a festival that's held here dedicated to the delicious tuber at the end of August and the beginning of September. Hence the reason why gnocchi, served with tomato sauce, simply with butter and sage or with a meat or kid ragù, are never lacking.

Emanuele lives in a territory where traditions have been preserved intact. *"Here it's a quiet life and I try to get this serenity, which lies at the bottom of everything, across in my restaurant, in the service and cuisine."* He increasingly thinks about the figure of an ethical chef, who believes in certain values of sincerity and transparency. *"In my restaurant whatever a customer eats, my son also eats."* He also thinks about humility. *"Although our work is currently under the spotlight, we're still just people who put pans on the hob."*

As a starter for the menu for this book, he has chosen a warm tartare of sea bass, *musetto*, and horseradish. For the first course, there's bread soup with salt cod tripe and popcorn. *"I began with the bread soup, or panade, which is a traditional bread soup that is cooked slowly on a spolert, a typical wood-burning stove. It contains chicken and beef stock, to which a raw egg yolk and pork finocchietto are added at the end. I use fish stock and I like to serve it with salt cod tripe and crispy salt cod popcorn."* The meat course offered is cured veal cheeks, served with celery root puree and *picecui* mustard, the name for dog rose berries in Friulian dialect. In Friuli-Venezia Giulia this shrub grows at the edge of woodlands, in clearings, and hedges, along country and hill roads. Its fruits are traditionally used to make herbal teas, infusions, syrups, and preserves. The dessert, called *Zamò & Nonino dessert*, pays *"tribute to two people who have done wonders for food and wine in Friuli: Giannola Nonino of the historic family of grappa distillers and the producer of Tullio Zamò wines."* This dessert, which consists of Vola Vola ice-cream, a raisin dessert wine from the Zamò vineyards, and chocolate custard with Nonino grappa, also pays tribute to the name of the restaurant. In Friuli, the pleasure of having a chat with friends while enjoying a glass of wine or grappa is sacrosanct.

WARM TARTARE OF SEA BASS, *MUSETTO*, AND HORSERADISH

Ingredients for 4 people
Preparation time: 20' – Cooking time for *musetto*: 2 h – Oil butter: 48 h

TARTARE
3½ oz (100 g) musetto* (previously cooked and diced)
1 wild sea bass, weighing about 1 lb (500 g)
Salt, for seasoning
Freshly ground black pepper, for seasoning
Chives, chopped
Fresh horseradish, grated
Radish sprouts
Extra-virgin olive oil

* The best-known Friulian sausage, *musetto* is a ground seasoned pork mixture Stuffed into sausage casings. *Musetto* is made from lean pork snout meat (where its name comes from), the tastiest and most delicious part of the whole pig, mixed with a bit of firm lard.

OIL BUTTER
1 cup (250 g) Carso extra-virgin olive oil, or other good-quality olive oil

Method

OIL BUTTER
Pour the oil into a container and keep it in the freezer for 24 hours. Chill in the refrigerator for 1 day.

TARTARE
Simmer the *musetto* in its casing very slowly over low heat for about 1½–2 hours. Cut into small cubes.
Transfer the *musetto* cubes to a large pot and heat them through.
Cut the sea bass flesh into small cubes and season with salt and pepper. Toss with the chives and fresh horseradish.
Mix the sea bass with the musetto and warm (but take care not to cook the eel) over low heat.

Serving

Arrange the tartare in the center of the plate using a pastry cutter; top with the radish sprouts. Finish with a quenelle of oil butter.

Wine pairing

Sauvignon del Collio – White
Winery: Attems – Lucinico (GO)

BREAD SOUP WITH SALT COD TRIPE AND POPCORN

Ingredients for 4 people
Preparation time: 1 h – Cooking time for soup: 3 h – Drying the tripe: 24 h

FUMET
Fish trimmings
Vegetables (such as carrot, celery, and mushroom stalks)
Onion
Garlic
Herbs (bay and parsley)
Salt
White wine
Peppercorn

SOUP
1¾ oz (50 g) shallot
2 salt-cured anchovy fillets
Garlic-infused extra-virgin olive oil
1 sprig of thyme
4oz (125 g) dry white bread
5 cups (1.2 kg) fish fumet
Salt, to taste
Freshly ground black pepper, to taste
Dill

*SPICY TOMATO SAUCE
4 tablespoons extra-virgin olive oil
2 onions, chopped
3 cloves garlic, chopped
½ cup (125 g) tomato passata
2 lb (1 kg) tomatoes, cut into cubes
½ cup (125 ml) red wine
1 tablespoon traditional balsamic vinegar
1 teaspoon brown sugar
1 tablespoon (15 g) parsley, chopped
1 chile pepper

SALT COD TRIPE
14 oz (400 g) salt cod tripe
1⅔ cups (400 g) spicy tomato sauce*

POPCORN
14 oz (400 g) salt cod tripe
Salt, for seasoning

Method

FUMET

This concentrated fish stock is made by cooking fish trimmings with vegetables, salt, and herbs for a long time. Gut the fish (medum and large-sized fish are preferable as they are rich in collagen) and cut the fish bones into pieces. Add the bones, head, tails, and flesh to a saucepan with the carrot, celery, onions, mushroom stalks, garlic, bay leaf, and parsley. Cover the mixture with water and white wine and cook for at least 1 hour, Skim the foam occasionally. Add the peppercorns at the end. Let rest for at least 15 minutes before straining.

BREAD SOUP

Chop the shallot. Rinse the anchovies and cook over low heat in a little garlic-infused oil. Add the thyme, which will be removed at the end, and bread. Mix well and add enough of the fumet until it all ingredients are covered.
Cook over low heat (if possible, use a flame tamer to help evenly distribute the heat of the burner) for 3 hours until the bread starts to stick to the bottom of the pan. Season with salt and pepper to taste and add the chopped dill.

SPICY TOMATO SAUCE

Heat the oil in a large pot. Add the onions, garlic, and chile pepper. Cook over medium heat for 5 minutes. Add the tomato passata and cook for 3 minutes, mixing occasionally. Pour in 2 cups (500 ml) of water with the tomatoes, wine, vinegar, and sugar. Bring to a boil, stirring often. Lower the heat and simmer for 25 minutes, until the mixture thickens.
Finish with the remaining parsley 2 minutes before removing from the heat.

SALT COD WITH TOMATO SAUCE

Use a knife to remove the skin from the tripe and blanch in plenty of water. Add the tripe to the tomato sauce.

SALT COD POPCORN

Peel the tripe and cut into ¾-inch (2-cm) squares. Place in a dryer at 85°F (30°C) for 24 hours. Remove and store in an airtight container until ready to use.
Let the tripe burst into popcorn in oil heated to 350°F (180°C), making sure that it tripled in volume. Drain and season with salt.

Serving

Ladle the soup in the center of each plate. Place a tablespoon of tripe in tomato sauce on top and finish with a piece of salt cod popcorn.

Wine pairing

Malvasia istriana – White
Winery: Cantina Produttori di Cormòns – Cormòns (GO)

SALTED VEAL CHEEKS WITH CELERY ROOT PUREE

Ingredients for 4 people
Preparation time: 3 h – Marinating: 24 h

10 fresh veal cheeks*
Salt
Curing spices

* *To cook the cheeks, a multi-functional oven or a Roner digital thermostat should be used, pieces of equipment that maintains the water in a container at a set temperature.*

PICECUI MUSTARD
7 oz (200 g) picecui (dog rose berries)
1 cup (250 g) white wine vinegar
1 cup (250 g) white wine
¾ cup (150 g) sugar
Zest of 1 lemon
Zest of 1 orange

2 bay leaves
1 cinnamon stick
5 cloves
1 shallot
1 quince
Salt and peppercorns

CELERY ROOT PUREE
8 oz (250 g) celery root, cut into short lengths
Salt, for seasoning
Freshly ground black pepper, for seasoning
Scant ½ cup (100 g) extra-virgin olive oil, plus additional, for drizzling
Scant ½ cup (100 g) whole milk

Method

Sprinkle the cheeks with salt, followed by the curing spices. Seal them in a vacuum pack and let marinate in the refrigerator at +35.5°F (2°C) for 1 day. Cook at 200°F (85°C) for 2 hours in the oven.

MUSTARD
Cut the berries in half, removing the seeds and washing them carefully under running water to remove any thorny residues.
Boil all the ingredients (apart from the berries) for 5 minutes and then strain. Add the berries and simmer over medium heat for 10 minutes.

PUREE
Season the celery root with salt and pepper. Drizzle with extra-virgin olive oil. Seal in a vacuum pack and bake in the oven at 200°F (90°C) for 30 minutes. Open the pack and pour the contents into a food processor. Blend with the milk and extra-virgin olive oil to make a puree. Keep warm.

Serving

Slice the warm veal cheeks and serve with a generous spoonful of celery root puree and a spoonful of mustard.

Wine pairing

"Schioppettino di Prepotto" nei Colli Orientali del Friuli – Red
Winery: Azienda agricola Hilde Petrussa Mecchia – Prepotto (UD)

ZAMÒ & NONINO DESSERT

Ingredients for 4 people
Preparation time: 1 h

ICE-CREAM
Generous 3 cups (625 g) sugar
3 cups (650 g) Vola Vola (raisin dessert wine)
1¼ cups (300 g) Vola Vola syrup, (see recipe, below)
2 cups (500 g) milk
1 cup (250 g) fresh cream
Scant ¼ cup (50 g) egg yolks

CHOCOLATE AND NONINO
ANTICA CUVÉE CUSTARD
Generous 1¼ cups (320 g) cream
⅓ cup (80 g) milk
8½ oz (240 g) couverture chocolate, chopped

⅔ oz (20 g) egg yolks
Generous 2 tablespoons (35 g) aged grappa (Nonino Antica Cuvée)

NOUGAT
2 oz (60 g) fondant
Scant 3 tablespoons (40 g) glucose
2 tablespoons (30 g) ground hazelnuts
Scant 3 tablespoons (40 g) Jivara cocoa

SERVING
Dried fruit
Cantucci cookies
Oranges
Grappa

Method

VOLA VOLA ICE-CREAM
Heat the sugar and 2 cups (500 g) of Vola Vola until the volume has reduced by half. When it has cooled, it should have a honey-like consistency. Heat the milk and cream and slowly whisk the mixture into the egg yolks, which have been mixed beforehand with the syrup and gently heated in a saucepan to 175°F (80°C). Cover and let infuse, refrigerated, overnight.
The next day, add the remaining ¼ cup of Vola Vola and churn in an ice-cream machine according to the manufacturer's instructions.

CHOCOLATE AND NONINO ANTICA CUVÉE CUSTARD
Bring the cream and milk to a simmer and pour over the couverture chocolate. Beat in the egg yolks and finally the grappa.

NOUGAT
Heat the fondant and glucose to 330°F (165°C). Add the ground hazelnuts and Jivara cocoa. Pour the mixture over two sheets of parchment paper to form a thin, even layer. Bake at 250°F (120°C) for 3 minutes. Shape into a low ring.
Marinate the dried fruit in the Vola Vola and the segments of orange, peeled, in the grappa.

Serving

Arrange a tablespoon of crumbled cantucci cookies and dried fruit marinated in Vola Vola on one side and the orange in grappa on the other side. Place the nougat ring on top of the oranges and a top with a spoonful of the Nonino custard. Place a scoop of Vola Vola ice cream on top of the cantucci cookies and the dried fruit marinade. Serve.

Wine pairing

Vola Vola IGT – Dessert wine
Winery: Le Vigne di Zamò, Località Rosazzo – Manzano (UD)

THE CUISINE OF EMILIA-ROMAGNA

Via Aemilia crosses Emilia-Romagna from one end to the other. The Po, the Adriatic Sea, and the Apennine ridges mark the region's boundaries. The ancient artery was created between BC 191 and 187, perhaps based on previous routes, by the consul Emilio Lepido, from whom it takes its name, unites Piacenza with the sea.

However, this large, fertile region, one of the richest areas in terms of Italian food and wine, is actually divided by an invisible border traced by history. In Emilia there were the Longobards, with their specialties cooked in a cast-iron pan, as well as charcuterie, cheese, and fried pastry (*gnocco*). In Romagna, there were the Byzantines, with dishes made on a terracotta plate, *castrato* (castrated sheep) and *piadina* (flatbread). All of this was colored by the long reign of Rome (hence Romagna) that lasted until halfway through the ninth century.

A magical land, Emilia-Romagna, which stretches out from the wide and winding curve of the great river, the Po, to the immense delta where its waters merge with the Adriatic, offering an ideal refuge to a variety of fish which is luxuriant and still untouched nature, and to the wooded mountain range.

All this is scattered with cities which are rich in art and history.

Ravenna, the former capital of the Holy Roman Empire, glimmering with mosaics and memories of the Byzantine era, is renowned for its *vino di bosco* (forest wine), produced in the vineyards which extend alongside the coastal pine forests. It's red and particularly good served with eel. Indeed Ravenna is also well-known for the fish and eel of the marshes of Comacchio.

Bologna, the ancient Etruscan center of *Felsina*, followed by the Roman *Bononia*, home to the oldest university in the world, is the region's capital with a beautiful historic center rich in architectural gems, containing glimpses of the medieval, Renaissance elegance, and Baroque monuments: the two towers, the complex of Santo Stefano, the old university buildings, and arcades. In the background there are the hills with their walled villages, the endless arcade of San Luca, and the surrounding plain. It is also the capital of Mortadella (see box) and tortellini, made by the skilled hands of the *sfogline* (pasta-making women).

The cuisine of this region is delicious, rich, yet simple at the same time, based on a few genuine ingredients rather than complicated recipes. The fruits of this generous land are important features in the recipes. In Romagna there are vast orchards, extensive breeding of cows for their meat, of which the Romagnola breed is one of the best-liked, as well as pigs. Turkey and capon are also commonplace, reared with selected feed, and young cockerels. Huge varieties of fish and shellfish arrive on the table from the sea, including lobster, red snapper, sole, mullet, turbot, and the tasty eel from the marshes of Comacchio.

An upbeat and generous people, the Romagnols love to linger at the table, which sees homemade tagliatelle, cappelletti (whose filling contains purely capon in Romagna unlike in Bologna), tortelloni filled with meat and herbs, the "passatini" of breadcrumbs and Parmesan cheese cooked in stock, green lasagne served with mushrooms, grilled castrated sheep chops, roasted suckling pig, originally from this land but adopted by the food of Rome and Lazio, spit-roasted game, and other delicacies, traditionally served with *piada sfogliata* or *piadina*, the typical thin, round unleavened bread, cooked on a terracotta *testo* over the lively flames of a wooden fire. The wines – mainly Sangiovese and Albana – are of a good quality, robust and sparkling, with aromas that marry happily with the regional dishes. The Sangiovese – produced in forty-six Italian provinces – comes from Predappio and is an excellent wine to accompany the entire meal, with a ruby color and a robust flavor, which withstands long ageing periods and improves over the years. Albana is one of the few wines in the world containing sugars which do not ferment, so that it preserves a certain mellowness, even in the drier types. It has a clear golden color, a high alcohol content, and an aroma that recalls the perfume of lilies. It is also one of a few white wines recommended for serving with roasted meats, yet still pairs happily with a piadina flatbread.

The region pushes on to the west, coming across new towns and new flavors.

Ferrara, capital of the House of Este, elegant and refined, illuminated by the metallic flashes of the paintings of Cosimo Tura and his school, is home to *Salama da Sugo*, the incomparable cooking salami of Renaissance cooking (see box) and *Coppia Ferrarese*, the aromatic and unmistakable bread that has earned the Protected Origin Denomination. Here there are dishes that let you relive the feasts of court and the specialties of Jewish cuisine.

Modena is the hometown of Enzo Ferrari and Luciano Pavarotti, the incarnation of Italian *bel canto*, and is also home to the military academy, which has been located in the seventeenth-century *Palazzo Ducale* of the House of Este since 1862, which governed the city until the mid-nineteenth century. The cathedral with its sculptures by Wiligelmus, a superb example of Romanesque architecture and a UNESCO world heritage site, is dominated by the 86-meter-high Ghirlandina, the bell tower on the city's urban horizon. Modena's food scene is rich and is rightly famous for *Zampone* (see box), *Cotechino*, and salami in general, the traditional balsamic vinegar (see box), the true gastronomic jewel whose origins are deep-seated in history, and tortellini, which tradition has them cooked in capon stock. Modena-style lasagne are green, with the addition of spinach, and served with Béchamel sauce and meat ragù. Tagliatelle with ragù and Ricotta-filled tortelli are also widespread in the nearby provinces of Bologna and Reggio Emilia. Among the typical desserts, Amaretti cookies and Bensone cake should be mentioned, as well as the dessert liqueurs Nocino and Sassolino. Wine production is significant in the area, especially the Lambrusco di Sorbara, Lambrusco Salamino, and Lambrusco Graspa Rossa.

Then there's Reggio Emilia, a city with Roman origins, a free commune in the Medieval era, with Modena it was part of the Duchy of the Este until the unification of Italy. The *Sala del Tricolore* (Room of Three Colors) is situated here in the eighteenth-century town hall with its arcades, where the congress of the cities of Emilia chose the green, white, and red as the standard on January 7, 1797, proclaiming the Cispadane Republic. This banner later became the Italian national flag. The cuisine of Reggio Emilia cannot disregard the production of food linked to the Emilian territory: Parmigiano Reggiano, charcuterie, and sausages.

Typical specialties of Reggio are cappelletti, herb-filled tortelli, *chizza* (pastry flavored with lard and Parmesan cheese), *erbazzone* (savory pie with chard), *gnocco fritto* (fried dough), and mountain Pecorino cheese. In terms of the charcuterie, there's *Salame di Canossa, Pancetta Canusina*, and *Zuccotto di Bismantova*. We should also mention the traditional balsamic vinegar. Among the various desserts, there's *Spongata di Brescello*, which is perhaps Roman in origin with hints of Jewish culinary influence, and Biscione, an almond-based dessert, which is served at Christmas time, and rice cake. These dishes are served with the area's most typical wine, Lambrusco, made from a grape, which was once called *la brusca* due to its sharp flavor, as well as other white wines from San Ruffino and Scandiano.

Parma is a medieval splendor. It showcases an admirable square where the Romanesque cathedral and the baptistry by Antelami stand, known as a cradle of the Renaissance, with the Correggio domes and *Teatro Farnese*, the small capital of the duchy with its neoclassical style. It boasts an independent gastronomy, which has matured over the centuries around the ducal court in comparison with other European countries, with its local ingredients par excellence which are known all over the world. It is now deservedly known as the "Food Valley" of Italy. We have dedicated a separate chapter solely to Parma and its territory especially for its characteristics.

For those coming from the north, Piacenza is the first ambassador you come across of the Emilian food scene, yet it's rich in interesting influences and Lombard, Piedmontese, and Ligurian fusions, which make its cuisine more delicate and less heavy. The typical dishes are *pisarei*, gnocchetti with a bean sauce, *bomba di riso* (rice timbale), *tortelli con la coda* (herb-filled tortelli), and a variety of *anolini* which are particularly rich in cheeses. The typical charcuterie is also worthy of a mention: coppa, pancetta, and salamis. There are also a range of cheeses, including Provolone Val Padana PDO, Robiola, and Grana Padano PDO. In the River Po, small fishes called *stricc* are caught, as well as eels, which play an important role in the food of the riviera. The wines produced in the hills of Piacenza (Gutturnio, Bonarda, Trebbiano, Malvasia, etc.) deservingly accompany the area's dishes.

Emilia-Romagna is the land of fresh filled pasta. Some of the most famous and renowned Italian pasta dishes were created here, including tortellini, anolini, cappelletti, the historic Bologna-style lasagna, fettuccine with ragù, and herb-filled tortelli. The Romagnol and Emilian pasta dishes (the homemade sheets of pasta rolled out by hand) are closely attached to family tradition and are still made according to the old recipes, which are jealously guarded and handed down from one generation to another. Every province has its own special interpretation in terms of the filling.

Emilia-Romagna should however also be remembered for its typical products, known and enjoyed all over the world: the extraordinary Parmigiano Reggiano cheese, the succulent Prosciutto di Parma, and a whole range of excellent cured meats.

ACETO BALSAMICO TRADIZIONALE DI MODENA PDO

The must, obtained from Lambrusco and Trebbiano vines and other grapes grown in the province of Modena, is cooked over low heat until it is highly concentrated and dark brown in color and is then left to rest to start the natural fermentation process. With the peculiar pouring technique, implemented in special and characteristic ageing environments called *acetaie*, created in the attics of houses, where the temperature drops close to zero during the winter months or becomes torrid in the summer and the humidity penetrates it all where there's rain or fog, the cooked must reduces in volume, matures, ages, and refines. 100 liters of must are needed to make a couple of liters of traditional balsamic vinegar. A good balsamic vinegar requires at least 12 years before being ready for consumption and becomes sublime after 30 or 50 years. The process takes years and needs constant application and attention, which justifies the expensive price tag.

MORTADELLA DI BOLOGNA IGP

Mortadella is a cooked salami with a striking pink color and an exquisite aroma. It is a smooth mixture made from second-class pork with diced gullet fat and herbs. It is also made in colossal sizes, which help the tastiness of the mixture.

SALAMA DA SUGO FERRARESE IGP

Queen of the Ferrara food scene for over five centuries, Salama da Sugo, with its mature flavor that is stronger and, at the same time, more elegant and persuasive, than the rest of Italian charcuterie. *Coppa di collo*, pancetta, liver, tongue, wine, and lard all feature in its mixture.

ZAMPONE DI MODENA IGP

The Zampone di Modena PDO, made from lean meat, belly and shoulder rind, and gullet fat, is traditionally packed into a pig's trotter, which has been thoroughly cleaned and emptied. It is eaten after being cooked for a long time in water with its rind, served with spinach and zabaglione.

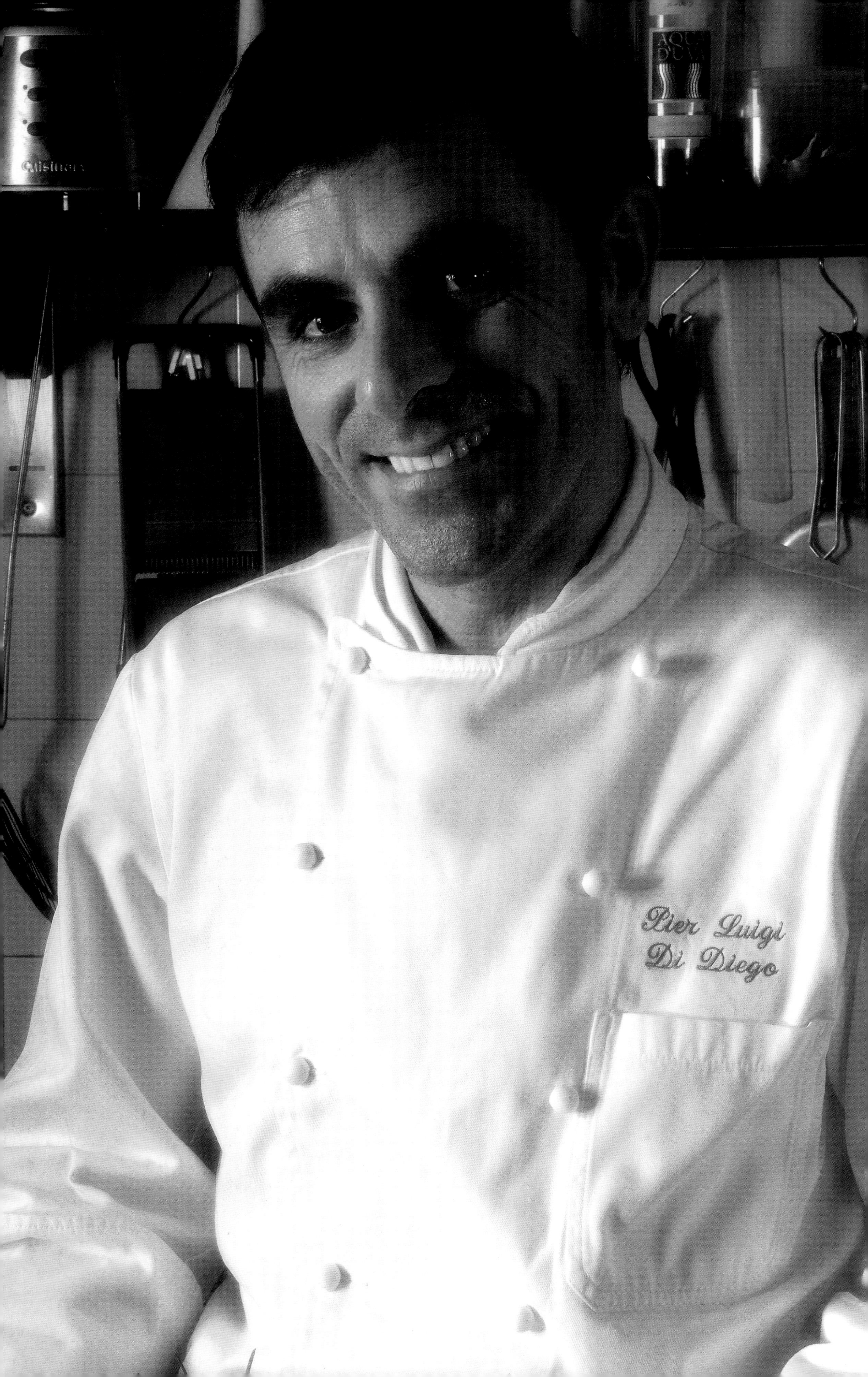
Cuisinart
Pier Luigi
Di Diego

PIER LUIGI DI DIEGO

RESTAURANT IL DON GIOVANNI - FERRARA

Forget about clay, Pier Luigi Di Diego, chef and co-owner with Marco Merighi of the restaurant *Il Don Giovanni* in Ferrara, sculpted fresh pastry when he was a child. On tiptoe, he stretched out his little hand on the work surface where his mother Carmela was working and took a small piece of dough to make lots of little *piadine*. It's no coincidence that he now focuses on pasta dishes and that he rolls out pastry every day in his restaurant.

The restaurant, situated in the eighteenth-century *Palazzo dell'ex Borsa di Commercio*, is right in the center of Ferrara. The eatery is opposite the fourteenth-century *Castello Estense*, with its four defensive turreted towers and surrounded by a moat, It is the hub of the historic center, with its network of medieval streets, and the Renaissance area, with its valuable homes, like the famous *Palazzo dei Diamanti*, designed by the architect Biagio Rossetti and named in honor of the diamond-cut stone walls.

"*The restaurant·has an informal atmosphere, but with an awareness of what's going on,*" Marco, the maître d'hôtel, observes. "*The space is undoubtedly elegant and may perhaps inspire awe at first. It has all the qualities needed to be an international environment. However, it has a dynamic air. Refined bodywork, but with a free-range engine.*" The masters of the house behave in a warm and welcoming manner, with a sense of genuine familiarity. "*We do our best for our guests.*" The environment is fairly modern, without being hi-tech, preserving more than just a friendly feel, especially with the use flowers. Marco arranges the blooms in the dining room and Pier Luigi keeps his eye on them from the kitchen. "*What we're trying to communicate is the meeting of the rational aspect with the emotional element. It's deliberate then that there's a Chiavari red wall, while the others are cream in color.*"

The restaurant opened in November 1998, in Marrara, the last part of the borough of Ferrara headed towards Ravenna. Just four months prior to opening, Pier Luigi and Marco had decided to make the entrepreneurial leap and they renovated an old country house within a month, bestowing it with more than just one shade of color. They did it all by themselves, working like madmen, even at night. They didn't have a cent at the beginning, just vast amounts of professional experience. When they had to think up a name, they asked themselves, "What do we like about life?" The answer was beautiful women and music, good food and wine, and what better than the name of Don Giovanni, the character who embodies all these pleasures? *"We added the definite article "Il" because we thought it seemed too pretentious to call it after Mozart's great work."* The restaurant got straight into gear. Although it's located in an off-the-beaten-track locality in the countryside of Ferrara, it was featured in the leading food guides right from the start. Within less four years, it had earned a Michelin star, the first in the history of the municipality of Ferrara.

In 2003, also in November – *"the restaurant was born as a concept in the fall, perhaps because it's the season when the products of our land are their most numerous"* – Il Don Giovanni moved into town. Here the two owners designed the environment, styling it to suit their personalities and halving it into a small restaurant with 20 covers, only open in the evening. Patrons are seated in a lounge that looks into the kitchen and with direct access into the cellars, and in a wine bar with 35 covers and 55 covers in the covered courtyard (spaces which become 350 when gala dinners are organized). It is just the right size to offer haute cuisine with a more accessible price-quality ratio.

In the restaurant there are historic dishes which are constantly on offer. There's one dish in particular that is the pride and joy of Italian cooking, although a twist of the Po Valley has been added: spaghetti *alla chitarra* with garlic, oil, and chile pepper on a Parmigiano Reggiano fondue. A simple dish, but one where it's important that you're able to manage the temperatures to sublimate the ingredients, making them truly appetizing and digestible. Inevitably, there are also some successful dishes which have taken their cue from the Ferrarese tradition. For example, another of the restau-

rant's classics, made from the pumpkins grown in the garden that Marco and Pier Luigi have kept in Marrara: pumpkin pudding with pumpkin crisps and a *Saba di Fortana* reduction. The soft consistency and the sweet flavor of the pudding contrast with the slightly bitter, crunchy slices of fried pumpkin. The *saba*, or cooked wine, obtained from a variety of Ferrarese DOC grape, ripened on the sandy soils of the initial Adriatic hinterland, with its sweet-sour flavor, not only cleans the palate of any fatty notes of the pudding and crisps, but balances both flavors.

However, the cuisine of Ferrara and therefore the food at *Il Don Giovanni* isn't based on pumpkin alone. *"I use many local products in my kitchen, even though my cuisine is traditional, but not strictly territorial. I don't shut myself within the city walls of Ferrara,"* chef Pier Luigi asserts. *"I always try to understand the ingredients that I have available and not to distort them. If that's ever the case, I prepare the ingredients with my up-to-date knowledge of processes and cooking methods."* He only ever offers *Salama da Sugo* in the winter and obviously only if he finds it produced homemade and of high quality. Then there's eel from the marshes of Comacchio, the striking heart of the Po Delta and one of the most important lagoon complexes in Italy and Europe, as well as Goro clams, the picturesque village of fishermen in the deltaic area, with the brightly colored houses that stand out brilliantly amid the fog and water vapors, and all the fish that comes from Porto Garibaldi, a locality in the Ferrarese lidos known for the disembarkation of the national hero Giuseppe Garibaldi in the area in 1849: mantis shrimp, large shrimp, baby squid, and so on. When it's in season, he also uses game: duck, teal, partridges, woodcock, etc. In terms of fruit, he uses melon and local strawberries of the Rossana variety. *"I tend to cook what I'd like to eat. Herein lies the secret: being generous and honest. I don't want to amaze people. There are other chefs who do just that. I want to excite people. There are no special effects, just the content. I think that people trust you if you give them transparency, simplicity, and linearity."* After all, he thinks along the lines of Duke Ercole I d'Este, who expanded Ferrara with a system of straight streets in the second half of the fifteenth century.

He would never give up the typical dishes of the Emilian city, where the food traditions are so deep-seated: pumpkin cappellacci, *salama da sugo* with mashed potato, macaroni pie, *tagliolina* pie with almonds, and *tenerina* chocolate cake; Pier Luigi only offers them when he has the right ingredients. *"But without revising them; on the contrary, trying to get their genuine flavor across. For us tradition means experimentation that is consolidated over time."* For example, he serves pumpkin cappellacci simply with butter and sage, and not with a walnut or almond sauce or ragù, as is the custom in Ferrara. *"I want to be able to taste the pumpkin. If it's good, it doesn't need anything else."* "Healthy and delicious" is his way of interpreting cuisine. *"Every dish is like a film. It must have a leading star and very few bit parts."* When he was young he also liked the idea of becoming a journalist, although the kitchen won in the end, *"as for me it's like riding a half line. You know when and how to start, but you don't know how and when you'll finish."* So if journalism had won, Pier Luigi would have been one of those reporters of the English speaking world who write clear and simple articles; only a few concepts that are expressed well.

"When I have a product – I never buy ingredients that aren't in season, so it's often the case that the menu is drawn up on a weekly basis with daily variations based on the availability of the products *– I start to think about how I'd like to eat it and try to cook it for myself. It's not like I sit at a desk with a pen and paper to create a new dish. I need to look at what nature's offering me with its aromas and colors, and then trust my senses and experience."* In short, he has to do the shopping and then listen to himself, looking at what's in the bags. *"I usually get someone I trust to fetch me the fruit and vegetables from the market in Bologna. As regards the fish, I go and get it myself on Tuesdays and Fridays. I head towards Porto Garibaldi at around 2:30 pm, about 55 kilometers from our restaurant, where our supplier arrives who has the role of bringing me the fish that the Adriatic Sea has to offer from the market. On the other hand, other ingredients, always of the highest quality, are delivered to me from outside of the province, such as prosciutto from the province of Parma."*

Born in 1967 to parents originally from Abruzzo, Pier Luigi lived in the Milanese hinterland for about 20 years. After attending the hotel institute of Milan, he started to work during the summer and winter seasons in the various tourist resorts at the age of 15. When he was 20 he went to work on cruise ships, then he came back on land and started to gain experience in hotels. *"I wanted to see and experiment with various ways of being in the kitchen to find out what suited me the most."* Finally, in 1991, he arrived in Argenta, in the hive of talent of *Il Trigabolo*, where he stayed until the restaurant closed. This was the turning point of his experience for the future. Here he met Marco and they started to plan the idea of opening a restaurant together. This is where he began to get attached to the Ferrara area and to create the place where he wanted to live and cook. He likes the city very much. *"Ferrara is fascinating. The fact that the Ferrarese people are traditionalists and conservatives has been a great asset to the city, which is still well-preserved today. I find it seductive, not only in terms of its architecture, but also due to its well-appointed size. The quality of life is high. I have a great life here. I don't think I'd be able to live in Milan again."*

The dishes chosen for this book pay thanks to the land of Ferrara. The starter is a mantis shrimp terrine in crudités with tomato confit with three pestos (basil, Taggiasca olive, sun-dried tomato). *"One of restaurant's classics, but also a regional dish as we're able to get mantis shrimp from Porto Garibaldi all year round, apart from in July and August."* For the pasta course, there's slightly spicy spaghetti *alla chitarra* with Goro clams and stewed greens. This type of pasta comes from his roots in Abruzzo, the greens from his memories of Milan, but there's also the candid flavor of the Adriatic. For the main course, we've got a fricassée of Comacchio eel and chanterelle mushrooms with bay, pecorino, and anchovy emulsion, where the main fish from the delta dominates. For dessert, there's a Ferrarese Violina pumpkin and fresh Ricotta di Bufala frangipane. A crystal-clear menu aimed at emphasizing the in-house rule that pushes ingredients towards turning into complete perfection. Cosimo Tura would like it, the most alchemic of fifteenth-century painters from the Ferrara area, who freed himself from material inertia in great magical works like the organ shutters in Ferrara cathedral.

MANTIS SHRIMP TERRINE WITH TOMATO CONFIT AND THREE PESTOS

Ingredients for 4 people
Preparation time: 20' – Tomato confit: 2h 20'

16 large mantis shrimp, or other shrimp
Drizzle of extra-virgin olive oil
Freshly ground salt, to taste
Freshly ground pepper, to taste
Several drops of red wine vinegar
Mixed fresh herbs
Basil leaves, as needed

TOMATO CONFIT
4 ripe tomatoes
Generous ¾ cup (200 ml) extra-virgin olive oil
10 g fresh thyme

2 cloves garlic, thinly sliced
Splash of red wine vinegar
Salt, to taste
Freshly ground black pepper, to taste
1 teaspoon (5 g) sugar

SERVING
Taggiasca olive pesto, as needed
Basil pesto, as needed
Sun-dried tomato pesto, as needed
Basil leaves, for garnish

Method

Shell the raw mantis shrimp; use scissors to butterfly them, cutting them halfway open along the length of the back Arrange them on a stone plate at 95°F (35°C). Drizzle with oil and season with salt and pepper. Add a few drops of vinegar and fresh herbs. Let marinate for 3 minutes.

TOMATO CONFIT
Cut a cross in the bottom of each tomatoes; blanch the tomatoes for a few seconds in boiling water and peel them. Cut into quarters and remove the seeds. Arrange the peeled tomatoes on a baking sheet; toss with oil and thyme, placing a slice of garlic on top of each. Add the salt, pepper, and sugar. Let soften in the oven at 200°F (90°C) for 2 hours and 20 minutes.

Fill the molds in the following order: tomatoes, mantis shrimp, basil, tomatoes, basil, mantis shrimp, and basil again to finish.

Serving

Turn out a mold in the center of each plate, drizzling with the three types of pestos and the cooking juices of the mantis shrimp. Garnish with fresh basil on top and the heads of the mantis shrimp.

Wine pairing

Trebbiano d'Abruzzo, 2005 – White
Winery: Azienda Agricola Emidio Pepe – Torano Nuovo (TE)

SLIGHTLY SPICY SPAGHETTI ALLA CHITARRA WITH GORO CLAMS AND STEWED GREENS

Ingredients for 4 people
Preparation time: 20'

1⅓ lb (600 g) Goro clams, or other good-quality clams
Coarse salt, as needed
Extra-virgin olive oil
1 clove of Voghiera garlic or other garlic, crushed
7 oz (200 g) greens, cut into short lengths
Fresh green chile pepper, sliced, to taste
11 oz (320 g) spaghetti alla chitarra
Chopped parsley, for garnish

Method

Purge the clams under cold running water with a handful of coarse salt for at least 30 minutes in the dark and covered. Choose them, letting them fall one by one into an empty container.
You can tell if the clams are empty or not by the noise they make as they fall.
Discard those leaking sand. Cook the clams, covered, in a frying pan with the oil, garlic, and a splash of water until they open (discard those that don't open). Shell the clams immediately and set clam meat aside. Strain and reserve the cooking water.
Make the sauce: In a large frying pan, sauté the clams with the oil, greens, and garlic over medium heat. Add the strained clam water and the clams. Simmer for 5 minutes. Add a few slices of fresh green chile pepper (cut using scissors so that the juices are not lost).
Cook the spaghetti in plenty of salted water until al dente. Drain and finish cooking in the pan with the sauce. Drizzle with a little oil and garnish with the chopped parsley.

Wine pairing

"Il Templare" 2001 – White
Winery: Montenidoli – San Gimignano (SI)

FRICASSÉE OF EEL AND CHANTERELLE MUSHROOMS WITH BAY, PECORINO, AND ANCHOVY EMULSION

Ingredients for 4 people
Preparation time: 40'

EMULSION
1 oz (30 g) aged pecorino
6 bay leaves
1 anchovy fillet in oil
Generous ¾ cup (200 ml) extra-virgin olive oil
Salt and pepper to taste

MUSHROOMS AND EEL
7 oz (300 g) fresh chanterelle mushrooms
Salt , to taste
1 eel, weighing about 1½–1¾ lb (700/800 g)

Method

EMULSION
Chop all ingredients and place them in a blender. Blend for only a few seconds to avoid overheating the mixture.

MUSHROOMS
Clean and chop the mushrooms. Sauté them in a little oil in a frying pan for a few minutes with salt and some bay leaves. Keep warm.

EEL
Clean the eel and open it up (ask your fishmonger to do this for you). Cut into 4 pieces lengthwise. Roast in the oven at 400°F (210°C) for about 15 minutes.
Fillet it, keeping the skin to be used as a garnish. Cut into small morsels.

Serving

Mix the mushrooms, which have been cooked with the eel, in a steel terrine.
Place a medium-sized cookie cutter in the center of the plate and fill with the eel and mushrooms, pressing down lightly with your fingertips.
Drizzle with a little sauce and garnish with the bay leaves and roasted eel skin.

Wine pairing

Vernaccia di San Gimignano "Fiore" 1995 – White
Winery: Montenidoli – San Gimignano (SI)

PUMPKIN AND RICOTTA FRANGIPANE

Ingredients for 4 people
Preparation time: 1 h 20' – Resting time: 1 night

8 oz (250 g) Ferrarese Violina pumpkin, uncooked
¾ cup (180 g) fresh Ricotta di Bufala

FRANGIPANE
Scant ¼ cup (50 g) cold hazelnut butter
2 whole eggs
¾ cup (150 g) superfine sugar
⅓ cup (50 g) ground almonds
2 tablespoons (30 g) milk
2 tablespoons (30 g) fresh cream

SHORTCRUST PASTRY
3⅓ cups (500 g) flour
2 egg yolks
1 whole egg
Generous ¾ cup (170 g) superfine sugar
1¼ cups (300 g) butter, at room temperature
¼ teaspoon (2 g) yeast
Pinch of salt

Butter, for pan
Superfine sugar, for pan

Method

Clean and peel the pumpkin. Cut into small to medium-sized cubes.
Melt a pat of butter in a large pot over low heat. Sprinkle the sugar into the bottom of the pot and gradually add the pumpkin, turning up the heat and brown for a few minutes. Set aside in a container.

FRANGIPANE
Melt the hazelnut butter in a saucepan until it starts to color. Let cool slightly (but do not let it solidify). Beat the eggs and sugar in a steel bowl until frothy. Add the almonds and the remaining ingredients, followed by the melted butter. Cover and let rest in the refrigerator overnight.

SHORTCRUST PASTRY
Sift the flour and make a hollow in the center.
Add all the ingredients to the hollow. Knead the mixture as quickly as possible (using a pastry cutter so that the mixture isn't overheated by your hands) to make a smooth pastry. Chill dough in the refrigerator for 3 hours before use.

Serving

Butter a cake pan and sprinkle with superfine sugar, making sure that you tap the sides lightly to remove any excess sugar. Roll out the pastry to ⅛-inch (3-mm) thick and transfer to the prepared pan. Top with the pumpkin. Mix the frangipane with the Ricotta in a bowl until smooth. Pour the mixture into the cake pan. Bake at 350°F (180°C/gas mark 4) for about 15 minutes. The cake is done when a toothpick inserted in the center comes out clean. Let cool for a few minutes before turning cake out of the pan. Serve at room temperature or slightly warm.

Wine pairing

Moscato passito 2001 – Dessert wine
Winery: Cascina degli ulivi – Novi Ligure (AL)

FEDERICO TONETTI

OSTERIA LE MASCHERE - SARSINA (FORLÌ-CESENA)

At Osteria Le Maschere in Sarsina, a bewitching town founded by the Romans on the high hills of Cesana, which now boasts archaeological relics and a beautiful Romanesque cathedral, good food and wine are a form of classical theater. The great Latin poet and playwright Titus Maccius Plautus would have happily eaten here. Not only because the restaurant is situated in his hometown, but also because Federico Tonetti, the chef and co-owner with Giordana Cattani, maître d'hôtel, shares his shrewdness and vivacity. A genuine, passionate, and free spirit, he crafts culture everyday with his dishes. They are culinary representations whereby the history, art, creativity, and fresh air in this area of the Romagnol Apennines merge in a vast and precious work of civilization, which is both 1000 years old and contemporary.

"Le Maschere, as much as it is prestigious, isn't just a restaurant, but rather an establishment that chose not to be purely a commercial business in order to set out along the inaccessible path of feelings and sentiments where cuisine and tables laden with food mix in a unique ambience of human hospitality. Individual personal differences merge here in those fascinating moments of divine inspiration which only friendship and natural ingredients can turn into flavors and the panacea of life," Federico affirms. The idea is to offer a place that relates to the soul, perhaps even with time for a dinner. Here, as in the plays of Plautus, "every rite of human existence is a lovely mixed salad, meat that bleeds, throbs, and desires, fish that talk and wine that purifies," as you can read on the restaurant's website. And catharsis is possible: "Each ingredient is an actor with a personal, uninhabited role, and there's the joy of being in a place where you can consume a moment of normal daily life with an extraordinary potential quality, uniqueness, and pleasure." Even professional actors come and eat in his restaurant, important names on the Italian theater scene. "They act like ordinary people and, on the contrary, ordinary people stage and convert their daily efforts."

The osteria, called *Le Maschere* in honor of Plautus. – *"We liked this character so debunking and a desacralizer of power and all the conventions whose actuality lies in the fact that the human condition hasn't changed, although centuries have passed by,"* – is located in a narrow street that leads into the town, which is very lovely and closed to traffic, where there's the possibility of arranging tables under the porticos in the summer. It stays open until late all year and until the dead of night when there's a summertime theater festival. Opened in 1990, Federico's unusual personality immediately made it into *"a reference point for free thought where we always put ourselves to the test."* However you can also breathe in the peace of true intelligence. Despite his strong and bearded resemblance to a fire-eater, the host – he doesn't feel like the term chef suits him – releases the same sweet serenity as the medieval artist who sculpted the marble slab depicting Christ on the throne in between the archangels Gabriel and Michael, which embellishes the altar of Sarsina cathedral, erected 900 years ago.

"Towards the beginning, we gave the restaurant a theme by hanging some masks on the walls, which we got in a Venetian handicraft workshop where they make masks for Commedia dell'Arte. Then some of the customers and the boys started to bring me masks from all over the world. Now we have an impressive collection, even though we physically don't have the space to display them all." In fact, the restaurant is tiny: 20 to 25 covers and small, bistro-style tables like along the River Seine in France. The kitchen is on show and overall the space is in proportion to good taste and comfort at the table, without excessively showy decorations, in terms of the ambience and service.

"Over the years, the walls with the masks have also become a testimony to the many plays of Plautus which have been staged here in Sarsina. As we welcome theatrical companies, we give them the chance to pen some words or a drawing on the wall."

It is an informal establishment that's full of warmth, where research and experimentation in the kitchen do not border on the obsessive. Siphons and foams haven't reached here yet and who knows if they ever will; what matters is the enhancement of the precious local ingredients and the chance to eat at a reasonable price. Federico offers, *"What is called a simple cuisine, which is linked to what the land has to offer, transforming dignified poverty into unpretentious gastronomic fantasy that is healthy and intelligent. A cuisine that doesn't cry out, but is personalized, typical of authentic and guaranteed flavors, able to mix the art of living well liturgically."* His land offers a variety of truly remarkable products, which he gathers together and uses liberally. Like one day, while the bishop Vicinio, the patron saint of Sarsina, went into the silence of the mountains to pray, a devout and reverent oak tree bent its branches down to the earth, bowing down to his holiness, the land of Sarsina winks at Federico whenever he cooks.

This inspired host of the Apennine people of the Val di Savio loves the wild herbs that coat the rocky slopes, the rustic field bulbs, the freshwater river crayfish, all the products of the kindly undergrowth, mushrooms, truffles, fruits of the forest and forgotten fruit, such as the local *pera cocomerina* (watermelon pear) with its pink pulp, which is used to make delicious preserves to be served with cheeses or with meat. Indeed *"there are no words to describe the meat of the robust beef of the Bianca Romagnola breed, our geese, the pigs of the Mora Romagnola breed, and the lambs from the park with the spectacular Rupe della Moia, close to the beech forests of Monte Fumaiolo, hung with wild hops, which are still hand-picked."* There are many typical cheeses, from the soft ones, such as Raviggiolo, Casatella, and Squaquerone, to the aged cheeses like Pecorino and Formaggio di Fossa, whose ripening caves are located just 20 kilometers from the restaurant at Sogliano al Rubicone. For example, Federico uses Raviggiolo to fill the classic *polifemi*, a type of pasta created halfway between Sarsina and Mercato Saraceno by an innkeeper who wanted to make one large cappelletto to free women from the slavery of making many small ones. He called them this on account of the single eye of the giant who Ulysses came across in *The Odyssey*. He serves Formaggio di Fossa, *"the most intriguing of them all,"* in many ways. For Easter, he serves it with the traditional Easter *pagnotta* and caramelized figs. *"It is a sweet bread made with sultanas from the middle Sarsina valleys, which was once taken by people when they went on their first springtime trips to the countryside, eating it with a bit of cheese, charcuterie, and fava beans."*

Born here – *"I am a man in the flesh and blood whose innate compulsions of social justice and peaceful cohabitation come to fruition among the clods and copses of this piece of Apennine land, the hard-earned paternal property, the Mandriole, situated a few hundred meters from the Plautin arena of Sarsina"* – ever since he was a boy he always loved being in the kitchen trying things. *"It's not like I decided to be a chef. I did it because I feel at home in the kitchen. I don't find it tiring and it comes naturally to me."* After having graduated from the hotel institute of Marebello, he started to travel around Europe, in France, Germany, England, and Spain, always taking part in the life of the place like any other citizen. Meanwhile, he worked for a few seasons in some Italian tourist resorts, from Sestrière to the Costa Smeralda. After the professional experience he gained abroad, *"I surrendered myself to the urges and appeals of my homeland. I went home to the haystack of familiar memories and feelings that I find essential to give meaning to a life that deserves to be lived."* Herein lies his intuition of taking back the area's products – *"cuisine is the land that blossoms and regenerates in a person's life"* – always matched with great or simple, yet fundamental, wines (he has a superb cellar), with an awareness that *"there is a second side to the Made in Italy coin: the small great Italy of the provinces, the Italy of the most populated mountains in Europe, whose feet are bathed in the saltiness of the sea."* When he goes to do the shopping for the restaurant every morning around 7:30 a.m, he first makes a trip into town, to the greengrocer's and butcher's, then he goes down to the sea, to Rimini and Cesenatico, to stock up on fish. Yet again, ingredients rooted in his homeland; in this case, the excellent fish of the Adriatic Riviera.

There are some historic dishes of his osteria to which he's particularly attached. For example, the mixed salad with medicinal herbs *"because it brings back my childhood memories. My grand-mother and aunties went to gather these wild herbs, such as salad burnet, mizuna, chervil, wild arugula, or mountain celery. They brought them home and used them in the kitchen."* Another dish of the past that's on the menu, although not all year round as you can't always find the ingredients, is the tartlet of field herbs, cooked au gratin and refined with white truffle. However, there's also the *polifemo, "only filled with cheeses as is the custom in Alta Romagna, a poor, mining area where the introduction of meat in filled pasta occurred later when economic wellbeing also arrived."* He serves this type of pasta all year round, though he alternates the filling. The basis is always Ricotta, Parmesan, Raviggiolo, or Squacquerone, to which asparagus is added in the spring, walnuts and basil in the summer, potatoes and pumpkin in the autumn, and radicchio in the winter.

The dishes of the menu for this book *"actually mean being in this area to me"*. For the starter, he chose mixed salad with herbs and browned lamb sweetbreads and fried custard. *"When you taste the flavor and smell the aroma of some herbs, it's as if you're walking along a path in our gul-lies."* For the pasta course, Romagna-style cappelletti, only filled with cheeses, candied citron, and nutmeg, served with fois gras and sweet onion from Sant'Arcangelo, a town on the Apennine stretch between Forlì and Rimini, which are stewed in Albana passita, one of the most famous products from the vineyards of Romagna. *"The coming together of these ingredients shows the desire to transmit the idea that, yes, we are attached to the area and we use our own excellent products, but that we also want to aim at other foods par excellence that are available in Europe."* There's pigeon on offer for the meat course, *"a bird that we often cook in our area,"* stuffed with mushrooms and sausage, a pate toast made from the pigeon's liver, poached eggs, and fried sage. For dessert, there's an almond basket with rosolio custard and wedges of sweet flatbread, a little known version of the classic *piadina romagnola*, a wheat flour dough cooked traditionally on a ter-racotta plate called a *teggia*. A canvas of flavors, colors, and aromas are here to supply a full-house culinary demonstration.

MIXED SALAD WITH HERBS AND BROWNED LAMB SWEETBREADS, FRIED CUSTARD AND TRADITIONAL BALSAMIC VINEGAR

Ingredients for 4 people
Preparation time: 1 h 15'

2 cups (500 ml) + 1¼ cups (300 ml) whole milk
1 vanilla pod
Lemon zest
3 egg yolks
Generous ½ cup (125 g) sugar
⅔ cup (100 g) flour + 2 tablespoons
14 oz (400 g) mixed salad (such as lettuce, radicchio, lamb's lettuce, curly endive, gentilina, arugula)
5 oz (150 g) herbs (such as chives, tarragon, lovage, cress, chervil, salad burnet, dill, cilantro, mint)
10 oz (300 g) lamb sweetbreads
1¼ cups (300 ml) milk
2 eggs
2 tablespoons of olive oil
Edible flowers

Method

CUSTARD
Bring the milk to a boil in a small saucepan with the vanilla and lemon zest. Mix the egg yolks with the sugar in a bowl. Add the flour, mixing constantly, making sure that no lumps form. Pour the milk into the prepared egg mixture, whisking constantly. Return mixture to the heat over low, mixing until the custard becomes fairly thick. Pour the custard onto a sheet of parchment paper; spread to a ¾-inch (2-cm) layer and let cool.
Wash and chop the mixed greens with the herbs; dry the mixed salad.
Rinse the sweetbreads under cold running water. Blanch in water and milk for about 5 minutes. Let cool.
Make a batter consisting of 2 tablespoons of flour, 2 tablespoons of olive oil, 1 egg, and a pinch of salt.
Cut the sweetbreads into ⅓-inch (1-cm) thick medallions, dip in the flour, followed by the batter. Fry in plenty of olive oil. Cut the chilled custard into diamonds. Dip in the flour, followed by the beaten egg and breadcrumbs. Fry in plenty of oil.

Serving

Arrange the salad, herbs, and edible flowers on the plate. Place the sweetbreads in the center with a couple of custard diamonds on the side and a few drops of traditional balsamic vinegar.

Wine pairing

Spumante Extra Brut Metodo Tradizionale
Winery: Bruno Giacosa – Neive (CN)

ROMAGNA-STYLE CAPPELLETTI WITH SWEET ONION, FOIE GRAS, AND ALBANA PASSITA

Ingredients for 4 people
Preparation time: 1 h

STOCK
1½ lb (700 g) beef
1 lb (500 g) veal
1 onion
1 carrot
1 stalk celery
Salt
1 bay leaf

PASTA
4 cups (600 g) all-purpose flour
5 whole eggs

FILLING
3½ oz (100 g) Parmesan

1 cup (250 g) Ricotta cheese
⅔ cup (150 g) Raviggiolo cheese
1 egg
Candied citron zest
Nutmeg
Salt and pepper

TO SERVE
Butter
1 sweet onion
1 cup (250 g) foie gras
Scant ½ cup (100 ml) Albana passita
Pistachio nuts
Pepper, to taste
Shaved truffle, optional

Method

STOCK
Put the meat in a large saucepan and cover with cold water. Bring the water to a boil over medium heat, covering it with a lid. When the water comes to a boil, skim the froth, season with salt, and add the whole vegetables, salt, and the bay leaf. Lower the heat, cover again, and simmer for about 2½ hours. Let cool and chill for at least 3 hours. Before using the stock, remove the layer of fat that will have solidified on the surface.

PASTA
Sift the flour onto a wooden surface and shape into a mound. Make a well in the center. Pour the eggs into the hollow and beat them using a fork. Knead until the dough is smooth. Let rest under a cloth for 20 minutes.
Meanwhile, combine the filling ingredients to make a smooth, thick mixture.
Use a long rolling pin to roll out a sheet of pasta until it is fairly thin, almost see-through (or use a pasta machine). Cut into about ¾-inch (2-cm) squares. Place small amounts of the filling in the center and fold in half diagonally to make a triangle. Take the two ends and join them together to make filled, hat-shaped pasta.

Serving

Melt the butter in a frying pan. Add the onion, cut into julienne, and add the Albana passita. Let evaporate and add the foie gras, cut into ⅓-inch (1-cm) cubes and brown slightly. Season with salt. Cook the cappelletti in meat stock; drain and toss in the pan. Spoon the cappelletti into a preheated plate. Garnish with chopped pistachios and pepper. If in season, add shavings of truffle.

Wine pairing

Pignoletto Vendemmia Tardiva Permartina
Winery: Fattoria Vallona, Fraz. Fagnona – Castello di Serravalle (BO)

STUFFED PIGEON, SERVED WITH LIVER PATE TOASTS, POACHED EGGS, AND FRIED SAGE

Ingredients for 4 people
Preparation time: 1 h

4 pigeon eggs
2 pigeons, boned
3 slices of day-old bread
Scant ½ cup (100 ml) brandy
3½ oz (100 g) sausage
3½ oz (100 g) porcini mushrooms
1 egg
1¾ oz (50 g) Parmesan cheese
Livers from the pigeons
Salt, to taste
Pat of butter
1 clove garlic
Rosemary, sage, spinach or wild spinach

Method

POACHED EGGS

Bring plenty of water to a boil with salt and vinegar in a large pot. Lower the heat as much as possible, break one egg at a time in a dish and carefully add to the water. Boil the eggs for about 3 minutes until the whites are firm and completely enclose the yolk. Use a slotted spoon to drain the eggs and arrange them on a dry tea cloth. Remove any foam from the whites using a sharp knife.

PIGEON

Season the pidgeon meat with salt and pepper. Soften a slice of bread in ¼ cup (50 ml) of brandy, then crumble it up and add to the sausage and porcini mushrooms not needed to garnish the dish. Add the egg and Parmesan. Stuff the pigeons with this mixture. Seal them up and arrange on a baking tray with sprigs of rosemary and sage. Bake in the oven at 350°F (180°C/gas mark 4) for 20-25 minutes, basting them occasionally with the white wine and its cooking juices.
Sauté the livers in a frying pan with the onion. Drizzle with ¼ cup (50 ml) of brandy and let it evaporate. Season with salt to taste. Puree in a blender with a pat of butter and spread on toasts (freshly made); top with the poached eggs.
To finish, sauté the porcini mushrooms (*boletus edulis*) with 1 clove of garlic and keep warm. Sauté the spinach and arrange in the center of the plate. For each serving, form a wreath, alternating the porcini mushrooms and fried sage. Cut half a pigeon into small, thin slices and arrange in a fan shape. Drizzle with the cooking juices and serve with the liver pate toast.

Wine pairing

Sangiovese di Romagna riserva ombroso
Winery: Azienda Agricola Giovanna Madonia – Bertinoro (FO)

ALMOND BASKET WITH VANILLA CUSTARD AND SWEET FLATBREAD

Ingredients for 4 people
Preparation time: 1 h 20'

BASKET
1 cup (200 g) superfine sugar
2½ cups (240 g) slivered almonds
Mixed berries, to garnish

CUSTARD
2 cups (500 ml) whole milk
1 vanilla pod
Lemon zest
3 egg yolks
Generous ½ cup (125 g) sugar
2 tablespoons (30 g) flour

Semisweet chocolate shavings
Rosolio

SWEET FLATBREAD
6⅔ cups (1 kg) flour
1½ cups (300 g) sugar
2 tablespoons (30 g) vanilla baking powder
Generous ¾ cup (200 g) lard
3 eggs
Lemon zest
1 cup (250 ml) whole milk

Method

BASKET
Melt the sugar in a small saucepan. Add the slivered almonds and let them caramelize until the mixture turns a cinnamon color. Pour the mixture onto a sheet of parchment paper, creating interwoven and overlapped circles. Let cool to lukewarm and form them into a basket shape (using an upside-down small bowl as a mold).

CUSTARD
Bring the milk to a boil in a small saucepan with the vanilla and lemon zest. Mix the egg yolks with the sugar in a bowl. Add the flour, mixing constantly, making sure that no lumps form. Pour the milk into the prepared mixture, whisking constantly. Return to the heat (low), stirring until the custard becomes fairly thick. Let cool to lukewarm and pour into the basket, which has been drizzled with rosolio.

SWEET FLATBREAD
Sift the flour onto a wooden surface and shape into a mound. Make a well in the center. Add all the remaining ingredients. Knead together and let rest. Shape the mixture intolarge balls the size of a fist. Roll out with a rolling pin, forming rounds that are ⅓-inch (1-cm) thick. Cook on the typical Romagnolo terracotta *testo* (a circular heated plate). Cut the flatbread into 8 wedges and serve 2 of them per basket. Decorate with mixed berries.

Wine pairing

Albana passita "Scacco Matto"
Winery: Fattoria Zerbina – Marzeno di Faena (RA)

THE CUISINE OF PARMA

Nicknamed the Food Valley of Italy, Parma boasts an undisputed supremacy in the world of food, with roots are based in history that actually begins in the pre-Roman era when the region was already well-known for rearing pigs and preserving meat, assisted by local sources of salt water.

The economic boom of the thirteenth century and the vast reclamation efforts of the marshy areas of the plain, begun by the monastic orders, allowed permanent pastures to be extended and set up the requirements for the implementation of manufacturing technologies for Parmesan cheese. The growth of the cheese industry also brought with it in turn the development of the breeding of pigs, which discovered the leftovers from the production of Parmesan to be an excellent raw material with which to feed the animals.

The happy territorial and cultural marriage has permitted the fine-tuning of top-class typical products over the centuries, such as the charcuterie. First and foremost, there's Parma ham (see box), Parmigiano Reggiano cheese (see box), derivatives from the processing of tomatoes, and pasta – Barilla, the world's leading pasta manufacturer is based in Parma – as well as the development of technologies for the processing and preservation of general foodstuffs.

The city has known how to treasure its gastronomic innovations since the sixteenth century, which were achieved due to the presence of a court – initially, the Court of Farnese and then the illuminated Marie Louise of Austria, Napoleon's wife. With foreign diplomatic influence came foreign staff, accompanying its products of quality, taste, and refined elaboration in order to make Parma into a gastronomic region apart, characterized by a luxury and highly French soul, one could even say Parisian, which makes its way in the pleasure-seeking and gourmet tradition of wealthy Emilia. The influence of the transalpine culinary culture has remained until this day and age, bringing special customs to local habits which range from the table service to recipes, their own true food techniques, and the many words associated with French cuisine which have become grafted to and turned into the dialect of Parma.

The history, culture, and long-lasting tradition of top class products is dominated by the presence of his majesty the pig, whose processing was depicted on the doorway of the cathedral back in the eleventh century. The low-lying plain – marked by the rows of poplars, ploughed fields, and large farmyards and skirted by the great Po – is the homeland of Fiocchetto and the prized Culatello di Zibello (see box), enshrouded with winter fog and summer sultriness. Typical of another town in the province of Parma, is San Secondo, or cooked pork shoulder, which was preferred by Giuseppe Verdi. He gave it dutifully to his friends with instructions on how to prepare it: made into a sausage, it is cooked in water and wine. It is excellent served warm with Fortana, a sweet, sparkling wine, and perhaps with slices of aromatic fried cake. Salame di Felino, another sausage, is made in the hilly area, a stone's throw from the superb sixteenth-century *Castello di Torrechiara*. It is sweet and delicate in flavor, refined with careful and loving ageing. Coppa, pancetta, and other tasty salamis also dominate the cuisine of Parma.

Parma has two jewels in terms of pasta dishes: the summer herb-filled tortelli, made with a filling of Ricotta, Parmesan, and mild chard, and the winter anolini, filled with stewed meat sauce and covered with typical fresh egg pasta. Roasted meats, boiled meats, stews, and the popular Parmesan tripe are all traditional too. Exquisite wild produce comes from Parma's mountainous area, the Apennines, which are thick in woods and rich in pastures. The mountains yield delicacies such as Borgotaro porcini mushrooms (noted in the mid-eighteenth century and exported over seas for over 100 years), the only ones sealed by the Protected Geographical Indication, and the black truffles from Fragno (a small fraction of the Val Baganza), which are exceptional stars of the most sumptuous recipes of the Court. Spongata is a Christmas dessert that is ancient in origin, and Parma has significant variations, with its spiced filling covered in sweet pastry. Among the liqueurs, Nocino, an infusion of unripe green walnuts rigorously gathered for June 24th, the festival of Saint John the Baptist, is quite notable. Produced in Noceto, Nocino is excellent as a digestive after the lavish gastronomic explorations that this city, much loved by the French writer Stendhal, allows every palate to make.

PARMIGIANO REGGIANO PDO

ALREADY MENTIONED BY GIOVANNI BOCCACCIO IN THE DECAMERON AND ENJOYED OVER THE CENTURIES BY MANY ILLUSTRIOUS PALATES, IT IS THE UNDOUBTED CHAMPION OF THE ITALIAN CHEESE INDUSTRY. A COMPACT AND FINE-GRAINED CHEESE (HENCE THE TERM GRANA), WITH A DETERMINED, YET NOT SPICY, FLAVOR, IT IS PROCESSED AND AGED (FOR UP TO THREE YEARS) IN THE PROVINCES OF PARMA, REGGIO EMILIA, MODENA, BOLOGNA (ON THE LEFT BANK OF THE RIVER RENO), AND MANTUA (ON THE RIGHT BANK OF THE PO). WITHOUT USING ANY ADDITIVES, IT IS MADE WITH THE MILK FROM TWO MILKINGS, ONE OF WHICH IS SEMI-SKIMMED, FROM CATTLE FED WITH SELECTED FORAGE. AFTER A STRICT CHECK, THE SUITABLE CHEESES ARE BRANDED BY THE PARMIGIANO REGGIANO CONSORTIUM AS A STAMP OF AUTHENTICITY AND QUALITY.

PROSCIUTTO DI PARMA PDO

ONE OF THE MOST FAMOUS CURED MEATS IN THE WORLD, THIS PROSICUTTO HAS A SWEET AND DELICATE FLAVOR AND UNMISTAKABLE AROMA. MADE IN LANGHIRANO AND THE VALLEYS OF PARMA, BAGANZA, AND TARO, IT IS PRODUCED FROM FRESH LEGS OF PORK, WHICH ARE REFINED WITH THE SIMPLE ADDITION OF SALT AND LEFT TO AGE FOR 10-12 MONTHS IN THE TYPICAL PRODUCTION AREA. TO GUARANTEE THAT THE PRODUCTION CONFORMS TO TRADITION, AT THE END ONLY THE HAMS WHICH HAVE PASSED THE CONTROL INSPECTION ARE BRANDED WITH THE TYPICAL DUCAL FIVE-POINTED CROWN OF THE CONSORTIUM.

CULATELLO DI ZIBELLO PDO

THE MOST PRIZED CHARCUTERIE PRODUCED IN EMILIA, ITS PRAISES WERE ONCE SUNG BY GABRIELE D'ANNUNZIO, THE ITALIAN POET AND STATESMAN. **CULATELLO DI ZIBELLO** IS MADE FROM THE BEST CUT OF THE HEALTHIEST LEGS OF PORK: THE *CULATTA*, THE REAR MUSCULAR PART OR RUMP, FROM WHICH THE RIND AND BONE HAVE BEEN REMOVED. IT IS AGED IN A NATURAL PORK BLADDER FOR AT LEAST 12 MONTHS IN THE RIPARIAN AREAS OF THE PO AND BASSA PARMENSE. IT HAS A UNIQUE AROMA, A BRIGHT RUBY COLOR, AND A SOFTNESS THAT LITERALLY MELTS IN THE MOUTH. **FIOCCHETTO** (TYPICAL OF THE PROVINCE OF PIACENZA) IS MADE FROM THE MEAT THAT REMAINS AFTER MAKING THE CULATELLO THROUGH A SERIES OF CAREFUL STAGES. IT IS TIED UP, SALTED, TENDERIZED, WASHED WITH WINE, SPRINKLED WITH SALT AND PEPPER, STUFFED INTO A NATURAL PORK BLADDER, DRIED, AND LEFT TO AGE FOR ABOUT EIGHT MONTHS. IT IS A LEANER PRODUCT THAN CULATELLO, BUT JUST AS EXQUISITE. **STROLGHINO,** A SALAMI WITH A SWEET AND AROMATIC FLAVOR, IS MADE FROM THE TRIMMINGS OF CULATELLO.

MARCO PARIZZI

RESTAURANT PARIZZI (PARMA)

The cuisine of Marco Parizzi, owner and chef of restaurant Parizzi in Parma, has the same spirit as the great medieval sculptor and architect Benedetto Antelami. Just like Antelami embraced the solid Romanesque tradition to rise towards the subtle Gothic suppleness (as he masterfully accomplished a stone's throw away from the restaurant, in the superb baptistery in Piazza Duomo), so too, does Marco keeps his feet welded to the ground to achieve elegance.

Anchored to the local robust flavors, he makes them lighter to bring them up to date. *"As I was born in Parma, I have a fairly strong sense of flavor, like our products,"* he tells us. *"My cuisine is always strong and well-defined, with an extra pinch of salt rather than one less."* Even when he prepares fish, he makes dishes with a vigorous composition, reducing them to the dense heart of the Po plain, with its quiet and opulent landscape of poplars, ploughed fields, and large farmyards. But the dishes remain light, while *"putting the strong flavor sensation forward again with herbs and spices."* However, he's not in favor of replacing one ingredient with another, for example, replacing butter with oil, just because there's a trend of doing it. *"Ingredients should only be substituted if there's a reason for doing it. Herb-filled tortelli with Parmesan need butter."* So the pasta filled with Ricotta and herbs, served with melted butter and Parmesan, are left well alone, which tradition has it are eaten in Parma al fresco on the evening of June 23. It is one of the typical dishes of Parma that restaurant Parizzi always features on the menu. *"In terms of charcuterie, I chose prosciutto and culatello to represent our land, thereby excluding the others, as they are the only ones for which I'm able to find good constant high-quality production. Among the pasta dishes, as well as tortelli, I offer anolini in meat stock all year round. For the meat course, I offer Parmesan beef stew and nut-crusted guinea fowl with potatoes and green onions, which is the Piatto del Buon Ricordo – we became members of the association (the Piatto del Buon Ricordo) in 1990. For dessert, we serve a crème brulée that my mother used to make. It is alternated with vanilla or a special, exquisitely-flavored licorice that is sent to me from Amarelli in Calabria."*

The restaurant is not only located in the historic center along the route of the Via Aemilia, the ancient Roman consular road that crosses the entire region from Piacenza to Rimini, and in a sixteenth-century building, but it also has a long history attached to Parma. Three generations have followed one another: an innkeeper, a restaurateur, a chef: *"It doesn't really matter if we've served you with a ladleful of stock, two slices of shank, or a glass of ginger ale; we put our hearts into our job and we were happy to do so."*

Marco's grandfather, Pietro Parizzi, and his wife Luigina opened an osteria in another part of the city back in 1946, which then moved here to Via Repubblica, 71, in 1956. *"The restaurant was a long corridor, which had formerly been the building's stables. On the street side, there was a delicatessen shop, with a lounge at the back."* A delicatessen with homemade takeaway food andonly a few tables to play cards or to drink a *bianchino* (a shot of white wine). In 1967, Marco's father, Ugo, took over the management of the restaurant, he met Graziella and together they decided to plan what would become restaurant Parizzi. *"They made another room out of the courtyard that was connected to the interior of the building and they gave up the delicatessen to concentrate exclusively on cooking for 120 covers."* It became one of the city's leading restaurants. *"My father organized it in a modern way, employing a staff consisting of chefs and sous chefs, as well as the inevitable* rezdore *(the female cooks who closely guard Parma's culinary secrets). In the dining room, the waiting staff were dressed in jackets and bow ties."* In 1980, on being awarded with a Michelin star, Ugo planned the renovation of the restaurant, which, with fewer tables and a more elegant style, started to appeal to a more elite clientele.

Marco began working in the restaurant when he was a boy. *"When I was only 11 years old, I helped my parents as a waiter when I wasn't at school until I started to work there on a permanent basis at the age of 19."* His training actually began in the kitchen. Fresh from his accountancy studies, the kitchen was a world waiting to be discovered by him. *"After four and a half years working as an apprentice for the chef Gino Giulianotti, I preferred to choose people who could introduce me to a less classical type of cooking. I hired chefs such as Davide Oldani and, especially, my main teacher, Patrik Massera, who worked here for two years, from 1994 to 1996."* Massera was the one who helped him to develop his skills as a chef. At the end of an intense and profitable experience, Marco took up the reins of the kitchen and became a member of the *Jeunes Restaurateurs d'Europe* association.

It was thanks to a food-based television program on a leading Italian TV channel, in which he took part once a week for nine years, that he was able to free himself once and for all from his father's glorious past, establishing his own identity. *"Following in your father's footsteps obviously has its pros and cons. On one hand, it's complicated; on the other hand, it helps."* His television experience also allowed him to be identified with his city and to become a cornerstone of haute cuisine. *"Now people come to my restaurant not to eat a certain dish, but a dish that I've cooked; it doesn't matter which. It's an important change. It gives value to my profile as a chef and allows me to be free."*

On the wishes of Marco and his wife Cristina, sommelier and restaurant manager, the restaurant's recent renovation has undoubtedly contributed towards arousing people's curiosity in his cuisine and, above all, modernizing the image of Parizzi as a restaurant that's a bit pompous and instills a certain fear. *"The space is extremely modern and fairly minimalist."* Yet it's a special kind of minimalism. Only in a city with a neoclassicism that's full of warmth, like what can still be made out in the

ducal garden of the court architect Ennemond Alexandre Petitot, which has recently been restored to the essential and refined eighteenth-century layout, it never slips into an ascetic purism; also because the new arrangement has wisely added value to the oldest parts of the restaurant, emphasizing the wooden beams and curtain walls. *"A very clean, yet elegant, style, bedecked with works of art – the largest art gallery in Parma loans us works to be displayed as if this were a museum – and famous pieces of furniture, made by established companies of Italian design."* An environment suitable for a restaurant that has just proudly become a member of the prestigious *Le Soste* association, which includes the elite of the Italian food scene.

Within the restaurant, Marco's tasks involve collecting ingredients, creating new dishes, and checking the service performed by the kitchen staff. His working day starts at 8:30 a.m. and ends at 1 a.m.. *"Everyday I go and do the shopping personally. In the evening, I send faxes of the orders to the various suppliers and I go and collect the products in the morning. At 10 am I arrive at the restaurant, unload the car, and attend to a few things. I eat at 11 am, then I go into the kitchen for the lunchtime service. I have a break from 3:30 to 6:30 when I go home. Then I come back to the restaurant, have some dinner and start again with the evening service."*

Restocking the ingredients, which is done within the radius of the city and province, where Marco has discovered the best suppliers, isn't like it once was. *"It's increasingly difficult to source high-quality products, but you shouldn't give up trying to find them. The most important relationship of which the chef has to be careful is with the ingredients, followed by the rapport with the customer. My grandfather ate beef five times a year and it was exquisite; now although we can eat it everyday, it's hard to find it that delicious [...] I've managed to do it. I buy an animal from a breeder who rears ten in total. They are animals which are three and a half years old that have had a good life, have been grazed well, and are eaten well [...]"*

In choosing the ingredients, Marco is guided by the season, not according to a calendar, but the effective seasons of nature. *"I buy from producers who are farmers, supplying me directly. They don't have a greenhouse and they work the land themselves. Therefore I have a menu that may change suddenly based on the products at my disposal, even four dishes in one day or dishes which are off the menu for a month and a half."*

Precedence is always given to seasonal products from his land, such as the porcini mushrooms from Borgotaro and the black truffles from Fragno, wild produce that comes from the green mountains in the province of Parma, thick in forests and rich in pastures, and also to typical artisan products, *"the only ingredients that I offer without manipulating them in any way"* such as Parmesan, prosciutto, and Culatello di Zibello, the three glories of food and wine in Parma, each intimately linked to the territory. All are great products for a demanding and highly technical cuisine like Marco's, where the processing of the ingredients and the preparation of the dishes are groomed from the cooking processes to the temperature and the final presentation.

"I've never really been driven towards research. My cuisine consists of cooking .It's a slower movement that isn't state-of-the-art, but of the here and now. I may use an old technique for a new dish or rework an old dish with a new technique," he explains. This is the ideal for a city that looks toward the future, but posesses food traditions that are deep-seated and still alive. A city of which Marco is proud: *"It is a small, yet gourmand province, where people love to go out for lunch and dinner. The sensation of pleasantness moves me. It's small enough city to go out and see lots of people you know, but, at the same time, large enough not to know everyone."*

In the menu chosen for this book, *"the bond with the area is evident in all the courses."* For starters, a *"Pork fillet that we have smoked ourselves with aged vinegar, Fragno black truffle and Parmesan shavings,"* which features the meat of the pigs found everywhere in the low-lying areas, proving that these pigs are not only used to make exquisite sausages. Then there are Parmesan crowns with a veal ragu and tomato confit, in which the mainstay of Parma cuisine is used, followed by a skewer of stewed beef with fried polenta, a typical dish, that is presented differently here, with its crunchy polenta sheets layered with small medallions of beef stew and held together with a skewer. To finish, a Parma-style Italian trifle, an Alchermes-laced version of the traditional dessert.

All are dishes that speak of Parma, not only by way of their intrinsic typicality, but also because of their inspiration. Thanks to Marco's refined cuisine, they express the pleasant art of Correggio, combined with the modernity of Parmigianino—the city's two Renaissance souls, which bring splendor to the cathedral, the churches of San Giovanni Evangelista and Santa Maria della Steccata, and the National Gallery, their works standing right next to Marco's restaurant in a celebration of form and color.

SALAD OF SMOKED PORK FILLET WITH BLACK TRUFFLE AND AGED VINEGAR

Ingredients for 4 people
Preparation time: 30' - Smoking: 40'

Food-grade beech wood chips
2 quarts (2 liters) water
7 oz (200 g) sea salt
3½ oz (100 g) mixed spices (black pepper, cinnamon, cloves, juniper)
2 pork fillets
12 asparagus

7 oz (200 g) spinach
Generous 1 tablespoon (20 g) lard
3 tablespoons (50 g) extra-virgin olive oil
3½ oz (100 g) mixed herbs
⅓ oz (10 g) Parmesan cheese
4 quail's egg
vinegar and truffle

Method

Bring the water to a boil with the salt and spices. Let cool. Add the pork fillets and let marinate for 4 hours. Cold-smoke it (see directions below).
Blanch the asparagus in a pot of salted boiling water, leaving them crunchy. Transfer immediately to a bowl of ice water to preserve the brilliant green color.
Clean and wash the spinach. Sauté the spinach with the lard in a frying pan over medium heat. Add the asparagus and a vinaigrette of the aged vinegar, which is made by first dissolving the vinegar with the salt and then emulsifying it with extra-virgin olive oil. Cut the fillet into thin slices. Arrange the spinach on the plate, followed by the mixed herbs, asparagus, fillet, Parmesan, truffle, and the egg (previously hard-boiled), cut in half. Drizzle with the remaining vinaigrette (optional).

COLD SMOKING

Create a smoking chamber (an oven that's turned off works well).
Arrange the beech chips in a roasting pan and heat until it becomes red-hot. Season with herbs, such as rosemary, bay leaves, and lavender. Cover with a tight-fitting lid and position at the bottom of the oven. Place a baking tray containing ice on the upper shelves and above that a tray with holes containing the items to be smoked: meat, fish, oil, and salt all seasoned in the bowls and anything else you would like to smoke.

Wine pairing
Sauvignon "vulcani" fumé – White
Winery: Inama Azienda Agricola – San Bonifacio (VR)

PARMESAN CROWNS

Ingredients for 4 people
Preparation time: 30'

TOMATO CONFIT
6 oz (180 g) tomatoes
1¼ cups (300 ml) extra-virgin olive oil
1 teaspoon (5 g) thyme
Garlic, thinly sliced
Generous 1 tablespoon (20 g) salt
Pepper
Generous 1 tablespoon (20 g) sugar

PASTA
3⅓ cups (500 g) flour
5 large eggs

FILLING
5 oz (150 g) Parmesan cheese
5 oz (150 g) Provolone cheese

Generous 3 tablespoons (50 g) fresh light cream
Generous 3 tablespoons (50 g) meat stock
Grated zest of ½ lemon
Nutmeg

SAUCE
5 oz (150 g) veal, cut into cubes
2 tablespoons clarified butter
Generous 3 tablespoons (50 g) tomato confit
1 teaspoon (5 g) thyme
Generous 3 tablespoons (50 g) veal cooking juices
Generous 3 tablespoons (50 g) stock

Method

TOMATO CONFIT
Make a cross in the base of the tomatoes; blanch the tomatoes for a few seconds in boiling water and peel them. Cut into quarters and remove the seeds. Arrange the tomatoes on a baking sheet with oil and thyme, placing a slice of garlic on top of each. Add the salt, pepper, and sugar. Let soften in the oven at 200°F (90°C) for 2 hours and 20 minutes.

PASTA
Sift the flour onto a wooden surface and shape into a mound. Make a well in the center. Pour the eggs into the hollow. Knead until the dough is smooth and even. Let rest for 1 hour in a cool place.

FILLING
Mix all the filling ingredients in a bowl, including the grated Parmesan and Provolone cheeses, until smooth.

SAUCE
Brown the veal in the clarified butter. Add the tomato confit, thyme, veal cooking juices, and the stock.

Serving

Roll out the sheet of pasta in a pasta machine and place small amounts of the filling on the pasta. Seal well and cut using a round pastry cutter.
Cook the pasta in plenty of boiling water. Serve hot with the sauce.

Wine pairing

"Nabucco" – Red – Made from Barbera (70%) and Merlot (30%)
Winery: Monte delle Vigne – Ozzano Taro (PR)

PARMA-STYLE SKEWER OF BEEF STEW

Ingredients for 4 people
Preparation time: 3 h 30'

10 carrots
4 onions
1 stalk celery
1 head of garlic
Extra-virgin olive oil
1 shoulder of beef*
3¼ cups (500 g) flour
3 quarts (3 liters) full-bodied red wine
5 cloves
1 cinnamon stick
1 teaspoon (5 g) peppercorns

Cut of meat from the front quarters of the cow, which is found between the fesone di spalla (shoulder clod - at the back) and the girello di spalla (shoulder round - in front).

POLENTA
Generous 1¾ cups (450 g) salted water
⅔ cup (100 g) *polenta taragna* (a mixture of cornmeal and buckwheat)
Butter, for molds

Method

Chop the vegetables and brown them in extra-virgin olive oil in a large pot. Sprinkle the meat with the flour. Brown the meat in a frying pan. Season with salt. Add the meat to the vegetables and pour in the red wine. Add the spices. Cover and bake at 300°F (140°C) for 3 hours.
Remove the meat. Let cool in the refrigerator. Strain the sauce and reduce in a saucepan until fairly thick.
Bring the salted water to a boil. Add the polenta, mixing constantly. Cook over low heat for about 40 minutes. Add a pat of butter and pour into molds (the shape of the molds is optional).
Slice the meat to a thickness of ¾-inch (2 cm) and cut slices into 12 rounds with a diameter of 5 cm using a round pastry cutter. Spoon a little sauce over the meat and heat them just before serving.
Remove the polenta from the molds and fry.

Serving

Assemble the skewer as shown in the photo, taking care that the meat doesn't break and alternating it with the polenta.
Sheets of polenta can also be made to garnish the dish. Spread out the polenta dampened with a drop of water on a sheet of parchment paper. Bake at 175°F (80°C) for 2 hours, or until it has dried out completely.
Serve hot with plenty of sauce.

Wine pairing

Barolo "Monfortino" – Red
Winery: Conterno Azienda Vitivinicola, Fraz. Ornati – Monforte d'Alba (CN)

ITALIAN TRIFLE

Ingredients for 4 people
Preparation time: 1 h 30'

LADYFINGERS
⅔ cup (150 g) egg yolks
2 tablespoons (30 g) sugar
8 (210 g) egg whites
1¼ cups (180 g) sifted flour

OLD-FASHIONED PASTRY CREAM
1 cup (250 ml) milk
½ vanilla bean
Zest of ½ lemon
10 (250 g) egg yolks
¾ cup (150 g) sugar
Scant 3 tablespoons (40 g)
sifted flour
1 cup (250 ml) cream

CHOCOLATE CUSTARD
2 cups (500 ml) milk
Scant ½ cup (100 g) egg yolks
¾ cup (150 g) sugar
⅔ cup (100 g) cocoa
3½ oz (100 g) chocolate

DIP
Scant ½ cup (100 g) water
½ cup (100 g) sugar
1⅔ cups (400 g) Alchermes liqueur
1 vanilla pod
Liqueur-soaked cherries and fresh fruit
Whipped cream, to decorate
Broken chocolate, to decorate

Method

LADYFINGERS
Beat the egg yolks with the sugar in a bowl. In a separate bowl, beat the egg whites with the sugar. Fold in the egg yolk mixture and the flour. Make a ⅛-inch (0.5-cm) layer on a baking sheet that has been buttered and floured. Bake at 350ºF (180ºC/gas mark 4) for 10 minutes. Remove from the oven and cut into ¾ x 2¾-inch (2 x 7-cm) rectangles.

OLD-FASHIONED PASTRY CREAM
Bring the milk to a boil with the vanilla bean and lemon zest. Beat the egg yolks and sugar together in a bowl. Add the sieved flour and mix. Pour in the hot milk. Pour the mixture back into the pan that contained the milk and bring to a boil for 2 minutes. Pour the custard into a bowl and let cool.

CHOCOLATE CUSTARD
Follow the same instructions given to make the old-fashioned pastry cream. Beat the egg yolks and sugar together in a bowl. Add the boiling milk and return to a boil. Add the cocoa and chocolate and mix until it has melted completely. Pour the custard into a bowl and let cool.

DIP
Bring the water to a boil with the sugar. Let cool and stir in the Alchermes.

Serving

Make a layer of soaked (in the dip) ladyfingers, then an initial layer of one custard, another of ladyfingers, another one of chocolate custard, and another one of ladyfingers to finish. Cut into squares. Decorate with liqueur-soaked cherries, fresh fruit or whipped cream and pieces of chocolate. Serve cold.

Wine pairing

"Ala Marascato" – Flavored liqueur wine
Winery: Duca di Salaparuta – Marsala (TP)

THE CUISINE OF LIGURIA

Embraced between the sky and sea, Liguria is an arch of stony mountains engulfed in the Tyrrhenian Sea from the wooded slopes of the Apennines mountain range. The narrow sunken valleys have been transformed through the thousands of years of men's hard work into a series of steep terraces where the prized land has been wrestled from the rock to be cultivated. This hard land – hard like its people and like its cuisine, characterized by long and complicated recipes – is the kingdom of the olive tree. Olive oil pervades a gastronomy that's capable of blending the products of the sea and fruit of the mountains, the flavors of the water and the land in an original and one of a kind way, fragrant with unique aromas and perfumes.

Genoa, one of the four flourishing Maritime Republics once governed by Doges, center of important trading and one of the leading Mediterranean ports, preserves many traces of its glorious past in the sumptuous homes of the merchant aristocracy. The highest glory in Genoese cooking is its pesto, a sauce made from the basil that's cultivated on sunny balconies, in small gardens at the back of houses or inland, which is *pestato* (ground up) in a marble mortar with coarse salt, garlic, and Parmesan cheese (Pecorino Sardo was added at a later time) and mixed with extra-virgin olive oil (see box). It is the ideal sauce to add flavor to vegetable minestrone soups and many fillings, and excellent served with pasta.

Ligurian pasta deserves a special mention. Genoa, the historic pasta capital after Palermo and Sicily (and undoubtedly before Naples), owes its fame to the climate and the configuration of the territory. Here the waters of the steep torrents provided the power to grind, knead, and bronze-die the durum wheat that arrived by sea. Here the sea breezes blew intermittently, towards the coast or towards the sea, drying the various forms of durum wheat pasta to perfection. *Trenette* come from here, a sort of flattened spaghetti, ideal when combined with pesto (but those benefiting from a dark color are perfect in minestrone), as well as *troffie,* a type of pasta curl, which is especially enjoyed in Camogli with pesto, potatoes, and green beans; the triangular *pansotti,* a specialty of Rapallo; *picagge*, fettuccine with a characteristic green color due to the borage that's added to the dough, a herb with wide, hairy leaves which are also tasty battered and fried; *corzetti*, discs of pasta made using molds decorated with the coats-of-arms of each family. We also mustn't forget rice, a common ingredient in vegetable minestrones, herb stock, and the local recipe for *riso arrosto,* which is cooked in a meat sauce with peas, artichokes, sausages, and mushroom, baked, unmixed in the oven and emerging fluffy, light, and full of flavor.

Inevitably fish has a vital role in the cuisine of Liguria, always prepared with the local oil. All types of Mediterranean seafood appear on the Ligurian dinner table. The delicious *Ciuppin,* the exquisite fish stew ladled on top of a layer of bread toasted in oil, is made with small-sized shellfish, generally whatever was left over at the end of the market for the fishermen. *Cappon magro,* the apotheosis of Ligurian cooking, is made with garden-grown vegetables, eggs, olives, and fish, rich in flavors and aromas. In spite of the reputation of the Genoese and Ligurians as being miserly, they are not at all parsimonious in this dish. Here there are cabbages, green beans, celery, carrots, beets, artichokes, and potatoes, green olives, fine-textured fish (sea bream or gurnard), lobsters, shrimp, salt-cured anchovies, *mosciame* (dolphin fillet, which is no longer allowed sun-dried and then cut into very thin slices), capers, cucumbers, mushrooms, garlic, pine nuts, hard-cooked eggs, bread, and plenty of olive oil. Another typical fish dish is *buridda,* a stew made from stockfish or shellfish and seafood. However, the most common seafood recipe is undoubtedly the fried fish, golden and crispy, which can be eaten anywhere in the small villages overhanging the sea and in the big coastal towns. Camogli is now famous all over the world for its fried fish festival, made in the giant pan set up in the square, on the day of San Fortunato (celebrated on the second Sunday in May), the town's patron saint, and San Prospero. Many fried fish, such as mullet then end up being marinated in *scabeccio* (a type of sweet and sour sauce). Anchovies, fished according to tradition by lamplight, are instead preserved under salt. They are pressed with a slate *ciappa,* the symbolic stone of Liguria, as they lose water.

Frying isn't just limited to fish. Ligurian cooking also fries meat (the mixed fried meat with veal chops, liver, brain, and sweetbreads) and vegetables. They also fry desserts (*Frisceu*, a batter containing apples and sultanas and *latte brusco*, hard milk) as well as other strange, yet delicious, things: ground sage, wisteria flowers, borage leaves, zucchini flowers, swollen focaccette of leavened pastry, which are curiously called aria *fritta*, or fried air.

There is a love of fillings all over Liguria, in terms of meat (the typical breast of veal stuffed with a delicate aromatic herb mixture) and vegetables: artichokes, onions, eggplants, cardoons, mushrooms, and especially zucchini loan themselves to be stuffed with meat, fish, and vegetable-based mixtures.

Vegetables are also the main ingredients in the oven-baked pies: a vegetable-based filling in between very thin layers of puff pastry. Easter pie, or *torta pasqualina*, is the most classic of these, made from chard (and not artichoke as many wrongly think), dried mushrooms, and eggs. Artichoke, mushroom, and herb pies are also delicious. Herb pie is a specialty of Imperia.

Also baked in the oven, there's the classic *fugassa* or Ligurian *focaccia*, bread dough pricked with a fork, soaked with olive oil, sprinkled generously with salt and aromatics. Every riverside town makes it with its own variation, spreading it with sliced onions, flavoring it with sage, oregano, or rosemary, filling it with cheese (in Recco and Pieve Alta). The *farinata* is also traditional: a dough made from garbanzo bean flour and water, baked in the oven in a shallow, wide tray drizzled with lots of oil.

Desserts in Liguria are represented by almond cake; *pandolce*, a type of panettone with a very dense pastry, rich in sultanas and candied fruit; and sweet ravioli filled with a candied fruit based paste, another unbeatable specialty of Genoa. Frisciolata, a cake made from garbanzo bean flour, *castagnaccio*, made from Gabbiana chestnuts from the Val Bormida in the province of Savona, and candied sour orange tart are also important specialties, served with sweet, aromatic wines from the Cinque Terre.

Here among the peaks that dominate the picturesque towns hanging onto the rock face on the eastern strip of Liguria, which ends with the lovely town of Porto Venere, the sun ripens and sweetens the bunches of vines cultivated in the steep terraces that overhang the sea. Sciacchetrà is made here, with its amber color that turns brown with ageing, aromatic and velvety. The dessert wine is remembered by Andrea Bacci (1524–1600), author of *De naturali vinorum historia*, published in 1595, and the personal doctor of Pope Sixtus V, as *"the utmost nutrition for the elderly, helpful to the healthy and poorly alike."*

OLIO EXTRAVERGINE D'OLIVA RIVIERA LIGURE PDO

DUE TO THE PRESENCE OF EXQUISITE OLIVE VARIETIES, INCLUDING THE TAGGIASCA (BLACK, IT TAKES ITS NAME FROM THE TOWN OF TAGGIA, IN THE PROVINCE OF IMPERIA, AND IS PRESERVED IN BRINE AS AN APPETIZER), LIGURIA EXTRA-VIRGIN OLIVE OIL IS DESERVING OF ITS PROTECTED DESIGNATION OF ORIGIN. THE PRODUCTION OF OIL OF THE LEVANTE IS DISTINGUISHED FOR ITS COLOR, WHICH TENDS TOWARDS GREEN AND AN AVERAGELY SWEET FLAVOR, WITH A POSSIBLE FINAL PIQUANT AND BITTER NOTE. THE OIL OF THE PONENTE, ON THE OTHER HAND, STANDS OUT DUE TO ITS YELLOW COLOR AND CLEAR AND RIPE ORCHARD AROMA. THERE IS AN EXTRAORDINARY MUSEUM DEDICATED TO THE OLIVE TREE IN THE CENTER OF IMPERIA, WHICH TRACES THE THOUSANDS OF YEARS OF HISTORY OF THIS PLANT THAT WAS SACRED TO THE GODS AND ITS VARIOUS USES.

LUCA COLLAMI

RESTAURANT BALDIN - SESTRI PONENTE (GENOVA)

The restaurant and the chef were established together; in 1969 chef Luca Collami was born in Genoa, and in Sestri Ponente, a small municipality on the Genoan cost, a couple opened Trattoria Baldin. Without one knowing about the other's existence, what would later become his own restaurant grew at the same time as he did. They came across one another later on just before his eighteenth birthday. *"I took over the trattoria, whose name comes from the owner's nickname, Mr. Teobaldo, in 1989 by sheer chance,"* Luca recounts. *"As a boy I lived in Pegli and the restaurant's owners were my neighbors. As they needed help at a certain point, I came to work here and then became their employee at the age of 18 and a half. Within less than a month, with my parents' guidance I decided to become a shareholder, buying the first share, given that the restaurant was working well. Within less than six months, I also acquired a second share and at the age of 20 I find myself managing the trattoria, assisted by my mother Maria."*

Luca hasn't followed in his father's footsteps. *"I was the first one in my family to do this job, but when I was 11 years old I was already saying, 'When I grow up, I'll be a chef and open a restaurant."* And that's how things have worked out. *"I attended a hotel institute and then did some apprenticeships in various places during the summer seasons and a year and a half in a leading restaurant in Genoa, but that's all. I'd call myself self-taught. I've tried to broaden my love through reading, studying, traveling, experimenting and, above all, by drawing comparisons between myself and my colleagues, often people who are more authoritative than me. In this sense, becoming a member of the Jeunes Restaurateurs d'Europe association has really helped me."*

In managing Trattoria Baldin, Luca started off low-key, while however also being aware of the fact that he had the edge over other restaurateurs: *"In my case, the owner and the chef were the same person."* The real turning point occurred in 1999 when he decided to completely renovate the restaurant, entrusting the work to the skill of his architect friend, who was able to give substance to his needs. He also would have changed the name of the restaurant, *"but I was sorry for the previous two owners."*

So with a French-style idea and great humility, he simply added his name beneath the historical name of the restaurant. Indeed, it would have been a shame to erase Baldin; like Sant'Alberto da Genova, patron saint of Sestri Ponente and cook at the *Abbazia di Sant'Andrea* before becoming a hermit in a cave in the Sestri Levante area, who discovered his calling in life when he was a boy when he was present at the sacred representation of the conversion of the ascetic Teobaldo, for Luca it was another Teobaldo who set him off along the right path.

"When the restaurant was renovated, something clicked inside of me and, slowly but surely, I started to become what I am today." He doesn't regard himself as somebody important, *"but it's certainly a pleasure to do my work and I devote a lot of time to it, although it's difficult, not so much being in the kitchen where I have fun, but rather taking care of managing the restaurant from a bureaucratic point of view."* He'd like to work full-time as a chef as he's got real talent in the kitchen. *"New dishes come to me instinctively. I plate up the idea without doing many tests and counter-tests. Once it's done and has been tasted, any number of things may happen to make me change the composition or arrangement of the elements. Furthermore, my dishes are never the same. I owe this inconstancy to my continued search for improvement."*

It's not so much the type of cuisine, which has always been *"extravagant, though linked to tradition,"* as the way in which it's offered, which has changed over these ten years. The chef's touch has become refined and has achieved an uncommon style. The clientele has also changed and peo-

Baldin Ristorante chef Luca Collam

ple have started to come from outside of the region. The restaurant's image has become more lumi-
nous, modern, and groomed. Restaurant Baldin, which Luca manages with his wife Barbara, sommelier and manager, not only of the dining room, but also of the line of desserts and *petits fours*, *"is
an informal, lively atmosphere, also frequented by young people, where there is, however, an air of
professionalism."* It is situated in a seventeenth-century building, in a small square that has a
Parisian feel about it in the oldest part of Sestri, in a populated corner of alleyways and *straduzze*
(narrow streets), a stone's throw away from *Basilica di Nostra Signora dell'Assunta*. Consecrated in
1602, when Sestri was still lapped by the sea, it was practically built on the beach and faced in a
north-south direction rather than west-east, as tradition decreed that the faithful faced towards
the east during mass to prevent the seawater from entering the church during storms. Luca is
happy to live here. *"I like the fact that we're on a hill, but you can see the sea. The whole of Liguria
has this promiscuity between the sea and mountains that I find fascinating."*

The restaurant has vaulted ceilings in an ecru color, dark, hard wooden floors, and well-spaced
light Finnish birch wooden paneling on the walls. The lighting system is state-of-the-art, purposely
designed to emphasize the various dishes. The tables and chairs are in light-colored bent wood
with traditional lines. In the niches of the walls, there's simple shelving for the excellent wines destined to accompany the cuisine. A simple atmosphere, yet warm and effective.

From 1999 to the present day, there are historic dishes which Luca continues to offer. For example, spaghetti with lobster, *"a classic dish and perhaps a little obvious compared to my current
cooking, but I think it's always impressive and I'll never take it off the menu."* Then there's *zuppet-
ta imperiale,* which is a combination of seafood – razor clams, scallops, clams, mussels, hard clams,
and so on – in a tomato and rosemary soup, as well as scabbard fish in a potato crust, which stays
crispy on the outside and seems steamed on the inside, and the raw/cooked variation, a sequence
of 25 fish appetizers (oysters and anchovies, gurnard, scabbard tartare, mussels, bottarga, tuna
tataki, salt cod flan, a lobster salad, home-smoked moreno fish, and so on), a true tasting experi-

ence, presented in a splendor of colors. There's also oven-fried mullet served with cheese and vegetables, which changes according to the season, with a Provolone fondue and sautéed artichokes or Parmesan and porcini mushrooms, or Emmental and ovules. The chef has been arousing and satisfying his customers' tastes for years.

"My cuisine has tradition at its base in terms of its aromas and products, but also in its flavors, given that they're rather decisive, Ligurian and Mediterranean. For me the territory is sacred, but using this as the premise I am strictly creative and innovative." Like Genoese food and wine uses the raw materials of the land, but in dishes which reflect the echoes of a past of trading and contact with faraway peoples, Luca interprets the ingredients of a dish and tends to play with the local elements to recreate it. However, he does this with expert intuition and without ever losing his head. For example, salt cod – widely used in Ligurian cuisine – is offered cooked at a low temperature and served with a pea and black truffle puree when in season. Alternatively, there's his stoccafisso alla darsena, another classic regional fish that's offered in an endless number of recipes. The chef steams the stockfish and then sautés it in a pan with all the flavorings: garlic, anchovies, capers, etc. It is a lighter dish than the so-called accomodata version where the stockfish is cooked for hours. He also offers a reworked version of cappon magro that's restructured, hot, and unusual. It is a typically cold Genoese starter, a tile layered with vegetables, which are almost always potatoes, green beans, cauliflower, and white fish, usually gurnard and end shellfish, served with a rich sauce made from garlic, anchovies, pine nuts, capers, olives, hard-cooked egg yolks, parsley, oil, and vinegar. Luca serves it in a new combination: open, laid out flat on the plate, with lighter vegetables like zucchini, carrots, or asparagus and a wider range of types of fish.

Apart from the fish caught in the Ligurian Sea, among the regional products that are always used there are undoubtedly the herbs, especially basil, which is the main ingredient of the famous pesto in Liguria, the delicious sauce made from garlic, pine nuts, cheese, and extra-virgin olive oil, and marjoram, which is used to add flavor to the different traditional regional dishes, from stuffed mussels, called muscoli here, to the torta pasqualina, a savory pie made with boiled chard, curdled milk, and eggs, served during the Easter period, from the famous *cima ripiena*, made from stuffed veal to *tomaxelle*, rich veal rolls stewed in white wine, stock, and tomatoes.

Luca is the one who does the shopping every morning before going to the restaurant to set up the day with the kitchen boys and to make the bread, grissini, crackers, and the famous Genoese focaccia, flavored with rosemary, sage, oregano, and onion, which he serves freshly baked twice a day. He chooses the ingredients, paying special attention to the quality and seasonality. He cooks them in ways which do not kill the flavors. *"Here right next to us, after many years of research, I'm lucky to have found a well-stocked fishmonger's, which has a huge supply of fishermen able to guarantee local products and some real pearls. Also close to the restaurant, there's a greengrocer from whom I buy everything I need on a daily basis. Every now and then, if I need some early fruits, I also go and stock on fruit and vegetables from the eastern market in Genoa, which is lovely and picturesque. I also have a trusted butcher, but I tend not to cook much meat; mine is essentially a fish restaurant."*

The dishes chosen for the menu in this book are traditional recipes. *"For starters, I chose zucchini flowers stuffed with stockfish, served with tomato mayonnaise and a sauce made from garlic, Ligurian extra-virgin olive oil and salt-cured anchovies."* An appetizing new take on the classic stuffed vegetables in Ligurian cuisine. *"For the pasta course, there's potato gnocchetti with white fish, Taggiasca olives, and marjoram."* Here he's played with the aromas of the classic potato gnocchetti, which are often served with pesto in the Genoa area, given that marjoram is a typically Ligurian herb. He has also played on the use of the esteemed black olives of the Imperian town of Taggia. *"For the main course, locally sourced squid stuffed with porcini mushrooms. The mushrooms are excellent in our area."* The low temperature cooking allows him to make the dish particularly fragrant and elegant. *"For dessert, Genoa-style cookie base – which, despite its name, is a soft sponge cake – served with a coffee and gianduja mousse."* The last two flavors are not strictly Ligurian, but as Genoa was the birthplace of Christopher Columbus, the man who discovered the Americas, featuring aromatic coffee and the divine flavor of cocoa among the ingredients is certainly in line with local History, with a capital "H."

ZUCCHINI FLOWERS STUFFED WITH STOCKFISH SERVED WITH A TOMATO, OIL, AND ANCHOVY MAYONNAISE

Ingredients for 4 people
Preparation time: 50'

1⅓ lb (600 g) stockfish
Generous 1 tablespoon (20 g) capers
1 clove garlic
Generous 1 tablespoon (20 g) anchovies
8 tablespoons (80 g) Ligurian extra-virgin olive oil PDO
1 egg white
12 zucchini flowers
10 oz (300 g) cherry tomatoes

SAUCE
Cherry tomatoes and extra-virgin olive oil

Method

Bring a saucepan with plenty of water to a boil over medium heat. Add the stockfish and let it soak for 10 minutes until ready. Remove from the water; remove the skin of the fish and remove fish from the bones. Transfer to the food processor and add the capers, garlic, anchovies, and a scant 3 tablespoons (40 g) of oil to make a smooth and even cream.
When the fish has cooled, add the egg white, which has been beaten to stiff peaks.
Wash the zucchini flowers. Use a pastry bag to fill the flowers with the prepared mixture. Wrap them in aluminum foil and cook in a double boiler for 10 minutes.
Clean the tomatoes. Using a handheld immersion blender, emulsify them with 3 tablespoons of oil. Strain through a fine-mesh sieve to remove the seeds. Heat the remaining 2 tablespoons of oil.

Serving

Arrange the zucchini flowers diagonally on the plate with the tomato mayonnaise. Drizzle with the hot oil.

Wine pairing
Vermentino Colli di Luni DOC 2006 – White
Winery: La Felce – Ortonovo (SP)

POTATO GNOCCHETTI WITH WHITE FISH, TAGGIASCA OLIVES, AND MARJORAM

Ingredients for 4 people
Preparation time: 1 h

1 lb (500 g) potatoes
Salt
1⅓ cups (200 g) flour
1 clove of garlic

1 white fish fillet
2 tablespoons Taggiasca olives
8 cherry tomatoes
Marjoram

Method

Boil the potatoes with the skins on in plenty of salted water. Peel them when they are still hot and puree with a potato masher. Season with salt and add the flour.
Knead together quickly on a floured surface to make a soft dough in the shape of a sausage. The sizes suggested can be adjusted based on the quality of the potatoes and may change as needed. Test them by immersing a small piece of the mixture in boiling water. If the consistency of the dough isn't good enough, add more flour and test again.
Cut the dough into portions and use your hands to roll them out into cylinders about 1-inch (2.5-cm) thick. Cut crosswise into ¾–1¼-inch (2–3-cm) gnocchi.
Press the gnocchi briefly under the prongs of a fork for decoration and to give them more shape. Arrange in a single layer on floured or parchment-lined baking sheets.
Bring plenty of salted water to a boil. Add the gnocchi. They will cook quickly; drain them as soon as they rise to the surface.
Sauté the chopped garlic in the oil in a frying pan. Add the fish, Taggiasca olives, and cherry tomatoes. Cook for a few minutes. Sauté the gnocchi in the sauce and add the marjoram.

Wine pairing

"Pigato" Costa de Vigne, 2006 – White
Winery: Massimo Alessandri – Ranzo (IM)

SQUID STUFFED WITH PORCINI MUSHROOMS

Ingredients for 4 people
Preparation time: 40'

12 squid
7oz (200 g) porcini mushrooms
1 zucchini
½ onion
1 clove garlic
⅓ cup (40 g) breadcrumbs

1 egg
Salt to taste
Pepper to taste
Scant 3 tablespoons (40 g) Ligurian
extra-virgin olive oil PDO
Parsley, to garnish

Method

Clean the squid, removing the heads which will be used in the filling.
Set 3 whole squid aside per portion (12 altogether).
Make the filling: Chop up the squid and the leftover heads. Dice the porcini and chop up the zucchini, onion, and garlic. Mix all the ingredients together in a bowl. Add the breadcrumbs and egg. Season with salt and pepper.
Stuff the squid with the filling and secure them with toothpicks. Arrange them on a baking sheet and drizzle with a little oil. Bake at 325°F (160°C/gas mark 3) for 7 minutes. Chop the parsley.
Serve the hot squid with a drizzling of extra-virgin olive oil and the parsley.

Wine pairing

Rossese 2006 – Red
Winery: Massaretti – Albenga (SV)

GENOA-STYLE COOKIE WITH COFFEE AND GIANDUJA MOUSSE

Ingredients for 4 people
Preparation time: 1 h – Resting: 3 h

GENOA-STYLE COOKIE BASE
6 whole eggs
2 egg yolks
1 cup (150 g) flour, sifted
Generous ¾ cup (180 g) sugar
Scant ⅓ cup (40 g) starch
Scant 2 tablespoons (25 g) butter, plus
additional for molds

COFFEE OR GIANDUJA MOUSSE
Generous ¾ cup (200 g) light cream
Scant ¼ cup (50 g) glucose
1¼ cups (300 g) gianduja or ½ cup (125 ml) of espresso coffee
1¼ cups (300 g) whipped cream

Chocolate, for serving

Method

GENOA-STYLE COOKIE BASE
Heat the whole eggs and yolks in a saucepan, whisking until heated to 115–120°F (45–50°C). Transfer to a food processor, preferably an electric mixer, and beat with sugar. Fold in the flour, the starch, followed by the melted butter. Bake in the oven in buttered molds at 375°F (190°C/gas mark 5) for 35–40 minutes.

GIANDUJA MOUSSE
Mix the glucose with the light cream in a saucepan and let boil over medium heat. Blend the gianduja in a mixer, adding the hot cream mixture. When the mixture has cooled, fold in the whipped cream.

COFFEE MOUSSE
Follow the same method used to make the gianduja mousse, replacing the gianduja with ½ cup (125 ml) coffee.

Serving

Use a round pastry cutter to cut the cookie base. Completely line the molds with the cake. Fill the lined molds with a little gianduja mousse, followed by the coffee mousse (the same method for gianduja ganache). Freeze for at least 3 hours. Decorate with chocolate before serving.

Wine pairing

Ala – Dessert wine
Winery: Duca di Salaparuta – Marsala (TP)

THE CUISINE OF TUSCANY

Announced by the clear Mediterranean light that fills your eyes as soon as you cross the Apennines, this region contains the age-old lake basins of Lunigiana, Garfagnana, Mugello, and Casentino, thick with forests, pastures, chestnut groves, and fields of spelt. This was cradle of Italian civilization, the land where the Renaissance was at its most splendid. It was home to the literary greats, from Dante Alighieri, to Giovanni Boccaccio, Giotto, Brunelleschi, Botticelli, Michelangelo, and Leonardo da Vinci. Tuscany offers a gentle and relaxing landscape that is mostly hilly. It offers sensations, colors, and aromas that can be enjoyed among rows of cypress trees and explosions of broom, extensive vineyards, and prized olive groves. It is the region of Chianti, with its many villages and isolated townships; the restless, solitary, and wooded Colline Metallifere ("metal hills"); the Crete Senesi with its vast expanses of sunflowers; and the Val di Chiana with the herds of cows from which the infamous Florentine T-bone steak is taken; the Maremma, among fields of wheat and domestic pine trees with their umbrella foliage. There's also the coast, with its market gardens, pine groves, coastal lakes, charming riverside towns, and the islands of the archipelago like pearls flung among the waves, from the enchanting Elba to the small isle of Giglio. However, there's much more than just the beauty of nature. There are staggeringly beautiful towns like Montepulciano and San Gimignano and spectacular cities that are rich in art and history, from Renaissance Florence to Medieval Siena, Arezzo with the frescoes of Piero della Francesca, the Leaning Tower of Pisa, and Volterra with its Etruscan cemeteries. A leading contender in regional cuisine, with its pure, sanguine flavors like the nature of its people, is undoubtedly the Toscano IGP extra-virgin olive oil, which is produced in particular around Lucca. The color varies from green to golden yellow and its flavor is fruity with aromas of almond, artichoke, and ripe fruit. The locally made cheeses are abundant, and are the pride of the area. In particular, Pecorino Toscano PDO (see box), but also Caciotta, produced above all in the Maremma, and Marzolino del Chianti, a sheep's cheese with a well-defined flavor, which errs on the spicy side with ageing. Tuscan starters consist of a selection of local cured meats, from lardo to Finocchiona, Soppressata, including the famous game liver and spleen pate toasts, which are softened with hot stock. The standard bearer of the Tuscan cured meat specialties is without a doubt lardo di Colonnata, originally from the small village of the same name in the Apuane Alps. A few artisans continue to age this lard there today, using herbs and spices from the Mediterranean scrub. The meat is cured for at least six months in tanks that are carved in marble. It is delicious cut thinly on slices of toasted Tuscan bread. Tuscan ham is also important, with its distinctively tasty meat. Typical of Florence and Siena, there is the soft finocchiona, pork salami flavored with wild fennel seeds. According to tradition, Tuscans have always been soup-eaters or *minestrai*. There are many vegetable and bean soups, as well as soups prepared with day-old bread such as *pantrito, pappa col pomodoro,* and the inevitable *acquacotta.* Rice and dried pasta are often served with a meat sauce. Florentine-style rice is even cooked in the sauce or in tomato sauce, which is enriched with chicken liver for special occasions. In Tuscany, locally sourced beef is especially eaten, famous for its goodness. In Tuscan family cooking, it is common to cook whole cuts of meat rather than cutting them into slices. There are therefore many recipes for cooking whole cuts of meat in sauces that are delicious and full-flavored. There is also the Florentine T-bone steak, strictly from Chianina cows, it follows the Tuscan tradition with its thick cut and remarkable size. A particularly delicious pork is used to prepare roast loin of pork, or *Arista,* which takes its name from the loin cut in contact with the thigh, with sprigs of rosemary and garlic rolled in salt and pepper. There is a special place for offal in Tuscan cooking, whose dishes are some of the best-known. Chicken livers are used to create *cibreo di rigaglie* (an offal omelet), which has resonances of the Piedmontese *finanziera.* Beef or veal tripe is prepared in the Florentine style, that is to say with the tastier and thicker stewed sauce, which tradition has it was sold by the hawkers along the river Arno and eaten on slices of Tuscan bread; pig's liver, almost always cooked in pieces wrapped in its netting; Arezzo-style liver, which was once preserved in glazed earthenware pots and covered in lard. In the Maremma, game-based dishes are the norm. There's pappardelle pasta with Scansano wild boar or hare sauce and wild boar stew with chocolate. Along the Tyrrhenian coast of Tuscany, beaches alternate with reefs and coastal lagoons, encouraging the wide range of fish and seafood Seafood provides the basis of *cacciucco*, Leghorn's typical soup, which was once prepared by fishermen's wives with leftovers from the market, characterized by adding red wine and the spicy flavor of chile pepper. Mullet is also excellent at Leghorn, first fried and then stewed in a fresh tomato sauce or baked in foil if large in size with mushrooms and Tuscan ham. Alternatively, there are cèe, little fish that are prepared in a refined manner. We also mustn't forget the clam soup, cooked using clams from the Tyrrhenian, which tradition would have cooked in seawater trapped in the shells with tomato and eaten on slices of Tuscan bread, which has been fried in extra-virgin olive oil or toasted. Tuscan vegetables, tender and tasty, are the fundamental ingredients of many dishes. Artichokes are usually eaten dipped raw, leaf by leaf, in a *pinzimonio* of oil, vinegar, salt and pepper or fried with a filling of their stalks. Typical vegetables also include peas, asparagus, or the delicious, thin asparagus, and Tuscan cabbage, unmistakable in minestrone, but which is also eaten *alla certosina*, boiled and served with oil, salt, and pepper on toasted homemade bread. There are many dishes made using pulses. Garbanzo beans are served with tripe, pork rind, and pig's trotter, and beans are served stewed with tomato. With their unique flavor and extremely sought after due to their reduced production, there are the Sorana beans and Zolfini beans from Pratomagno. In Tuscany, there are many dessert specialties, especially in terms of cookies, which range from the Cantucci di Prato, simple cookies made from almonds and flavored with anise, to Ricciarelli made from almond paste, and the Sienese Cavallucci, enhanced with fennel seeds. In Siena, the famous Copate are also produced, which are made from a special almond paste that remains soft for a long time, squeezed between two large wafers, as well as the internationally renowned Panforte, made from almonds, candied fruit, and honey. Special sugared almonds come from Pistoia, with a soft and spongy filling. At Lamporecchio, not far from Vinci, the birthplace of Leonardo, anise-flavored wafers called Brigidini are cooked on red-hot plates. The infamous Zuccotto comes from Florence, a frozen dessert prepared in a typical mold, with sponge cake soaked in Alchermes liquor and Italian pastry cream, chocolate, nut brittle, candied citron, and whipped cream. Above all, however, Tuscany is a land of fine wines. Chianti, the most famous Italian wine worldwide, produced in a restricted mountainous and hilly area between the basins of the rivers Arno and Ombrone bridging the provinces of Florence and Siena, which has been defined since 1932. From Montalcino, in the province of Siena, come the great Brunello and Moscatello, which is a dessert wine. Vernaccia di San Gimignano, with its straw yellow color and a refreshing, crisp flavor, with a slightly bitter head, is especially suitable with fish. Produced for centuries and served at the tables of popes and kings, its praises were sung by the Buonarroti the young, nephew of the great Michelangelo, according to whom Vernaccia *"burns, licks, bites and hits."* The Tuscan archipelago has exceptional wines: the Procanico elbano (red and white from Elba), Aleatico from Portoferraio, recommended with desserts, Ansonica from the island of Giglio, perfect with fish, whose production also continues on the Argentario promontory, and Vin Santo, perfect for desserts, which is created from the long fermentation of strained Trebbiano and Malvasia grapes that are ripened for at least four years. It is one of the best fortified wines in the world.

PECORINO TOSCANO PDO

CREATED FROM PURE SHEEP'S MILK AND FORMERLY LAUDED BY PLINY THE ELDER, PECORINO TOSCANO TAKES ITS AROMATIC FLAVOR, WHICH IS MORE MARKED WHEN AGED YET STILL BALANCED, FROM THE FRAGRANT PASTURES OF THE TUSCAN HILLS. PRODUCED IN TWO TYPES, WHEN SLICED OR GRATED, IT CAN BE A SOFT, WHITE CHEESE OR A SEMI-HARD CHEESE THAT IS TENACIOUS WHEN CUT WITH A STRAW YELLOW COLOR. EXCELLENT WHEN SERVED WITH A GOOD ROSSO DI MONTALCINO.

GAETANO TROVATO

RESTAURANT ARNOLFO - COLLE VAL D'ELSA (SIENA)

"My dishes are always hiding in a book as if they were architectural drawings," chef Gaetano Trovato explains. What else could he call his restaurant then, given that it stands a stone's throw away from where Arnolfo di Cambio was born, the celebrated Tuscan architect and sculptor who worked on the plans of the cathedral of Santa Maria del Fiore in Florence? It had to be Arnolfo, named with a great sense of pride.

The restaurant is set in a sixteenth-century building in the historic center of Colle Val d'Elsa, the small medieval town known for its handcrafted glass, and overlooking the gentle, immobile expanse of the Sienese hills of Chianti. It was recently restored with the aristocratic simplicity of Arnolfo's architecture, dense with an old use of space and dotted with modern elements. *"The restaurant, which lets you experience a medieval feeling when you step in from the town combined with the Tuscan countryside, which is truly splendid, is a real home with lounges on different floors. It is also a hotel, where the customer can benefit from a room for the night."* The atmosphere is crisp and basic. There are white-on white tones, walls in slaked lime, marble dust and beeswax, crystal chandeliers, light-colored leather seats, white Flanders linen tablecloths, a few selected pieces of old furniture, and modern artwork. A sober, informal, yet distinctive, atmosphere, characterized by transparency, cleanliness, and strictness: *"My brother, Giovanni, sommelier and maître d'hôtel, and I inherited the attention to these values from our family and these are the same values which are also reflected in my cooking – passing on quality, but without pomp."*

The restaurant was established in 1982 in the small town centre of Val d'Elsa. *"My mother Concetta and my sisters offered homemade cooking, but with a strict focus on the ingredients. It was therefore local cuisine, but not offered as haute cuisine like it is today. Giovanni and I pointed it out during the mid-Eighties, thereby radically changing the philosophy."*

Thinking about them now, these were difficult times, he reflects. *"My parents sometimes told me off, then they slowly started to support me as I received my first Michelin star at the age of 26 in 1987."* He received another one in 2000, which confirmed his tendency towards local cuisine based on incessant research.

"My philosophy is the evolution of the tradition seen today with local products." An innate classical beauty, which it perhaps derives from the Tuscan Renaissance in which it is immersed, taking the best from the past to make it thrive in the present. Gaetano has historical dishes on the menu that he continues to offer, but which are presented in new and more interesting ways, like the roasted meats that are a classic of Tuscan cuisine, from the Medici reign to the present day. *"For example, we serve mother's pigeon dish in a more contemporary way, constantly challenging ourselves with the same ingredient, with two or three cooking methods and modern combinations. Roasted breast with cacao beans and a bittersweet chocolate-based sauce, for example, takes us back to the traditions of the past, but it's been renewed for the present day."* Chianina beef, the crowning point of the adjacent Val di Chiana, is another ingredient that is constantly interpreted in different ways. In the summer, there's steak cooked in Brunello di Montalcino, one of the area's leading wines, a tartare made from Chianina fillet, and aspic consisting of the animal's less noble parts. In the autumn, on the other hand, the restaurant serves Chianina raw, cooked, and stewed, or *"stracotto"* and, in the winter, boiled Chianina with a coffee infusion and braised, or *"brasato."* *"It is interesting to follow the season's trend with local products and discover new cuts every time to offer them in different ways."*

Gaetano enjoys constantly discovering new ideas, producers, and food businesses. This year he has uncovered some breeders of a heavy lamb, called "pomarancino" as they come from the town of Pomarance, which live outdoors and eat the wild forage in the fields, from those chalky crags in the nearby Balze di Volterra, which with their gullies and undulating fields have helped to make the Sienese countryside unique worldwide. *"It's a meat with a sublime aroma."* The same applies for

the kid from the Crete Senesi, roundish rock formations perfumed with thyme and calamint. *"I found an organic company that allows me to serve this exceptional meat with Tuscan Morello artichokes."* Despite being situated inland, the restaurant also serves fish. *"At certain times of the year, the fish market in Piombino supplies us with incredible products, such as the swordfish caught between the islands of Elba and Capraia, aromatic and extremely tender, which I offer to my guests from June to September."*

Naturally, the menu changes every month. *"I like to work in this way as it never becomes monotonous. After 25 years, I am still having a ball being a chef, even though it isn't easy. At the end of the day, I'm an Aquarian and I need stimuli to enjoy life."* He is meticulously careful in choosing the products that are used and he respects them greatly. His adoration of ingredients, including preserving their genuine flavors, is something that was impressed upon him in his childhood. With his Sicilian origins, he moved to Tuscany at the age of 6. *"In Ragusano, my grandparents and parents had a commercial farm where they produced oil and vegetables. From a very young age, I was used to only eating foodstuffs in season and of high quality."*

Throughout his career, Gaetano has started with the most ordinary, but most symbolic, of foods: bread. *"As a boy, when I attended high school, to top up my summer pay I went to work in an old wood-burning bakery where they made bread with cultured yeast: its aromas invaded the narrow streets of Colle Val d'Elsa. This experience left its mark on me and it has stayed with me. Today, we serve freshly baked bread to our clients that we have made on the premises with cultured yeast twice a day."* After this spell at the bakery, he had the chance to enjoy some impressive training. He attended the St. Moritz school of hotel management and worked at Kulm, the oldest hotel in the famous locality of Engadina. He also worked in the Côte d'Azur for a chef with several Michelin stars and in Paris with a famous patisserie chef to learn his secrets. After having finished various internships in other European countries and before becoming the chef at his family's restaurant, he was fortunate enough to enjoy a fantastic experience with Angelo Paracucchi: *"With him, every day was a challenge in sourcing the best products offered in the local area: a school of life.*" And even today, "*I am moved every time I go to visit our bio-dynamic companies and organic producers. This high-class product gets to me with its freshness and naturalness.*" Every Thursday, Gaetano gets up at the crack of dawn and goes to the market at Novoli or San Lorenzo to choose the very best produce. "*I sometimes take a student with me to spread this culture of the quality of ingredients. I enjoy it very much as I see the products personally. We have trusted suppliers that have understood our philosophy, also because they have eaten at least once here in the restaurant as my guests – so much that we list them all on the last page of the menu and wine lists, both for the local area and in terms of creativity.*"

You can sense that Gaetano puts his soul into his work to the point at which he enjoys telling us: "*Local cooking is a great treasure that we must preserve, restore, and relaunch, just as you do with monuments, offering the flavor once more, yet making it fresher and lighter, more suitable for today.*" In the kitchen he directs the staff, which is made up of chef de partie and commis, like an orchestral conductor. No detail escapes his attention. When creating a dish, it is the substance that counts, certainly, but also innovation, color schemes, presentation, and new cooking technologies. His cuisine is well-considered, in terms of the construction of the dishes and its style, essential and precious. A rare and natural fruit together, which recalls the elegant yet smooth Byzantine solidity of the great Maestà by Duccio di Buoninsegna, which can be admired in the *Museo dell'Opera del Duomo* in Siena.

He has a humanist temperament. "*Not only do I plan my courses on paper before making, tasting, and improving them, but I have also designed some plates for my courses. I have always personally selected – I am an aesthete by nature and a perfectionist – plates, cutlery, glasses, and also tablecloths by keeping an eye on the leading Italian companies.*" Not content with having a hobby, he follows it in all its turns and explodes it into its many aspects; he manages it from the beginning

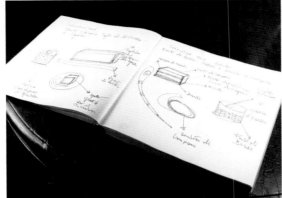

to the end. Above all, he utilizes his artistic vein. It's no wonder that he's proud of the place where Arnolfo was born. He knows that if his restaurant is now featured in the leading food guides worldwide and is visited by an international clientele, it owes this to nearby Siena, a real treasure chest of art and the perfect room with a view for every traveler, set as it is among vineyards and olive groves, expanses of wheat and aromatic meadows, bewitching medieval towns, and neighborhoods of Roman and Etruscan origin.

The courses for the menu in this book *"are my expression of the local area today."* As a starter, rabbit with apricots and almonds, a dish based on a meat that is found all over Tuscany, which uses the entire animal: the fillet, the breasts stuffed with dried apricots and goose liver, and its liver served with an apricot purée and almond foam. The sheep's Ricotta tortelli with herb and light tarragon pesto with Ricotta flan is actually an early link to the Medici family. *"I enclose the Ricotta – many shepherds bring us cheeses of extreme quality on a daily basis – in a layer of fresh pasta and offer it with a tarragon-infused sauce, a herb which grows in the Crete Senesi since Catherine de' Medici took it to France because she preferred it in her food, with Pisan pine nuts, Tuscan Pecorino cheese, and Terre di Siena extra-virgin olive oil PDO."* For the meat course, *"a variation of Chianina, the most interesting interpretation available from inland Tuscan cooking"*, the classic Florentine T-bone steak revisited without the bone, then the tartare tenderized with a knife with herbs and a poached quail's egg, and aspic served cold with baby vegetables.

For a sweet finish: *Zuccotto* with Pisan pine nuts. *Zuccotto* is a traditional Tuscan dessert, but Gaetano revamps it by serving it with a raspberry and Alchermes sauce, *"a typically Florentine liquor, made in the pharmacy of Santa Maria Novella by infusing cochineal."* A product created in another Florentine church, which, according to Giorgio Vasari, could have the mark of Arnolfo di Cambio. Yes, him again...

RABBIT WITH APRICOTS AND ALMONDS

Ingredients for 4 people
Preparation time: 1 h and 45'

1 locally sourced rabbit, weighing about 3 ⅓ lb (1.5 kg), with its liver and kidneys
1 oz (30 g) dried apricots
1¾ oz (50 g) fois gras
Scant ½ cup (100 ml) brandy
1 small bunch of herbs (such as chives and wild fennel)
Salt and pepper
1 quart (1 liter) extra-virgin olive oil
2 shallots

Scant ½ cup (100 ml) white wine
2 cups of beef stock
2 juniper berries
2 cloves
1 cinnamon stick

ALMOND FOAM
Generous ¼ cup (50 g) blanched almonds
Pinch of soy lecithin
Salt

Method

RABBIT
Use a sharp knife to cut the two loins from the saddle and remove the bones from the thighs (or ask your butcher to do this for you). Lay it all out on plastic wrap, fill with the dried apricots, roll it up, and let it rest.
Cut the fois gras into thin strips and add the brandy and chopped herbs. Season with salt and pepper. Marinate it for 30 minutes. Roll the two loins up tightly with a piece of aluminum foil to form two cylinders and arrange them in a baking dish. Bake in the oven for about 12 minutes at 275°F (140°C/gas mark 1). At the end of the cooking time, let cool completely.
To make the sauce, brown the rabbit bones (broken in pieces), 2 chopped shallots, 2 juniper berries, 2 cloves, 1 cinnamon stick in the extra-virgin olive oil in a casserole. Add the wine and let it evaporate. Pour in the stock. Cook for about 1 hour. Strain the sauce through a fine-mesh sieve and keep warm.
Brown the two loins, liver, and the thigh meat split into four parts in extra-virgin olive oil in a frying pan. Season with salt and pepper.

FOAM
Crush the almonds in a mortar, then mix them into 2 cups of warm water. Let the mixture infuse for about 1 hour. Strain the liquid into a bowl and add the lecithin and a pinch of salt. Whip with a mixer just before serving.

Serving

Pour the apricot puree onto four warm dishes, then arrange two slices of the thigh, about ¾ inch (2 cm) high and alternate with three slices of saddle of rabbit. Add a piece of liver, drizzle with the sauce, and garnish with the almond foam.

Wine pairing

Vernaccia di San Gimignano riserva, 2001 – White
Winery: Giovanni Parizzi – San Gimignano (SI)

RICOTTA TORTELLI WITH TARRAGON SAUCE AND PECORINO FLAN

Ingredients for 4 people
Preparation time: 55'

FRESH EGG PASTA
⅔ cup (100 g) semolina flour
⅔ cup (100 g) all-purpose flour
0.07 oz (2 g) egg yolks
1 whole egg

FLANS
Scant ¼ cup (50 g) fresh Ricotta
Generous ⅓ cup (50 g) fresh Pecorino, grated
1 egg white
pinch of nutmeg and pinch of salt

FILLING
Generous ¾ cup (200 g) sheep's Ricotta
Scant ½ cup (100 ml) extra-virgin olive oil
½ beaten egg
Small bunch of chopped herbs (such as chives, marjoram, wild fennel)
Pinch of nutmeg
Salt and pepper to taste

TARRAGON SAUCE
½ oz (100 g) tarragon
2 ice cubes
1¾ oz (50 g) aged Pecorino
Generous 3 tablespoons (50 ml) Terre di Siena extra-virgin olive oil PDO
Generous 1 tablespoon (20 g) pine nuts
1 pat of cold butter
Salt and pepper to taste
1¾ oz (50 g) aged Pienza Pecorino, to be grated over the tortelli

Method

PASTA
Sift the flours onto a wooden surface and shape into a mound. Make a well in the center. Pour the eggs into the hollow and knead until the dough is smooth and even. Let rest for 30 minutes in a cool place.

FLANS
Mix together the Ricotta and Pecorino. Then fold in the lightly whipped egg white with a pinch of salt. Spoon the mixture into buttered individual molds and bake in the oven for 20 minutes in a bain-marie at 275°F (140°C/gas mark 1).

FILLING
Combine the filling ingredients. Roll out the sheet of pasta using a pasta machine. The sheet must be thin and elastic. Cut it into rounds with a 3-inch (8-cm) diameter pastry cutter. Spoon a walnut-sized amount of the filling in the center, close in a half-moon shape, press down the edges, and join the two ends together.

TARRAGON SAUCE
In a blender, puree the tarragon leaves with two ice cubes, so that they don't oxidize and turn black. Blend in the Pecorino, olive oil, pine nuts, butter, salt, and pepper.

Serving

Cook the tortelli in a pot with plenty of salted boiling water for about 2 minutes. Spread a thin layer of the tarragon sauce in the bottom of the dish. Arrange six tortelli on top per person and garnish with the Pecorino flan.

Wine pairing

Chardonnay Capannelle 2004 "James Sherwood" – White
Winery: Capannelle – Gaiole in Chianti (SI)

CHIANINA BEEF, TARTARE, ASPIC, AND CARVED STEAK

Ingredients for 4 people
Preparation time: 4 h

STOCK
1½ lb (700 g) beef
1 lb (500 g) veal
1 onion
1 carrot
1 celery stalk
1 bay leaf
Salt

BEEF GRAVY (MAKES 1 LITER)
2 lb (1 kg) beef bones with
some meat, broken into
walnut-size chunks
10 oz (300 g) meat scraps, fat
removed
2½ oz (70 g) onions, diced
1¾ oz (50 g) celery, diced
1¾ oz (50 g) carrot, diced
Small bunch of bouquet
garni (sage, rosemary, stalks
of parsley and a bay leaf)
1 cup (250 g) dry white wine

Generous 1⅓ cups (350 g)
ripe chopped tomatoes
Peppercorns
2 quarts (2 liters) water
Salt

TARTARE
5 oz (150 g) steak fillet
Small bunch of herbs (thyme,
sage, and rosemary), chopped
Salt, for seasoning
Pepper, for seasoning
Ginger
Juice of ½ lemon
1¾ oz (50 g) lamb's lettuce
¾ oz (20 g) watercress
4 quail's eggs
Fleur de sel, for finishing

ASPIC
1 cheek
1 onion, chopped
1 celery stalk, chopped

2 sheets of gelatin
1 quart (1 liter) beef stock
1¼ cups (300 ml) beef
cooking juices

CARVED STEAK
1 onion
1 quart (1 liter) red wine
1 clove
1 bay leaf
5 black peppercorns
3 juniper berries
1 cinnamon stick
1 Chianina beef steak,
weighing about 1 lb (500 g),
fat and bone removed
Extra-virgin olive oil
2 cloves garlic
1 sprig of rosemary
Small seasonal vegetables to
accompany the carved steak
Fleur de sel, for finishing

Method

STOCK

Place the meat in a large saucepan and cover with cold water.

Bring the water to a boil over medium heat, covering it with a lid.

When the water comes to a boil, skim the froth, season with salt, and add the whole vegetables and the bay leaf.

Lower the heat, cover again, and simmer for about 2½ hours.

Let cool, then strain and chill for at least 3 hours.

Before using the stock, remove the layer of fat that will have solidified on the surface.

GRAVY

In a cooking pot, put beef bones, meat scraps, fat removed, onion, celery, and carrot, and a small bunch of bouquet garni. Roast it all in the oven, stirring often, until it has turned golden brown.

Skim any fat and pour in the white wine. Add the tomatoes, some peppercorns, and a little salt; pour in the water. Let simmer for 4 hours, skimming the fat continuously. Strain stock through a fine-mesh sieve.

TARTARE

Use a sharp knife to finely chop the fillet steak and mix with the chopped herbs. Season with salt and pepper, ginger, and lemon juice. Serve the dish alongside the steak, placing the beef tartare in a 2-inch (5-cm) diameter circle, pressing down the meat. Arrange the lamb's lettuce around the meat, garnish with bits of watercress, and place an hard boiled quail's egg on top of each tartare. Season with a pinch of *fleur de sel*.

ASPIC

Place the chopped onion and celery and the beef cheek with 3 quarts of water in a pot. Bring to a boil and simmer at approximately 250°F (120°C) for about 4 hours. Remove the cheek. Filter the stock, dissolve the gelatin in 1.5 liters of it. Adjust the salt and let cool slightly. Cut the cheek, fat removed, into 4 even pieces and arrange it in four disposable molds with a carrot brunoise and a zucchini. Fill to the brim with the stock and cool in the refrigerator.

CARVED STEAK

Sauté the coarsely chopped onion in a saucepan. Add the red wine, spices, and bay leaf. Let the wine evaporate almost completely. Pour in the beef gravy and cook over low heat until a runny sauce forms. Strain liquid into a pot and keep warm.

Sear the beefsteak in a hot, heavy, cast-iron pan with extra-virgin olive oil, clove of garlic, and rosemary for about 2 minutes on each side. Bake in the oven for about 3 minutes at 400°F (200°C/gas mark 6). Let rest for about 10 minutes, covering it with foil to keep it warm before carving it. Carve the steak, arrange on warm plates with the sauce underneath. Add seasonal vegetables. Season with *fleur de sel* and extra-virgin olive oil.

Wine pairing

Chianti classico "Poggio alle Rose" 1998 Coralia Pignatelli della Leonessa – Red
Winery: Castell'in Villa – Castelnuovo Berardenga (SI)

ZUCCOTTO WITH ALCHERMES AND PISAN PINE NUT ICE-CREAM

Ingredients per 8 persone
Preparation time: 40' – Resting time: 24 h

BISCUIT BASE
3 tablespoons (45 g) all-purpose flour
3 tablespoons (45 g) ground almonds
3 eggs yolks
Generous ¼ cup (60 g) sugar

ALCHERMES DIP
⅔ cup (150 g) sugar syrup
Generous ⅓ cup (83 g) Alchermes
Generous 2 tablespoons (37 g) water

FILLING
4 egg yolks
1 whole egg
½ cup (100 g) sugar
Generous ¾ cup (200 ml) water
1 cup (250 g) cream, whipped
Grated zest of 1 lemon
Juice of ½ lemon

PISAN PINE NUT ICE-CREAM
Generous 1⅓ cups (350 g) fresh milk
Generous ½ cup (110 g) superfine sugar
1 tablespoon glucose
2 teaspoons (10 g) powdered milk
Scant ½ cup (80 g) Pisan pine nuts, well toasted
⅔ cup (150 g) cream

SAUCE
2 cups (200 g) raspberries
½ cup (100 g) sugar
Generous 3 tablespoons (50 ml)
Alchermes, scant 2 fluid ounces

Plain yogurt, for serving
Fresh raspberries, for serving

Method

BISCUIT BASE

Beat the egg whites to stiff peaks with the sugar. Fold in the 3 egg yolks, the flour and the ground almonds until well combined. Spread the batter out to ⅛ inch (5 mm) thick on a parchment-lined baking sheet. Bake in the oven for about 10 minutes at 350°F (180°C/gas mark 4). Let cool completely. Line the disposable spherical molds with the biscuit base.

FILLING

Beat the egg yolks and egg in a bowl with a mixer. Meanwhile, cook the sugar and water in a small saucepan over medium heat to 250°F (120°C). Use a whisk to gradually beat the sugar syrup into the eggs until the mixture has cooled completely. Fold in the whipped cream and grated lemon zest and juice.
Fill the molds lined with the biscuit base and freeze.

ICE-CREAM

Place the milk, sugar, glucose, and powdered milk in a pan and cook to 175°F (80°C). Toast the pine nuts and stir them into the mixture to infuse for 24 hours. Gently reheat the mixture, strain, setting the pine nuts aside (stir them back into the ice cream at the end). When the ice-cream has become creamy, mix in the whipped cream. Pour the mixture into an ice-cream machine and churn according to the manufacturer's instructions.

RASPBERRY SAUCE

Place the raspberries and sugar in a saucepan. Bring to a boil and cook until syrupy. Puree and strain the sauce when it has cooled, then stir in the Alchermes.

Serving

Unmold the zuccotto onto plates with the raspberry sauce and plain yogurt. Decorate the Pisan pine nut ice-cream with fresh raspberries and plain yogurt.

Wine pairing

"Solalto" 2004 late vintage – Dessert wine
Winery: Fattoria Le Pupille – Istia d'Ombrone (GR)

FRANCA CHECCHI

RESTAURANT ROMANO - VIAREGGIO (LUCCA)

What moves her emotionally is also the inspiration of her cooking. *"It gets to me when I reach the end of the quay on my bike in the spring or when fall has just begun and I turn around to admire the view of the Apuane Alps, especially at sunset,"* Franca Checchi confides, chef and co-owner, with her husband Romano Franceschini, of the restaurant *Romano* in Viareggio, the elegant social capital of Versilia. Viareggio is famous not just for its beautiful beaches and green pine forests, but also for its remarkable Liberty Style and Art Deco buildings. For Franca, the combination of the products from the plain and mountains with those from the sea is the pièce de résistance of her local cuisine.

"'A lovely family, an affectionate, yet not affected, staff, a terrific cellar and, above all, extremely delicious food.' This is how the director of a well-known food guide began a review of our restaurant, filling us with satisfaction and pride. We believe that these few words are the exact snapshot of the 42 years of our business." So many years of business riding on the crest of a wave are no joke, but they bear witness to a love that hits the spot, which does not lose luster, but continues to improve itself over time. *Da Romano* was established on December 15, 1966. *"It was given this name because it was the tradition at that time to name the restaurant after the person who managed it. My husband and I opened it; we were just kids at the time, he was 23 and I had just turned 16."* Romano had already worked as an employee in various restaurants in Viareggio, where he behaved as if they were his own. *"He never questioned his shifts and never asked for an increase in his wages because the most important thing was for him to learn to run a restaurant."* From the outset, Romano managed the dining room, while Franca took care of the kitchen. They are now helped by their son, Roberto, an expert sommelier, who works in the dining room with his father.

"In 2001, to maximize the space and revamp the look, the restaurant was closed from January to the end of June for complete renovation. Up until then, the two dining rooms were just the one space, while the number of tables was reduced from 23 to 15, and the kitchen was moved to the back of the building." Also here, in Franca's realm, many changes were made. "The workspace was extended and new ovens and machinery were installed to make it as easy as possible for those working behind the scenes."

The style of the new *Romano* makes use of the colors of the enchanting coast of Versilia and its charming hinterland, from the rustic mountains of Garfagnana to the calm Lucchesia, from the Valdarno strip to the plateau of the Pizzorne. "Frosted blue glass doors, which recall the shades of the sea, act as an entrance into the restaurant. Other dividing walls in worked glass, which depict the elements of air, water, earth, and fire, split the restaurant into groups of tables, with magnificent colors that add warmth to the atmosphere. A nod to the beach of Viareggio is given by the walls in a sand finish color. The entrance is enhanced by sculptures by Igor Mitoraj and paintings by Riccardo Benvenuti. And that's not all. The restaurant also puts art on the menu, reproducing the painting "Beach at Viareggio" by Moses Levy on the front cover, which looks impressive in the dining room."

Special care is also given to the table settings. "A range of shapes and materials are combined from time to time with the different dishes, depending on the composition and color of what is served. Crystal glasses best enhance the many wines on offer in the cellar; while the tablecloths in quality beige linen emphasize the colors of the floor in light teak and travertine, materials which are typical of the area, associated with the maritime world." After all, *Romano*, with its Michelin star and membership in the prestigious Le Soste association, is like a boat that sails towards a cuisine, the only thing that hasn't altered after the restaurant's makeover, consisting of the aromas and flavors of Versilia, with recipes old and new that are alternated in the kitchen. "The restaurant's long-standing dish par excellence is baby squid stuffed with vegetables and shellfish."

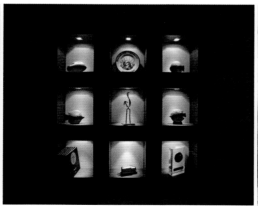

Given that the restaurant is actually in Viareggio, which, in addition to being a seaside resort, is a town also famous for its carnival. The carnival started in 1873 and is regarded as the most significant of its kind in Italy and Europe with its allegorical papier-mâché carriages that parade along the seaside promenade. However, Franca doesn't go over the top to amaze, apart from the dishes that she makes with her own hands. *"I'm not looking for artifice; on the contrary, I strive to make the dishes reach the diner through a series of easily identifiable processes, which are done simply and with transparency."* This doesn't mean "straightforward" cooking, but achieving the main aim of your research with simplicity. In short, if your cooking style has an urban setting, it would be based on the symmetry of a chessboard like that of Pietrasanta, the most historically and artistically interesting town in Versilia, known all over the world for its marble carving since the sixteenth century with Michelangelo.

"Everything that's served owes its success to the widespread appeal that I am able to give to the dishes and the first-class quality of the products I use. Our cuisine is traditional, appetizing, light, and innovative from certain perspectives; innovative in terms of how it's presented and the original combination of ingredients that aims to win over customers." A moving experience, like being in the center of the famous Piazza del Mercato in Lucca, with the houses laid out in the oval shape of the ancient Roman amphitheater. Here ingredients appear on the plate, complying with the historical outline and placing one beside another in perfect unity; often they come from the land and the sea. For example, fried zucchini flowers stuffed with scampi, where homegrown vegetables are combined with shellfish, or mantis shrimp served with lard of Colonnata, a small village in the Apuane Alps, and a flatbread (*farinata*) containing Tuscan cabbage, a vegetable that is often found in Tuscan food. Franca also pays tribute to the variety coming from her territory's landscape in the Garfagnana spelt soup with vegetables and fish, which is the restaurant's *Piatto del Buon Ricordo*, and the Lucca-style *Garmugia*, a typical spring stew with monkfish, and turbot with Empoli artichokes, mint, and other herbs.

"There aren't many traditional dishes from Viareggio, also because we're not allowed to prepare certain ingredients any longer as they have been 'outlawed' in accordance with the directives of the European Union, such as date shells and salted dolphin meat, or musciame". In terms of the dishes that have survived, Romano serves some of these in paper as tradition commands, without altering them at all. There are the spaghetti with arselle (donax clams), stewed maruzzelle (whelks), Viareggio-style fish stew – "it's based on the dish from Leghorn, cacciucco, but we add fish removing the bones and, while being a succulent stew, it has a more delicate flavor" – stuffed muscoli (mussels), cicale di mare (mantis shrimp) soup, and spaghetti with coltellacci (razor clams) sauce. On the restaurant's sweet trolley, there is room for scarpaccia viareggina, which is a sweet cake made from zucchini, and an Easter cake with rice and chocolate. "There are other typical dishes that are still prepared in the area, such as clams with egg, a clam broth with rice, a peasant's fish broth, stockfish alla marinara, salt cod eaten with leeks, pasta tordellata (homemade pasta with ricotta, Swiss chard and meat sauce), matuffi or pallette (rather soft polenta with meat sauce on top), and stuffed chicken neck."

The chef makes other delicacies for those who don't like fish. These dishes are always prepared using strictly Tuscan ingredients, from Chianina beef to lamb from Zeri, bred in the village of the same name in Lunigiana, from Bruciato Cinta Senese pigs to the season's game, from the white truffles of San Miniato to the classic Lucchesia vegetable soups, the homeland of Romano, which are also the ideal basis to taste uncooked extra-virgin olive oil, one of the food products that this province is rightly famous for.

Franca's training was speeded up by her talent. "At the beginning, I worked for a while alongside a chef who Romano had employed when the restaurant opened. We worked in parallel, I was still very young and I had to find the right rhythm. After a couple of years, when the first chef left and after several attempts to work with other chefs, I decided to take control of the situation." She has never worked or done any training at other restaurants. "I can regard Franco Colombani as a teacher, the founder and creator of *Linea Italia in Cucina*, one of the first associations of selected restaurants in Italy. We became part of the association in 1980, which brought together the then élite of Italian catering, the only member restaurant south of the Po at that time. We met every month to talk about our experiences and to spread the 'faith' in a high-quality regional cuisine. I listened to my colleagues as if they were elder siblings and I compared myself to them in terms of cooking techniques and practices and the ingredients they used, thereby learning a lot despite not working in other restaurants."

Romano takes care of provisioning the ingredients for the restaurant. *"Every morning, when he leaves home to go to the markets in Viareggio, he has shopping lists in his pocket that I prepare for him the evening before. He goes around the fishermen, fish warehouses, and fishmongers, and doesn't come back until he's found the fish that gives back in terms of the right kind of quality. On his travels, he always pays a visit to the area around the Burlamacca canal, where the boats that have cast their nets during the night come ashore."* He does the shopping several times a day, when the fishing boats return in the morning and at sunset, and so on all week long. This is his routine even on Saturdays and Sundays, when the big boats do not go out fishing, but the little ones do. *"The shopping ritual ends up in the kitchen, where the fish is immediately cleaned and prepared, despite being cooked later to order."* On the other hand, the majority of vegetables come from small farmers in the areas of Capezzano, Camaiore, and Pietrasanta, a small flood plain behind Viareggio, where the *schiaccioni* beans stand out in terms of quality, which Franca loves to cook with mantis shrimp.

The four dishes chosen for this book are all linked to the area. As a starter, there's baby squid stuffed with vegetables and shellfish. The pasta course is spaghetti with arselle and Viareggio-style fish stew features as the main. For dessert, there's Tuscan cantuccini semifreddo with Vin Santo di Carmignano custard. A menu for a king, it would even bring color back into the cheeks of the gentle Ilaria del Carretto, who has been entombed for centuries in the superb marble masterpiece by the sculptor Jacopo della Quercia in the Cattedrale di San Martino in Lucca.

BABY SQUID STUFFED WITH VEGETABLES AND SHELLFISH

Ingredients for 4 people
Preparation time: 40'

2 lb (1 kg) baby squid
5 oz (150 g) carrots
5 oz (150 g) zucchini
8 mantis shrimp, or other large shrimp
Extra-virgin olive oil
2 clove garlic
Chile pepper, salt, and pepper, to taste
2 basil leaves
5 large calamint or mint leaves
2 slices of bread, crumbs removed

Method

Clean the baby squid carefully, removing the eyes and the quills, but leaving the tentacles attached. Clean the carrot and zucchini and chop them finely; set aside.

Clean the mantis shrimp carefully, peeling and deveining them (but leaving heads and tails on). Saute the shellfish in a pan with 2 tablespoons of extra-virgin olive oil, 1 colve of garlic, and chile pepper for a few minutes.

Remove the shellfish from the pan, and remove the heads and tails, leaving only the meat; reserve the cooking oil in the pan.

Place the carrots, zucchini, basil leaves, calamint, and garlic in the shrimp cooking oil. Sauté over low heat until the vegetables have softened. Add the bread, cut into small pieces, and cook until they have softened and absorbed the liquid from the vegetables.

Process the shellfish meat briefly in a food processor. Add the vegetable, bread, and oil mixture from the pan and blend for several seconds.

Wine pairing

"Montecarlo" DOC 2007 – White
Winery: Franceschini – Lucca (LU)

SPAGHETTI WITH ARSELLE

Ingredients for 4 people
Preparation time: about 30'

2 lb (1 kg) live arselle clams
1 clove garlic, crushed
Extra-virgin olive oil
1 chile pepper, seeded and finely chopped
Calamint or mint
¼ cup (60 ml) good-quality dry white wine
14 oz (400 g) spaghetti
1 sprig of parsley, finely chopped

Method

Carefully clean and wash the arselle under running water after having
soaked them beforehand for 24 hours in seawater, or very salty water.
Sauté the garlic in the oil in a deep frying pan for 1 minute.
Add the chopped chile, calamint leaves, and arselle.
Cover the pan and cook for 3 minutes, shaking the pan occasionally
to open the arselle.
Add the white wine and cook, uncovered, for 5 minutes until it has
evaporated.
Meanwhile, cook the spaghetti in boiling water until not quite al
dente. Drain; add pasta and parsley to the pan with the clams; saute
until pasta is al dente.

Wine pairing

Candia dei Colli Apuani 2007 DOC – White
Winery: Cima – Romagnano (MS)

VIAREGGIO-STYLE FISH STEW

Ingredients for 4 people
Preparation time: 1 h

1½ lb (700 g) mollusks, such as cuttlefish, octopus, and baby squid
8 spottail mantis shrimp, or other large shrimp
3⅓ lb (1.5 kg) fish with bones, such as gurnard, weaver, scorpion fish, stargazer,
dogfish, or conger
1 piece of spicy chile pepper
2 cloves garlic, lightly crushed
⅓ cup (80 g) extra-virgin olive oil
Scant ½ cup (100 ml) white wine
1¼ cups (300 g) fresh tomatoes
Salt
Freshly ground black pepper
Chopped parsley
Fish stock or water, as needed
8 slices of farmers' bread, toasted

Method

Carefully clean the mollusks, removing the eyes and quill. Cut the cuttlefish into
pieces; leave the tentacles of the octopus whole. Peel the shrimp, leaving the heads
attached.
Clean, gut, scale, and fillet the fish carefully (or ask your fishmonger to do this for you).
If they are large, cut them into pieces.
Sauté the chile and the garlic in the extra-virgin olive oil until the garlic turns pale gold.
Discard the garlic and add the mollusks, letting them getting the flavors. Pour in the
white wine and cook until evaporated.
Add the tomatoes. Season with salt and pepper. Cook over low heat for 15 minutes.
Add the fish and shrimp.
Cook over low heat for 10 minutes more, without stirring to avoid breaking up the fish.
Add the parsley halfway through and add a little fish stock or water, if needed to finish.
Ladle the stew evenly into serving bowls, topping each serving with two slices of toast.

Wine pairing

"Chianti Classico" Castello di Ama 2005 – Red
Winery: Castello di Ama – Gaiole in Chianti (SI)

TUSCAN CANTUCCINI SEMIFREDDO WITH VIN SANTO DI CARMIGNANO CUSTARD

Ingredients for 4 people
Preparation time: 1 h – Resting time: 12 h

SEMIFREDDO
4 egg yolks
½ cup (100 g) sugar
Scant ½ cup (100 g) milk
3½ oz (100 g) nougat paste (can be purchased in specialist food stores among the ice-cream products)
3½ oz (100 g) Tuscan cantuccini cookies, broken into small pieces
1¼ cups (300 g) whipping cream, whipped

CARMIGNANO CUSTARD
1 cup (250 g) milk
4 egg yolks
Generous ¼ cup (60 g) sugar
Generous 1 tablespoon (20 g) Vin Santo di Carmignano

Method

SEMIFREDDO
Beat the egg yolks and sugar in a metal bowl. Bring the milk to a boil in a small saucepan over medium heat. Slowly whisk the hot milk into the egg mixture; transfer to the top of a double-boiler to cook. Remove the mixture from the heat when it is about to boil. Pour immediately into a mixer and beat until it becomes quite thick and smooth. Pour into a large bowl and whisk in the nougat paste (a little at a time to avoid lumps from forming) and the cookies. When the mixture has been well combined, slowly fold in the whipped cream with a wooden spoon. Pour the semifreddo into individual silicon molds and freeze for at least 12 hours.

CUSTARD
Bring the milk to a boil. Use a whisk to beat the egg yolks and sugar in a bowl. Continue whisking, slowly mixing in the boiling milk. Pour the mixture into a saucepan. Cook, whisking constantly, until it reaches 185-195°F (85°-90°C). Remove from the heat; let the temperature drop to 160°F (70°C) and add the Vin Santo, mixing with a wooden spoon. Let cool before serving.

Serving

When you are ready to serve, remove the semifreddo from the freezer and let stand several minutes at room temperature. Turn it out onto a plate and decorate with some crumbled cantuccini and the Vin Santo di Carmignano custard.

Wine pairing

Vin Santo di Carmignano – Dessert wine
Winery: Tenuta di Capezzana – Carmignano (PO)

Curiosity

Almond cookies, also called *cantucci*, are one of the most famous desserts in Tuscany. It is still tradition today to serve them, accompanied with Vin Santo, for special occasions or to send them around the world as a Christmas gift. They are ancient in origin. Some say that they are direct descendants of the melatelli, which were made in medieval times with wheat flour, water, and honey; eggs and almonds have been added to this mixture over the centuries. The recipe, then as now, was noted in the eighteenth-century cookbook by Amadio Baldanzi, but the distribution of these rustic cookies is owed to Antonio Mattei, nicknamed Mattonella, who opened a bakery for the preparation of pasta and desserts in the mid-nineteenth century on the main street in Prato.

FRANCESCO BRACALI

RISTORANTE BRACALI - MASSA MARITTIMA (GROSSETO)

Francesco Bracali, chef and co-owner, with his brother Luca, maître d'hôtel, of the restaurant *Da Bracali* certainly isn't lacking in imagination and courage. The restaurant is in Ghirlanda, a small fraction of Massa Marittima, the precious town situated in the heart of the Colline Metallifere ("metal hills"), in the Tuscan Maremma. The structural complexity and brave combinations of Francesco's dishes recall the town's splendid and unusual Piazza del Duomo. Like the irregular star-shaped space has a strong visual impact due to the asymmetrical view of the most important buildings, such as the imposing cathedral of San Cerbone, a masterpiece of Pisan Romanesque. In Francesco's dishes, every ingredient creates surprising flavors due to atypical combinations and unusual perspectives.

"My cuisine," he asserts, "is fairly creative. I include four or five ingredients in the same dish. It certainly isn't simple, but I believe that the technique helps, when done exclusively and in the right measure, to make sure that a traditional dish is given a new life, which is more suited to our times and our food trends." Reworking a dish "doesn't mean interrupting the link with the territory, but finding a way to offer it in a more elegant and original way, without uprooting it." On one side, his dishes reflect the origins of Maremma; on the other hand they demonstrate innovative aspects. "I love to try out new culinary marriages, uniting tastes, consistencies, and cooking methods. The final result is perhaps a little complex, but I think it's balanced. In the end, my dishes must blend together into a single flavor, without ever needing further explanations. The message of a great chef, like a great artist, must reach one and all." After all, if he hadn't decided to go down the catering route, he would have definitely chosen a job of an artistic nature. "Working as a chef, my aesthetic part flows out that was already there deep-seated inside me. As I see it, cooking is an art in the true sense of the word as it goes beyond merely preparing a recipe, but to its creation, structure, and presentation."

Francesco also put his creative nature to work in the restaurant's latest makeover, which took place in 2004. *"While maintaining some rustic characteristics, such as the old beams on the ceilings and the Tuscan terracotta floor, the restaurant is furnished with a neoclassical feel, with lots of trimmings that recall the style of Versace."* Pure white Flanders tablecloths, bag hooks, and flecked wall coverings, which contrast with the mother-of-pearl walls, black wooden columns and golden friezes. The armchairs and console tables are juxtaposed with silk gauze drapes that vary from bordeaux to orange, and cream-colored sideboards. An elegant environment, yet played down by the large window through which one can see the state-of-the-art kitchen, where steel is the undisputed main feature.

The restaurant, which resembles an English cottage externally immersed in the wooden hills of Grosseto, was taken over by Francesco's parents, when he was still a child. At the time, given its scenic location, it was a classic country trattoria with a tobacconist's shop and a bar. The initial leap towards a different type of catering, which coincided with the first renovation of the establishment, was in 1997 when Francesco and his brother took on the management of the restaurant. *"The transformation wasn't easy at the beginning. It went from being a business with a very high income and low labor costs to one with 20 covers and 10 employees, as well as a type of cuisine that was rather innovative at that time, which wasn't easy to offer in a place far away from built-up areas. However, we were lucky to have two parents who, despite the many difficulties, always supported us and were rightly proud of us when we were awarded with a Michelin star in 1999."*

Francesco is *"100 per cent self-taught,"* not having attended hotel institute or any courses or having done any internships in Italy or abroad. *"I've always been very involved in my parents' business. It's inevitable that you become sucked into it when the restaurant is family-run."* In the beginning it was his mother who taught his the basics of the trade and who gave him some of the area's typical recipes, from stewed wild boar, the main star of the cuisine of Grosseto, to the classic Maremma-style tortelli filled with spinach and Ricotta and served with meat ragù. *"Ever since I was*

a child, I did however know that if I were to do this job, I would do it in a personal way." That's why

his cuisine is genuinely traditional, while not being that straightforward. It offers a glimpse of times

gone by, but lives on refined contemporary research. A bit like the *Parco dell'Uccellina*, a sanctu-

ary of the Maremma landscape, where the elegant lyre-horned cows graze beneath the tall umbrel-

la pine trees and, in the swamps of the River Ombrone, you can see horses in the wild and many

migratory birds. It's a natural habitat, yet one that's organized in terms of its landscape.

Francesco only uses local ingredients, such as Tuscan extra-virgin olive oil, local vegetables and

herbs, lamb – confirming the strong pastoral nature of the Maremma – Chianina beef, the many

homemade cheeses, and fish and shellfish from the nearby Tyrrhenian coast. There are also the top

quality guinea fowl from Leghorn, pigeons, which are one of the best-loved birds in Tuscan cuisine,

capocollo, a typical regional salami, and chocolate, which he purchases from the famous Pistoia-

born chocolatier Roberto Catinari. *"On the day when the restaurant is closed every week I concen-*

trate on going to visit various suppliers in the Grosseto and Pistoia areas. In some case, given that

we're far away from the towns, I'm obliged, as it were, to turn to large companies, although they

always supply me with top quality products. However, when I have the time, I go and discover the

small-scale producers in the area. It's great to have personal contact with them, especially to find

out more about the ingredients that we go on to buy." He also uses more difficult products, offer-

ing them in a top class restaurant, such as *lampredotto*, a special type of tripe that's the tradition-

al peasant dish of Florentine cuisine. *"For example, we currently have red shrimp on the menu, which are cooked* sous vide *at a low temperature, with a cornet of onion stuffed with* lampredotto *and Mozzarella di Bufala.*"

Francesco looks after the ingredients he uses. He demonstrates the same finesse as his Etruscan ancestors – Massa Marittima stands in a place loaded with history, next to the so-called *Riviera degli Etruschi*, from the nearby necropoli of Vetulonia to the archaeological excavations of Ansedonia – who seemed to rear their pigs to the sound of the flute because the animals were happier and therefore their meat was more exquisite. "*I studied the breading of pork in great detail. I fished out some old books on Tuscan herbs and set out to find them, from lavender to rosemary, drying them. Then I added other dried flavors, such as tomatoes, onions, olives, and garlic. Using precision scales I made a mixture of decidedly Tuscan herbs and flavorings to mix into the grated, dried bread with which to bread the pork.*"

The chef passes his whole working day in the kitchen. "*I get up around 8 am and come straight here to make fresh bread, including the bread made with sourdough starter and the more modern breads with olives or tomato. I take the shortest of breaks in the afternoon, which is more often than not filled up with other tasks related to the restaurant, from updating the website to writing out a recipe for a magazine or creating a new dish with ingredients for the next season. Once the service has finished in the evening if some of our customers stop in the lounge for spirits and cigars, I'll happily have a chat with them.*" He immediately sees the dishes in his mind's eye and they don't usually change much when he prepares them. "*The idea remains the same, therefore so do the combined flavors, perhaps the presentation and composition alters.*"

The dishes of the menu for this book also came about out of intuition. The starter is a triptych of Chianina beef carpaccio with three sauces. "*Tenderized with a knife and prepared traditionally, Chianina beef is served in three different ways: topped with grated, dried bread and chopped olives, accompanied with a chive sauce; as a meatball with a brunoise of pear and sundried toma-*

toes inserted in the center, with a green sauce; and topped with ground dried mangoes and a roll of ginger-flavored phyllo pastry, served with classic mayonnaise."

For the pasta course, there's rigatoni pasta filled with *capocollo*, served with a Lucchesia spelt sauce. Made using typically Neapolitan pasta, but dressed in a Tuscan style. *"The unique element of the dish is that a very thin layer of raw scallop is laid on top of each piece of pasta with a drizzling of licorice-flavored oil when the rigatoni come hot out of the oven. The saline hint of the sea goes together very well with the pasta's outstanding filling."* The sauce is a classic spelt soup, the flagship of regional gastronomy, blended and beaten with the area's extra-virgin olive oil.

For the meat course, there's roasted chicken cooked in two ways; a new take on the classic roasted chicken served at family Sunday lunches in Tuscany. *"I flavor the legs with the classic herbs used in a Tuscan roast. It's then placed in a vacuum pack and I let it cook overnight. I then put it through a salamandra, a special tool used to cook foods au gratin. That's how a leg stays soft and juicy on the inside, but is crispy on the outside. The same applies to the breast, which is wrapped in Cinta Senese pork cheek and then browned in a frying pan just before serving. I then make a double stock with the chicken bones, which I use to whip up a celery root puree with Tuscan extra-virgin olive oil."*

In Tuscany, *"the zuccotto is the only traditional dessert that I find interesting, apart from certain types of dry cookies like cantucci."* In this instance, he makes it with a white chocolate mousse and raspberry jelly inside, served with a dill sauce. He often uses herbs, vegetables or pulses in his desserts. For example, he also makes a rice tart with a white bean and lemon sauce and coffee ice-cream. *"As the zuccotto is rather 'loaded' in terms of its calorie content, dill, a classic herb in my area, helps to make it lighter and more digestible."* A menu in which Francesco sets new ideas alongside old designs, a little like the architects Alessandro Manetti and Carlo Reishammer did in 1836 when they designed the neoclassical church of San Leopoldo in the nearby town of Follonica, the only church in Italy to have cast iron porticoed entrances, rose windows, and apses.

A NEW TAKE ON CHIANINA BEEF CARPACCIO

Ingredients for 4 people
Preparation time: 1 h

12 oz (350 g) sirloin steak
4 tablespoons soy sauce
Salt and pepper, to taste
4 tablespoons extra-virgin
olive oil

GREEN SAUCE
4 oz (120 g) parsley
3 anchovy fillets
2 cloves garlic
1 tablespoon salt-cured
capers
Scant 1 cup (50 g) fresh
breadcrumbs
Generous 3 tablespoons
(50 g) vinegar
Scant ½ cup (100 g) extra-
virgin olive oil
Pepper to taste
2 hard-cooked egg yolks
Pinch of sugar

THREE TYPES
OF MAYONNAISE
•*Classic*
1 egg yolk
Pinch salt
1 tablespoon cider vinegar
Scant ½ cup (100 g) oil
•*Chive*
Classic + 2 chive stalks,
chopped
•*Green*
Classic + green sauce

GINGER-FLAVORED
PHYLLO PASTRY
8 phyllo pastry squares,
measuring
1½-inches (4-cm) on each
side
Ginger-infused oil

FRIED BREAD WITH OLIVES
1¾ oz (50 g) bread
4 olives, chopped
1 clove garlic
1 bay leaf

TOMATO TARTARE
4 quenelles of tomato
tartare

TO SERVE
Herbs, such as chives,
Dried ground mangoes
2 teaspoons (10 g) pear,
diced
1 teaspoon (5 g) sun-dried
tomatoes in oil
Pane carasau (Italian
flatbread)
4 whole Pachino or cherry
tomatoes

Method

Cut up the sirloin with a knife. Drizzle in the soy sauce and oil. Season with salt. Use your hands to work the meat and create three different shapes for each portion: a cone, cylinder, and square.

GREEN SAUCE

Prepare the parsley, removing the large stalks and only keeping the best leaves. Wash, dry, and chop it finely with a *mezzaluna*. Chop the anchovies (having already removed the bones and washed them if salt-cured), garlic, and capers (rinsing them well to remove any excess salt).
Dampen the breadcrumbs with the vinegar. Squeeze out any excess and push through a strainer. Mix all these ingredients together well with the oil. Season with salt and pepper to taste. Add, if desidered, the hard-cooked egg yolks, which have also been pureed.

THREE TYPES OF MAYONNAISE

Beat the egg yolk with a pinch of salt and some of the vinegar. Gradually pour in the oil, whisking until the desired consistency is reached. Season with salt and add more vinegar to taste.
Divide the mixture into three parts. Leave 1 portion plain, add the chopped chives to the second part, and add a teaspoon of green sauce to the last portion.

GINGER-FLAVORED PHYLLO PASTRY

Spread 4 squares of phyllo pastry with the oil infused with the ground ginger and top each square with another pastry square.
Wrap the phyllo pastry around cylinders used to make four small cannelloni. Bake in the oven at 350°F (180°C/gas mark 4) for 5 minutes.

FRIED BREAD WITH OLIVES

Grate the bread. Brown in the oil with the garlic and bay leaf in a frying pan for 10 minutes. Season with salt and pepper. Turn the mixture out onto kitchen paper to remove the excess oil. Add the chopped olives.

TOMATO TARTARE

Cut a cross into the bottom of each tomato; blanch them in boiling water for several seconds. Cool them immediately in ice water and remove the skins and seeds.
Chop the pulp finely with a knife. Season with salt and sugar. Let drain in a strainer for 10 minutes.
Use two teaspoons to shape the drained tomatoes into small quenelles.

Serving

Dip the carpaccio cylinder in the fried bread with olives. Arrange on a plate, accompanied with the chive mayonnaise, a chive and a tomato quenelle to decorate.
Arrange a carpaccio cone on the plate and sprinkle with the dried ground mangoes. Drizzle with the plain mayonnaise and serve with a small roll of ginger-flavored phyllo pastry.
Cut a small pocket in the center of the carpaccio square and insert a pear and some chopped sundried tomatoes. Garnish with wild fennel and spoon the green mayonnaise into the remaining space on the plate.
Serve the carpaccio with the pane carasau in the center of the plate and a whole tomato to garnish.

Wine pairing

Franciacorta brut *couvée* Annamaria Clementi 1998 – White spumante
Winery: Ca' del Bosco – Erbusco (BS)

RIGATONI FILLED WITH CAPOCOLLO AND LUCCHESIA SPELT SAUCE

Ingredients for 4 people
Preparation time: 1 h 40'

24 durum wheat rigatoni pasta tubes
4 scallops
Salt

FILLING
5 oz (150 g) Tuscan *capocollo*
5 oz (150 g) Mozzarella di Bufala or Burrata

SPELT SAUCE
1 cup (100 g) *farro lucchese* (spelt)
2 onions
2 stalks celery
2 carrots
1 clove garlic
1 bay leaf
1 sprig of rosemary
⅓ oz (10 g) Cinta Senese pork cheek
Scant 3 tablespoons (40 ml) extra-virgin olive oil
2 cups (500 ml) vegetable stock, as needed
Salt

ORANGE REDUCTION
1 orange
2 peppercorns
1 bay leaf

LICORICE OIL
Scant 2 tablespoons (25 g) extra-virgin olive oil
½ teaspoon (3 g) Amarelli powdered licorice

TO GARNISH
2 stalks celery
Extra-virgin olive oil
Salt and pepper
Orange zest

Method

FILLING

Grind the capocollo with the Mozzarella or Burrata cheese in a meat grinder and mix well. Cover with plastic wrap and keep in the refrigerator.

SPELT SAUCE

Soak the spelt in cold water overnight.

The next day, drain. Cook the spelt in water with whole 1 carrot, 1 celery stalk, 1 onion, garlic, bay leaf, rosemary, and salt for 2½ hours.

Drain the spelt and reserve the cooking water.

Brown the diced pork cheek in a little oil. Add the finely chopped carrot, celery, and onion left. Sauté over medium heat for 5 minutes.

Add the drained spelt. Cook for a few minutes. Add half the cooking water and vegetable stock to cover the spelt. Cook for about 40 minutes. Puree in a blender and season to taste, adding water, if needed, to reach the desired consistency.

ORANGE REDUCTION

Cook the orange juice with the peppercorns and bay leaf in a small saucepan over low heat until it has reduced to one-third.

RIGATONI

Cook the pasta in unsalted boiling water for 10 minutes.

Let cool and stuff them with the filling. Heat them in a steam oven for 4–5 minutes.

CELERY

Cut the celery into small diamonds. Blanch in boiling water for 1 minute. Cool immediately under cold running water. Sauté in a little oil with a pinch of salt.

Serving

Cover each hot rigatoni with a slice of raw scallop and drizzle with a little licorice-flavored oil.

Pour the spelt soup in the bottom of the plate and position the rigatoni in a spoke-like pattern radiating out from the center. Between one piece of pasta and another, add a drop of the orange reduction and two celery diamonds.

Garnish with the orange zest in the center and a drizzle of extra-virgin olive oil.

Wine pairing

"Bianco" 2003 – White
Winery: Massa Vecchia – Massa Marittima (GR)

ROASTED CHICKEN COOKED IN TWO WAYS

Ingredients for 4 people
Preparation time: 2 h

1 chicken, weighing about 4
to 4½ lb (1.8–2 kg)

BREASTS
Salt and pepper
1 small branch of rosemary
2 sage leaves
10 slices of Cinta pork cheek
Extra-virgin olive oil, for
sauteing

LEGS
Salt and pepper
1 small branch of rosemary
1 small branch of marjoram
2 sage leaves
⅓ cup (80 g) chicken stock
Generous 1 tablespoon (20 g)
Marsala
2 teaspoons (10 g) white
wine
2 tablespoons (30 ml)
extra-virgin olive oil

ROASTED POTATOES
2 potatoes
Extra-virgin olive oil
Salt and pepper

CHICKEN STOCK
Chicken bones and leftovers
1 onion
1 carrot
1 stalk celery
2 stalks parsley
1 bay leaf
Peppercorns
Ice
Salt

CELERY ROOT PUREE
1 celery root
½ onion
Generous 1 tablespoon (20
ml) extra-virgin olive oil
Generous ¾ cup (200 ml) milk
Concentrated chicken stock

Salt and white pepper

LEMON OIL
1 bunch of lemon balm
Generous 3 tablespoons
(50 g) extra-virgin olive oil

TOMATO TARTARE
1 tomato
1 teaspoon chopped green
onions
8 capers
4 black olives
2 basil leaves
Generous 1 tablespoon (20
ml) extra-virgin olive oil
alt and pepper

CHILE PEPPER TEMPURA
2 green chile peppers
Ice-cold water
Flour (for tempura)
Oil, for frying
Salt, to taste

Method

Bone the chicken and separate the breasts from the legs. To cook the breasts, season with salt and pepper. Arrange the skinless breasts on top of the herbs and wrap in the pork cheek slices. Place in a vacuum pack for sous vide cooking. Cook in a steam oven at 143°F (62°C) for 4 hours. When the time has passed, remove the breasts from the pack, reserving the cooking liquid. Sauté the chicken in a little oil in a frying pan until the pork cheek becomes crispy. Keep warm.

LEGS

Divide the two legs into quarters. Season with salt and pepper. Add the chopped herbs. Make a marinade with the stock, Marsala, and white wine, and a little extra-virgin olive oil. Place the legs in a vacuum pack with the marinade. Cook at 143°F (62°C) for 12 hours. At the end of the cooking time, remove the legs from the pack, reserving the cooking liquid. Bake the chicken legs in the oven with the potatoes cut into ⅓-inch (1-cm) cubes, seasoned with salt, pepper, and oil, at 375°F (190°C/gas mark 5) for 15 minutes. Adjust the flavor of the cooking liquid in a small saucepan over low heat and reduce if needed.

CHICKEN STOCK

Brown the vegetables with the herbs in a little extra-virgin olive oil. In a separate pan, brown the chicken bones and leftovers. Add the vegetables and ice. Cook for 2 hours, skimming the foam occasionally. Strain and let cool.

CELERY ROOT PUREE

Peel and dice the celery root. Sauté ½ chopped onion in the oil in a small saucepan. Add the celery root. Season with salt and pepper. Cover with the milk and bring to a boil. Drain and puree in a blender. Spread out the puree on a sheet of parchment paper. Let dry in the oven at 175°F (80°C) for about 2 hours. Transfer the dried mixture to a bowl. Re-hydrate with the chicken stock and puree with a handheld immersion blender, gradually adding the extra-virgin olive oil.

LEMON OIL

Blanch the lemon balm in boiling water for 10 seconds. Let cool immediately in ice water. Drain, dry, and puree with the oil. Emulsify in a bowl using a handheld immersion blender.

TOMATO TARTARE

Cut a cross in the bottom of the tomatoes; blanch them in boiling water for a few seconds. Remove the skins and seeds. Cut up the pulp with a knife. Season with salt and sugar. Add the remaining ingredients. Shape the tomatoes into 4 small quenelles.

CHILE PEPPERS

Cut the chile peppers in half lengthwise. Dip in the flour and cold water mixture. Fry in very hot oil. Drain and dry on kitchen paper. Season with salt and arrange the tomato quenelles on top.

Serving

Arrange the legs and ½ breast in the center of each plate. Pour the reserved cooking sauce over the top. Place the chile pepper on the side with the roasted potatoes. Finish with the celery root puree and lemon oil.

Wine pairing

Chianti classico DOCG 2001 – Red
Winery: Castello di Ama – Gaiole in Chianti (SI)

WHITE CHOCOLATE AND RASPBERRY MOUSSE ZUCCOTTO WITH DILL SAUCE

Ingredients for 4 people
Preparation time: 1 h + 1 night resting

SPONGE CAKE
5 oz (150 g) egg yolks
⅓ cup (70 g) sugar
Generous 1 cup (270 g) egg whites
Scant 1 cup (135 g) all-purpose flour, sifted

DIP
Generous 3 tablespoons (50 g) water
⅓ cup (70 g) sugar
2 teaspoons (10 g) Maraschino

WHITE CHOCOLATE MOUSSE
1 sheet gelatin
4 oz (125 g) white chocolate
Generous ¾ cup (200 g) cream

RASPBERRY JELLY
1 sheet gelatin
Generous ⅓ cup (100 g) raspberry puree
Generous 1 tablespoon (20 g) sugar

DILL SAUCE
5 egg yolks
Generous ⅓ cup (85 g) sugar
Generous ¾ cup (200 g) milk
1 small bunch of dill

TO DECORATE
1 tray of fresh raspberries
Small chocolate or caramel decorations

Method

SPONGE CAKE

Beat the egg yolks with half of the sugar. Beat the egg whites with the remaining sugar to stiff peaks. Fold the beaten whites into the egg yolk mixture. Fold in the sifted flour. Spoon the mixture into a pastry bag fitted with a smooth tip. Pipe out in lines on parchment paper to form a solid rectangle.
Bake in the oven at 400°F (200°C/gas mark 6) for 6–8 minutes.
Remove from the oven and immediately cut out 4 rounds using a pastry cutter for the base of the dessert.

DIP

Make a syrup by heating the water and sugar. When it comes to a boil, remove from the heat and let cool. Add the Maraschino.

MOUSSE

Soak the gelatin in cold water. Drain and squeeze dry.
Melt the chocolate in the top of a double boiler.
Heat half the cream in a separate pot and stir in the gelatin until dissolved.
Add the remaining cream to the melted chocolate, whisking. Add the cream and gelatin mixture and let mousse rest in the refrigerator for at least 1 hour.
At the end of this time, the mixture will have set. Whip until it forms a soft mousse.

RASPBERRY JELLY

Soak the gelatin in cold water. Drain and squeeze dry. Heat 3 tablespoons of raspberry puree with the sugar. Stir in the gelatin until dissolved. Add the remaining puree and spread out on a baking sheet to form a film. Set in the refrigerator.

SAUCE

Beat the egg yolks with the sugar until foamy.
Bring the milk to a boil and gradually pour over the beaten yolks, whisking constantly.
Return the mixture to the heat and heat to 185°F (85°C).
Remove from the heat, add the dill; let marinate for 10 minutes.
Transfer to a blender and puree; strain through a fine-mesh sieve.

Serving

Dip the sponge cake rounds in the Maraschino syrup. Use them to line the zuccotto molds. Fill the molds, alternating with layers of mousse, raspberry jelly circles, and fresh raspberries. Top the zuccotto with the white chocolate mousse.
Leave overnight in the refrigerator.
Turn the zuccotto out upside-down onto a plate. Serve with the dill sauce, some fresh raspberries, and the chocolate and caramel decorations.

Wine pairing

Moscato d'Asti "Bricco Quaglia" – Dessert wine
Winery: La Spinetta – Castagnole Lanze (AT)

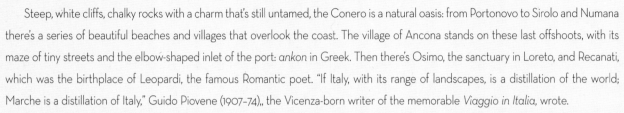

THE CUISINE OF MARCHE

The first sight you usually have of Marche is the Adriatic Coast, a long ribbon of golden sand. The only interruption is Monte Conero, once an island and now, due to years of erosion, a promontory, which, according to the locals, has assumed the appearance of an enormous whale ready to dive into the billows. At the end of the Conero strip, there are the unique Scoglio della Vela and the Due Sorelle, small stacks which can only be reached by sea.

Steep, white cliffs, chalky rocks with a charm that's still untamed, the Conero is a natural oasis: from Portonovo to Sirolo and Numana there's a series of beautiful beaches and villages that overlook the coast. The village of Ancona stands on these last offshoots, with its maze of tiny streets and the elbow-shaped inlet of the port: *ankon* in Greek. Then there's Osimo, the sanctuary in Loreto, and Recanati, which was the birthplace of Leopardi, the famous Romantic poet. "If Italy, with its range of landscapes, is a distillation of the world; Marche is a distillation of Italy," Guido Piovene (1907-74),, the Vicenza-born writer of the memorable *Viaggio in Italia*, wrote.

Gentle and undulating, the smattering of hills between the sea and the Apennines is the most representative stretch of Marche. The area was once a forest; it became a small strip of cultivated land until the Roman era, when small towns and villages blossomed. Each one with its own personality: Ascoli, noble and austere, the ancient villages with their towers and cobbled streets, Urbino, the ancient capital, elegant and distinctive, and Camerino, the ancient university town. There's also the village of Montefeltro among cultivated fields, woods, and fluvial gravel. Here history speaks to us through perched castles, glimpses back in time, and scenes of everyday life long gone in the past, as if time had stood still, maintaining the charm of distant and genuine flavors. This is the taste of the region.

Indeed Marche, as indicated by the plurality of the name, preserve the different realities which they forged, a land of many peoples, of dukes and *signorie*, with a free spirit, a treasure trove of culture and art scattered here and there: castles, fortresses, monasteries, and sanctuaries; sea and land. The cuisine is as varied as the territory, which combines simple, homemade flavors with the memory of foreign influences.

Extremely rich and substantial, the soups from Marche are reminiscent of the region of Emilia with the widespread use of fresh egg pasta, often served with sauces made from fresh or dried mushrooms and chicken giblets. There's a whole range of recipes for rich baked lasagne, which are also called *incassettate* here. The most famous is the typical *vincisgrassi*, oven-baked pasta with very thin, almost seethrough sheets of pasta, which seems to owe its name to Windischgratz, the Austrian prince, conqueror of the siege of Ancona. Oral history tells us the dish invented by his chef to celebrate the end of the hostilities. A specialty of Ancona is the delicately flavored *minestra di lumachelle*, small pellets made from a mixture of breadcrumbs, ox marrow, cheese, eggs, and a little nutmeg. Tripe soup is also part of the repertoire of Marche, which is cooked with chopped lard and aromatic herbs, with plenty of marjoram.

The coastal area is abundant in fish and the food scene is a celebration of fish and seafood dishes. The masterpiece of marine cuisine in Marche is the *brodetto*, made in numerous variations. In Ancona 30 different varieties of fish are used, which are generally small in size: baby mullet, baby sea bream, mackerel, monkfish, baby eel, baby cuttlefish,. All the smaller fish are caught when they gather together in the bottom of the nets. The fish are floured and cooked with plenty of red vinegar and arranged on a bed of toasted bread just before serving. In Porto Recanati, the *brodetto* is based on cuttlefish, with tope, cod, and striped mullet, without the use of flour and vinegar, but with the strong flavoring of wild saffron and garlic, rubbed on bread that hasn't been toasted. There are also many types of mollusks, shellfish, and seafood. *Pauri* are prickly, horrible-looking yet delicious crabs, which are excellent when boiled. Oysters, seafood, and *crocette* (a type of clam) are often cooked *in porchetta*, one of the region's typical recipes, fundamentally the same as stockfish *in potacchio*, a sauce made from garlic, oil, rosemary, white wine, and tomatoes, which is also served with chicken. *Muscioli* are large mussels, particularly succulent, from the sea around Ancona. They are oven-baked *alla marinara* (with parsley and lemon juice) .

The other type of Marche cooking is meat-based, especially lamb and kid, generally cooked simply, roasted or on a spit. It is the aromatic herbs and which give these dishes an extremely special character. Here the use of *pilotto* is widespread, a cooking technique wherin a piece of lard is wrapped in butcher's straw paper and lit on fire and placed over roasting meat. The melted fat drips onto the meats being cooked on the spit below. Flavor is also given to chickens and pigeons, which are called *pistacòpi* in Marche, in this traditional way.

Pork is one of the best-loved meats of the region. Roast suckling pig is regarded as one of their most delicate and delicious specialties. Here it is cooked in an original way, rather than whole on a spit, like in Romagna, Lazio, and Umbria. In Marche, suckling pig is completely boned, laid out flat and seasoned with salt and black pepper. It is then stuffed with aromatic herbs, including *erba cavallina*, a type of wild fennel that smells of aniseed, reassembled and stitched up and cooked in the oven for several hours. In Macerata, *Vitellino al Chianti* is made with tender milk-fed calf, called *Mongana*. Among other masterpieces, the recipe for *Tournedos alla Rossini*, beef medallions with Gruyère, prosciutto, Bechamel sauce, and truffle, is attributed to the great Pesaro-born Gioacchino Rossini (1792–1868), the internationally renowned composer.

The leading typical cheese in Marche is the rich and delicious Casciotta di Urbino PDO. After ninety days of ripening, it stands out due to its strong and pronounced greasiness and an intense and persistent aroma with a slight sweet fragrance. Other cheeses are: Pecorino, with its marjoram-flavored curd; Slattato; and Raviggiolo, which is typical of Montefeltro. The charcuterie is also important, sustained by the widespread breeding of pigs: Prosciutto di Carpegna PDO, delicately flavored with juniper; the salami and soppressate from Fabriano, the old capital of paper; the sausages from Filottrano, inland from Ancona. However, the most typical is undoubtedly *Ciauscolo* (see box) due to its recipe and special flavor.

The vegetables grown in Marche are delicious: from the *cardi gobbi*, cardoons which are particularly tender, white, and fleshy, the fundamental ingredient for the traditional Macerata-style *Parmigiana di Gobbi*; to the Jesi cauliflowers in their early variety, compact, white, and delicate; as well as the tasty, thorn-less purplish artichokes; and the *paccasassi*, an aromatic herb that is exclusive to these lands, and is pickled in vinegar like bell peppers; *rinci*, sweet cardoons with a flavor similar to turnip; *roscani*, long and thin, similar to forest asparagus, ideal with eggs. Finally, it's impossible to forget the area's famous olives, the delicious specialty of Ascoli. They are large, sweet, and tender, served stuffed, breaded, and fried.

There are many old recipes for desserts from Marche of a rather rustic nature. *Migliaccio* is a pie made from pig blood with sugar and orange zest. There's *Frustega*, a simple cake made with flour, eggs, and sugar, served with *sapa*, a sauce consisting of must, which is used in many of the region's desserts. *Lattaiolo* is a cream of milk and flavored sugar, whereas *ciambellone* is a traditional aniseed-flavored ring. *Sughetti*, soft cookies made from polenta flour, and *becciate*, decorated with sultanas and pine nuts, should also be remembered. In Macerata, a special *cicerchiata* is made, a ring consisting of small balls of leavened dough the size of garbanzo beans – hence the name in Italian (*ceci* means garbanzo beans) – soaked with white honey, made solely from Sulla flowers, a spring herb that flourishes in the region.

The most famous wine in Marche is Verdicchio, with a greenish-yellow color – hence the name (*verde* means green in Italian) – with an alcohol content that varies between 11 and 13 degrees. It's produced in the area of Castelli di Jesi: Cupramontana, Monteroberto, Castelplano, and Castelbellino. It is one of the prized wines to be served with fish, and is excellent when aged for more than three years. Other local wines include Sangiovese delMarche, the delicately flavored, dry, and slightly sour Bianchello, and the curious *Vin Cotto*, made from concentrated must, hence its very high alcohol. One of the most famous Italian liqueurs is also produced in Marche: Anisetta, distilled with aniseed with its extremely intense aroma, cultivated on the hills of the hinterland.

CIAÙSCOLO

The singular name comes from the Latin *CIBUSCULUM*, meaning small food. It consists of a fine pork mixture flavored with garlic, herbs, thyme, and fennel, which has been ground several times. Initially common in the provinces of Macerata, Ascoli Piceno, and Ancona in particular, it is now produced by a few craftsmen in Visso and in the areas close to Abruzzo. Its consistency recalls the tradition of spreadable French pates. It should be served with young red wines with a sharp acidity, good alcohol content, and mid structured. Lacrima di Morro d'Alba and Colli Pesaresi Novello and Rosso are ideal.

MICHELE BIAGIOLA

RESTAURANT ENOTECA LE CASE - MOZZAVINCI (MACERATA)

Biagiola, the chef of the restaurant *Enoteca Le Case* in Mozzavinci, a small municipality of Macerata, is well-considered, yet not overly thoughtful, linked to the past, but brimming with new sensations. It recalls the painting of Lorenzo Lotto who depicted an ancient miracle in the famous *Annunciation*, which can be seen in the *Museo Civico* of Villa Coloredo Mels in the nearby town of Recanati, with everyday naturalness and anxious modern revisitation. *"My cuisine is well thought-out, without necessarily resorting to the scientific aspect that the art of cooking seems to require today,"* he explains. *"This doesn't mean that I don't feel up-to-date. My approach is inevitably young, given that I'm only 35 years old. However, when I learn a new technique, I'm not as excited as when I'm able to rework a dish from my land using basic techniques."* He means land in terms of his memories. *"I was born in Macerata and my cuisine renews all those flavors which I'm able to develop mentally as I've known them since I was a child, flavors which belong to my past."*

Enoteca Le Case is situated in the beautiful Le Case tourist center, a small farming village. The business includes a restaurant with traditional cooking, a hotel, a few small apartments immersed in greenery, and a *Beauty and Wellness* oasis. A stone's throw away from the splendid natural paths, the riviera of Monte Conero, the Monti Sibillini national park, *Grotte di Frasassi*, and places of great artistic and historical interest, like the medieval parish churches of San Claudio and Santa Maria in Val di Chienti, the complex is set in the bewitching landscape of the Marche hills, cultivated as though they were private gardens, in between the blue of the Adriatic Sea and the mountain ridge of the Central Apennines.

Only open in the evenings, the *Enoteca* has been groomed down to the last detail and transmits a pleasing rustic ambience to the customer – terracotta floors, beamed ceilings – while also being elegant and bedecked with modern furnishings. It has a professional service, a cellar where over 1,000 labels of wine coming from all four corners of the earth are stored and two sommeliers in the dining room, but it also has a youthful feel, which is perhaps due to the young owner, Francesca Giosuè. Opened in 2005, the *Enoteca* already shines with a Michelin star. Over the course of a few years, the restaurant has become one of the best in Marche. *"We have achieved certain goals which fill us with satisfaction and I'll take the recognition as regards the cuisine. However, there's an entire organization without which I wouldn't have been able to achieve any type of result, from Mrs Elvia Pelagalli and her husband Marcello Giosuè, who deserve recognition for their business skills, to daughter Francesca, the true heart of the whole complex, who manages the dining room in an impeccable style, with enthusiasm and obstinacy, and sous chef Giacomo Messi and the boys who work with me everyday, putting energy and love into what they do, as well as all those who have worked and contributed to the development of this restaurant over the years before going on to choose different paths."* He sometimes feels as though he's the student of his staff. *"I consult them and, if somebody doesn't like a new dish, I may decide not to include it on the menu."*

After having graduated from hotel institute, Michele, who was fascinated and intrigued by the possibility of learning and discovering new ingredients, did *"some important work experience placements with Vincenzo Cammerucci at restaurant Lido Lido in Cesenatico, Marc Veyrat at Megève in Haute-Savoie, and David Zuddas at Digion in Burgundy."* He continues to do internships today, despite having been executive chef of *Le Case* for eight years.

When the *Enoteca* opened, Michele was already working in the restaurant, where he offered traditional, *" we understood that they were the dishes that people would continue to order,"* and innovative dishes, despite still being attached to the area. *"At a certain point, the management decided to separate the two types of catering in order not to mix the environments and clientele."*

Today the restaurant's customers find the so-called typical dishes, as if you were going for a meal at your grandmother's. For example, for Sunday lunch, there's *vincisgrassi* on the menu, the traditional Macerata-style lasagne, made with offal and various herbs. This is an historic dish, which was mentioned by Antonio Nebbia, the famous chef from Macerata, in his eighteenth-century recipe book, the pinnacle of food and wine to which the majority of the area's restaurants aspire. Michele offers this dish as it was, *"while trying to personalize it as little as possible."* On the other hand, those who choose the *Enoteca* are seeking a traditional, yet creative, cuisine, *"made with the same quality ingredients: organically grown products with special focus on ingredients of the cooking of the past and wild herbs. As she's a botanist, Mrs Pelagalli is the one who procures all our herbs, which are used in our dishes."*

Among the house specialties are *"the 'egg that's solid on the outside and liquid inside', served depending on the time of year with the ingredient that excites us the most, and the 'garden on a plate,' our welcome dish for customers, which is the daily expression of what we're growing at that time."* The latter consists of a pea and green onion puree, on which sorrel stalks and red beets, sprigs of marjoram, mint and holy basil, lovage leaves, fava and wild spinach leaves, stalks of fool's parsley, borage and mallow flowers, thinly sliced asparagus, and blanched and shelled field beans are all arranged, drizzled with extra-virgin olive oil and finely chopped wild fennel, with tomato toasts on top. *"My creed of cooking is to be led by the hand through the seasons, uniting culture, personal experiences and love for the products of our land and making sure that you can gather a different aroma and flavor in every teaspoonful."* Like in the church of the Cistercian monastery of Santa Maria di Chiaravalle in Fiastra, a few kilometers from the *Enoteca*, the simplicity and poverty makes the call to contemplation and prayer stronger, the 'garden on a plate', in its essentiality, makes one concentrate on the priceless range of vegetables that the land offers us. *"All tastes being equal, Francesca and I prefer making vegetarian dishes. Nowadays people go over the top with meat and fish and there's a sort of lasciviousness at the table. For a while now, we've had a vegetarian menu that we groom with the same love – if not more than others."*

Since the beginning, the *Enoteca* has also featured reworked traditional dishes on the menu, such as pigeons, called *pistacòppi* here, stuffed *"according to Ermete's recipe,"* a historic shopkeeper in Macerata who passed away in 1983, *"as a tribute to this character who was deeply attached to the city. When housewives asked him how long they should cook the pulses for, he answered: 'Have a walk around the walls and when you get back, they'll be cooked'."*

Michele favors local ingredients in his cuisine. *"There's such a wide range of products that I find it hard to use them all."* As well the *ciauscolo*, the soft salami that is typical of Macerata, Marche offer excellent cheeses, such as the pecorino from Monti Sibillini, prized meats like *Vitellone Bianco dell'Appennino Centrale*, an extraordinary variety of fruit and vegetables, from the Macerata apricots to the Fano and Jesi cauliflowers, the large Ascoli olives, and the extra-virgin olive oil. *"Working with these ingredients everyday, it's often the case that I revise a local classic in passing in a spontaneous way. It just happens."*

The chef's working day starts at dawn and ends at sunset, if not physically, then definitely mentally. *"If a dish comes to mind, I certainly don't let it go, not even when I'm sleeping."* He pursues and tweaks it until it has the same refined composure, innovative drive, and the capacity to respect the classic equilibrium of the *Palazzo Ducale* of Urbino, the town in Marche that acted as the gathering place of the Italian Renaissance. *"In the morning I plan the day's organization with the staff. A traditional restaurant is also open at lunchtime, but I don't often take care of the lunch service. I follow the purchases instead and experiment with some new dishes for the Enoteca, on which I actively work from the afternoon onwards."* In terms of fish, he's in close contact with a supplier who goes to the fish market at Civitanova Marche everyday. *"I often go with him, at 4:00 am, not so much to buy the fish directly, but to understand what the sea has to offer."* As regards the vegetables and meat, *"we actually buy very little and always from commercial farms located near to us. Le Case has 25 hectares of land that almost completely covers our needs."* It is home to the rearing of wild boar, calves, sheep, rabbits, capons, goats, donkeys, and pigs. There are also market gardens, olive groves, and a herb garden, as well as a lake with ground water for river crayfish and lake sturgeons.

The menu for this book is the happy outcome of a revamped memory. The starter of sandy seafood salad with old-fashioned dressing, *"came from a memory that I had of a seafood salad with pickled vegetables that I ate in the kiosks along the beach when I was young."* It is made in the traditional way and presented on a bed of edible sand, made from semolina, tapioca starch, and durum wheat flour, oil, and seaweed. *"It represents our sea bed, which is particularly sandy, but it's also a sort of payback for all those times when we haven't enjoyed a fish dish due to the sand that's ended up between our teeth."*

In the *spaghetti with Porto Recanati and San Benedetto chowder*, the chef has fused together the recipe for a fish stew from these two areas on the coast of Marche, a typical traditional maritime dish. *"In Porto Recanati, they make it with* zafferanella, *which is a sort of wild saffron, and cherry tomatoes; while in San Benedetto del Tronto, it's made with green tomatoes and bell peppers."* In the meat course, the stuffed pigeon is made according to Ermete's recipe, *"the acidity of wild strawberries and the iron of wild spinach or buon Enrico has been added"* to the full flavor of the stuffing, which features *ciauscolo*, eggs, and local herbs, such as mountain savory herb.

In the dessert menu, the upside-down Rosa gentile apple tart is offered. The caramelized fruit is arranged in the center of the plate and topped with pastry cream, vanilla and cinnamon granita crystals, and crumbled shortcrust pastry. It's ,made with an old variety of apple from inland Marche.

it's a long-lasting tradition of food. It's a menu that Father Matteo Ricci, the sixteenth-century Macerata-born Jesuit missionary, mathematician, and cartographer, who lived for many years in China, would happily have presented to the court of the Ming. Certain of showing the innovation of Italian cuisine, which has evolved because it is respectful of its history.

SANDY SEAFOOD SALAD WITH OLD-FASHIONED DRESSING

Ingredients for 4 people
Preparation time: 40'

SAND
1 tablespoon (15 g) semolina
1 tablespoon (15 g) durum wheat flour
1 tablespoon (15 g) tapioca starch
2 teaspoons (10 g) dried seaweed, finely chopped
1 tablespoon (15 g) extra-virgin olive oil

PICKLED VEGETABLES
1 quart (1 liter) white wine vinegar
¼ cup (50 g) sugar
3 tablespoons (50 ml) extra-virgin olive oil
Scant 3 tablespoons (40 g) salt
⅓ oz (10 g) asparagus, washed and cut into short lengths
⅓ oz (10 g) red bell peppers, washed and diced small
⅓ oz (10 g) yellow bell peppers, washed and diced small
½ oz (15 g) shallot, washed and cut into wedges
⅓ oz (10 g) eggplant peel, washed and diced
½ oz (15 g) green beans, washed and cut in half lengthwise

FISH
4 mantis shrimp, or other large shrimp
4 medium scampi
8 oz (250 g) small-medium cuttlefish, cleaned

TO SERVE
Small pieces of seaweed
Extra-virgin olive oil
¼ oz (2 g) chopped parsley

Method

SAND
Mix together all the ingredients to make a smooth mixture.
Wrap it in a piece of parchment paper and freeze to -0.4°F (-18°C).
Break up the frozen mixture, scraping it with the blade of a knife. Bake in the oven at 350°F (180°C/gas mark 4) for 12 minutes.

PICKLED VEGETABLES
Bring the vinegar, sugar, oil, and salt to a boil in a saucepan. Cook each vegetable separately, keeping them crunchy.
Remove each vegetable with a slotted spoon and let cool in ice water. Drain and dry with a cloth.

FISH
Steam the mantis shrimp and scampi for 3-4 minutes. Shell them and set the flesh aside. Boil the cuttlefish for 10 minutes and cut into strips.

Serving

Mix together the fish, pickled vegetables, parsley, the seaweed, oil, and crispy sand.

Wine pairing
Verdicchio di Matelica 2007 – White
Winery: Fattoria Colle Stefano – Castelraimondo (MC)

SPAGHETTI WITH PORTO RECANATI AND SAN BENEDETTO CHOWDER

Ingredients for 4 people
Preparation time: 1 h 30'

½ oz (15 g) yellow bell peppers, blanched, peeled and diced small
½ oz (15 g) red bell peppers, blanched, peeled, and diced small
5½ oz (160 g) green tomatoes, peeled, seeded, and diced
5½ oz (160 g) red tomatoes, peeled, seeded, and diced
40 mussels, cleaned
3½ oz (100 g) cuttlefish, cleaned and diced
3½ oz (100 g) green onions, cleaned and chopped
2 teaspoons (10 g) garlic, chopped (peeled and green central part removed)
2 dried chile peppers

4 sprigs of parsley, washed
Generous 3 tablespoons (50 g) extra-virgin olive oil for the sauce
Salt to taste
4 oz (120 g) weever fish (or other chowder-appropriate fish), filleted, reserving bones
25 wild saffron strands
4 mantis shrimp, or other large shrimp
4 medium scampi
9¾ oz (280 g) spaghetti
2 fresh basil leaves
¾ oz (20 g) fresh marjoram, washed
1 tablespoon (15 g) extra-virgin olive oil, for finishing

Method

Open the mussels, and remove the beards that grow between the half-shells. Scrape the mussels well to remove any barnacles and calcium deposits. Wash well, changing the water several times. Cook the mussels in a little water in a saucepan, covered, over the heat. As soon as the mussels open, remove from the heat and remove the half-shells.

Cook the cuttlefish, chopped onion, garlic, chile peppers, parsley, and the diced tomatoes and bell peppers in the oil in a large saucepan over medium heat for about 6-7 minutes. Season with salt and pour in 3 cups (750 ml) of cold water. Add the weever fish bones and bring to a boil.

Remove the bones and add the mussels, saffron strands, mantis shrimp, scampi, and weever fish fillets at the same time. Cook for another 2-3 minutes.

Remove and set aside all the fish, apart from the cuttlefish.

Cook the spaghetti in plenty of salted boiling water until three-quarters cooked. Drain and transfer to the chowder and cook for another 3-4 minutes. Add the reserved fish at the end, as well as the basil, marjoram leaves. Drizzle with oil to finish.

Wine pairing

"Podium" Verdicchio dei Castelli di Jesi classico Riserva 1999 – White
Winery: Garofoli – Loreto (AN)

PISTACOPPU WITH STUFFING, STUFFED PIGEON INSPIRED BY THE RECIPE OF ERMETE, A MASTER SHOPKEEPER IN MACERATA

Ingredients for 4 people
Preparation time: 45'

4 pigeons

SAUCE
1 green onion
1 carrot
2 tablespoons (30 g) extra-virgin olive oil
1 quart cold water
2 sprigs of mountain savory, or regular savory
12 wild strawberries
Cooking juices of the cooked pigeon

ROASTED STUFFED PIGEON
Breasts, legs, wings, hearts, and livers of the pigeons
1 teaspoon (5 g) prosciutto
¼ cup (60 g) extra-virgin olive oil

Scant ½ cup (100 ml) vino cotto
2 teaspoons (10 g) ciauscolo salami, or other salami
8 sprigs of mountain savory or regular savory
1 egg
Pinch of ground nutmeg
16 thin slices of pork cheeks
Salt to taste

TO SERVE
3½ oz (100 g) wild spinach, blanched in plenty of salted water for 1 minute
2teaspoons (10 g) extra-virgin olive oil
12 wild strawberries
Salt to taste

Method

SAUCE

Use a sharp knife to bone the pigeons, splitting up the legs, breasts, and wings; set aside. Brown the green onion, carrot, and the pigeon bones and cavities in the oil in a saucepan over medium heat. Turn up the heat and cook over high heat for about 7–8 minutes. Pour in cold water and the sprigs of savory. Bring to a boil, reducing it all to make a thick sauce. Add the wild strawberries. Strain through a fine-mesh sieve and reserve the liquid (you will combine it later with the pigeon cooking juices).

PIGEONS

Cook the livers, hearts, and prosciutto in the oil over high heat for 2 minutes. Add the vino cotto and let it evaporate. Add the ciauscolo, savory leaves, and egg. Cook for 1 minute. Add the nutmeg and let cool. Chop them up finely with a knife. Stuff the legs with the filling, wrapping them with the slices of pork cheek. Bake in the oven at 350°F (180°C/gas mark 4) for about 12 minutes. Brown the pigeon wings in oil in a separate frying pan. Add the breasts and cook for another 2 minutes. Season with salt. Bake in the oven at 350°F (180°C/gas mark 4) for 4 minutes.

Serving

Arrange the wild spinach on the bottom of the plate and dress with oil and salt. Top with the various pieces of pigeon, fresh strawberries, and the natural cooking juices combined with the pigeon sauce.

Wine pairing

"Kurni" Marche rosso IGP 1998 – Red
Winery: Oasi degli Angeli – Cupra Marittima (AP)

UPSIDE-DOWN ROSA GENTILE APPLE TART

Ingredients for 4 people
Preparation time: 2 h - Freezing granita: 2 h

SHORTCRUST PASTRY
2¾ cups (400 g) flour
1 egg yolk
¼ cup (50 g) sugar
½ cup (75 g) all-purpose flour
Scant 2 tablespoons (25 g) butter

CARAMELIZED APPLES
Scant ⅓ cup (70 ml) water
¾ cup (150 g) sugar
2 tablespoons (30 g) butter
1¾ lb (800 g) Rosa gentile apples, peeled and diced
½ teaspoon (3 g) powdered agar agar

VANILLA AND CINNAMON GRANITA
Generous 1 tablespoon (18 g) sugar
Generous 3 tablespoons (50 ml) water
⅕ cinnamon stick
⅕ vanilla pod

PASTRY CREAM
Scant ½ cup (100 ml) milk
1 teaspoon (5 g) lemon zest
1 egg yolk
Scant ½ cup (70 g) all-purpose flour
Scant 2 tablespoons (25 g) sugar

Method

CRUMBLED SHORTCRUST PASTRY
Mix the flours, eggs, butter and sugar together until crumbly. Bake at 350°F (170°C) for about 30 minutes.

CARAMELIZED APPLES
Warm the water and sugar in a small saucepan over medium heat to 275°F (135°C). Turn off the heat, add the butter and let it melt. Add the apples and return to the stovetop over low heat for 2–3 minutes, mixing constantly. Remove from the heat and finish with the agar agar, mixing it well. Divide the apples, placing them in 4 molds of the desired size. Let cool in the refrigerator for at least 30 minutes.

GRANITA
Mix the sugar and water in a small saucepan. Bring to a boil and add the cinnamon and vanilla. Remove from the heat, cover, and let cool to room temperature. Strain through a fine-mesh sieve and pour the liquid into a container to about ⅓-inch (1-cm) thick. Freeze to –0.4°F (–18°C). Break it up into small pieces just before serving.

PASTRY CREAM
Bring the milk to a boil with the lemon zest. Meanwhile, beat the egg yolk with the flour and sugar. Slowly whisk the boiling milk into the egg mixture. Return to the pan in which the milk was boiled and cook cream gently to 180°F (82°C) over low heat, whisking constantly, until it has thickened. Let cool to 37.5°F (+3°C).

Serving

Turn the apples out in the center of the plate. Serve with the cream, granita, and the crumbled pastry.

Wine pairing

"Tor di Ruta" Verdicchio dei Castelli di Jesi Passito DOC 2001 – Dessert wine
Winery: Terre Cortesi Moncaro – Montecarotto (AN)

THE CUISINE OF UMBRIA

Umbria is an ancient landscape that is rich in spirituality. Gentle green hills are bound with small medieval stone villages among vineyards and olive trees. Splendid and harsh mountains stand tall in the heart of the Apennines, perfumed with forests, crystal-clear waters, and silence. There's the enchanting mirror of *Lago di Trasimeno*, which preserves Etruscan and Roman relics, valleys of poplars, holm and downy oaks, and numerous country homes immersed in the sun-kissed peace of the countryside.

And yet in Umbria, the homeland of Saint Benedict, Saint Francis, Saint Rita, and Saint Clare, not only do you feel the charm of the transcendent, but also that of the material culture, the flavors and art of cooking in particular.

The cornerstones of Umbrian food and wine, which are created by the combination of a remarkable variety of environments, lie in the Umbrian extra-virgin olive oil PDO, which has a color that varies from green to yellow depending on the olive variety and a fruity flavor, which also ranges from light to strong and from bitter to piquant. Also of importance is the truffle, the true regional pièce de résistance, black in Norcia and Spoleto, white in the Eugubino Gualdese area; these are almost as famous as the Alba truffle, and are hunted down with dogs and also pigs which posess a keen sense of smell. Norcia, the hometown of Saint Benedict, also owes its fortune to the Umbrian pig, with its delicious and compact meat thanks to its diet of forest acorns. It's a beautiful town with a backdrop of severe mountains and framed by solid fourteenth-century walls, a true gourmet destination and the capital of pig breeding. Its fame is such that *Norcino* (that is to say, a resident of Norcia) has become a synonym of a butcher's shop throughout Central Italy. In the north, the *Norcini* were the skilled craftsmen who moved from farm to farm. They knew how to butcher and prepare meat for salamis.

The widespread presence of meat in the cuisine – which also includes veal, calves which are roasted, young bulls and pigs as roasted suckling pig, typical of Lazio, but even tastier and aromatic here – has sustained the fine tuning of special cooking methods, such as *alla ghiotta*. The *ghiotta* or *leccarda* is the shallow tray that is placed beneath the spit to collect the grease that drips down during cooking. Red wine, vinegar, slices of lemon, sprigs of sage, and black olives are also added to the container. This is done to release aromas as the grease drips into the tray that then penetrate the meat and flavor it like a sauce at the end of the cooking time.

Soups in Umbria are simple and rustic, aromatic with herbs. The spelt soup is of note, cooked in a stock made with the bone of a leg of pork. Maccheroncini are famous in terms of dried pasta, made from strips of pasta wrapped around knitting needles and served with truffle sauce. *Risotto alla Norcina* is also famous, with the aroma of black truffle. The use of *pizze* made from bread dough is typical of the area, enriched with lots of cheese, mild or strong, prosciutto and salamis.

Charcuterie also plays an important role, especially Prosciutto di Norcia IGP, with its lingering flavor. It is made from mainly lean meat, taken from fresh legs of pork and seasoned with salt, pepper, and garlic for about one month and then aged for one year. Charcuterie is the basis of excellent starters and is used in making ragù, fillings, pizzas, and savory pies. The salami, characterized by rather large lardons, stand out in the midst of the finer-grained meat mixtures. Produced in the winter, the *mazzafegati* are very characteristic, made with pork liver sausage and orange zest, pine nuts, and golden raisins and seasoned with sugar. This is the legacy of Renaissance cuisine, where sweet and savory are blended together in unique flavors.

Originating in the mountains, there's a product that owes all its goodness to the particular geology and climate of its homeland: the exquisite Castelluccio di Norcia lentils with protected geographical indication (see box). There are also many cheeses, especially in the Norcia and Valnerina areas, such as Pecorino with its strong flavor, Ricotta Salata, and mixed cow's Caciotta. Fall brings a large amount of game to Umbrian tables, which is made traditionally, mainly roasted or in *salmì*. There's hare, partridge, lark, and thrush from the Apennines, which smell of truffle and are stuffed with the herbs gathered in the woods, giving the dish a delicate aroma and a definite flavor of the forest. Roasted turkey stuffed with lark is another local delicacy.

Teeming with fish, *Lago di Trasimeno* provides excellent fish, carp, pike, and bleak, which were served up to the popes in bygone centuries. When the bleak are in season, which are fished in quantities in the lake's abundant waters, a large festival is held that is similar to another in the town of Camogli, with a colossal frying pan outdoors on the shores of the lake.

The traditional Umbrian desserts, simple and rather rustic, mostly consist of cakes that aren't decorated, made from genuine and very fresh ingredients, such as *ciaramiccola*, a ring drizzled with *Alkermes* liqueur and covered with tiny multicolored sugar sprinkles; *stricchetti*, marzipan cookies; and *pinoccate*, made from sugar and pine nuts that are easy to make. *Rocciata d'Assisi*, a *spongata* cake with mixed flavors marries well with the region's dessert wines, such as Montefalco Sagrantino Passito.

Finally, there's the curious predilection for chocolate of the region's capital, Perugia, one of Italy's most beautiful cities, renowned for the frescoes of Perugino and the sculptures of Nicola and Giovanni Pisano, the home of the world-famous *Baci* chocolates and the Chocolate Museum.

However, Umbrian cuisine not only distinguishes itself by its exquisite food, but also by its remarkable range of wines. The best-loved is Orvieto, produced on the border between Umbria and Lazio and famous for centuries. It is said that Pinturicchio (c. 1454–1513), called upon to fresco Orvieto cathedral, demanded a clause in his contract that he would be served wine free of charge whenever he asked for it throughout the duration of the job. Two different types of Orvieto wine are produced: one is fairly sweet, with a finish of sweet almonds that's gained in the cold fermentation in caves. It's perfect as a dessert wine. The second variety is dry, recommended with fish dishes and starters. The old cellars in Orvieto are fascinating, carved into the tufa bank that supports the town, in the form of long galleries dating back to the sixteenth century, the ideal environment to age the town's wines. The red Montefalco, Sacrantino, Greco di Todi, red and rosé Torgiano, and Cabernet Sauvignon are also famous. In Torgiano, there's the extremely comprehensive Wine Museum, established on the wishes of the Lungarotti Foundation to safeguard the extraordinary historical and cultural heritage of Umbrian wine.

LENTICCHIE DI CASTELLUCCIO DI NORCIA IGP

WITH THEIR VERY SMALL GREEN SEEDS, THEY ARE UNIQUE IN TERMS OF THEIR FLAVOR AND QUICK COOKING TIME, MAKING THEM RENOWNED. THE LENTILS ARE CULTIVATED IN RESTRICTED HIGH-LYING PLATEAU AREAS, ESPECIALLY AROUND CASTELLUCCIO DI NORCIA (THEY ARE ALSO PRODUCED AROUND ANNIFO AND COLFIORITO), WHERE THE SOIL AND THE CLIMATE LEND THEM THEIR SPECIAL QUALITIES. THEY ARE THE LEADING PRODUCT OF UMBRIAN COOKING. BEING DELICATELY FLAVORED AND ERRING TOWARDS THE SWEET, THEY GO WELL WITH STRUCTURED CRISP WINES WITH A MEDIUM AROMA.

MARCO BISTARELLI

RESTAURANT IL POSTALE - CITTÀ DI CASTELLO (PERUGIA)

FROM A GARAGE FOR COACHES IN THE EARLY 1930S TO AN ORIGINAL REFUGE FOR GOURMETS OF THE THIRD MILLENNIUM: THE RESTAURANT *IL POSTALE* IN CITTÀ DI CASTELLO, IN THE MAGNIFICENT GREEN-BLUE LANDSCAPE OF THE NORTHERN UMBRIAN VAL TIBERINA, SCATTERED WITH OLD VILLAGES WHICH HAVE MIRACULOUSLY BEEN PRESERVED, IS UNDOUBTEDLY AN ENVIRONMENT *SUI GENERIS*. A SIMILAR REUSE OF THE ORIGINAL ARCHITECTURAL STRUCTURE COULD ONLY TAKE SHAPE IN THE HOME-TOWN OF AN ARTIST LIKE ALBERTO BURRI, WHO PAINTED SALVAGED MATERIALS WITH A PAST, FROM SACKS TO PLASTIC, DURING THE TWENTIETH CENTURY.

"IT'S A SPECIAL AND FASCINATING RESTAURANT, ACTUALLY, BECAUSE IT'S LOCATED IN A GARAGE. FOR EXAMPLE, WE USE THE OLD PETROL PUMP OUTSIDE THE RESTAURANT AS A LECTERN TO DISPLAY THE MENU," MARCO BISTARELLI AFFIRMS, CHEF AND CO-OWNER OF THE RESTAURANT WITH WIFE BARBARA, THE MAÎTRE D'HÔTEL. *"WE CALLED IT IL POSTALE BECAUSE IT WAS THE NAME OF THE FIRST COACH THAT TRANSPORTED PASSENGERS AND LETTERS FROM CITTÀ DI CASTELLO TO FANO IN LE MARCHE."* THERE'S A LARGE DINING ROOM, SPARSELY FURNISHED AND EQUIPPED WITH PERFECT ACOUSTICS AND TABLES THAT ARE WELL-SPACED OUT TO ENSURE INTIMACY. BENEATH THE WOODEN TRUSSES OF THE CEILING, WHICH HAVE BEEN LEFT ON SHOW, A SYSTEM OF SUSPENDED WIRES HAS BEEN CREATED THAT HOLD SPECIAL LAMPS INTENDED TO ILLUMINATE THE CENTER OF EVERY TABLE, LEAVING THE OUTER SPACE IN A MORE SUFFUSED LIGHT. *"WE HAVE RECENTLY MADE OVER THE RESTAURANT'S LOOK, WITH SMOOTHED PLASTER TOTALLY IN GOLD AND BLACK, WHICH IS PARTICULARLY SPECTACULAR AT NIGHT, AND A LOUNGE DIVIDED FROM THE MAIN ROOM WITH COLORED GLASS PANELS TO BREAK UP THE RESTAURANT'S SINGULAR ENVIRONMENT A BIT."*

MARCO'S LOVE FOR COOKING CAME LATER IN HIS LIFE, BUT IT WAS A FORM OF EMOTIONAL SURVIVAL. *"I LEFT AFTER THREE YEARS AT THE HOTEL INSTITUTE WITH A SPECIALIZATION AS A MAÎTRE D'HÔTEL. AFTER A COURSE OVERSEAS AND VARIOUS EXPERIENCES AS A WAITER IN HOTELS ALONG THE ADRIATIC RIVIERA, I CAME BACK TO CITTÀ DI CASTELLO BECAUSE MY FATHER HAD ASKED MY TWIN BROTHER SANDRO AND I, WITH WHOM I WORKED – WE WERE INSEPARABLE – TO TAKE OVER A PIZZERIA HE OWNED. THAT'S HOW WE ROLLED UP OUR SLEEVES FOR THE FAMILY RESTAURANT: A BUSINESS THAT HAD 80,000 COVERS PER YEAR. THEN, IN 1990, AT THE AGE OF 25, I LOST MY BROTHER IN A ROAD ACCIDENT AND EVERYTHING CHANGED FROM THAT POINT ON."*

To allow Sandro to live on in himself, Marco decided to start a training course as a chef, just as his brother who was more interested in cooking would have wanted for himself. *"The most important experience was at La Grotta in Brisighella, where there was the great chef Vincenzo Cammerucci, who I regard as my teacher and, after many years, is almost like a brother to me."* Having returned to Città di Castello, in 1992 he started to manage the restaurant of the established *Hôtel Tiferno*, achieving flattering results. Unfortunately, the management costs of the restaurant eventually turned out to be too high for the hotel and Marco and his wife decided to start looking for their own restaurant. In 1996 they fell in love with the town's old coach garage and they renovated the old derelict hanger a year later, opening the restaurant, and earning a Michelin star shortly afterwards. *"I was so focused on giving my all to my work that I didn't understand quite how important this recognition was straightaway. Only later on did I get that it was a huge achievement."*

Marco, former president of *Jeunes Restaurateurs d'Europe* Italy, offers *"contemporary and creative cuisine based strictly on local products."* He believes that the magical element of each of his dishes comes *"through a great technique that I acquired during my training with other chefs. This allows me to create an almost perfect transformation of the ingredients and a symbiosis between the past and future without ever losing elegance."* Like the church of *Santa Maria della Consolazione* in Todi designed by Donato Bramante, one of the most successful temples with a centralized layout in the Italian Renaissance, expresses the ideals of perfection, balance, and special unity, Marco masters his culinary talent to such a level that he deciphers it in remarkably executed dishes, where the flavor, *"doesn't come from the innovation of the techniques, but from history."* This is because, to paraphrase Leibniz, the seventeenth-century German philosopher and scientist, *"cucina non facit saltus"* (cooking does not make sudden jumps). *"Tradition isn't a stumbling block, but the path that one follows to create great modern cuisine."*

The dishes of *Il Postale* are constantly changing, *"because we realize that new offerings are created depending on certain cooking methods or by concentrating on something different."* However,

there are some classics, such as roasted pigeon with stuffed legs, escalope of fois gras and crunchy vegetables, *"an established dish: many people come to our restaurant just to eat it,"* and *pappa al pomodoro* with salt cod tripe, which takes a local dish as the starting point and uses a typical regional fish that's often cooked with garbanzo beans and onion. Another dish that's always on the menu is quail with *roveja*, an ancient Umbrian pulse that's similar to the pea, which is being discovered again now, raw baby spinach and tomato confit. There are also kid-filled tortellini with cherry tomato confit, fresh fava beans, and slightly smoked Norcia Ricotta. There are many dishes in which *"we are still able to maintain all the prerogatives of healthy and local food through state-of-the-art cooking techniques – for example, we cook ox tongue at a low temperature, then browned in a pan, which remains mousse-like on the inside and crispy on the outside."*

There is an abundance of Umbrian products which Marco uses. First of all, there's extra-virgin olive oil, *"I think it's the best in the world due to its very low acidity,"* and he always uses the oil produced by a friend of his. *"The oil weighs on the flavor of a dish to the extent of 35 per cent. When the customer is used to the taste of a certain oil, there's no need to change it."* Then there's pork, the flag bearer of typical regional products, *"for example, pork cheek that locally consists of 50 percent lean meat and 50 percent fatty meat, which is what's needed to lend true flavor to a dish,"* explains Marco. There's also beef that bears the brand "5 erre," or rather the five breeds of the Central Apennines: Chianina, Marchigiana, Romagnola, Toscana, and Marrone. *"We use them all from calf cheek to the shank and offal, perhaps the cheapest part of the animal, but unfairly for-*

gotten." *Il Postale* also features fish-based dishes on the menu, obviously of top quality, but that come from outside of the region 80 kilometers away.

Green beans from *Lago di Trasimeno*, Umbria's small inland sea, are also a constant feature in Marco's cooking, as well as the prized lentils from the nearby village of Castelluccio, and truffles, the true glory of the Umbrian food scene. He also uses the produce grown in the garden. *"We have a friend who has a garden that covers 8,000 square meters, where he grows top-class produce. It's strictly organic and has an extraordinary flavor—that makes a difference in a dish in my opinion. The garden is extremely important. It's futile to use quality ingredients if you then go and ruin them by using them with low quality vegetables [...]"* Marco goes and does the shopping for the restaurant every day. *"We stock up on the wild herbs of the past, like the common brighteye that we use raw in salads and to add flavor or garnish our dishes, as well as many vegetables like chicory and cabbage."*

Il Postale offers many traditional dishes. *"In terms of game, for example, there's wild boar ham on the menu that's prepared homemade by some hunter friends, and I cook the classic wild boar loin, as well as a few pheasants tied up with juniper, sage, and lard, and woodcock cooked in a pot like in the past."* Marco has an almost ethnographic interest in the gastronomic traditions of his land. *"A new dish is created from the ingredients available in the area and based on what's in season, but also by asking the elderly people about what they used to cook."* He likes to go around the villages when festivals have been organized, such as the festival of the *gota del cipollotto e erba sul pignatto*, field herbs and mixed boiled spinach, which is then cooked with garlic, chile pepper, and pork cheek sautéed with fresh green onions. *"A ridiculous dish, usually you end up drinking until 6 am to digest it!"* It's clear that a dish like that couldn't be offered anymore, but Marco has created *"a Cinta suckling pig with porcini mushrooms, cooked at a low temperature, so a type of butter remains in the mouth, served with a hot sandwich of pork liver and bay leaf, which imitates the flavor of the livers with caul fat and bay leaf cooked on a spit. Foods of yore are eaten, they are just looked at from today's perspective."* His cuisine seems to come straight out of the hands of Perugino, the Renaissance artist who knew how to blend together theoretical and empirical space, mediating them through the gentle yet pragmatic methods of Umbrian painting. This can be seen in many of the canvases preserved in the *Galleria Nazionale di Perugina*. In the kitchen, Marco is able to merge the clear and solid idea of the past with the ever-changing and toned-down present through the frank cordiality of dishes which are as close as possible to tradition in their current state.

The menu chosen for this book looks dearly and lovingly to the land. The starter is calf's tripe with fresh fava beans and Pecorino. Pulses are a source of local pride and sheep's Ricotta is the main produce of Umbrian cheese-making. As a pasta course, there are the characteristic strangozzi with pigeon ragù. Strangozzi are the regional type of pasta par excellence. They are made from a mixture of flour and water without eggs and kneaded roughly on a work surface, and then lengthened one by one. For the meat course, there's leg of lamb from Monte Sibillini with green onions and sweet garlic sauce. This is the area's typical meat, which comes from the mountainous area located between Le Marche and Umbria, along the central Apennine chain. It has been a national park since 1993, but it's been the fascinating scenery of pagan cults since ancient times. Legend has it, in a grotto that's since caved in, there was the hellish cavern of the sorceress Sibyl, who took refuge here after the spreading of Christianity of the Roman Empire. The dessert is a lavender cream served in a crispy roll on a pink grapefruit and lemon thyme sauce: *"Lavender is a wild herb in our land that, given that it was traditionally used to protect linen from moths, has an aroma that is reminiscent of grandma's drawers [...]."*

It is a menu that shines with its intelligence and tact. As in the nearby town of Gubbio, where, during the Christmas period, Monte Ingino is completely lit up by the world's tallest Christmas tree, so it is with Marco: The whole of Umbria gathers at the table to enjoy the cooking into which Marco pours his soul; it's the largest table around.

CALF'S TRIPE WITH PECORINO AND FAVA BEANS

Ingredients for 4 people
Preparation time: 30' – Cooking time for tripe: 4 h

1 lb (500 g) calf's tripe
3½ oz (100 g) celery
3½ oz (100 g) onion
3½ oz (100 g) carrot
2 teaspoons (10 g) spices
Scant ½ cup (100 g) vinegar
Generous ¾ cup (200 g) white wine
2 teaspoons (10 g) bay leaves
7 oz (200 g) fresh fava beans
Salt, pepper, and extra-virgin olive oil, as needed
3½ oz (100 g) Pecorino di Fossa cheese
Fleur de sel to taste
Toasts, for serving

Method

Wash the tripe well in warm water.
Make a court bouillon from celery, carrots and onions. Add the vinegar and bay leaves.
Simmer the tripe in the court bouillon for 4 hours until tender. Drain and cut tripe into small triangles. Set aside.
Clean the fava beans and blanch for 5 seconds. Shell, and drizzle with a little extra-virgin olive oil in a bowl. Fry the outer side of tripe in a nonstick pan until crispy. Keep warm

Serving

Serve the warm tripe and fava beans on a flat plate. Grate a little Pecorino di Fossa over the top.
To finish, sprinkle with *fleur de sel*, freshly ground black pepper and serve with toasts.

Wine pairing

Campo del Guardiano 2003 – Red
Winery: Palazzone, Loc. Rocca Ripesena – Orvieto (TR)

STRANGOZZI PASTA WITH PIGEON RAGÙ

Ingredients for 4 people
Preparation time: 45' – Resting time: 2 h

PASTA
3⅓ cups (500 g) flour
Generous 1⅓ cups (350 g) water
Egg white
Salt
Extra-virgin olive oil

PIGEON RAGÙ
4 pigeons, each weighing 1–1⅓ lb
(500-600 g)
2 red onions

leek
2 carrots
1 stalk celery
2 cloves garlic
Scant ½ cup (100 ml) red wine
Drizzle of brandy
1 sprig of rosemary
1 sprig of thyme
1 tablespoon tomato paste
Salt and pepper to taste

Method

PASTA
Knead all the pasta ingredients together on a wooden surface to make a smooth dough. Shape into a ball and let rest in the refrigerator for at least 2 hours

PIGEON RAGÙ
Bone the pigeons, cutting them into 4 breasts (or ask your butcher to do this for you). Set the carcasses aside, removing the livers and hearts. Skin and dice the legs and any other meat remaining on the bones
Dice the onions, leek, carrots, and celery.
Sauté the garlic in the oil in a large pot over medium heat. Brown the carcasses and diced meat for a few minutes until browned. Add the red wine and a drizzling of brandy and let evaporate. Add the vegetables. Let soften for 5-6 minutes. Add the herbs and add a little water.
Add the tomato paste and cook for 10-15 minutes.
Meanwhile, in a pasta machine or by hand, roll out the pasta to ¾–1 inch (2-3 mm) thick (not too thin) and let dry for a while.
Roll up pasta sheets; cut crosswise into long, thick spaghetti using a large knife. Unroll and separate strands to let them dry.
Cook the pigeon breasts, keeping them pink on the inside. Season with salt and pepper. Remove the carcasses from the ragù (they will have released all their flavor into the sauce).
Cook the pasta in plenty of salted water for 5-6 minutes. Drain it and toss it in the pigeon ragù.

Serving

Arrange four nests of pasta in the center of a plate. Lay the scalloped pigeon breast on top and garnish with the herbs.

Wine pairing

Rubesco DOCG 2001 – Red
Winery: Lungarotti – Torgiano (PG)

LEG OF LAMB FROM MONTI SIBILLINI WITH GREEN ONIONS AND SWEET GARLIC SAUCE

Ingredients for 4 people
Preparation time: 1 h 10'

1 leg of lamb
Salt and pepper to taste
⅓ cup (80 g) extra-virgin olive oil
Generous ¾ cup (200 g) butter
Mixed herbs
3½ oz (100 g) garlic
8 green onions
2 cups (500 g) light cream
Drop of lemon juice

Method

Cut the leg of lamb into quarters. Season with salt and pepper. Sear the meat in the oil and butter in a nonstick pan with the herbs and 2 cloves of garlic.
Brown the lamb on all sides over high heat. Let rest in the oven at 225°F (100°C) for 40 minutes.
Meanwhile, clean the green onions and cut in half. Spread them out on a baking sheet. Season with salt and pepper. Drizzle with oil. Bake at 350°F (180°C/gas mark 4) for 8 minutes. Remove from the oven and keep warm.
Cut the remaining cloves of garlic in half, removing the inner green part. Blanch in boiling water 6 or 7 times, changing the water every time.
Reduce the cream in a saucepan over medium heat. Add the blanched garlic, a drop of lemon juice, and transfer to a blender to puree until smooth.

Serving

Arrange a nest of braised green onions in the center of a plate. Drizzle the garlic sauce on the sideand place the lamb on top. Drizzle with a little extra-virgin olive oil.

Wine pairing

Sagrantino di Montefalco DOCG 2004 – Red
Winery: Arnaldo Caprai – Montefalco (PG)

LAVENDER CREAM IN A CRISPY ROLL
WITH PINK GRAPEFRUIT AND LEMON THYME SAUCE

Ingredients for 4 people
Preparation time: 40' - Resting: 5 h

¾ teaspoon (4 g) gelatin
1 cup (250 g) sweetened light cream
Generous 1 tablespoon (20 g) lavender
flowers
3 eggs, separated
½ cup (100 g) superfine sugar

SUGAR ROLL
2 cups (500 g) freshly squeezed orange
juice
¼ cup (50 g) superfine sugar

⅓ cup (50 g) flour
Generous 3 tablespoons (50 g) butter,
softened

SAUCE
2 pink grapefruit
¼ cup (50 g) sugar
¾ teaspoon (4 g) potato starch
Lavender flowers
Lemon thyme
Lavender flowers, for garnish

Method

Soak the gelatin in cold water. Drain and squeeze it dry. Bring ½ cup (125 g) of cream
to a boil over medium heat in a small saucepan with the lavender flowers. Simmer for
2 minutes. Strain mixture through a fine-mesh sieve and let cool.
Beat the egg yolks and sugar in a metal bowl. Add the lavender cream and return to
the heat. Simmer gently, whisking constantly until thickened, heating it to 176°F (80°C)
for 2 minutes. Add the gelatin. Let cool to room temperature. Beat the egg whites to
stiff peaks. Fold the beaten whites into the lavender mixture. Whip the remaining ½
cup cream and fold into the mixture. Spoon into a disposable pastry bag. Chill in the
refrigerator for 4-5 hours.

SUGAR ROLL
Mix all the ingredients together to make the sugar roll batter. Wrap in plastic and chill
in the refrigerator for 1 hour. Line a baking sheet with parchment paper. Spread the
sugar roll mixture evenly on the tray, making 4 stripes measuring 4 x 2⅓ inches (10 x 6
cm) each. Bake at 350°F (180°C/gas mark 4) for 6 minutes. Remove from the oven. Trim
with a knife, wrap in a cylinder, and leave to cool and dry out.

SAUCE
Peel the grapefruit with a potato peeler and cut the peel into cubes. Juice the fruit,
and strain the juice. Heat the grapefruit juice and pulp with the sugar in a saucepan.
Reduce over low heat. Add the potato starch and add the water, whisking to make
a thick liquid. Add a few lavender flowers, lemon thyme, and grapefruit zest, having
removed the white pith and blanched in water and sugar 2 or 3 times.

Serving

Fill the rolls with the lavender cream and arrange in the center of the plate. Drizzle
sauce over each roll and garnish with a lavender flower.

Wine pairing

Vendemmia Tardiva 2005 IGT Umbria – White
Winery: La Palazzola – Stroncone (TR)

THE CUISINE OF LAZIO

""*When you're seen Rome, you've seen everything,*" wrote the great German poet Johann Wolfgang Goethe (1749-1832). The eternal city dominates the country with its historical, artistic, religious, and architectural splendor. *Roma caput mundi,* or Rome, capital of the world, has built itself and its myth over 27 centuries of time. Encountering it is like abandoning oneself completely to the murmurs of history: emotion, surprise, and stupefaction are the almost inevitable reactions of tourists. It is the only European capital that has preserved its ancient defensive walls. It is the city of the Coliseum, the Imperial Forum, the Capitoline Hill, squares, elegant streets, fountains, and the Vatican. This is a city par excellence.

When you leave Rome headed towards the nearby Tyrrhenian, it is a journey through the ancient testimonies of imperial power and myth, a crossing that touches upon the lands of the Etruscan people to the west and the Abruzzo to the east. In the Valle dell'Aniene, the tributary of the more famous Tiber River, time has forged beautiful, old villages, medieval remains, traces of past settlements, and artistic masterpieces that important names have left as a legacy.

There are many people who believe that the real heart of Lazio is the Ciociaria. From here to the Agro Pontino region, art and mystic introspection created unforgettable acropolises on the hills and sacred architecture of haunting simplicity. But there's also the Tuscia Romana, an Etruscan imprint of a heritage that's only partly preserved. It is a world of incomparable worth and a testimony of daily life, with funeral and religious costumes and cultural changes.

The landscape of Lazio is different from every angle, like the towns, though they're often offered up for comparison with the capital, have their own unique identities: Tivoli, Cerveteri, Sabaudia, Gaeta, and Viterbo. Each is indisputably beautiful in their own right and attached to their own origins and traditions, just like the cuisine, which offers a wide selection of common dishes.

The cuisine of Lazio, just like Roman food, stands out by consisting of only a few simple and rustic elements. Sophisticated complexities are alien to this way of eating, despite the contribution and influences of the many chefs who have arrived in the capital from all over Italy.

In the most classic of menus a plate of spaghetti *cacio e pepe* is always featured or Roman-style gnocchi, baked spring lamb, oxtail vaccinara, *pajata* (calf intestines), beans with pork rinds, Roman saltimbocca, and Jewish artichokes, with the Canino and Sabina extra-virgin olive oils as a condiment.

The food from Lazio consists of simple, tasty, and traditional dishes. Elaborate and sophisticated recipes are rarely offered, as they are not a feature of regional tastes.

With regards to meat and vegetable soups, the preferred cooking methods are always quick and as simple as possible. Perhaps the only exception is the making of pasta sauces in which pancetta or pork cheek, herbs, sautéed vegetables, eggs, cream, butter, oil, or lard often make an appearance. With spaghetti or fettuccine (the favorite types of pasta in this region), we find sauces based on onion, garlic, and oil, with a whole range of well-known names: *all'amatriciana* (from Amatrice, a town situated on the border between Lazio and Abruzzo) whose fundamental ingredient is pork cheek, *alla carrettiera, alla prestinara, alla carbonara,* and so on.

Typical of peasant cuisine, there are numerous soups, in which short or broken-up pasta is combined with beans, garbanzo beans, broccoli, and other filling ingredients, always flavored with a sautéed base of onion, carrot, celery, and garlic.

As in other regions of central Italy, rice isn't used much: just a delicious risotto made from chicken giblets and tomatoes, filled *supplì* with stringy Mozzarella, or also with a *finanziera* made from giblets and sweetbreads.

Among the most commonly used meats, in addition to beef, due to the sheep-farming tradition that is widespread in this region, there's also lamb or spring lamb and kid. They are cooked in various ways: baked in the oven, on a spit, in a sauce with rosemary served with olives and anchovies, or as a fricassee (two egg yolks mixed with lemon juices are poured into the cooking juices). Pork is also enjoyed, a dish which developed in Romagna, Umbria, and the Marches as suckling pig, that it has now been incorporated into the cuisine of Latium as Roman-style suckling pig.

Romans often use chicken, which is one of the local favorites for recipes served with bell peppers and tomatoes. It is also cooked on a spit or char-grilled.

Due to the particular composition of the land, rich in mineral components, the farming industry provides Lazio with some exquisite vegetables, among which fava beans, served fresh with young Pecorino cheese, and artichokes excel in terms of their quality and flavor (cooking enhances them in many recipes), as well as peas, broccoli, cauliflower, fennel, celery, and others. The lentils from Onano and Gaeta olives are particularly high in quality.

Capitoni, a fat, tasty variety of eel, and common eels arrive on tables (especially for Christmas) from Lake Bolsena. From the Tiber, there are the small *Ciriole* eels, eaten pan-fried with tomatoes, garlic, and parsley. Salt cod is also found in some recipes, especially fried in batter.

In addition to Pecorino, other quality cheeses enjoyed are Ricotta, a rich ingredient for fillings or desserts, and Mozzarella di Buffala that accompanies the industry in Campania.

Among the charcuterie, there's pork cheek, pancetta, Mortadella di Amatrice, Salsiccia di Monte San Biagio, lard, prosciutto, and small salamis with their intense and spicy flavors.

The desserts of Latium follow the tradition of simplicity: *Maritozzi,* doughnuts of leavened pastry, rice fritters, Ricotta tarts, *Nociata,* with a walnut filling, and a special pie that contains macaroni pasta in a sweet pastry and is sprinkled with lots of sugar when it comes out of the oven.

Under the name of Castelli wines, we find the production of dry, amiable, and sweet white and red wines. Undoubtedly worth a mention are the famous Falerno wines and Est Est Est from the areas of Bolsena and Montefiascone.

RICOTTA ROMANA

THE TRUE PEARL OF LATIUM PRODUCTION IS RICOTTA ROMANA, ONE OF THE OLDEST CHEESES OF THE REGION, WHICH DISTINGUISHES ITSELF FROM OTHER PRODUCTS DUE TO ITS LARGER GRAINS AND FLAVOR.

THE FIOR DI LATTE, A SOFT, FRESH CHEESE WITH SPUN CURDS, ALSO DESERVES A MENTION, WHICH IS MADE FROM THE FULL-FAT MILK FROM THE PROVINCES OF FROSINONE AND LATINA. THE PDO RECOGNITION IS IN THE PRELIMINARY STAGES.

AGATA PARISELLA

RESTAURANT AGATA E ROMEO - ROMA

At about 2:00 am when the restaurant closes, she looks up towards Santa Maria Maggiore and thinks about how incredibly beautiful it is, lit in the moonlight so majestically, but perhaps she never considers how much it resembles her way of understanding cuisine. Of all the great basilicas in the capital city, Santa Maria Maggiore is the one in which different architectural styles blend together with the utmost grace and sobriety, from the fifth century mosaics to the Romanesque bell tower, from the Renaissance coffered ceiling to the seventeenth century dome. Agata Parisella, chef and co-owner with husband Romeo Caraccio, of the restaurant *Agata e Romeo* in Rome, mixes the most authentic Roman traditions with the new requirements of presentation and creative combinations in a simple and harmonious way.

"I'm very attached to the area and the traditions of Roman and Latium food," she recounts, *"and, although there have been many developments in the world of catering and there will be more to come in the future, I will never abandon our typical dishes."* On the menu, she offers many of the most characteristic offerings of her food culture, recipes of the peasant classes which express the honest, rustic, and vibrant soul of Rome, often created in the trattorias around the butchers' shop where the workers picked up the parts of meat which couldn't be sold and called "the fifth quarter" in the local vernacular. However, she no longer serves them like in the past. *"I no longer offer oxtail alla vaccinara like my mother made it, with pieces of meat attached to the bone, but in a terrine instead. I stick to the traditional recipe and use all the classic ingredients which are there to give the right balance to the dish, such as pine nuts, sultanas, cocoa, and lots of celery, but I serve it in a more elegant way. In short, it can be eaten with a knife and fork and not with one's hands as was the case 40 years ago."*

It's also sometimes the case that Agata combines an ingredient that comes from another region with the traditional dishes.

"For example, when I make fettuccine pasta with chicken giblets, one of our city's typical dishes, I add a sprinkling of Parmesan. Or when I make spaghetti cacio e pepe, a classic Roman dish, instead of Pecorino Romano, I use a Pecorino that I have delivered from Sicily, Piacentino di Enna. As it's light yellow in color because it contains saffron, it allows me to obtain a colored dish."

Agata and Romeo's restaurant is located in the Esquiline Hill neighborhood, the largest and highest of the capital's seven hills, in one of the most interesting areas of the city. It's an area with many churches, from Santa Prassede with its magnificent Byzantine mosaics to San Pietro in Vincoli where you can admire Michelangelo's *Moses*, but it is also one of the most populated and popular districts where you can still breathe in the spirit of old Rome. The restaurant is situated in an historic district, one whose appearance has changed over time. In the 1930s, it was Agata's grandfather's *osteria*. It was the last stop for all the carriages, which transported the barrels of wine before reaching Via Appia and returning to the *Castelli Romani*. *"It was an osteria which only served wine, frequented by the so-called* fagottari, *the people who brought food from home in a* fagotto (bundle)." Over the course of time, he also began to serve bread and roasted suckling pig with the wine of *Castelli Romani* and, slowly but surely, it became a true osteria, then a trattoria with Agata's parents. *"Da Gabriele was one of those typical trattorias which were all the rage in Rome in the 1950's and 60's, open seven days a week, with traditional Roman fare, from oven-baked pasta to spring lamb. My mother was in the kitchen, my father in the dining room, and we kids came to help out when we got home from school."*

Agata and Romeo took over the trattoria in 1974. *"Although I'd been nourished on catering at home since I entered the world, my further education was unrelated to cooking. Having finished middle school, my father wanted to send me to the hotel institute of Stresa, but I dug my heels in. I said to him, 'I'd never do your job because it's too much like hard work!'"* And yet, you can't escape destiny. *"When I was about 20 years old, out of five children, I was the only one who offered to continue my parents' business."* A choice in which she also involved her future husband, who she met at

university. *"He abandoned his medicine studies to take care of the dining room and the restaurant's cellar."* Now 30 years on, Romeo is one of the most sought-after sommeliers in Italy and his cellar is award-winning. *"We worked really hard to do all this, but I was guided by my DNA. My grandmother Agata was an amazing chef and I remember that I loved to be in the kitchen with her when I was a child. I still make all the desserts she taught me following her recipes, such as pastry puffs, sponge cake, and pastry cream."* A love that she's never denied: *"I love to cook, also when I'm at home for my friends. I do it naturally with love and gentleness as for me it's a dream come true."*

After the basics that were passed down in her family – *"the strongest impression was left by my grandmother and mother"* – Agata traveled considerably from the age of 22 and she also did internships abroad to learn the techniques of other culinary cultures. Then she returned to the family restaurant and with her husband and she slowly transformed it from a trattoria with home cooking into one of the pillars of the Capitoline food scene, frequented by an international clientele. There are many satisfactions; Michelin-starred Agata is a member of a privileged circle of chefs called upon to cater receptions for heads of state and visiting foreign heads of government in Italy. She also exports her talent overseas, where she has often been invited to cook. Member of the *Jeunes Restaurateurs d'Europe*, she is a true ambassador of Italian food culture in the world.

Agata e Romeo is a particularly welcoming restaurant. *"Our customers tell us that they feel at home here."* It isn't very large – 35 seats at the most – and it's simple while being elegantly furnished at the same time. On the walls Agata's collection of old teapots is displayed, as well as many portrait photos of her in the kitchen, calm and smiling. The tables are large and well spaced out and the staff are trained and friendly. From the ceiling flowers or aromas could well descend on the guests as, according to Suetonius, happened in the nearby Domus Aurea belonging to Nero, one of the most fabulous places of antiquity. This is an establishment where the customer is truly sacred. *"We* try to offer the utmost hospitality. It pleases us that people spend a relaxing and pleasurable evening here. Exactly like they would eat at home, yet being served and with the chance to eat dishes that are a little different."

Among the dishes that Agata often has on the menu, during the winter there's pasta and broccoli soup in skate stock, a classic local food, which uses a fish from the Tyrrhenian Sea and a typical Roman vegetable. *"It's a cheap dish, yet so good that my customers often ask for seconds!"* There are, however, also dishes which are Latium in tradition. *"My maternal grandmother came from Fondi, a town in southern Lazio, and the excellent curly endive soup with cannellini beans is typical of her land, which I offer every now and then at the end of spring and the beginning of summer when I can use the freshest of ingredients. It's a simple dish, but with all the flavor of seasonal produce."* As a tribute to her husband, who comes from the province of Benevento, in Campania, Agata also adds a few traditional Samnite dishes.

"My cuisine is regional where practically only products from the land of Latium are cooked, featuring on a menu that is changed four times a year based on the seasons." As well as cheeses, meat, and fish, she also uses pulses like fava beans, beans, peas, and garbanzo beans, and vegetables, such as Roman artichokes and *puntarelle*, chicory tips. *"Also on the menu, there are some creative dishes in which I use a range of products from all over Italy, from the veal of the Langhe to Parmigiano Reggiano and the Pendolino cherry tomato from Vesuvius."* Like the emperor Hadrian had the Greek and Egyptian buildings rebuilt, which had bowled him over during his journeys, in the garden of his splendid villa at Tivoli, having building material and statues sent from Egypt and Greece, Agata does not restrict her freedom as a chef and has products delivered from every region of Italy. *"Our country has such a wealth of excellent food products that the whole world envies us."* Not only does Agata seek the utmost quality in her ingredients – *"They are the most important thing in making a dish. As we say in Rome, 'you can't do it on a shoestring'"* – but she also tries to get to know her sup-

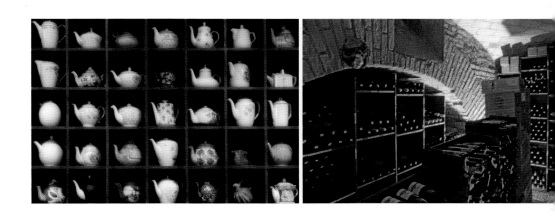

pliers directly. *"Our vacations are often linked to food and wine. Wherever we go we try to make contact with those who produce the best ingredients in the area. We prefer to meet the person who produces what will then be delivered to us."* It follows then that she's the one who checks what's ordered and delivered to the restaurant by her loyal suppliers every morning and takes care of the shopping. *"We have two markets in the squares of Rome where we've been going to for a long time: one is the historic market of Campo de' Fiori and the other one is Testaccio, two of the most vibrant and exuberant in the city."*

The morning is also the time when Agata tries the dishes with her kitchen staff for the tasting menu, which changes every month, aligning them with the seasons. Instead in the evening when the service has finished, she follows all the business that revolves around her work: she tweaks some recipes, researches a new menu, flicks through a few food magazines. On the other hand, on the days when the restaurant is closed given that she's an art lover she makes the most of them to experience the city on foot and to discover it in all its charm. *"For me every corner of Rome is exciting as it recounts over 2,000 years of history. Many are the times when Romeo and I have gone for a walk heading towards the historic center and we've come across forgotten alleyways, which are marvelous. In fact, just yesterday I saw the Fountain of the Tortoises for the first time, a jewel of Renaissance sculpture."* The dishes chosen for this book come from her deep love of Rome. The starter is a tartlet of anchovies and white curly endives, an historic offering of Capitoline cuisine. The first course is Pasta and Broccoli in Skate Stock, followed by Oxtail Vaccinara Terrine. To finish, for dessert there's Agata's millefeuille, her specialty, *"made using traditional ingredients, but served in a different way."* This is a menu that moves from dishes that are an appropriate and sublime reinterpretation of history to others that make the past more come to life with a breath of innovation. In her own seemingly magical way, Agata balances the two Baroque souls of Roman architecture; on one side, the impeccable Bernini of Sant'Andrea al Quirinale and, on the other side, the ingenious Borromini of Sant'Ivo alla Sapienza.

ANCHOVY AND CURLY ENDIVE TARTLET

Ingredients for 4 people
Preparation time: 35'

2 lb (1 kg) fresh anchovies
2 lb (1 kg) yellow-white curly endives
Salt, pepper and lemon juice
Fennel seeds
Cherry tomatoes
Ligurian extra-virgin olive oil
Breadcrumbs
Curly parsley
Pepper, to taste
Wild fennel, for garnish
Tomato wedges, for garnish
Parsley sprigs, for garnish
Basil leaves, for garnish

Method

Remove all the bones from the anchovies. Cut the endives into thin
strips. Let marinate in the salt and fennel seeds for about 1 hour.
Oil the disposable individual molds. Cover them completely with the
raw anchovy fillets, letting them partly stick out.
Cut the cherry tomatoes into quarters and place in a small bowl,
setting 4 aside. Drizzle with the oil and season with salt and pepper.
Fill with the marinated endives and press down. Top with a few pieces
of anchovies and the seasoned tomatoes. Top the tartlet by placing
the anchovies that are sticking out in the center. Drizzle with the oil,
some breadcrumbs, and a crushed tomato in the center, which will
help to keep the tartlet moist. Bake in a bain-marie in the oven at
350°F (180°C/gas mark 4) for 10 minutes.
Make a sauce by beating together the oil, lemon juice, and fennel
seeds. Season with salt and pepper to taste.

Serving

Serve the hot tartlet with the sauce. Garnish with raw wild fennel,
a few cherry tomato wedges, a sprig of parsley, and a basil leaf.

Wine pairing

"Racemo" DOC 2006 – White
Winery: L'Olivella – Frascati (RM)

PASTA AND BROCCOLI SERVED WITH SKATE STOCK

Ingredients for 4 people
Preparation time: 1 h

2 lb (1 kg) whole *arzilla* (skate)
Salt
1 onion
1 stalk celery
2 cloves garlic
Parsley
Garlic
Chile pepper
1 anchovy fillet
Generous 3 tablespoons (50 g) extra-virgin olive oil
Generous ¾ cup (200 g) peeled and chopped tomatoes
White wine
10 oz (300 g) Romanesco broccoli
7 oz (200 g) Ave Maria pasta or broken-up spaghetti
Grated Parmesan (optional)

Method

Clean and wash the *arzilla* (and place in a fish kettle with cold water. Add the salt, onion, celery, and a whole clove of garlic. Cook for about 30 minutes. Drain and remove the head and the cartilaginous part. Return the removed parts to the cooking pan and cook for another 20 minutes. Strain stock into a bowl.
Sauté the chopped parsley, garlic, a little chile, and anchovy fillet in the oil in a frying pan. Add the peeled and chopped tomatoes. Add the white wine and cook for 20 minutes.
Separate the broccoli into florets and cut the larger ones into quarters. Blanch in salted boiling water for 3 minutes; drain. Add the florets to the pan with the anchovy. Cook, adding the stock. Add the pasta halfway through the cooking time.
Pour mixture into a soup tureen and serve with a sprinkling of Parmesan, if desired. The *arzilla* fish can be dressed with oil and lemon, chopped garlic, and parsley and served as a main course. According to tradition, it was added to the soup, thereby making it a nice filling meal.

Wine pairing

"Frascati DOC Superiore" 2007 - White
Winery: Cantina Principe Pallavicini – Colonna (RM)

OXTAIL VACCINARA

Ingredients for 4 people
Preparation time: 1 h – Minimum cooking time: 3 h

CELERY ROOT PUREE
14 oz (400 g) peeled, boiled, and diced celery root
¾ cup (180 g) butter, softened and cut into pieces
Salt
White pepper

OXTAIL
2 lb (1 kg) oxtail and cheeks
onion
2 cloves garlic

1 celery stalk
chile pepper
carrot
White wine
1½ lb (700 g) peeled tomatoes
Salt, to taste
Generous 1 tablespoon (20 g) golden raisins
Generous 1 tablespoon (20 g) pine nuts
Generous tablespoon bittersweet cocoa
Tablespoon tomato paste

Method

CELERY ROOT PUREE
Cover a potato masher with a cloth and use it to puree the celery root . Mash the vegetable several times, pressing down lightly, so that as much water as possible is removed. It is important to remove the majority of the juice contained in the celery to make a firm, dry puree. You could gather the juice that the celery gives out and use it in other recipes. Transfer the celery puree into the bowl of a food processor. Season with salt and pepper. Blend until a smooth and creamy mixture forms.
The consistency of the puree depends on how watery the vegetables are. The more juice you're able to extract, the firmer and drier the mixture becomes.

OXTAIL
Ask your butcher to cut the oxtail into its various vertebra and the cheeks into even pieces. Wash well. Chop the onion, garlic, celery stalk, and parsley. Sauté the chopped mixture in the oil in a large pot. Add the oxtail and cheek pieces and brown them. Add the white wine and let it evaporate. Add the peeled tomatoes. If they don't cover the meat completely, add hot water. Cover and bring to a boil. Lower the heat and simmer.
The cooking time is very lengthy and depends on the size of the oxtail pieces. It will vary from 3 to 6 hours. 30 minutes before the end of the cooking time, add the remaining celery, cut into small sticks. Season with salt and add the raisins, pine nuts, the cocoa dissolved in water and the tomato concentrate. When cooked, bone the oxtail and arrange the meat in a terrine mold. Let rest.

Serving

Serve the oxtail cut into slices with the celery root puree cooked with shallots, oil, and cream. Blend, served with julienned celery hearts.

Wine pairing

"Montiano" IGT 2005 – Red
Winery: Falasco, Montefiascone (VT)

AGATA'S MILLEFEUILLE

Ingredients for 4 people
Preparation time: 1 h 15'

PUFF PASTRY
3⅓ cups (500 g) all-purpose flour
2 cups (500 g) butter
Pinch of salt
Water, as needed

CUSTARD
5 egg yolks
¾ cup (150 g) sugar
Generous ⅓ cup (60 g) sifted all-purpose flour

2 cups (500 ml) milk
1 vanilla pod, split
2 cups (500 ml) whipping cream

DECORATIONS
confectioners' sugar, as needed
3½ oz (100 g) extra bittersweet chocolate, chopped
½ cup (50 g) slivered almonds

Method

PUFF PASTRY
Make the initial dough on a wooden surface: mix 2½ cups (375 g) of all-purpose flour, a pinch of salt, and enough water to make a soft dough. Knead it. Let rest under a cotton cloth while you make the second dough.
Make a ball of dough with ¾ cup (125 g) of flour and all the butter. Let rest under a cloth. Roll out the first dough and the second into a rectangle and place the second dough over the first. Fold into three. Repeat (rolling out and folding into three) this method six times every 15 minutes, making sure that you always keep the dough under a cloth in the lowest part of the refrigerator. The puff pastry will then be ready to roll out to ⅓-inch (1-cm) thick. Bake in the oven at 350°F (180°C/gas mark 4) for 15–20 minutes. When ready, sprinkle the pastry with plenty of confectioners' sugar. Caramelize in the oven at 400°F (200°C/gas mark 6) for about 5 minutes. Cut into large pieces when it has cooled.

PASTRY CREAM
Beat the egg yolks with the sugar and flour in a copper pot. Whisk without beating. Meanwhile, in a separate small saucepan, bring the milk to a boil with the vanilla pod. Slowly whisk in the egg yolks and cook gently for 5–6 minutes, heating the mixture to 175–180°F (80–85°C). Let cool, preferably in a blast chiller. Whip the cream and fold into the custard.

DECORATIONS
Melt the chocolate in a double boiler. Form 10 leaves in small cones of parchment paper. Freeze for 5 minutes.
Toast the slivered almonds at 350°F (180°C/gas mark 4) until golden brown, about 5 minutes.

Serving

Place a generous spoonful of the pastry cream in the center of the plate with a few pieces of puff pastry, the slivered almonds, and a sprinkling of confectioners' sugar. Finish with a chocolate leaf.

Wine pairing

"Moscato di Baselice" 2006 – Dessert wine
Winery: Santiquaranta – Torrecuso (BN)

THE CUISINE OF ABRUZZO AND MOLISE

The Gran Sasso mountain chain is a watershed region, located between the Adri-atic and Tyrrhenian Sea. Also the land of the classical poet Ovid, the writers D'Annunzio, Silone and Flaiano, and the philosopher Croce, Abruzzo is the hinge between the north and south of the Italian peninsula.

This striking land, which is almost completely above sea level (apart from the thin coastal strip), offers a landscape modeled on gentle hills and domineering mountains. This valuable constellation of breathtaking natural scenery that man-kind decided to preserve, is on display in the *Parco Nazionale d'Abruzzo*, the oldest national park in Italy, which is filled with forests, pastures, valleys, clear-ings, copious springs, and an abundant flora of beech forests and groves of dwarf pine. It is also home to the fauna of the Marsican brown bear, Abruzzo chamois, and Apennine wolf.

Untamed and far away from the mass tourism resorts, Molise is a solitary region of farmers and shepherds. From the mountains to the sea, the land gradually de-scends. Rich in natural and instant charm, it is awash with rivers, old villages where you can still breathe in the air of bygone times, and hills that slope down to the beaches. These Adriatic beaches, like Capomarino and Petaccio, have been wrongly over-looked. A particular beach town jewel is Termoli, an old town that has preserved its charm over the years, with a vibrant port where one used to barter for fish.

The region's capital, Campobasso, extends from the mountain region and is a place where one can enjoy beautiful scenery. It is also the home to the important archaeological sites of the ancient *Saepinum*. In the old town, which watches over the new town from on high, the fifteenth-century castle stands tall, a massive presence and impressive in its elegance.

Marked by a genuine and authentic hospitality, Molise welcomes visitors all year round. The traditions, folklore, and constant hospital-ity go hand-in-hand with a varied geography.

Combined with the region's double dose of nature, mountain and marine life, there is a rich and nevertheless simple culinary tradition consisting of carefully prepared, simple dishes, and quality ingredients.

Pasta has a prestigious place in these regions, and is often served with rich ragù or cooked in the form of timbales. The region's tradi-tional pasta shape is the so-called spaghetti *alla chitarra*, obtained from a sheet of homemade egg pasta using a special tool, the *chitarra* (Italian for "guitar"), which consists of a small frame on which steel wires are stretched out (this is where its association with the musical instrument comes from). It creates an unusual, square-shaped spaghetti. A range of vegetable soups are also widespread across the region, which are always flavored with excellent condiments such as Aprutino Pescarese extra-virgin olive oil and lard. They are often served with fried slices of bread or egg.

Typical seasonings from Abruzzo are the fiery hot chile peppers called *diavoletti* and, in the L'Aquila area, saffron, the spice that has been cultivated for centuries. Although not particular to the regional cuisine, saffron has long been a typical symbol of Abruzzo.

Among the traditional salamis, the Mortadelline di Campotosto is worth noting. It is a specialty of the slopes of the untamed Appenine mountain Monti della Laga, where pigs still live in the wild. The Mortadelline are made from the leanest pork meat with a piece of ham lard in the center. Other sausages include the Ventricina di Crognaleto and Vastese (see box), which consists of pork flavored with bell pep-pers, fennel and orange zest, and sausages from L'Aquila prepared with pig's liver, pistachio nuts, and diced candied citron and orange, which are joined together in a ring and are eaten roasted. Another typical pork dish is suck-ling pig, exported to nearby Lazio, which remains one a much enjoyed roasted meat.

Cows and sheep are bred in the region, too, especially in the area of Rocca di Mezzo, in particularly aromatic mountain pastures. One classic lamb dish is defined by the cooking method: lamb cooked in a *cotturo* (a copper pot), born out of the need for the extended boil-ing of old animals and tough meat over fire in days of yore, which were flavored with herbs.

Fish dishes vary from chowders, sauces and fried versions and are often made with freshwater fish, such as trout and tench, which are caught in Lago di Scanno. The bisque of Pescara is a long-standing tradition, enriched with *diavolillo*, a fiery red chile pepper. At Vasto, another traditional fish dish is prepared, marinated with vinegar and flavored with a type of saffron called *scapece*.

Typical farm products in the area are the white cardoons and celery; the cardoons are served with butter, cheese, and egg at Christmas. Given that both black and white truffles are widespread in the Aquilan Mountains (so much that Abruzzo is the region with the largest production of the prized tuber in terms of quantity and quality), Abruzzo makes truffle oils, perfect for enriching a range of dishes.

Like all regions where sheep farming takes place, the production of cheese de-serves a mention. Here an excellent scamorza *appassita* is produced, made from cows and goat's milk, as well as caciocavallo (see box) and outstanding ricotta (the areas of production are Revisondoli, Ovindoli, Alfedena, and Pescocostanzo, among others) and burrino, a type of butter made from whey, which is shaped into a ball during processing and covered with caciocavallo paste and then placed in brine. A very thin crust forms when it is ready. It has an intense, yet delicate flavor. Burrino is produced all over the region and especially in the Apennine area. Pecorino di Farindola a unique cheese that is prepared using pig rennet. It is marinated for 3 months in wine, salt and pepper. Incanestrato, a fresh sheep's cheese, is obtained by pressing the curd in bulrush baskets, which lends a sweet, grassy flavor to the product.

Honey is one of the main ingredients used in Abruzzese desserts It is produced locally and is featured in chocolate nougat, *scarponi* cookies made from ground almonds and cooked grape must, and *malterrata*, a dessert consisting of almonds, sugar, and chocolate. In addition to the traditional and attractive sugared almonds *(confetti)* of Sulmona, a special type of cassata is prepared, with a filling that doesn't contain the traditional ricotta, and therefore keeps for much longer. *Parrozzo*, a soft dessert covered in chocolate, is a specialty of Pescara.

The leading wines are mainly from Abruzzo: Cerasuolo d'Abruzzo, Montepulciano d'Abruzzo, Trebbiano d'Abruzzo. Molise does however offer two famous Registered Designation of Origin wines: the eminent Biferno, which comes from the vineyards of the Campobasso plains, and the inexpensive Pentro d'Isernia, whose production is located around Agnone and Venafro, in the province of Isernia.

One should also not miss the traditional liquors: Aurum, a sweet Italian liqueur, Centerbe, a liqueur made from the local herbs and prized for its medicial proper-ties , and *Milk*, a typical liquor from Molise.

VENTRICINA DI CROGNALETO AND VASTESE

ORIGINALLY FROM THE VILLAGE OF TERAMANO ON THE SLOPES OF GRAN SASSO, *VENTRICINA DI CROGNALETO* IS A SAUSAGE MADE FROM FINELY GROUND AND CHOPPED PORK CHEEK, SHOULDER, AND INTESTINES. IT IS COMBINED WITH SEASONINGS, ROSEMARY, AND BELL PEPPER; THE MIXTURE IS THEN PRESERVED IN A PIG'S STOMACH. IT IS EXQUISITE SPREAD ON BREAD. ANOTHER VARIETY, *VENTRICINA VASTESE*, IS A TYPICAL SAUSAGE FROM THE HILLY AND MOUNTAINOUS AREA OF VASTO. IT IS MADE WITH PORK MEAT (75% LEAN/25% FAT), WHICH IS THEN CHOPPED WITH A SHARP KNIFE AND SEASONED WITH SALT, SWEET AND/OR SPICY BELL PEPPER, AND FENNEL FLOWER. IN THE PAST, THE MIXTURE WAS THEN TYPICALLY PACKED INTO A PIG'S BELLY; NOWADAYS IT IS AGED IN A PIG'S BLAD-DER FOR AT LEAST FOUR MONTHS BEFORE BEING CONSUMED.

CACIOCAVALLO

EASILY IDENTIFIED BY ITS PEAR SHAPE, CACIOCAVALLO HAS A HARD, THIN, AND DARK SKIN, WITH RIPPLES OF MOLD IN THE MOST AGED FORMS. THE CHEESE IS COMPACT WITH SOME OOZING CRACKS AND AN INTENSE AROMA. THE FLAVOR CAN BE SWEET AND MELLOW BUT BE-COMES INTENSE AND SPICY WITH RIPENING. ITS PRODUCTION, WHICH PARTLY FALLS INTO THE REGISTERED DESIGNATION OF ORIGIN CACIOCAVALLO SILANO, IS PARTICULARLY HIGH IN THE CITY OF AGNONE. IT SHOULD BE SERVED WITH COMPLEX RED WINES THAT GROW IN STRUC-TURE, FROM BIFERNO ROSATO TO PENTRO DI ISERNIA ROSATO.

PEPPINO (GIUSEPPE) TINARI

RESTAURANT VILLA MAIELLA - GUARDIAGRELE (CHIETI)

A FORCE OF NATURE. THAT'S ONE WAY OF DESCRIBING PEPPINO TINARI, THE CHEF AND PATRON OF THE RESTAURANT *VILLA MAIELLA* IN GUARDIAGRELE, A CHARMING HISTORICAL TOWN AT THE FOOT OF THE MAIELLA MOUNTAINS, IN THE CHIETI HINTERLAND. IT ISN'T JUST A PERSONIFICATION OF THE NATURE THERE WITH ITS REMARKABLE NATURAL RESOURCES, CONSTANTLY NEW AND FULL OF ENERGY, THAT ABRUZZO WISELY PROTECTS IN ITS THREE LARGE NATIONAL PARKS OF GRAN SASSO, MAIELLA AND D'ABRUZZO AND IN THE REGIONAL PARK OF SIRENTE-VELINO, BUT IT IS ALSO AN EXPRESSION OF THE INSTINCTIVE CULINARY NATURE THAT THE REGION HAS PRESERVED FOR CENTURIES. IT IS SIGNIFICANT THAT ST. FRANCIS CARACCIOLO (1563-1608), THE PATRON SAINT OF COOKS, FOUNDED THE FIRST ITALIAN COOKING SCHOOL HERE AT VILLA SANTA MARIA, IN THE LOW VALLEY OF THE RIVER SANGRO.

IF *VILLA MAIELLA* PAYS TRIBUTE TO THE HISTORY AND DEVELOPMENT OF THE FOOD AND WINE OF ABRUZZO BY REVISITING THE AREA'S RESOURCES, THE RESTAURANT'S BLISSFUL SUMMER PATIO OPENS OUT OVER A VAST PANORAMA: FROM THE WHITE BEACHES OF THE ADRIATIC COAST TO THE MARKET GARDENS AND ORCHARDS OF THE COUNTRYSIDE, FROM THE GENTLE HILLS DOTTED WITH SILVER OLIVE GROVES AND VINEYARDS TO THE HIGHEST MOUNTAIN GROUP OF THE CENTRAL APENNINES, GRAN SASSO, AND MAIELLA. *"IT IS A LARGE, ELEGANT RESTAURANT,"* EXPLAINS PEPPINO, *"BUT CUSTOMERS IMMEDIATELY FEEL AT HOME AS SOON AS THEY STEP INSIDE AS WE WELCOME THEM IN A CALM AND FAMILIAR MANNER, WITHOUT BEING EXCESSIVELY FORMAL."* PEOPLE HAVE FELT AT EASE HERE SINCE 1968. IT STARTED OUT AS A SIMPLE BAR, WHICH WAS THEN TURNED INTO A RESTAURANT SPECIALIZING IN HOMEMADE COOKING BY PEPPINO'S PARENTS, WHERE REGIONAL DISHES WERE PROFFERED, FROM RABBIT COOKED UNDER A *COPPO*, AN OLD CONTAINER THAT IS SIMILAR TO A LID WITH AN IRON OR CAST-IRON HANDLE TO COOK THE DISHES UNDER THE ASHES IN THE HEARTH, TO ROAST KID WITH POTATOES AND *PALLOTTINE*, HORSE-MEAT MEATBALLS.

In 1984, at the age of 23, Peppino became actively involved in running the *trattoria*. With a solid training behind him, initially at the hotel institute of Roccaraso, where he understood for the first time what it meant to be a cook, and then by working at Hotel Cipriani in Venice, with the chef Giovanni Spaventa, who Peppino regards as his second tutor, after the teacher Domenico Stanziani, and his second father. Tired of living in the lagoon, he said, *"I really missed my home [...] When I worked in Venice, on the few occasions I came home to Guardiagrele, I found great pleasure in smelling the aromas of my father's allotment and my mother's cooking, that smell of charcoal that burnt in the hearth where the sauce was cooking in a terracotta pot [...]"* he went back to the family eatery and decided to turn it into a proper restaurant. *"I told my mother to remove the cutlery with plastic handles and the hospital-like tableware, and to use copper pans and redo the kitchen, equipping it with modern tools [...] And my mother supported me."* So he took the restaurant in hand, with his mother Ginetta and father Arcangelo, and began to gain customers who affectionately followed him in his venture. In 1985, the restaurant *Villa Maiella* was established. *"We called it Villa Maiella because that's the name of the area where it's situated in the Parco Nazionale della Maiella."* His wife, Angela, joined him in the kitchen. *"Initially she was a bit scared of cooking, as she'd never done it before, but over the years she has become better than me, especially in the art of pâtisserie."* In 1993, there was a qualitative leap. The restaurant was extended and a hotel with fourteen rooms was built above the eatery. *"This allows us to operate without doing banquets, which while lucrative, do not let me do the kind of catering that I aim to offer."*

Villa Maiella is now at the height of cuisine in Abruzzo, and Peppino has received many recognitions, the latest of which was the appointment as Official Knight of the Italian Republic. It is a well-deserved reward for his philosophy of work both as a caterer and as a businessman, always trying his best and asking for the maximum from himself and others. He clearly thinks like the builders of the splendid Romanesque *Basilica di Santa Maria di Collemaggio*, just outside the walls of L'Aquila, whose façade, clad in local pink and white stone, is a masterpiece of elegant work-

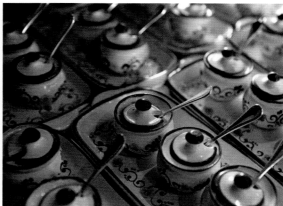

manship in terms of composition and decoration, with its three entrances and respective rose windows. For example, fifteen years ago, the restaurant was the first in Italy to have a total renewal air conditioning system. *"I stand by the fact that the air is always clean. When customers enter the building, they mustn't smell ham or Pecorino like in eateries, or a musty odor. When a customer tastes a dish or a wine, this should not be conditioned by other smells."* The kitchen, which is particularly spacious, has already been redone twice to have all the technologies and state-of-the-art equipment at one's disposal.

Peppino keeps himself constantly informed, setting himself the objective of keeping the quality high. *"I go around repeating to everyone, to myself, my wife, my co-workers, that we mustn't say that we've made it, but that we should improve every day."* He insists that his staff respect the ingredients, from when they arrive in the kitchen to when dishes are served, and respect the customers. He also asks them to work seriously and with a sense of commitment. In addition to this, he requests transparency from his suppliers, always ordering at least three of each type of product to guarantee constant quality at the restaurant. *"If I need a certain ingredient, that's what they must give me, and if it's right, I never try to make a saving or barter over the price."*

Peppino truly worships his ingredients. Wherever he is called to cook, in Italy or abroad, he always takes his own products with him, many of which he uses for his creations. For example, with others he financed a farmer who has a flock of sheep at Farindola, where the best-known pecorino in the region is produced. *"Every year, as if it were interest in the bank, we take back 10 per cent of the invested value as cheese."* On the other hand, in terms of pork: *"I personally follow my father and his friend's pig breeding and produce salamis for the restaurant."* He is also integrating five hectares of land to set up a commercial farm with his eldest son, Arcangelo jr., who is about to graduate in Food Technologies because *"products whose provenance we are certain of are used in the restaurant."* He errs on the safe side for veal: *"We use white veal from the Central Apennines, which has a highly controlled production process."* The region's lamb comes *"from small producers in the area and trusted butchers."* Rabbits and chickens are reared *"by some farming families."* He has even redeemed a 'lost' meat, ram, which belonged to the Abruzzo's gastronomic tradition, re-introducing the farming of these animals, and has busily intervened on the dairy front. *"The area's dairy industry has started making mozzarella, giuncata, and ricotta salata again, due to a course that I organized on how to make cheese."*

Traditional dishes always feature on the menu at *Villa Maiella*: spaghetti *alla chitarra (guitar)*, created with a typical tool from Abruzzo that is similar to the musical instrument, served with tomatoes, olive oil, and herbs, or with the typical lamb ragù, oven-baked rabbit with potatoes, grilled lamb chops, or *pallotte cacio e uova*, the classic meatballs consisting of Pecorino cheese, eggs, garlic, and parsley, which are fried and then served in a tomato sauce. The chef has also resurrected the use of the typical *vino cotto* from Roccamontepiano in the kitchen, which comes from reducing grape must (freshly pressed grape juice, used in wine-making) by boiling it and then adding fresh must. *"I use this wine, with its incredible aroma and a flavor that can be compared to a great Marsala, to prepare chicken in a cast-iron pot."* Some brand-new dishes are also offered on a regular basis, such as burrata-filled ravioli with saffron, and crispy lentils and veal rolls, grilled at low temperature, in a layer of lard on grilled fennel.

"I would describe my cooking style as being regional and personal. A style that I always try to interpret time and time again based on new ways of cooking, while never excluding traditional methods. If you know how to light a match, you can also use a computerized oven [...]" Beyond innovation, what matters most is the substance and the preservation of genuine flavor. His cooking goes back to basics: *"When there are three elements in a dish, that's already too much,"* but like the cathedral of Santa Maria Maggiore in Guardiagrele, built in the twelfth century completely in Maiella stone, which preserves the so-called *tesoro* (treasure) within its walls, consisting of precious gold-crafted works and medieval artistic imprints, he keeps the majority of his research hidden.

Peppino uses many products from the area, selecting them carefully and seriously. From forest products, like mushrooms, the different varieties of truffle from Abruzzo and wild strawberries, to earthy products, Peppino always respects the seasons. Then there's the honey from Abruzzo, the lentils from Santo Stefano di Sessanio and Caprafico, where you can also purchase barley and spelt, small mountain garbanzo beans, game, fish from the Adriatic coast and *Ventricina*, a typical salami from Abruzzo. He also procures the salamis produced in the Teramo area, which is spread on bread, and *Vastese* from the southern inland area of Teatino, a pig's bladder sausage. *"Financially assisting a small family that farms two pigs of its own and one of my own, and I have a product that is without comparison."* Peppino naturally used olive oil from Abruzzo, *"especially the oil extracted from the variety Gentile di Chieti, which is the most delicate of all oils,"* he says.

The menu chosen for this book includes the traditional cheese and egg fritters as a starter and chitarrina with fresh tomatoes and Maiella herbs as the pasta course, where the spaghetti alla chitarra, which are thinner than usual, are served with uncooked tomatoes, oil, garlic, and a little thyme, marjoram, oregano, basil, sage, and parsley. The meat course is a lamb shank with saffron sauce from L'Aquila, a spice grown for centuries on the plateau of the Aquilan mountains and the crowning point of the Abruzzo food specialties. Finally, the dessert is a chocolate cake semifreddo. *"Parrozzo is a 'pane rozzo', a round farmers' loaf from which it takes its name, consisting of cornflour or semolina, sweet and bitter almonds, sugar, butter, eggs, and bits of chocolate and then covered in chocolate. Given that it keeps for long periods, it is a dessert that shepherds often took with them during the old migratory herding from the plains to the mountains and vice versa along the sheep tracks, "* explains Peppino. Peppino's menu opens up the cuisine of Abruzzo from many perspectives. It recalls the geometric scale of the cubist roots of the sculptures by his fellow countryman, Pietro Cascella, the artist whose works in marble or stone, smoothed, rough or eroded, yet always disclosed, can be seen in many urban spaces in Abruzzo.

CHEESE AND EGG FRITTERS

Ingredients for 4 people
Preparation time: 35'

FRITTERS
2½ oz (75 g) day-old bread, soaked in milk
3 whole eggs
1 clove red or white garlic, finely chopped
Pinch of chopped parsley
1¼ cups (150 g) freshly grated pecorino cheese
2 cups (250 g) freshly grated semi-aged cow's cheese
Extra-virgin olive oil, for frying

SAUCE
Scant ½ cup (100 ml) extra-virgin olive oil
1 clove red or white garlic, lightly crushed
⅓ cup (10 g) finely chopped onion
Sprig of basil
1 cup (250 g) tomatoes, peeled, seeded, and cut lengthwise into thin strips
Vegetable stock
Pinch of salt

Method

FRITTERS
Squeeze the milk out of the bread. Beat the eggs in a bowl. Add the garlic, soaked bread, parsley, and finally the grated cheeses to make a thick mixture. Let rest for 30 minutes.
Use two tablespoons to shape the mixture into quenelles and arrange on a tray. The mixture should make about 20. (For the less expert cook, make the balls using your hands.)
Heat plenty of extra-virgin olive oil in a large, deep frying pan to 250–275°F (130–140°C). Fry the balls slowly until they puff up and are golden brown. Remove from the oil and let drain on a paper towel-lined baking sheet.

SAUCE
Heat the oil in a pot, preferably earthenware. Add the crushed garlic, then the chopped onion. Discard the garlic when it turns pale gold. Add the sprig of basil and tomatoes. After 5–6 minutes, add the fritters, arranging them evenly in the pot. Cover with the vegetable stock and cook for 5 minutes more. Season with salt to taste and serve.

Wine pairing

Trebbiano d'Abruzzo Castello di Semivicoli 2006 – White
Winery: Masciarelli – San Martino sulla Marrucina (CH)

CHITARRINA WITH FRESH TOMATOES AND MAIELLA HERBS

Ingredients for 4 people
Preparation time: 45'

PASTA
2⅔ cups (400 g) flour
4 whole eggs, lightly beaten
Pinch of salt

SAUCE
Scant ½ cup (100 ml) extra-virgin olive oil
1 clove red or white garlic, lightly crushed
Handful of finely chopped fresh herbs
1⅓ lb (600 g) tomatoes, peeled, seeded, and cut lengthwise into thin strips
Parsley, to garnish
Small fried basil leaves, to garnish

Method

PASTA
Sift the flour onto a wooden surface and shape into a mound. Make a well in the center. Pour the eggs into the hollow, add a pinch of salt, and knead until the dough is smooth and even. Wrap in plastic wrap and let rest for 30 minutes. Roll the dough out with a long pasta rolling pin to ¾-inch (2-mm) thick. Cut the sheet of pasta on the strings of the chitarra or use a pasta machine and pass the pasta through the cutter. Lay out the pasta on a tray and cover with a cotton cloth.

SALSA
Heat the oil in a large frying pan and add the crushed garlic. Discard the garlic when it turns pale gold. Add the chopped herbs to the pan. Immediately add the tomatoes, season with salt to taste, and cook for 10 minutes. Cook the pasta in plenty of salted water. Drain and sauté briefly in the sauce (given that it is fresh egg pasta, it absorbs a lot of the sauce). Serve at once, garnishing the dish with parsley and fried basil, which has been prepared in advance.

Wine pairing

Cerasuolo Pie' delle Vigne 2005 – Rosé
Winery: Cataldi Madonna – Locality Piano, Ofena (AQ)

LAMB SHANK WITH SAFFRON
SAUCE FROM L'AQUILA

Ingredients for 4 people
Preparation time: 1 h 25'

4 Small lamb shanks

HERBS AND AROMATICS
5 oz (150 g) onion
5 oz (150 g) celery
2 sprigs of rosemary
2 sprigs of thyme
4 sage leaves
1 bay leaf
3 cloves garlic
4 juniper berries
Salt and peppercorns, as much as needed
1 quart (1 liter) alcohol-free white wine*
Generous ¾ cup (200 ml) extra-virgin olive oil

50 saffron strands (soaked in scant ½ cup (100 ml) warm water for at least 1 hour before use)
* Bring the wine to a boil in a large pot. Carefully remove the wine from the stovetop, and light alcohol with a match or lighter. Let burn until flame has extinguished naturally, burning off all alcohol.

GARNISH
1 Small pearl barley flan
Vegetable puree (turnip or wild vegetables)
1 Candied tomato

Method

To prepare the lamb shanks, season them with salt, and brown in a casserole dish to seal the meat. Add the herbs and aromatics and cook them slowly. Then pour in the white wine and half of the saffron water. Cover and bake in the oven for 70 minutes at 325°F (170°C/gas mark 3), checking the level of the cooking liquid occasionally. At the end of the cooking, strain the cooking juices, and add the remaining saffron water. Place pot on the stovetop and simmer until reduced to the desired consistency. Season with salt to taste.

Serving

Arrange the shank on a plate and drizzle with the sauce. Garnish with the flan, vegetable puree, and candied tomato.

Wine pairing

Trebbiano d'Abruzzo "Edoardo Valentini" 2004 – Bianco
Azienda agricola: Azienda Agricola Valentini – Loreto Aprutino (PE)

CHOCOLATE CAKE SEMIFREDDO

Ingredients for 4 people
Preparation time: 20' - Resting time: 4 h

9 egg yolks
Scant 1 cup (180 g) sugar
2 cups (500 g) cream
4 oz (125 g) chocolate cake*, broken into
pieces
1¾ oz (50 g) chocolate

*CHOCOLATE CAKE
1 oz (30 g) almonds
4 tablespoons (60 g) sugar
3 eggs, separated
2 tablespoons (30 g) flour
2 tablespoons (30 g) cornstarch
Scant 3 tablespoons (40 g) butter
2¾ oz (80 g) melted dark chocolate
10 toasted almonds

Method

CHOCOLATE CAKE
Chop the almonds with a tablespoon of sugar. Whip the egg yolks with the remaining sugar, beat them, and add the chopped almond mixture. Sift in the flour and cornstarch. Add 2 tablespoons (30 g) of melted butter. Whip the egg whites and fold them into the mixture. Pour the batter into a buttered cake pan and bake in the oven at 350°F (180°C/gas mark 4) for 40 minutes. Let it cool, then turn the cake out onto a platter. Cover with the melted chocolate and the toasted almonds.

SEMIFREDDO
Use a mixer to beat the egg yolks with the sugar until they turn pale. Meanwhile, beat the fresh cream in a separate bowl until slightly thick. Mix the chocolate cake pieces into the beaten yolks with the chocolate, followed by the cream. Pour the mixture into a semifreddo mold or plastic-lined terrine and freeze for at least 4 hours.
Turn it out of the mold and cut into ⅓-inch (1-cm) thick triangles or slices. Arrange them on a dish and decorate as desired.

Wine pairing

White raisin wine "Terre di Chieti"
Dessert wine Winery: Cantina Tollo – Tollo (CH)

MARIA LOMBARDI

RESTAURANT VECCHIA TRATTORIA DA TONINO - CAMPOBASSO

"My cuisine is my mother's," Maria Lombardi affirms, chef and co-owner with husband Aldo Casilli, *maître d'hôtel*, of *Vecchia Trattoria da Tonino* in Campobasso. There could be no better definition. *"I'm not a fan,"* she asserts, *"of highbrow cuisine. I think that dishes have to come from the heart, not the mind. My mother's the emotion. I don't want to amaze, but give pleasure through an unexpected aroma, a forgotten flavor."* Maria offers local food, rich in flavor, with traditional Molisean recipes which have been reworked without betraying its spirit. She uses strictly local ingredients that have been carefully selected, and she serves portions like the ones you get at home, albeit presented with a eye for aesthetics and the design of the plate. That's not all: *"I pay close attention to the financial aspect. My dishes must always be high in quality, but at an affordable price."*

The restaurant is located right in the heart of the capital of Molise, in a beautiful late nineteenth-century building. *"The ceilings are rather high, the walls are light in color, and my collection of porcelain plates are on display. The ambience, well-lit and furnished in a unpretentious yet refined style, with colors ranging from peach to light green, is relaxing and comfortable."* There are no airs and graces and the customers feel *"as if they were guests in my own home."* What's the secret? *"We pay a lot of attention to courtesy: it's part of our culture. We often use the following two words in Molise: civility and manners. We try to offer these to whoever steps into our restaurant."*

In 1954, the restaurant, which has about 30 covers at its disposal, was formerly home to the delicatessens of Tonino Casilli, Maria's father-in-law. *"But it wasn't any old deli; even back then you could buy excellent Prosciutto di Parma or leading wine labels."* In short, the place was already dedicated to quality. In 1992, Tonino's son, Aldo, transformed it into a high-class restaurant, devoting himself to a difficult enterprise, which was however destined for success, from the acknowledgements of the trade publications that regard it as the gourmand cornerstone of the region (it has borne a Michelin star for years) to the esteem of the public. *"The greatest sense of satisfaction comes from the customers who thank me,"* Maria tells us.

Among the classics of the *Vecchia Trattoria da Tonino*, there are the variations of salt cod – creamed with extra-virgin olive oil and potatoes, as a escalope *arraganata*, with toasted bread-crumbs and oregano, as a fried skewer in rice spaghetti and in a *bauletto* (small vanity case) with Mozzarella in phyllo pastry – the *cannoncini* filled with fresh cheeses, the Ricotta and Mozzarella-filled eggplant rolls, cooked au gratin with tomatoes and Caciocavallo, or linguine pasta in salt cod sauce, a traditional Christmas Eve dish, which the chef has reworked, *"making it more delicious by adding a walnut sauce and a handful of toasted day-old breadcrumbs."* Her dishes demonstrate the best of the cuisine of Molise and allow something like a bird's-eye view of the region. Tasting them is like stepping onto the terrace of the fifteenth-century Castello Monforte in Campobasso, which dominates the city from on high. From here you can enjoy a panorama that's unique in its beauty and scale: the remains of the Oscan and Samnite walls, the fan-like shape of the old town, the new part of town, and the many surrounding villages, followed by the valleys of the rivers Biferno, Trigno, and Fortore, which gradually descend to the sea, among olive groves, vineyards, expanses of wheat, and orchards, and the green mountains of the Alto Molise.

"My cuisine is simple in terms of the ingredients and preparation, yet refined in terms of the raw materials." Home cooking is emphasized, perhaps also due to Maria's background. She has no hotel institutes on her CV, but attendance at a high school specializing in the humanities and an arts degree from the University of Naples. Afterwards, yes, it's true that she traveled around Italy, but not to go and work with illustrious chefs, but rather to follow her husband, who had to move

from the north to the south for his work. When they decided to take over Aldo's parents' deli and devote themselves to catering, Maria, a mother of two children, went from home cooking to the kitchen of *Vecchia Trattoria da Tonino*. Like in the traditional Molisean women's costume, her apron has become an essential item that has not only a decorative but also a deeply symbolic value. Maria's culinary skill is an integral part of her personality. *"I have always been curious about cooking and I've always liked to read and follow up on what I've read. That's how I was brought up. You could say that I've learnt with both my eyes and hands; I've seen and tried a lot. Of course, I've missed out on comparisons with structured environments, but when I started to cook as a job, I applied what I had already done at home: enhancing my knowledge and implementing it, making each dish with care."* Even today, she doesn't neglect her dual calling as a chef and scholar. On the contrary: *"I continue to read with great interest, perhaps fewer recipe books and more volumes dedicated to the history of food customs."* She is capable of balancing nature and culture, a little like the Molisean artist Paolo Saverio Di Zinno was able to calibrate the architecture of the traditional mysteries in the eighteenth century, which are paraded every year in Campobasso during the festivities of *Corpus Domini*, steel alloy structures placed on wooden bases and carried on the backs of groups of bearers, on which the mysteries of the Bible are displayed as well as people dressed as saints, angels, and demons.

Maria isn't part of the mundane circle of Italian cuisine, she does much more: she works lovingly. She works in the kitchen from 9:00 am to 4:30 pm and from 7:00 pm to midnight. In her afternoon break, she tends to her home, reminding us, *"I'm not just a chef, but also a housewife!"* Her day recalls the six placid and hard-working monks, carved almost completely in the round in the act of carrying out their religious functions in the niches of the parapet of the elegant thirteenth-century pulpit in the church of La Madonna del Canneto in Roccavivara. Along with her husband, Maria takes care of the shopping for the restaurant. The vegetables – *"The produce that I absolutely prefer like turnip greens, cauliflower, green, beets, spinach, zucchini, zucchini flowers, chicory. I love vegetarian food."* – are bought from a local supplier she trusts, as well as the pulses, such as the Capracotta lentils and

Paolina beans, a neighborhood of Riccia. The other ingredients are also delivered to her kitchen by small-scale producers in Molise, which are able to guarantee top quality products.

Although Molise has a short stretch of coastline on the Adriatic Sea, Maria only offers salt cod, anchovies, sardines, or herrings, *"which belong to the regional inland cuisine as they're preserved fish."* In terms of meat, she uses sheep the most, *"given that lamb, cooked in various ways, is a classic of the cuisine of Molise,"* from the ragù served with cavatelli, the traditional form of fresh pasta, to roasted *turcinelli*, the animal's offal gathered into a ball and grilled or char-grilled, as well as good quality veal when it is available. *"On the other hand, there's been a decrease in eating farmyard animals. For example, stuffed cockerel, whose sauce is used to dress homemade pasta, is only cooked on Sundays or for holidays."* On the Molise cheese front, Maria uses many of them: Mozzarella Fior di Latte, Caciocavallo, Ricotta di Pecora, fresh Caciotta, and so on.

"Our regional cuisine, having poor roots, consists of few ingredients. What makes the difference is the quality of the ingredients. I feel it's my duty to have a relationship with the land and to use its best produce as soon as it's in season. Indeed our menu varies according to the availability of the ingredients." For example, Maria makes ample use of the prized Molisean extra-virgin olive oil, *"especially the oil made from the Gentile di Larino variety, which is particularly delicate,"* as well as mushrooms and truffles – black, white, and *scorzone*, summer black truffle – which are mostly profuse in the province of Isernia. It is actually the genuineness of the products that makes sure that her dishes bestow infinite charms. A little like the *Monti del Matese*, which stand tall in western Molise, offer many landscapes: from the grottos with the incredible underground routes between Guardiaregia, San Polo, and Campochiaro, to the unexpected plateaus that open up at a high altitude among the protruding rocks and wooded ridges thick with beech and chestnut trees, and further down cerris and downy oaks, from the thousands of years of traces of the men who lived here to the fossil evidence of the geological infancy of these places.

The food traditions of Molise, a small and unappreciated region of Italy, absolutely must be defended: *"Forgetting them would be equivalent to killing the knowledge that is the proof of a civilization."* Maria not only protects it, but she even bestows upon it a touch of distinction, while she revives it, as occurs for example, in the orange, herring, and pomegranate salad with olive pâté, *"a delicious winter dish that I serve with the utmost elegance."* It's her land and she loves it, not only in terms of its cuisine, but also *"in its small villages which are medieval in origin, fairly well preserved, with their narrow little streets and the small houses in dark stone, yet gladdened with lots of flowers."* And for its genuine nature, like an earthly paradise still unaccustomed to mass tourism, and the *Parco Nazionale delle Mainarde* and UNESCO biosphere reserve: *"It's an unspoiled region. Often I feel on top of the world when I behold certain views, with fields of heather, brooms, ferns, and so on,"*

The menu chosen for this book starts with sheep Ricotta and cured sausage flan with a sauce of turnip greens, which features a traditional type of sausage, as well as the typical cheese – with *soppressata, capocollo,* sausages, and *la ventricina,* it confirms how *"the pig is a source of flavor for the people of Molise"* – and a vegetable that is often used in regional cooking. For the pasta course, there's a new take on a customary dish: linguine with salt cod sauce, served with walnut sauce and fried breadcrumbs. For the main course, tenderloin of veal with Caciocavallo and native Tintillia red wine reduction, in which an extremely robust indigenous red wine is used, *"obtained from an old vineyard that arrived in Molise in the wake of the Spanish."* For dessert, miniature sponge cakes filled with pastry cream and styled to resemble a peach, a typical Molisean dessert that originated in convents, made for weddings, baptisms, communions, and confirmations. One of the two liqueurs par excellence from Molise is used to make this sweet, the *Crema Milk,* produced from sheep's milk and saffron, dating back to the end of the eighteenth century. *"The other one is Poncio, whose name is a deformation of the English word punch. It's served as a grog or neat poured over ice-cream."* Maria offers an 'historic' yet vital menu which reminds one of sitting on the stone seats in the theater of the ancient sacred center of the Samnites at Pietrabbondante, on the slopes of Monte Caraceno, still home to leading theater productions during the summer today.

SHEEP RICOTTA AND CURED SAUSAGE FLAN WITH A SAUCE OF TURNIP GREENS

Ingredients for 4 people
Preparation time: 50'

BATTER
2 cups (500 ml) sparkling mineral water, iced
1⅓ cups (200 g) flour

SAUCE
1 lb (500 g) turnip greens
Salt
Water
Extra-virgin olive oil

RICOTTA FLANS
1¼ cups (300 g) sheep Ricotta
Salt
Pepper
Generous ⅓ cup (50 g) Pecorino Dolce, grated
3½ oz (100 g) Mozzarella appassita (Scamorza appassita)
½ cup (50 g) cured sausage in oil, diced
1 small bunch of parsley, chopped
3 eggs, separated

Method

BATTER
Blend the very cold sparkling mineral water with the flour in a bowl. Let rest in the refrigerator until ready to use.

SAUCE
Clean and wash the turnip greens. Set aside 6 perfect leaves, which will be used as garnish.
Boil in plenty of salted water; drain greens (reserving some of the cooking liquid) and let cool in ice water to maintain the brilliant color. Drain and puree in a blender with extra-virgin olive oil. Adjust the thickness of the sauce by adding some cooking water if needed. Season with salt.

RICOTTA FLAN
Strain the Ricotta through a fine-mesh sieve. Season with salt and pepper. Add the grated Pecorino, the diced Mozzarella and sausage, a pinch of parsley, and egg yolks. Mix well.
Beat the egg whites to stiff peaks and fold into the mixture.
Pour the mixture evenly into 6 buttered molds. Bake in a bain-marie in the oven at 300°F (150°C/gas mark 2) for about 30 minutes.

Serving

Serve the flans on a spoonful of turnip greens sauce.
Garnish with fried turnip greens, which have been dipped in the batter.

Wine pairing

"Pecorino" IGT – White
Winery: Castaldi Madonna – Ofena (AQ)

LINGUINE WITH SALT COD SAUCE,
SERVED WITH WALNUT SAUCE AND FRIED BREADCRUMBS

Ingredients for 4 people
Preparation time: 1h 20'

1 lb (500 g) desalted salt cod fillet*
1 stalk celery
1 carrot
onion
1 clove garlic
2 spicy chile peppers
2 tablespoons (30 ml) extra-virgin olive oil
4 anchovy fillets in oil
¼ cup (60 ml) dry white wine
3⅓ lb (1.5 kg) peeled tomatoes
1 small bunch of parsley
1 sprig oregano
3½ oz (100 g) day-old bread, crumbled
Salt

Pepper

If you buy salt-cured cod, soak it in water for 2-3 days, changing the water regularly

WALNUT SAUCE
1 cup (100 g) walnuts
1¾ oz (50 g) day-old bread, softened in milk
clove garlic
1 small bunch of parsley
Salt
Pepper
Scant ½ cup (100 ml) extra-virgin olive oil
14 oz (400 g) linguine pasta

Method

Bone and skin the salt cod fillet. Clean, wash, and chop the celery, carrot, and onion. Peel the garlic.
Sauté the chopped vegetables in the oil with 1 chile pepper, the anchovy fillets, and the bones and skin of the salt cod in a large pot. Add the wine and cook until evaporated.
Add the tomatoes and cook over medium heat for 40 minutes. Add half the chopped parsley, the remaining seeded chile pepper, and a sprinkling of oregano. Let cool and puree using a food mill.
Transfer the sauce to a large pot. Add the salt cod fillet, cut into cubes, and cook over low heat for a few minutes until the ingredients are well mixed.
Toast the breadcrumbs in the oil in a nonstick pan and sprinkle with oregano. Season with salt and pepper.

WALNUT SAUCE
Chop the walnuts in a food processor with the bread softened in the milk and squeezed dry. Add the garlic, parsley, salt, and pepper. Gradually add the oil at the end.
Cook the pasta in plenty of salted water. Drain and add to the salt cod sauce.

Serving

Add the walnut sauce and the remaining parsley and cook over high heat for a few minutes, tossing. Divide evenly among the plates, sprinkle with the toasted breadcrumbs, and serve.

Wine pairing
"Maso San Valentino" DOC – Pinot Nero
Winery: Cavit – Trento (TN)

TENDERLOIN OF VEAL WITH CACIOCAVALLO AND NATIVE TINTILLIA RED WINE REDUCTION

Ingredients for 4 people
Preparation time: 20'

Generous ¾ cup (200 ml) Tintillia
½ teaspoon honey
1 sprig of sage
1 sprig of rosemary
1 sprig of thyme
1 bay leaf
1 veal tenderloin, weighing 7 oz (200 g)
Scant 3 tablespoons (40 g) butter
Generous 1 tablespoon (20 ml) extra-virgin olive oil
Generous 1 tablespoon (20 ml) brandy
Salt
Pepper
1 tablespoon light cream
Generous 1 tablespoon (20 ml) grated Caciocavallo cheese

Roasted rosemary potatoes, for serving
Sauteed porcini mushrooms, for serving

Method

REDUCTION
Pour the wine in a saucepan with ½ tablespoon of honey and herbs. Bring to a boil and cook over low heat until reduced by half.

TENDERLOIN
Brown the tenderloin on both sides in the pat of butter and the oil, keeping it rare.
Add the brandy and let it evaporate. Season with salt and pepper.
Place the tenderloin on one corner of a hot plate. Deglaze the cooking juices with about ¼ cup (50 g) of the wine reduction. Add a spoonful of cream.
Return the tenderloin to the pan, top with the Caciocavallo, and keep warm covered with a lid. The cheese will have melted and the cooking juice will be creamy after a couple of minutes.

Serving

Serve with roasted potatoes cooked with rosemary and sautéed porcini mushrooms.

Wine pairing

"Tintillia" del Molise DOC – Red
Winery: Cantina d'uva – Larino (CB)

PEACH-LIKE PASTRIES FILLED WITH LEMON CREAM

Ingredients for 4 people
Preparation time: 1 h

PASTRY
1 cube of brewer's yeast (25 g)
Scant ½ cup (100 ml) milk, gently heated
7 tablespoons extra-virgin olive oil
3⅓ cups (500 g) all-purpose flour
3 eggs
½ cup (100 g) sugar

LEMON CREAM
2 cups (500 ml) milk
1 organic lemon, zested

4 egg yolks
½ cup (100 g) sugar
4 tablespoons (60 g) all-purpose flour

TO DECORATE
Crema Milk (a liqueur from Molise made from sheep's milk and saffron)
Sugar syrup
Alchermes
Sugar
Bay leaves, for garnish

Method

PASTRY
Dissolve the yeast in the warm milk and oil. Sift the flour onto a wooden surface and make a well in the center. Add the eggs, sugar, and yeast mixture. Knead the ingredients to make a smooth, elastic dough.
Shape into balls the size of walnuts, flattening them at the bottom. Arrange them on a buttered and floured baking sheet. Let rise for about 2 hours, or until they have doubled in volume.
Bake in the preheated oven at 350°F (180°C/gas mark 4) for about 20 minutes.

PASTRY CREAM
Bring the milk to a boil with the lemon zest in a small saucepan over medium heat. Strain it. Use a whisk to beat the egg yolks and sugar in a metal bowl. Whisk in the flour, followed by the milk (add slowly to avoid curdling the eggs).
Cook over low heat for about 10 minutes, stirring constantly.
Make a hole in the flat part of the pastry balls and soak them in 1 tablespoon of Crema Milk and 1 tablespoon of sugar syrup. Fill with the pastry cream.

Serving

Stick 2 balls together (on the flat side) to form peach-like cakes. Brush with the Crema Milk and Alchermes and dip in the sugar. Finish with a bay leaf.

Wine pairing

"Moscato Apianæ" – Sweet white
Winery: Cantina di Maio Norante – Campo Marino (CB)

THE CUISINE OF CAMPANIA

An entire book wouldn't be enough to recount the beauty of a region that has charmed tourists for centuries since the time of the Grand Tour. The subject of song and art, it is loved and sometimes hated. It is a region that harmonizes light and shadow, torment and passion. A region that makes you fall in love at first sight and cultivates an interest in the history, culture, and social contradictions that it embodies. Among the undisputed pearls: Naples, along the Amalfi coast where Homer chose to recount the sirens that Ulysses came across on his travels; Sorrento, upon the sea of the gulf that faces the heart of Naples; Positano, a perched town that is mirrored in the waves below; ancient Amalfi; and the silent, elegant Ravello. Memories of the classics, the remains of civilization buried by lava at Ercolano and Pompeii and the islands of Procida, Nisida, Capri, and Ischia: Campania is a place of evocative names and extraordinary splendor.

Then there's the capital: the cradle of Neapolitan culture, which overlooks the belly of the Mediterranean, is an explosion of artistic masterpieces, scenery that leaves you breathless, and ambience. Naples is romantic and persuasive, stately and common at the same time. It is sun-kissed and overlooked by Vesuvius.

Even the *napoletanità*, a sort of Neapolitanism civility that has remained intact over the centuries, is vibrant and colorful. *"You can say or tell or paint whatever you like but in this place everything exceeds expectations. These shores, gulfs, inlets, Vesuvius..."* once noted the great German poet and playwright Wolfgang Goethe (1749-1832). The cuisine of Campania is nestled in this setting, which is inextricably bound to the sea, one of the most exquisite corners of Italy. The cuisine is like a two-sided coin: there is the food of the lower classes, which combines their resources with the art of making do that is typical of the people; and the aristocratic cuisine, which brings together the culinary traditions of the succession of different dominions in Naples: the Greeks, Romans, Austrians, and French. The symbol of local cooking is the pizza, which with spaghetti represents Italy around the world. Pasta and pizza are the two foods from Campania, which indeed embody the whole of Italy in the rest of the world.

Pasta, which arrived from Sicily and Arabian culture, found a suitable microclimate for its production in Campania and more precisely in the Gragnano region. The types of pasta preferred in Campania are the long varieties, such as spaghetti, vermicelli, and bucatini, but at least a hundred other shapes are produced. In the past, pasta could be defined as a street food, once offered by hundreds of mobile stands: the *Vermicellaro* served a plate of spaghetti dressed with just cheese and pepper for a small price, or with the characteristic *pummarola*. From Naples and Campania, pasta conquered practically the whole of Italy, becoming the country's most representative food with good reason, served with all the variants that the imagination and the products of 20 regions can create.

Before pasta, there was the vegetable, and the people of Campania had their fill of them, sometimes mixing them together in a soup called *maritata*, with pork rind to enrich the green leaves. Soups rich in seasonal vegetables and served with various sautéed bases to add flavor are still fairly common today.

As in Sicily, rice is often used to make few, yet exceptional, dishes, such as *Sartù*, a timbale filled with: Mozzarella, sausages, peas, chicken giblets, and meatballs.

Meat is also used to make ragù with its mythical cooking time of seven hours: a sauce still the pride and joy of every true Neapolitan housewife today. It is strictly prepared in a *coccio*, an earthenware pot, in which the bound meat is added to a chopped mixture of carrot, celery, garlic, onions, and rosemary sautéed in oil and lard, so that it can be cooked covered, with the addition of an excellent wine and a teaspoon of homemade *conserva*. Traditionally the sauce was served with ziti pasta.

Conserva is a tomato sauce cooked for a long time and then left to dry in the sun. In the winter it brings the aroma and flavor of summer tomatoes back to Neapolitan dishes.

Another cornerstone of this region's cuisine is pizza. Perhaps derived in its current form from focacce, which were made in Roman times and are characteristic of all Italian coastal peoples, they were enhanced following the American discovery of the presence of the tomato. On the other hand, it was the Longobards who introduced the breeding of buffalos to Campania, thereby promoting the production of that type of Mozzarella, a cheese with curd that was spun and cut off, or *mozzata* – hence the name – the main ingredient of pizza in Campania (see box). It is mainly produced in the areas of Battipaglia and Aversa. Nevertheless the Neapolitans also put the merit of the specialty of their pizzas down to the water with which the flour is mixed, as well as to their cooking in wood-burning ovens.

The pizza toppings are totally varied, but the classic versions include fresh tomatoes, garlic, and oregano or tomato, garlic, and fresh anchovies. The classic Margherita came about in the nineteenth century, with the red of the tomatoes, white Mozzarella, and green basil, in honor of the first queen of Italy with the colors of the national flag. Among the ingredients to top a pizza, there are also clams, onions, olives, and many others. The type of pizza that is folded over on itself to seal the filling takes the name *calzone* and is another typical recipe from this region.

In addition to meat, fish is the true king of the cuisine of Campania, with a vast variety that includes all types of seafood: clams, mussels, king shrimp, date shells, wedrazor clams, and oysters, which are traditionally eaten raw with a splash of lemon, or appear to dress spaghetti in a rich sauce. The variety also persists in the different cooking methods: fish is eaten baked in paper, grilled, fried, and stewed. There are also the fish soups, which distinguish themselves with the obligatory presence of the ugly scorpion fish. The tradition of street food also offers a whole range of delicious morsels: *panzerotti*, fried Mozzarella sandwiches, various fried vegetables and potatoes, croquettes, *arancini*, and *sartù*.

As well as Mozzarella di Bufala, the cheese industry in Campania also tallies up smoked and plain Provola (from Battipaglia), Scamorza, and Fior di Latte.

Among the charcuterie, the *Capocollo* made from rolled pork saddle is worth a mention, produced in the area of Nola, as well as *Cervellatine*, sausages which are Neapolitan in origin.

In the countryside between Sarno and Nocera, the San Marzano tomato is cultivated with its elongated shape and bright red color. Sour-sweet with few seeds and fibrous parts, it is delicious raw in salads or when used to make a sauce.

The climate of this region offers a large variety of fruit, from apricots to peaches, white and yellow melons, watermelons, figs, apples, citrus fruits, and walnuts, almonds, hazelnuts.

The desserts of Campania practically always go hand-in-hand with faith and tradition: *struffoli*, the typical almond-based Christmas sweets; the carnival *zeppole*, and the sumptuous Easter *pastiera*. We should also mention the filled *sfogliatelle*, sweet *taralli*, Babà—and the art of ice-cream making also offers real specialties here. Finally, the sweet nougat of Benevento is renowned.

Among the wines, the most famous is the white and red Falerno, with its ancient heritage. It is created from vineyards cultivated on volcanic land and in the past the Romans enjoyed it on their tables. On the enchanting islands of Capri and Ischia both white and red wines are produced, as well as the *Lacrima Christi*, a refined and aromatic wine, on the slopes of Vesuvius. Finally, we should also mention Aglianico, Taurasi, Corbara, Giovi, although in reality the wine list of Campania is endless.

The famous Sorrento walnuts are used to make the liqueur Nocino. The lemons used to make Limoncello, the liqueur that is still consumed chilled as a digestive, it is a delight for the palate that bears the flavor and color of the sun. Another famous liqueur that takes its name from the legend of the witches of Benevento, is *Strega*, a spirit made from herbs (about 70) flavored with orange zest and spices. In the nineteenth century it was created by the local Alberti distillery and in the twentieth century it gave its name to a well-known Italian literary prize.

MOZZARELLA DI BUFALA CAMPANA

PROTECTED BY A CONSORTIUM, IT IS THE MOST CHARACTERISTIC AND WELL-KNOWN OF THE DAIRY PRODUCTS FROM CAMPANIA. BACK IN THE TWELFTH CENTURY, THE MONKS OF THE MONASTERY OF SAN LORENZO IN CAPUA OFFERED A TASTE TO THE VISITING PILGRIMS. THE ORIGIN OF ITS NAME DATES BACK TO THE OLD METHOD WITH WHICH THE PASTA WAS CUT BETWEEN THE THUMBS AND INDEX FINGERS. IT IS ALSO PRODUCED IN PLAITS AND SMALL BALLS, WHICH ARE DELICIOUS MORSELS. CREAMY, SWEET, AND OVERFLOWING WITH MILK, THE FLAVOR AND CONSISTENCY ARE UNMISTAKABLE. IT IS USED TO PREPARE TYPICAL DISHES, BUT ABOVE ALL IT IS EATEN AS IT IS TO TASTE THE GOODNESS.

GENNARO ESPOSITO

RESTAURANT TORRE DEL SARACINO - VICO EQUENSE (NAPOLI)

Vico Equense, the striking town of Etruscan origin suspended on a rocky spur overlooking the Gulf of Naples, is a landscape of unique beauty. In 1787 Goethe wrote of it as a region: *"where everything exceeds expectations,"* and he may have ben referring to its wines which were celebrated even in antiquity. Now it's praised for the gastronomic temptations of the restaurant *La Torre del Saracino*, in the seaside village of Seiano. A coveted destination for anybody who wants to celebrate their otium, or leisure, to which the Ancient Romans had dedicated their numerous villas along this stretch of the Sorrento coastline through the pleasure of eating and a view that's unparalleled around the world.

Consisting of two rooms, one of which is in a seventh-century Saracen sighting tower and the other room is in an elegantly restored outbuilding, the restaurant also has two small terraces overlooking the sea. *"After 16 years of business, there's an air of a result obtained through a lot of hard work and time, a great atmosphere of quality and hospitality, those highly important values which I think that people should always come across in a restaurant,"* Gennaro Esposito asserts, chef and co-owner with Vittoria Aiello. *"At the beginning, the ambience was extremely simple, but we have gradually tried to make it nicer, above all, more Mediterranean, while maintaining that simplicity that is also an expression of our own style."* It has all the essence of the Neapolitan soul, aristocratic and common at the same time, which is evident in its details. *"With the architect Sabrina Masala we tried to create an environment that reflects our concept and features elements of our land."* Hence the white handcrafted terracotta from Ogliara or the precious materials from San Leucio, the utopian model colony founded in 1789 by Ferdinand IV of Bourbon for the workers of the silk factory with the intention of promoting their happiness rather than profit, which was then wrecked with the loss of the 1799 revolution.

Noted as the best restaurant in Campania by a well-known Italian food guide and Michelin starred, the restaurant owes its success not only to Gennaro's talent. *"I like to remember all those people who help me to achieve quality on a daily basis, colleagues who have worked with me for many years and share many aspects of this job with me, allowing me to experience it in the best possible way."*

Starting with Vittoria, who takes care of making the bread and desserts, the introduction and conclusion of every lunch or dinner at *La Torre del Saracino*, thanks go *"to the supporting cast in the dining room and kitchen: Ciro, Luciano, Enzo, Giovanni, Salvatore, and Sharon."*

The chef offers *"a cuisine that is an expression of the different cultures of this territory through using different local products."* A porous cuisine, like the tufaceous land on which the restaurant stands, set on using every product that Campania has to offer. *"I use vegetables which are all seasonal because my father cultivates quite a large allotment in Montechiaro."* After all, from an historical point of view, the Neapolitans, well before becoming famous as 'maccheroni-eaters', were called 'leaf-eaters' as they ate vegetables, especially broccoli. *"Then there are all the fresh cheeses which are typical of the area, from Monti Alburni, Monti Lattari, and Cilento, like Mozzarella Fior di Latte and Mozzarella di Bufala Campana, Ricotta, and Caciocavallo, and the typical dried pasta from Gragnano in its different forms. And all the fish, which is the star of our menu."* Also here he doesn't pursue the foregone conclusion of sea bass or scallops: *"We try to consider fish from every angle, from seaweed to small snails, especially in using fish that are perhaps little known as they are typical of only a few areas."*

After many years, *"we have excellent and well-established relationships with our suppliers, of which there's always more than one per product."* His father takes care of buying the fruit and vegetables during the months where his allotment doesn't produce what's needed. On the other hand, for fish, Gennaro relies on a few fishmongers which sort out the restaurant's order every day. *"Meat features in small quantities on our menu. We prepare it with great care, but there's less demand for it than fish."* The ingredients of his land, Gennaro treats them with the wise and tenacious grace with which Saint Jerome shows in the famous painting by Colantonio, the Neapolitan fifteenth-century master, which can now be seen in the *Museo Nazionale di Capodimonte*.. The painting depicts

the saint surrounded by the building chaos of his workshop, instead of by the frenetic activity of a kitchen, removing a thorn from the paw of a lion. Gennaro gets excited when he looks at the local ingredients. *"When I look into a case of fish, a world opens up to me and I start to think about how many dishes I could make from them. In our work, it always helps to have a wide range of possibilities in front of us."* Of course, you also need to study, *"but you also need to have that spontaneity that allows you to create a dish, experiencing the daily life of the kitchen not just as a routine, but as a pleasure. I believe that the important thing is to experience the kitchen*

everyday, not suffering it, but approaching it with a certain philosophy. That's what allows us to constantly gather suggestions, ideas, aromas, and so on. There's no such thing as a moment where someone's creative and then they're not." Although there's a moment during the day, in the morning, when Gennaro, with his staff, takes care of innovating what's on offer on his menu. The menu typically changes four or five times a year, with dishes that are substituted sometimes even more than once on the same menu.

From 1992 to the present day, the restaurant continues to offer many classic recipes, which have represented and still represent Gennaro's cuisine. For example, scabbard fish cooked with Parmesan, which raises a scarcely used fish that isn't thought of as particularly flavorsome up a rank, or soup made from Ricotta di Fuscella from Agerola with red mullet fillets from the Mediterranean, where the cheese is combined with the fish and special care is taken to balancing them. *"On the menu we have traditional dishes, which we happily rework from time to time while remaining loyal to the original recipe, and creative dishes, which are however inspired by the gastronomic heritage."* For example, the zucchini soup with red shrimp and a poached egg symbolizes a dish handed down through generations, yet has been revived in the traditional manner. *"It was once an offering made from a wealth of ingredients, from day-old bread to pancetta. We now offer it in a lighter version using the whole zucchini plant and serving it with red shrimp and a poached egg, which goes particularly well."* On the other hand, a more innovative dish as it is based on the new kitchen technologies are the swordfish ravioli, *"where the ravioli pasta is replaced with thin sheets of swordfish, filled with lightly blanched vegetables and then cooked at low temperature."* It's a more elaborate dish, yet recognizable in terms of its ingredients. *"For me the magic is created when a flavor or aroma is very close to the original one and loaded at the same time with the lives of all the previous generations."* Like the excellent state of preservation of Pompeii, submerged by a blanket of ash and lava during the eruption of Vesuvius in AD 79 which lets us reconstruct the city life, in Gennaro's dishes the transformation of the ingredients always respects their natural qualities.

"I have always had a great love of cooking, also because I was lucky to have a mother who was a fantastic chef. Working in the countryside, she always used quality products and ever since I was young I had the privilege of recognizing and tasting certain flavors." After this early childhood love due to the delicious dishes made by his mother Carmela, cooking became his *raison d'être*. The love with which he carries out his trade and stands as godfather to his dishes, with juxtapositions of flavors that are so close and on the mark that they practically emit light, as well as making one's mouth water. The food calls to mind Luca Giordano, the seventeenth-century Neapolitan painting wizard, knew how to do with his palette of colors, capable of flaunting a sense of color with a prodigious technique. *"I enrolled at the hotel institute and then started my training around Italy and Europe. Every stage of the journey was important; some even taught me what I shouldn't do."* The most important advice Gennaro received came undoubtedly from Gianfranco Vissani, *"who passed on to me respect, love, and an awareness of great ingredients,"* and from Alain Ducasse in Montecarlo and Paris, *"where I understood what perfect organization of work and a maniacal attention to detail stands for."* When the chance to open his own restaurant materialized, he went home – *"Given that I'd already worked in a kitchen for many years, I happily decided to give it a go with Vittoria, who also had considerable experience."* – and fully maximized the opportunity. *"When I came back here I recovered the identity of our land and tried*

to ennoble it in a way that wasn't banal." He did this with linear forward-thinking, yet effective, ability, similar to famous Parco della Reggia of Caserta, designed by the court architect Luigi Vanvitelli in the eighteenth century, one of the most significant examples of the so-called Italian garden. From that point, "my story is one of knowledge and awareness, especially through continual comparison with the experiences of my colleague friends." Member of the Jeunes Restaurateurs d'Europe association, since 2003 Gennaro has organised the Festa a Vico, "a chance to meet in my town for my chef friends who abandon their businesses for three days and become honorary citizens of Vico Equense."

The menu for this book features zucchini soup with shrimp and a poached egg. "Strongly evocative of the tradition, but presented in a guise that is closer to our conception of cooking, both in terms of the ingredients and the use of modern preparation techniques." For the pasta course, there's a timbale of ziti pasta served on Neapolitan ragù, made with classic Neapolitan pasta for a typical dish that's been revamped. "The ingredients are traditional, such as the renowned San Marzano tomato, only the cooking method and the preparation of the filling has been changed so that it can be inserted into the pasta." In the past, it was a sumptuous main course, like many of the traditional Neapolitan dishes, perhaps an exorcism to the city's atavistic famine, incarnated by its typical mask, Pulcinella. "If we have given a touch of great complexity to the pasta course, we'd like to emphasize the freshness in the main course." Salt cod cooked in tomato leaves, saffron stock, and citrus fruits is proffered. "A simple dish, but with the lovely charm of the South." To finish, there's a typical dessert: Neapolitan Babà, served with pastry cream and wild strawberries.

These are dishes where innovation fits smoothly into history, a little like the superb triumphal arch erected by Alfonso I of Aragón in the mid-fifteenth century, which is wedged in between the two crenellated monumental towers of Castel Nuovo of Naples, a tapestry of masterful workmanship in solid loving arms.

ZUCCHINI SOUP WITH SHRIMP AND A POACHED EGG

Ingredients for 4 people
Preparation time: 20'

VEGETABLE STOCK (1 LITER)
1 potato
1 white onion
1 carrot
1 stalk celery
1 quart (1 liter) water
Small bunch of herbs (thyme, bay leaf, wild fennel)
¼ teaspoon (2 g) coarse salt

ZUCCHINI SOUP
1 lb (500 g) whole, small zucchini, including leaves, stalks, sprouts, and flowers

1 tablespoon (15 g) chopped onion
Generous 2 tablespoons (35 g) extra-virgin olive oil
Generous 1 tablespoon (20 g) lard, diced
1¾ oz (50 g) new potatoes, peeled and diced
2½ quarts (2.5 liters) vegetable stock
8 red shrimp, shelled
2 teaspoons (10 g) salt
Pepper
4 fresh eggs
Extra-virgin olive oil, for drizzling
Pinch *fleur de sel*, for garnish

Method

STOCK
Clean and peel the potato. Peel the onion. Clean the carrot and trim ends. Clean the celery. Pour the water into a large pot and add the vegetables and herbs. Bring to a boil and add a generous pinch of salt.
Lower the heat to its lowest setting and simmer, covered, for 45 minutes. Remove from the heat; strain the stock and let cool.

SOUP
Clean the stalks, leaves, flowers, and sprouts well under plenty of running water. Blanch in boiling water and plunge immediately in ice water to stop the cooking. Drain, lightly squeezing zucchini parts dry; dice the zucchini.
Sauté the onion in the oil in a saucepan. Add the lard and potatoes and brown them. Add the all zucchini parts and vegetable stock. Cook over low heat for about 8 minutes. Heat the shrimp in a nonstick pan. Season with salt and pepper.

POACHED EGGS
Break one egg at a time into salted, boiling water, using a slotted spoon to make sure that the egg yolk and white fall one on top of one another. This will ensure that the egg remains in once piece when cooked, as shown in the photo. Poach until set, 3 to 5 minutes.

Serving

Ladle the soup into the center of a deep plate. Arrange 2 red shrimp in the center and place a poached egg on top. Garnish with a drizzling of oil and a pinch of *fleur de sel*.

Wine pairing

"Coda di Volpe" 2007 – White
Winery: Vadiaperti, Regione Campania – Montefrédane (AV)

TIMBALE OF ZITI PASTA SERVED ON NEAPOLITAN RAGÙ

Ingredients for 4 people
Preparation time: 1 h - Cooking time: 5 h

14 oz (400 g) beef eye of round
1 small bunch of parsley
Scant ⅓ cup (50 g) pine nuts
3 cloves garlic, sliced
1¾ oz (50 g) Pecorino cheese, grated
Salt and pepper
10 oz (300 g) pork rinds
1 medium yellow onion, chopped
1¾ oz (50 g) beef suet
1 lb (500 g) pork ribs
5 oz (150 g) shin of beef
⅓ cup (80 g) extra-virgin olive oil

3 cups (750 ml) dry white wine
6⅔ lb (3 kg) San Marzano tomato passata

FILLING
1 yellow onion
Scant ⅓ cup (70 g) extra-virgin olive oil
5 oz (150 g) ground meat (3½ oz/100 g lean beef and 1½ oz/50 g lean pork)
Generous 3 tablespoons (50 g) white wine
Generous ¾ cup (200 g) tomato passata
3½ oz (100 g) Mozzarella di

Bufala Campana cheese, chopped
⅓ cup (80 g) cream
Scant ½ cup (50 g) semi-aged Caciocavallo cheese, grated
2¾ oz (80 g) Burrata cheese, chopped
Salt and pepper

TIMBALE
1 lb (500 g) ziti pasta
4 molds, buttered and sprinkled with breadcrumbs
Generous ¾ cup (200 g) Ricotta cheese, cut into cubes
A drop of extra-virgin olive oil
Fresh basil leaves, for garnish

Method

Fill the beef eye with some of the parsley, pine nuts, sliced garlic, grated Pecorino, salt, and pepper. Roll up meat and secure with kitchen string. Make more rolls using the pork rinds and the remaining filling ingredients. Sauté the onion, garlic, and suet in a pot (preferably copper or earthenware). Add the rolls, pork ribs, and shin of beef. Cook for 5 minutes. Add the white wine and let it evaporate. Add the tomato passata and season with a little salt. Cook over very high heat for about 5 hours. Season with salt to taste.
Sauté the chopped onion and garlic with the oil in a frying pan. Add the ground meat and brown over low heat. Add the white wine and let it evaporate. Pour in the tomato passata and cook over low heat for about 20 minutes. When the meat has cooled, add the Mozzarella di Bufala, cream, Caciocavallo, and Burrata. Season with salt and pepper.

TIMBALE
Cook the ziti pasta carefully in plenty of salted boiling water in a deep saucepan. Cook for 3 to 4 minutes. Drain well using two slotted spoons. Spread the pasta out on a work surface and let cool. Cut the ziti to the height of the mold. Fill the molds individually with the mixture using a pastry bag. Arrange the ziti vertically in the mold. Bake in the oven at 350°F (180°C/gas mark 4) for about 8 minutes. Butter a baking sheet and arrange the ricotta. Drizzle with a little olive oil. Bake in the oven at 350°F (180°C/gas mark 4) for about 4 minutes.

Serving

Position a ladleful of hot ragù (meat sauce) in the center of the plate. Turn the timbale out on top of the sauce. Garnish with the ricotta and a few leaves of fresh basil.

Wine pairing

Falerno del Massico "Camarato" DOC 1999 – Red
Winery: Villa Matilde – Cellole (CE)

SALT COD COOKED IN TOMATO LEAVES, SAFFRON STOCK, AND CITRUS FRUIT

Ingredients for 4 people
Preparation time: 50'

4 slices of salt cod, each weighing about 100 g
8 large tomato leaves
Scant ½ cup (100 g) extra-virgin olive oil
Freshly ground pepper
1 oz (30 g) seaweed
Scant ½ cup (100 g) tomato water*
1 tomato, cut into 4 slices and broiled
1 orange
1 lemon
Steamed vegetables, such as zucchini, carrots, and green beans, for serving, optional
Pinch *Fleur de sel*, for garnish
2 saffron strands

* The tomato water comes from separating the passata. For 100 g of water, you will need at least 1 kilogram of tomatoes (we like to use Cuore di Bue tomatoes).

Method

Wrap each slice of salt cod in 2 tomato leaves. Place in the vacuum packs used for sous vide cooking, adding 2 tablespoons of oil and a grating of pepper. Seal and cook at 160°F (70°C) for 30 minutes.
Dehydrate the seaweed, so that it becomes more delicate; cook in the oven at 175°F (80°C) for about an hour. Soak in the tomato water with the saffron at 160°F (70°C) for 10 minutes. The temperature is fundamental as it alters the flavor and aroma.

Serving

Remove the seaweed and spoon a ladleful of the water in the center of a deep plate. Arrange a slice of broiled tomato with the salt cod on top. Grate the zest of the orange and lemon and sprinkle over the plate with a few crumbs of dehydrated seaweed. Garnish with steamed vegetables, if desired. Finish with a pinch of *fleur de sel* and a drizzling of extra-virgin olive oil.

Wine pairing

"Fiano di Avellino" DOCG, Vigne della Congregazione 2002 – White
Winery: Villa Diamante – Montefrédane (AV)

NEAPOLITAN BABÀ WITH PASTRY CREAM AND WILD STRAWBERRIES

Ingredients for 4 people
Preparation time: 45' - Leavening time: 2 h

BABÀ
3⅓ cups (500 g) manitoba flour (type 0)
⅔ cup (150 g) butter, softened
9 whole eggs
¼ cup (50 g) sugar
Generous 1 tablespoon (20 g) brewer's yeast
2 teaspoons (10 g) table salt

SYRUP
2 cups (500 g) water

1¼ cups (250 g) sugar
Orange and lemon zests
1 vanilla pod

PASTRY CREAM
2 cups (500 ml) milk
Orange and lemon zests
¾ cup (150 g) sugar
6 egg yolks
4 tablespoons (60 g) all-purpose flour

Method

BABÀ
Combine the flour, scant ½ cup (100 g) butter, 8 eggs, sugar, salt, and the yeast
in an electric stand mixer or a food processor. Mix until ingredients form a dough.
Knead in the remaining egg and butter by hand, adding a little at a time to form
a voluminous and elastic dough. Let rise for about 1 hour, or until doubled in volume.
Beat the dough again in a stand mixer or food processor. Use a pastry bag to pipe the
dough into buttered molds. Let rise for another hour. Bake baba in the oven at 400°F
(200°C/gas mark 6).

SYRUP
Bring the water to a boil with the sugar, orange and lemon zests, and vanilla pod
in a small saucepan. Let cool until lukewarm.

PASTRY CREAM
Bring the milk to a boil with the citrus zests. Beat together the sugar, egg yolks, and flour
in an electric mixer. Slowly whisk in the boiling milk; transfer mixture to the top of a
double boiler and cook gently, stirring constantly to ensure that the eggs don't curdle.

Serving

Soak the baba in the syrup before serving. Arrange the babà on a plate, served with
the pastry cream and the wild strawberries.

Wine pairing

"Zingarella" IGT, Moscato di Baselice 2005 – Dessert wine
Winery: Masseria Parisi – Baselice (BN)

THE CUISINE OF APULIA

From the extraordinary grandeur of the ruins of Greek civilization to the natural splendors bathed in light and colors, Apulia is a land of mysterious charms.

This is Apulia, from the land of Bari to the golden fields of wheat, to the Murge pierced with rocks and ravines to the Itria Valley, scattered with *trulli* (circular, conical-roofed whitewashed houses) It is the Salentine peninsula and the coasts lapped by the waves of the Ionian and Adriatic. Then there's the historical evidence: the cave settlements, Greek heritage, Roman roads, the Norman and Swabian castles, the Romanesque and Baroque. The white stone cathedrals that prosper, the high, rocky coasts of the Gargano which plunge into the Adriatic, and the archipelago of Tremiti, white fragments in a turquoise sea. In the balance between two seas it is yet another Italian masterpiece.

Describing Apulia's appearance isn't easy; and it's just as complicated to talk about Apulian cuisine. The abundance of recipes, products, and customs, each of which vary from area to area, make the cooking of the region a varied and complex art. There is a world of flavors in this land between the sea and the Apennine mountains, a mosaic of orchards and expanses of grain fields, vineyards, olive groves, and pastures. In 1222, Frederick II had already distinguished the land of Bari from the *Capitanata* (the area around Foggia) and the land of Otranto. Today, these three regions remain separate but similar in regards to their culinary traditions, sharing common threads, such as the chile pepper, which is used in almost all dishes of Apulia.

Among its typical products, Apulia's food heritage includes refined cheeses, salamis, and oil *(Terra di Bari, Collina di Brindisi, Dauno,* and *Terra d'Otranto* extra-virgin olive oils, all of which are PDO and well-known producers). Among the most popular cheeses is the cow or sheep's milk cheese *Fior di Latte*, a PDO cheese that is a fresh, moist spun cheese, made from full-fat milk. It has a rounded, plaited or prism shape. The cheese is white and soft, and oozes when cut. It has a fresh flavor and a fragrant aroma. Another popular cheese is *Canestrato* (also a PDO cheese), a cheese of far-reaching history that has been produced all over the Foggia and Bari areas. Pecorino and Ricotta cheese are also of note, as well as Provola di Bufala, Mozzarella, Scamorza, Caciocavallo, and the specialty of the Andria region, Burrata, which encloses morsels of cheese mixed with cream in a shell of spun curd (see box).

On the charcuterie front, there are many choices, from the *Capocollo di Martina Franca* to the *Soppressata di Martina Franca*, but undoubtedly the most curious salami in the whole of Apulia is *Salsiccia Leccese*, a mixture of veal and pork cured with spices, grated lemon zest, cinnamon, and cloves. It's perfect with Altamura bread, typical of the lovely rural town of Altamura in the Murge. Overlooking the town, there's a large cathedral surrounded by winding alleyways and secret courtyards from which wafts the unmistakable aroma of its bread, baked in a wood-burning oven according to ancient tradition. The leavening of this dough, made from durum wheat flour, salt, and water, is done naturally. The demand for this bread all over Italy is considerable, which also explains the intensity of the industrial production.

Bread and pasta are the basis of Apulian cooking and food: from the traditional homemade bread baked in large communal ovens to *Frisedde*, a type of bread ring baked and cut in half to be cooked further like biscuits in the oven. *Frisedde* are eaten slightly dampened and served with oil, salt, oregano, and cherry tomatoes. It's a type of food to be eaten *al fresco*, perhaps a relic of the old sheep-farming life. There's also a whole range of pizzas and focacce, almost always filled with vegetables, olives, or Pecorino cheese, baked in the oven like a calzone or fried in oil like the *panzerotti*.

The pasta types are also mainly homemade in origin: the orecchiette, the pride and joy of Apulian cuisine, is traditionally served with turnip greens or with a Bari-style ragù, or made with veal rolls stuffed with Pecorino and herbs and cooked with fresh tomatoes. The sauce from this dish is used to dress the pasta and the meat, and is then served as a deliciously rich main course. A baked maccheroni pasta pie is made for special occasions: a filling made from meatballs, diced salami, sliced hard-cooked eggs, cheeses like Pecorino, and seasonal vegetables is placed on a sheet of pastry. A sauce called *Ciambotto* (which means 'mixture' in dialect) is made in Bari with many types of fish used to serve the pasta, called *Ciabotta*. However, there are also *Cìciri e trya*, Tagliatelle and garbanzo beans, which continue to pass on the ancient name of the Middle Eastern pasta to document how the art of dried pasta became widespread in Italy during the Arab domination.

The use of meat other than beef comes from the pastoral tradition; beef is used almost solely in making meatballs or ragù. The most commonly used meats are lamb or kid, followed by farmyard animals and sometimes game.

The important fruit of this rich land of expanses of ancient olive groves is oil, with its unique flavor of almonds. It's not a random coincidence. Almonds are also extensively cultivated and these nuts, widely used in Apulian patisserie, are one of the region's most important products in terms of export.

The range of fish on offer is one of the richest in Italy. Taranto is famous for its cultivation of oysters, which are delivered to restaurants in the north. Bari's specialty is *pulpe rizze*, curly octopus, but the entire region offers fish stews, pasta with seafood, stewed mollusks, mussels, and more. There is also the rare *Tarantello*, a typical salami made from tuna belly.

Among the vegetables, one should not miss the *lampascioni*, a type of small wild onion that tastes best when boiled or baked.

Yellow and white melons, watermelons, and excellent grapes also grow in Apulia. The large-scale production of grapes makes the region among the richest in terms of wine, turning out blended wines, which improve many Italian wines because of their body and sugar content, and specialties like Sansevero del Tavoliere, Santo Stefano, Torre Quarto, Primitivo, Malvasia, Aleatico, and Moscato.

What's for dessert? *Carteddate, Cauciani, Mostaccioli, Scarcedda,* and *Susamelli* are recipes that range from a medium to high difficulty to make. Especially when they contain candied fruits, they marry extremely well with the sweet and particularly aromatic wines of this land.

BURRATA DI ANDRIA

THIS EXQUISITE APULIA PRODUCT MADE FROM SPUN CURD IS ORIGINALLY FROM ANDRIA, BUT IT'S MADE ALL OVER THE REGION. BURRATA IS A SPECIAL CHEESE IN TERMS OF ITS FLAVOR AND APPEARANCE. EXTERNALLY IT LOOKS LIKE MOZZARELLA, WHILE ITS CORE, MADE FROM THE SAME SPUN CURD, IS FINELY CHOPPED AND MIXED WITH FRESH CREAM. IT HAS A BUTTERY, MILKY FLAVOR. IT'S SERVED WITH WHITE OR RED WINES THAT ARE NOT TOO PERFUMED LIKE RED NARDÒ, CHARDONNAY, OR ROSÉ LAVERANO.

ANTONELLA RICCI

RESTAURANT AL FORNELLO DA RICCI - CEGLIE MESSAPICA (BRINDISI)

THE KITCHEN OF THE RESTAURANT *AL FORNELLO DA RICCI* IN CEGLIE MESSAPICA, AN OLD HILLY TOWN IN THE NORTHERN PART OF THE SALENTINE PENINSULA, IS FAIRLY TECHNOLOGICAL, SPACIOUS, AND WELL-LIT, AND STILL MAINTAINS, PRESERVED LIKE THE ICON OF THE GOD IN THE CELLS OF THE GREEK TEMPLES, THE STOVE THAT MADE THE RESTAURANT FAMOUS AND WHICH IS STILL FULLY OPERATIONAL TODAY. *"THE STOVE,"* ANTONELLA RICCI, CHEF AND CO-OWNER OF THE RESTAURANT WITH HUSBAND VINOD SOOKAR (WHO HAS WORKED ALONGSIDE HER IN THE KITCHEN FOR 11 YEARS) AND SISTER ROSSELLA (MAÎTRE D'HÔTEL AND SOMMELIER), EXPLAINS, *"IS A TYPICAL OVEN IN OUR AREA. IT'S STRUCTURED LIKE A NORMAL OVEN, BUT IT WORKS ON CHARCOAL AND WITH VERTICAL SKEWERS. BENEATH THE OVEN THE FAT IS COLLECTED IN A SMALL TANK, WHICH WE EMPTY EVERYDAY. IT WAS CONSTRUCTED TOTALLY IN STONE AND WE ONLY COOK MEAT IN IT. ONCE UPON A TIME IN APULIA, ALL THE BUTCHER'S SHOPS HAD ONE OF THESE STOVES, COOKING A CUSTOMER'S PURCHASES IN IT IMMEDIATELY."*

OVER 40 YEARS OF CATERING HAS TAKEN PLACE IN FRONT OF THE STOVE BELONGING TO THE RICCI FAMILY. *"THE RESTAURANT WAS ESTABLISHED IN 1967 AT THE WISHES OF MY GRANDMOTHER ROSA. HER HUSBAND, GRANDAD ROCCO, WAS A WELL-KNOWN FIGURE IN THE TOWN. HE HAD AN OIL MILL AND A SMALL STONE CAVE. AFTER WORK, HE REALLY ENJOYED INVITING ALL HIS FRIENDS AND COLLEAGUES HOME TO EAT TOGETHER. THEREFORE, MY GRANDMOTHER ALWAYS COOKED FOR LOTS OF PEOPLE."* WHEN SHE DECIDED TO DON AN APRON AS HER JOB, OPENING THE RESTAURANT WITH HER SON ANGELO AND DAUGHTER-IN-LAW DORA, *"THERE WERE VERY FEW DISHES OFFERED AND THEY CHANGED WITH THE SEASONS: HOMEMADE PICKLES, ORECCHIETTE, AND MEAT COOKED IN THE STOVE, DISHES WHICH STILL REMAIN ON THE MENU."* WITH THE PASSING OF TIME, THE REINS OF THE RESTAURANT WERE PASSED ON TO ANGELO, THEN TO ANTONELLA, WHO IS A MEMBER OF THE *JEUNES RESTAURATEURS D'EUROPE* ASSOCIATION, AND NOW TO HER HUSBAND AND SISTER AS WELL.

Over the years, the simple trattoria of its beginnings has been transformed into the high-class restaurant it is today. *"The visit of the great food and wine critic Luigi Veronelli at the end of the 1980s was a highly important moment in the restaurant's history; he rewarded the Veronelli sun symbol to the leg of kid with potatoes cooked in ashes. Also the Michelin star, which was given 15 years ago, marked a turning point in the continual pursuit towards quality, research, and hospitality."* These gifts are the legacy of Antonella's father, who died in 2006. *"Since he passed away, we've tried to carry on the restaurant that he wanted in the best possible way, continuing to follow his philosophy of cooking and hospitality."* Surrounded in the lovely scenery of the Lower Murge, a patchwork of farm land, olive groves, vineyards, and orchards, *Al Fornello da Ricci* is located in an old country home. *"There's an atmosphere of total relaxation in the restaurant. It is furnished in a rustic yet elegant style; the garden for summer dining is Mediterranean in style, filled with flowers and herbs tended by my mother, Dora. The table settings are unpretentious, the tables are spaced well apart, and we can sit 40 guests."*

Antonella's cuisine *"tries – and I emphasize tries – to bring heart and mind together,"* she explains. On the one hand, there's the genuine sensation of the typical flavors of Apulia, the historic *Dàunia* region; on the other hand, there's she knows how to manipulate food in a rational and modern way. It is a set-up that recalls the splendid *Castel del Monte*, built by Frederick II in Andria in 1240 as a hunting lodge or—more probably—as a temple of knowledge. It is geometrically perfect, the fruit of evolved mathematical and astronomical knowledge, and imbued with ancient esoteric symbols, starting with the octagonal base, the union of the square of the earth with the circle of the sky. *"My cuisine is in pure symbiosis with the land,"* Antonella says. *"I use all the products that I can choose in my Apulia: fruits and vegetables, dairy products and cheese, sausages, flour, meat – especially lamb, kid, offal, pork, and rabbit – and preserved fish like salt cod and salt-cured anchovies. It's important to say that you won't find any fresh fish on our menu. That's not because we don't want to serve it, but due to the fact that the restaurant was founded based on the stove for the cooking of meat and we have preferred to carry on in this direction.*" Moreover, the restaurant is located in inland Apulia, far away from both the Adriatic and Ionian coasts.

"*It's not that I'm fanatical about the indigenous ingredients, but I'm convinced that if somebody comes to eat here, then they want to taste what the place has to offer.*" After all, true innovation does not follow fashion, but the details of its own history and Antonella is attached to hers. Above all, she is moved by the ancient olive trees which sweep down to the Adriatic Sea from Ostuni, the famous 'white town,' so-called for its houses whitewashed in lime. "*With their silent wisdom they have articulated the passing of time,*" Antonella reflects. But she is also moved by the town of Ceglie Messapica, with its historic center that has remained intact: "*I love that silence that can be heard in the hot siesta hours in the early afternoon during the summer, which takes you back in time, while the aroma of ragù still drifts around the alleyways.*"

She uses Apulian products in many recipes. For example, when the Brindisi artichokes are in season she offers a classic recipe from the area. After stuffing them with soaked bread and serving them with capers, garlic, fresh Pecorino, parsley, mint, and pepper, she cooks them in a wood-burning oven with herbs, onion, carrot, and celery. "*On top it become soufflé-like and stays crunchy, while being soft on the inside.*" Another typical vegetable, the "*small Violetta eggplant with its slightly piquant taste,*" is prepared with garlic according to tradition. "*Here we also have the characteristic Sant'Anna beans, thus named as they're only found at the end of July.*" (St. Anna is venerated on July 26.) "*They grow to about 50 centimeters long, are very thin, and are a brilliant green color. At this time of year, we serve them with spaghettoni from a Neapolitan pasta manufacturer and with a sauce made from three types of tomatoes: vine, Fiaschetto, and Regina.*"

The traditional Apulian dishes vary according to the season. "*Our menu lasts for a couple of*

months at the most. In the spring, it's even less. That's because we use products, such as wild asparagus, peas, and fresh fava beans, which are only found for a short length of time." These dishes are always featured. "You can't have innovation without knowing the tradition." This is also taught by the cathedral of Ruvo di Puglia, a masterpiece of Apulian Romanesque, which rises above a hypogeum, where the remains of a Pre-Roman settlement are found. It is also home to Roman tombs, an early Christian basilica and a group of medieval homes. "Personally speaking, I don't really like revising traditional dishes. I enjoy using traditional products to create new recipes." She likes to serve the dishes that are deeply rooted to the land as they are, like leg of kid with potatoes cooked in ashes, or orecchiette (the main form of homemade fresh pasta in Apulian regional cooking, along with incanulate, cavatelli, troccoli, and strascinati) with fresh tomatoes, Cacioricotta, and basil or turnip greens.

Like the *trulli*, the characteristic conical-roofed buildings found all around the town of Alberobello, in the Itria Valley, which have been declared a UNESCO world heritage site, Antonella recognizes the Apulian culinary legacy in the historic dishes and protects them from being tampered with or plundered. In addition to the cornerstones of tradition, however, "there is a myriad of new dishes made solely from local products." Among these dishes, some have become classics in their own right. For example, *Crudaiola*, a dish of homemade burnt wheat pasta with strands of salami, crunchy vegetables, and shavings of Cacioricotta and Ricotta with almond-crusted figs and bitter cocoa sauce are two contemporary local favorites. "Our area has excellent figs and almonds," Antonella explains.

Antonella, following in the footsteps of her mother's family – "my grandfather Antonio was a chef in Brindisi. There was already cooking in my family's blood." – has an external student diploma from the hotel institute in Brindisi and has completed various internships in Italy and France, as well as a degree in Economics and Banking from the University of Lecce, "a gamble with myself to show that I, too, could be studious like my sister." She had helped out in her parents' restaurant since she was a child. After she graduated in 1995, she started to work full time in the kitchen. Since 1997, the exotic soul of Vinod, a famous chef from Mauritius, has offered her new suggestions. "As well as in terms of the presentation of the dishes, he has influenced me in the clever use of spices, which I have started to use in some marinades and fruit salads, and in the plated desserts. We don't really have a tradition of plated desserts. We stop at marzipan-based sweets and bocconotti, small pastries filled with custard and cherry preserves. I had already started to offer some plated desserts, but given Vinod's training in French food, we're offering even more."

It's Vinod who does the shopping. "He goes to the Ostuni market for the fruit and vegetables and around here for the rest. For example, at Cisternino, there's a small mill for semolina and durum wheat flour. On the other hand, we can only source the burnt wheat flour from a producer in a village in the Monti Dauni, which sends us regular supplies. There are small-scale producers who come and sell us some special products directly, such as wild vegetables, cardoncelli mushrooms, olives for frying, pulses, such as garbanzo beans, chickling vetch, lentils, and fava beans, which are often used in our cooking – or snails." The meat is bought in the masserie, the large, characteristic, and historic fortified farms that stand isolated in the Apulian countryside, as is the Ricotta, Pecorino, Burrata, and Stracciatella cheeses. "It's a meticulous selection process that takes time to do. We don't just buy everything that one supplier produces."

The dishes chosen for this book "are all associated with the area and represent the generosity and variety of our marvellous Apulian products." For starters, there are zucchini flowers stuffed with goat's Ricotta on a basil and Fiaschetti tomato puree, which uses Brindisi extra-virgin olive oil PDO. For the first course, Antonella chose a black olive and veal stew millefeuille with basil-flavored bean puree, "which sees the use of an indigenous variety of olives, which are very small and black." For the meat course, there's rabbit thighs stuffed with Cegliese almond mousse and spicy fruity salad, "which features semi-aged Canestrato Pugliese, a cheese made from whole milk from the Gentile di Puglia breed of sheep, similar to Pecorino." And for dessert: Upside-down fig tartlet with goat's milk ice-cream and almond brittle. A menu created with expert and precise hands, like those of Barisano in the magnificent portal of Trani cathedral, carved in the second half of the twelfth century; they modeled the bronze with the uncommon grace of a miniaturist.

ZUCCHINI FLOWERS STUFFED WITH GOAT'S RICOTTA WITH A BASIL AND FIASCHETTI TOMATO PUREE

Ingredients for 4 people
Preparation time: 40' - Resting: 1 h

TOMATO PUREE
10 medium vine-ripened tomatoes, cored and chopped
Generous ¾ cup (200 ml) Brindisi PDO extra-virgin olive oil, or other good-quality olive oil
2 teaspoons (10 g) sugar
1 bunch basil
Pinch of salt
Pinch of chile powder

ZUCCHINI BLOSSOMS
4 zucchini flowers
⅓ cup (80 g) goat's milk Ricotta cheese
2 small mint leaves
Pinch of salt
Pinch of nutmeg
Pinch of pepper
1 egg
1¼ cups (150 g) breadcrumbs
Slivered almonds
Olive oil for frying

Method

TOMATO PUREE
In a food processor or blender, puree the tomatoes . oil, sugar, basil leaves, salt, and chile powder.

Remove the pistil from the flowers and wash well. Let blossoms dry, on a paper towel-lined baking sheet, in the refrigerator for at least 1 hour. Mix the Ricotta, mint, salt, and nutmeg in a bowl. Fill the flowers with the Ricotta mixture. Dip them first in the beaten egg, followed by the breadcrumbs mixed with slivered almonds. Fry the flowers in a deep pan. Drain on a paper towel-lined plate.

Serving

Arrange a generous spoonful of tomato puree in the bottom of a plate and place the stuffed flowers on top.

Wine pairing

"Girofle" 2007 – Rosé
Winery: Monaci – Copertino (LE)

BLACK OLIVE AND VEAL STEW MILLEFEUILLE
WITH BASIL-FLAVORED *PIATTELLI* BEAN PUREE

Ingredients for 4 people
Preparation time: 45' - Resting: 2 h

5 whole eggs
1⅔ cups (250 g) flour
2 cups (500 g) milk
1 Salt
Scant ⅓ cup (20 g) black olives
Melted butter
2 zucchini
4 walnut halves
5 ice cubes
2 teaspoons (10 g) extra-virgin olive oil,
plus additional, for serving
1 bunch basil, plus additional leaves, for
serving
5 oz (150 g) diced veal stew meat
1½ oz (40 g) smoked Scamorza cheese
¾ oz (20 g) Parmigiano Reggiano

Scant 3 tablespoons (40 g) piattelli bean
puree (see recipe, below)
Pepper to taste
4 nonstick molds, about 2 inches (6 cm) in
diameter

PIATTELLI BEAN PUREE
5 oz (150 g) white beans, shelled
½ potato
½ carrot
½2 onion
½ stalk celery
Salt
⅔ cup (150 ml) milk
Scant 2 tablespoons (25 g) butter, diced
2 to 3 tablespoons light cream
4 oz (120 g) fried toast

Method

PIATTELLI BEAN PUREE
Place the beans in a saucepan with cold water, potato, carrot, onion, celery, and salt. Boil
until vegetables are tender. Drain, reserving 2 cups (500 ml) of the cooking liquid, Force all
drained vegetables through a food mill. Stir milk and reserved cooking liquid into the
puree. Return to the heat and cook for 20 minutes. Mix in the diced butter and a few
tablespoons of light cream. Whisk the eggs and flour in a large bowl. Gradually whisk in
the milk and season with salt. Blend the olives in a food processor with a little water. Stir it
into the milk mixture. Cover mixture and refrigerate for 2 hours. Strain through a fine-mesh
strainer. Make into thin crepes: Pour the mixture in a nonstick frying pan with a melted pat
of butter and heated, evenly covering the bottom of the pan. Blanch the zucchini in boiling
water for 1 minute. Let cool in ice water. In a food processor, blend three-quarters of the
zucchini with the walnuts, ice, oil, basil, and a pinch of salt to make a green puree. Cut the
remaining zucchini into small cubes. Cut the crepes into 2-inch (5-cm) squares. Place a
layer of crepes in the nonstick molds and alternate with the meat, Scamorza, and
Parmesan up to the brim. Bake in the oven at 350°F (180°C/gas mark 4) for 12 minutes.

Serving

Turn out onto a plate. Serve on the bean puree, pesto, and zucchini cubes. Drizzle with
a little extra-virgin olive oil and garnish with a few basil leaves.

Wine pairing

"Cappello di prete" Salento rosso 2006 – Red
Winery: Candido Sandonaci – Brindisi (BR)

RABBIT THIGHS STUFFED WITH CEGLIESE ALMOND MOUSSE AND SPICY FRUITY SALAD

Ingredients for 4 people
Preparation time: 45' - *Demi glace: 5 h*

STUFFED RABBIT THIGHS
4 rabbit thighs
Handful of herbs (thyme, rosemary, sage, parsley)
1 teaspoon (5 g) garlic
¾ cup (120 g) blanched almonds
1¾ oz (50 g) semi-aged Canestrato* Pugliese
cheese
5 oz (150 g) caul fat or 4 bamboo skewers
Generous 1 tablespoon (20 g) extra-virgin
olive oil, to brown
Scant ¼ cup (50 g) rabbit demi-glace* (made
using the thigh bones)
Pinch of salt
*Canestrato is a cheese made from whole
milk, similar to Pecorino.*

DEMI GLACE*
Rabbit bones and thighs
Scant 2 tablespoons (25 g) lard
2 carrots, 1 stalk of celery, 1 onion
1¼ cups (300 g) peeled ripe tomatoes
1 clove garlic and 1 small bunch of parsley

2 tablespoons (30 g) olive oil
2 teaspoons coarse salt. Pepper
Scant ½ cup (100 g) dry white wine
Generous 2 tablespoons (35 g) all-purpose flour
2 quarts (2 liters) water
Scant tablespoon (10 g) dried mushrooms

SALAD
3½ oz (100 g) mixed salad greens
2 strawberries, julienned
¾ oz (20 g) pineapple, peeled, cored, and
julienned
¾ oz (20 g) peaches, peeled, pitted, and
julienned
¾ oz (20 g) kiwi fruit, peeled and julienned
4 melon balls

VINAIGRETTE
1 tablespoon (15 g) extra-virgin olive oil
1½ teaspoons (8 g) cider vinegar
1 teaspoon (5 g) sugar
¼ teaspoon (2 g) chile powder
Pinch of salt

Method

Bone the thighs, taking care to leave the shank intact. Make the demi-glace with the bones.

DEMI-GLACE (2 CUPS/500 ML)

Soften the mushrooms in 1 cup (250 ml) of water. Dice the lard. Peel the carrots and clean the celery stalk. Chop up the carrots, celery, onion, the tomatoes, garlic, sage, and parsley.

Drizzle a little oil in a heat-proof casserole. Add the lard and the rabbit bones. Mix over medium heat and season with salt and pepper. Add the chopped vegetables. Bake in the oven at 350°F (170°C) for 20–30 minutes.

Return the dish to the heat. Add the white wine and flour and mix well.

Pour in the water and mix. Return to the oven.

Continue cooking for another 3 hours; return the dish to the heat and add the mushrooms, which have been drained and squeezed dry.

After another 30 minutes, remove the bones; strain sauce.

Return the sauce to the heat. Simmer for an additional 1½ hours to thicken. At the end of the cooking time, turn off the heat and let cool.

Wash and chop the herbs and garlic. Blend the almonds, Canestrato cheese, vegetables, garlic, and a drop of oil. Stuff the thighs with the mousse, sealing them with with the caul fat or a bamboo skewer. Heat the oil in a frying pan and brown the thighs. Transfer to a baking sheet. Bake in the oven at 350°F (170°C) for 15–18 minutes, or until cooked through.

Mix the salad , julienned fruit, and melon in a large bowl. Whisk together the vinaigrette ingredients.

Serving

Slice the thighs and serve with the hot demi-glace on top and the salad dressed with the vinaigrette on the side.

Wine pairing

"Sum" rosso da tavola 2005 – Red
Winery: Academia dei Racemi – Manduria (TA)

UPSIDE-DOWN FIG TARTLET WITH GOAT'S MILK ICE-CREAM AND ALMOND BRITTLE

Ingredients for 4 people
Preparation time: 1 h 30'

ICE-CREAM
2 cups (500 g) goat's milk
¾ cup (150 g) sugar
1 Vanilla bean, split open
2 tablespoons (30 g) powdered milk
1 egg yolk
Scant ½ cup (100 g) cream

ALMOND BRITTLE
Scant ¾ cup (100 g) blanched almonds
½ cup (100 g) superfine sugar
1 lemon
Oil

SHORTCRUST PASTRY
1 cup (150 g) all-purpose flour
Scant ½ cup (100 g) margarine
Scant 3 tablespoons (40 g) water
1 teaspoon (5 g) salt
4 individual aluminum molds
Scant 3 tablespoons (40 g) fig preserves
4 oz (120 g) figs, washed , patted dry, and sliced
⅓ cup (80 g) goat's milk ice-cream
1 tablespoon (15 g) almond brittle, broken into pieces

Method

ICE-CREAM
Heat the goat's milk to 195°F (90°C) in a saucepan over medium heat with the sugar and vanilla. Remove from the heat and add the powdered milk and egg yolk. Mix in the cream and beat well.

ALMOND BRITTLE
Coarsely chop almonds (or leave them whole). Spread out on a very clean baking sheet. Bake in a 350°F (175°C) preheated oven, toasting them lightly. Meanwhile, caramelize the sugar. Add a few drops of lemon juice and the toasted almonds. Mix well and pour the brittle onto a lightly oiled marble work surface.. Use a lightly oiled lemon to spread out the brittle to the desired height. Before it hardens completely, use a large knife to cut the brittle to the preferred size. Let cool.

SHORTCRUST PASTRY
Mix the flour, margarine, water, and salt a bowl. Let rest in the refrigerator for 1 hour. Use a rolling pin to roll out the pastry to ⅓-inch (1-cm) thick. Cut pastry into rounds and line each mold with pastry round. Spread the fig preserves on the bottom of the pastry and arrange the fig slices on top. Bake in the oven at 350°F (180°C/gas mark 4) for 15 minutes.

Serving

Serve warm with the ice-cream and almond brittle.

Wine pairing

"Nektare" primitivo di Manduria – Dessert wine
Winery: Soloperto – Manduria (TA)

CLAUDIO FILONI

RESTAURANT LA PURITATE - GALLIPOLI (LECCE)

The philosophy of the restaurant *La Puritate* in Gallipoli, which is set on the beautiful Ionian coast in the province of Lecce, is similar to the interiors of the Baroque churches of the Salentine peninsula, which strip themselves of the pictorial overabundance that characterizes this style in the rest of Italy to become more essential in character. Like the *Basilica di Santa Croce*, a masterpiece of the *barocco leccese* (Lecce Baroque), where there is a true tapestry on the facade carved into the soft and malleable local stone with its warm pinky yellow tones, but the interior is a pure basilican form, this restaurant, indicated by several parties as the best in the Salentine peninsula, likewise the restaurant offers honest and linear dishes, without yielding to the fashion that wants to process them in terms of the concept, recipe, and ingredients.

"My cuisine is simple, quick, and delicious," the chef Claudio Filoni asserts, who works at *La Puritate* six months of the year from June to November when the work increases and it becomes necessary to give the owners' daughter, Daniele Fedele, a hand. *"The ingredients mustn't be altered, from the addition of spices or flavors, processed as little and made as quickly as possible."* A clear and concise manifesto, with which the restaurant has successfully complied for over ten years. Opened in 1997 by Paolo Fedele, assisted by his father Ernesto, both *maîtres d'hôtel*, the restaurant has the backing of more than one generation of restaurateurs behind it. It was preceded by the simple osteria at the start of the twentieth century, the first of its kind in Gallipoli, to the trattoria during the Second World War with the attached grocer's shop. *"Traditionally it was always the women who cooked, my grandmother Lucia and my mother Anna,"* Ernesto remembers. *"As a boy, I remember that turtle meat still hadn't been prohibited and we cooked one a day, weighing 80 to 90 kilos. It was cut into fairly large pieces and left to simmer with some spices for a few hours, then cut into smaller pieces and put in the oven to finish cooking. It was the main dish of my father's trattoria. Here's a curious fact for you: the butcher who prepared the turtles wasn't paid in cash, but with the head, shell, and fat of the turtle. These were used to make soap. I wouldn't be brave enough to cook turtle anymore."*

Today's restaurant is located in the historic center of Gallipoli, the town known as the Pearl of the Ionian due to its pristine beauty, situated on an island that is chalky in origin, connected to the mainland by a seventeenth-century arched bridge. The restaurant is entitled *La Puritate* because it is located next to the historic *Chiesa di Santa Maria della Purità*, called *la Puritate* in dialect, whose fraternal order organizes the procession of Mary's Desolation with the Dead Christ at dawn on Easter Saturday, one of the most touching and characteristic parades of its kind in the south of Italy, and juts out over the popular, old *Spiaggia della Purità* (the beach of purity), to which the townsfolk are deeply attached.

The restaurant, which has 70 covers at its disposal, set up in an indoor lounge and in a conservatory that overlooks the sea, *"has an informal atmosphere,"* Claudio continues, *"where we try to offer the customers our utmost willingness. The feeling is that they really want to taste our strong Mediterranean flavors when they arrive. We also have the impression that they feel satisfied for the choice they've made when they leave."*

La Puritate offers an extensively thought-out seafood based cuisine, albeit one faceted with numerous pleasures. *"We almost exclusively serve fish."* This does not at all make light of the great wealth that the Ionian Sea offers in terms of cooking: hake, squid, cuttlefish, bonito, angler, mackerel, lobster, crab, red mullet, swordfish, tuna, and so forth. Like the remarkable tiny *Chiesa della Vergine degli Abissi* in nearby Otranto, the splendid eastern town of the Salentine peninsula, bathed in the silvery reflection of ancient olive trees, the restaurant isn't lacking in maritime decorations, from its mosaic floor, ornamented in the center with a traditional seafaring star, surrounded by figure of eight knots, to all the furnishings and the lighting system which recall the sea: sea horses, dolphins, anchors, shells, and so on.

"We don't use many vegetables. Our fish is so fresh that the customers are so satisfied by eating it that they don't feel the need for a side order. On the contrary, it would almost be a shame to ruin the palate with other flavors. At the most, customers might want some salad just enough

to cleanse the mouth." Although the cuisine in this area also offers dairy products and famous pulses – a typical dish with a thousand-year tradition is *ciceri e tria,* durum wheat tagliatelle and garbanzo beans served with onions sautéed in oil – in addition to the excellent vegetables, especially inland where it's a completely dense series of chalky stone expanses mixed with the deep red of the soil of the fields, Claudio does not attempt any side dishes. The fish, *"brought straight to our restaurant by a fisherman every morning when his boat comes back,"* must be served 'nude', without any culinary dressing. *"My idea is that you should be able to*

taste the fish for what it is, without preparing it before being eaten or serving it with any overly strong sauces. For example, I'll cut a slice of tuna and grill it, then I'll serve it with a drizzle of extra-virgin olive oil, a bit of lemon, a pinch of salt and freshly ground pepper." Like the dolmen, the prehistoric megalithic monuments which are dotted all over the Salentine peninsula, are formed simply of two large stone slabs that act as the support to a third slab that covers them, Claudio's cuisine stands tall on just one high-quality ingredient used in a simple and natural way.

"The few vegetables that we use are all produced locally. We are supplied by farmers in the area." They are used to accompany the pasta dishes. *"For example, in* linguine alla Puritate, *as well as the seafood, there are small pieces of zucchini; in* pennette in barcaccia, *also fish-based, there's garlic-marinated eggplant."* The pasta dishes also err on the side of simplicity. *"We don't use fresh pasta in the typical forms of Apulian tradition, like orecchiette and maccheroncini, as you need to have the time to make it and it also absorbs a lot of sauce. Also if it's egg-based, it can interfere with the flavor of the fish in the sauce. Instead we use an excellent bronze-died durum wheat pasta, which we only cook in four types: linguine, pennette, spaghetti, and rice."*

The menu doesn't change often precisely due to its universal character that is not led astray by creative experiments, *"but when we have fish available other than those shown – we work based on the day's catch – the waiter will let the customers know the new dishes."*

There are the house specialties which *La Puritate* has offered since it opened, such as *"tartare of tuna, our shelled pink shrimp, squid in balsamic vinegar, and filleted fish, without the blood and bones, as if you were eating a steak, Mediterranean spearfish, and amberfish."* There are also the local classics *"which always stay on the menu,"* such as the Gallipoli-style cuttlefish baked in the oven with breadcrumbs, one of the town's typical dishes; *Scapece*, where sardines or anchovies are fried and left to marinate between layers of breadcrumbs soaked in vinegar and saffron in a tub called a *calette* in dialect; the fish stew, which sees scorpion fish, grouper, sea bream, porgy, squid, cuttlefish, shrimp, and mussels all end up traditionally in a pot with a base of onion and vinegar; *purpu alla pignata*, stewed octopus with potatoes and tomatoes; and *'mboti*, rolls made from calf's lungs and liver. *"It is above all a fish-based cuisine. Here we eat precious little meat."*

There's no talk of innovation on the culinary legacy of the past. *"The tradition remains intact and isn't being subjected to any changes. That's the way it should be."* Like the cock with the crown that appears on the Gallipoli coat-of-arms surrounded by the Latin wording that quotes *fideliter excubat*, or "faithfully oversees," this is how Claudio conducts himself with the gastronomic heirloom. After all, in the Salentine peninsula, named Messapia ("land between two seas") in the past by the ancient Greeks, able to fascinate with its relics and the crossroads of the different cultures in the Mediterranean basin, intrigue with the magnificent works of the master stone-masters, and entice with the colors and landscapes of the sun, the culinary traditions are still alive. *"Just by walking around the narrow streets in the historic center of our town, you can breathe in the aromas of the past. But these flavors also make themselves felt in the air, particularly when the elderly talk among themselves."*

Claudio was born in Milan, with parents originally from Galatina, the delightful Salentine town with important churches like the Late-Romanesque *Basilica di Santa Caterina*, which has been declared a national monument for its enormous fresco cycles. *"In 1983 I worked in a restaurant in*

Germany for a few years; then I came back to Italy and with my brother-in-law, who was a great chef and a lecturer in a well-known hotel institute in Milan, I opened a restaurant on Elba Island. He taught me all the tricks of the trade; he was an excellent teacher. Then about 20 years ago while I was on vacation around here, I fell in love with a girl from Galatina, I got married, and decided to come and live here. I started to work in various restaurants in the province of Lecce. I must have covered the entire coastline from Santa Maria di Leuca to San Giovanni, until I found the ideal environment here at La Puritate in 2004."

The menu chosen for this book naturally sees the fish from the Ionian Sea take to the spotlight. For starters, there's fresh marinated mackerel, *"served with a drizzling of our local extra-virgin olive oil, which is fundamental with fish."* For the pasta course, linguine with bonito fish with diced tomatoes, followed by angler fish medallions with lemon for the main course, *"floured and lightly fried in oil – without being overly handled in the pan – and then served with lemon juice, a pat of butter, a sprinkling of parsley, and salt and pepper."* For dessert, there's *Torta pasticciotto*, *"one of our typical desserts, consisting of a very crunchy pie crust and filled with lemon pastry cream. It goes brilliantly at the end of a fish-based meal."* It is the custom of the people of the Salentine peninsula to eat the dessert, which was invented by a pastry cook from Galatina in the mid-eighteenth century, for breakfast when it's just come out of the oven, almost boiling hot.

This is a menu in which the sea breeze and the land of Salentine peninsula are perfectly united. It's reminiscent of the many coastal grottos which can be seen in the continuous change between soft, shallow sandy beaches and the rocky stretches along the crystal clear sea, from the Neolithic Grotta dei Cervi, one of the most important monuments of cave art in Europe, with over 3,000 pictograms, to the Grotta della Zinzulusa, a lively spectacle of light and clear waters which gambol among the tortuous stalactites and stalagmites.

FRESH MARINATED MACKEREL

Ingredients for 4 people
Preparation time: 30'

2 lb (1 kg) mackerel
6 lemons
Pinch of salt
Pinch of pepper
Parsley
1 quart (1 liter) extra-virgin olive oil

Method

Clean the mackerel, removing the insides. Use a sharp knife to cut into two fillets.
Use some small pliers to remove the bones remaining in the central part of the
fillet.
Place a saucepan full of water over medium heat. Add the juice of the lemons
and the lemons themselves. Season with salt and pepper. When the water comes
to a boil, add the fish and cook for about 8 minutes.

Serving

Drain the fish and arrange in a dish. Sprinkle with the chopped parsley and drizzle
with the extra-virgin olive oil.

Wine pairing

Uve di Verdeca in purezza – White
Winery: Leone de' Castris – Salice Talentino (LE)

LINGUINE WITH BONITO FISH

Ingredients for 4 people
Preparation time: 25'

7 oz (200 g) bonito fish
1 clove garlic
tablespoons extra-virgin olive oil
Salt, to taste
Pepper, to taste
5 oz (150 g) peeled and chopped tomatoes
7 oz (200 g) linguine pasta

Method

Sauté the bonito fish, cut into small strips, with the garlic in a little oil in a pan for a couple of minutes. Season with salt and pepper. Add the chopped tomatoes.
Meanwhile, cook the linguine in plenty of salted water until *al dente*.

Serving

Drain the pasta. Transfer to the pan with the sauce.
Cook for a few minutes over low heat and serve.

Wine pairing

Miere – White
Winery: Michele Calò e Figli – Tuglie (LE)

ANGLER FISH MEDALLIONS WITH LEMON

Ingredients for 4 people
Preparation time: 20'

7 oz (200 g) angler fish or monkfish, cleaned and cut into slices
4 tablespoons extra-virgin olive oil
Salt, for seasoning
Pepper, for seasoning
Flour to dust
4 tablespoons lemon juice
1 pat of butter
Parsley

Method

Skin the angler fish and cut into 1¼-inch (3-cm) thick slices.
Warm a little oil in a frying pan over medium heat. Season the fish
with salt and pepper. Dip them in the flour, shaking off the excess.
Fry the fish for 5 minutes in the heated oil in the pan.
Strain off the cooking oil. Drizzle the fish with the lemon juice and
add a pat of butter. Sprinkle with the parsley and season with salt
and pepper. Serve at once.

Wine pairing

Miere – Rosé
Winery: Michele Calò e Figli – Tuglie (LE)

TORTA PASTICCIOTTO

Ingredients for 4 people
Preparation time: 1 h

PASTRY CREAM
1 cup (250 ml) milk
½ vanilla pod
Zest of ½ lemon
1 cup (250 g) egg yolks
¾ cup (150 g) sugar
Scant 3 tablespoons (40 g) flour, sifted
1 cup (250 ml) cream

SHORTCRUST PASTRY
4 cups (600 g) flour
Generous ¾ cup (200 g) lard, diced
Scant ½ cup (100 g) butter, softened
1½ cups (300 g) sugar
2 whole eggs
2 egg yolks
Grated lemon

Method

PASTRY CREAM
Bring the milk to a boil in a saucepan with the vanilla and lemon zest. Beat the egg yolks and sugar in a metal bowl. Add the flour and mix well. Slowly whisk in the boiling milk. Return the mixture to the heat in the saucepan used to boil the milk. Bring to a boil for 2 minutes. Pour the custard into a metal bowl and let cool.

SHORTCRUST PASTRY
Mix the flour with the diced lard and softened butter on a work surface. Add the sugar, egg yolks, and grated lemon. Knead the mixture quickly.
Oil a cake pan. Roll out half the pastry and use it to line the pan. Pour the pastry cream into the cake pan. Roll out the remaining pastry and cover the pastry cream. Brush with beaten egg whites. Bake in the oven at 350°F (180°C/gas mark 4) for about 1 hour.

Serving

Serve very hot.

Wine pairing

Moscato grecale – Dessert wine
Winery: Florio – Marsala (TP)

THE CUISINE OF BASILICATA

Ancient Lucania, the setting of historic clashes between the Greeks, Samnites, and Romans, is mostly a mountainous land, studded with the peaks of the Apennines and lush woodland. From the faraway inactive volcano of Mount Vulture, now covered in the greenery of vineyards and chestnut groves, a short distance from the charming town of Melfi, a place thick with Byzantine memories and held dear by Frederick II, you reach the town of Pollino, the home of the national park of the same name, on the border with Calabria. The region overlooks the sea on the east and west sides, with short stretches of Tyrrhenian and Ionian coastlines. It boasts true scenic and architectural pearls, such as the attractive medieval town of Maratea, with its bunch of fishermen's houses on the *Golfo di Policastro* and perfumed citrus plantations.

This is a land that cultivates high-quality wheat, used locally and throughout the rest of Italy to make pasta: the old-fashioned *lagane* are the pride and joy of many areas in Basilicata, including Matera, Potenza, and Melfi on an industrial level.

In addition to the *lagane* with beans, garbanzo beans, breadcrumbs, or walnuts, the area is home to *maccheroni* and *cavatelli* with vegetable sauce or ragù, and spaghetti with garlic, oil, and chile pepper.

Simple soups such as *acquasale* are not absent in regional cooking They were made during breaks from working in the fields, with a little oil or nothing at all: bread, onions, tomatoes, garlic, a drop of oil, and salt, and boiling water; also popular are heartier soups of mixed vegetables and meats, and soups made from beans, cardoons, and pork rinds.

A delicious and hearty large bread is made locally from durum wheat flour, which was once kept in terracotta jars. There's also a recipe called *Roccolo* that combines bread dough with pork crackling.

The production of olive oil is also important in what is, arguably, the most scenic area by the Ionian Sea. Only limited amounts are produced, but the quality is just as good as Umbrian or Tuscan oil.

The entire Metaponto area produces and widely exports high-quality vegetables, especially tomatoes, but also bell peppers, eggplant, chicory, fava beans, and lentils, which are cooked together in typical recipes such as *ciammotta* or *ciambotta*, with bell peppers, eggplant, tomatoes, and eggs, or *ciaudedda*, which sees potatoes, onions, artichokes, and fava beans cooked in a meat stock flavored with pancetta. The production of pulses and vegetables (see box) is considerable and of recognized dignity, especially Sarconi beans, excellent with *lagane*, and Senise bell peppers, exquisite when dried and fried, and served with boiled salt cod with the addition of chile pepper.

Fishing takes place along the Maratea coast, mainly tuna and anchovies, which are enjoyed fresh or canned. In the lakes of Monticchio and Pertusillo, eel and freshwater fish are caught. Salt cod has also become part of Basilicata's food scene in many recipes, perhaps only second to Veneto, due to the fact that it keeps for a long time: one type is Potenza-style salt cod, with olives, capers, tomatoes, and onions. Another typical dish is *sarde in scapece*, sardines fried and pickled in vinegar, to be eaten the day after having been prepared. Basilicata has been a region dedicated to farming sheep for millennia and therefore has a prized tradition of dairy products. There are many typical cheeses and they can be eaten with the unquestioned leading wine of Basilicata: Aglianico del Vulture. Two mixed sheep and goat's milk products come from the province of Potenza: Pecorino di Filiano, with its unique and intense flavor, enhanced by cave-ripening, and Canestrato di Moliterno PDO, a uniform hard cheese, piquant, and straw-yellow in color. A variety of sheep and goat's milk Ricotta Salata, Cacioricotta, is also famous with a persistent flavor, which becomes more pronounced with ageing.

Another typical cheese is made from the milk of the Podolica breed of cow, reared in the Pollino and Volturino area, the Caciocavallo Podolico, whose ageing ranges from six months to one year. The product made from Caciocavallo spun curd, called *Manteca* or *Butirro*, contains a ball of butter. The version that comes from Pisticci is famous, the town situated among olive groves, vineyards, and strawberry cultivations in the striking province of Matera. This province ranges from the prehistoric landscape of the Sassi to the golden fields of wheat, the traces of important cities of the Magna Graecia, and the vegetable gardens of the coast.

The production of salamis is equally important and valuable. There's *Lucanica*, a spicy sausage whose origins are so old that it has the Latin name of the land of provenance, *Soppressata*, made from the leanest part of the local species of black pig, and *Pezzenta*, a rustic sausage used to add flavor to sauces, made from leftover pork, veal, and lamb and flavored with garlic, chile pepper, and various other spices. In Basilicata, it is customary to cook lamb according to the *alla buca*, or 'in a hole' cooking method, which is also done in identically the same way in Sardinia.

The warm climate and the need to preserve foods due to the certain isolation of the peoples led to the creation of many preserving techniques, the tradition of which still continues today: small sausages in oil, olives in brine or oil, fried and dried or plain dried, fish preserves, fruit preserves, including dried figs stuffed with almonds, dried marrons (or chestnuts), walnuts, and hazelnuts, dried pulses, vegetables and tomato sauces.

The dessert eaten for celebrations is *Mostacciolo*, made from flour, honey, almonds, and *vin cotto*, an alcoholic drink made from boiled grape must. *Vin cotto* is also needed to make *Cuccia*, or sweet wheat, as well as durum wheat, sugar, walnuts, pomegranate seeds, and chocolate. The basic ingredients of patisserie in this region are also almonds, walnuts, hazelnuts, candied citrus fruits, dried figs, honey, Ricotta, and so on.

In terms of wines, we should mention the ancient Lagarino cited by the Latin writer Pliny the Elder as one of the wines most enjoyed by his peers; as well as Aglianico, which also exists in a sparkling version, some muscatels, Aleatico, etc.

FAGIOLI DI SARCONI PGI AND PEPERONI DI SENISE PGI

CULTIVATED IN THE TWO ECOTYPES CANNELLINO AND BORLOTTO, SARCONI BEANS IGP, WHICH ARE PRODUCED IN THE TOWN OF THE SAME NAME AS WELL AS IN OTHER MUNICIPALI-TIES IN THE PROVINCE OF POTENZA, TEND TO BE SWEET AND ARE PARTICULARLY PRECIOUS. SENISE BELL PEPPERS IGP, CULTIVATED IN THE POINTED, TRUNCATED, AND HOOKED VARIETY IN THE VALLEYS OF THE RIVERS SINNI AND AGRI, THE TYPICAL PRODUCTION AREA, ARE ALSO A CROWNING PRODUCT OF CUISINE IN BASILICATA.

FRANCESCO RIZZUTI

ANTICA OSTERIA MARCONI - POTENZA

Francesco Rizzuti has gone from harangues to herrings, from possible prince of the court to prince of restaurateurs in Lucania. He is chef and co-owner of the restaurant, regarded as the best in Basilicata, *Antica Osteria Marconi* in Potenza, studied law with the intention of becoming a lawyer and setting his pots and pans aside as a Sunday hobby. However, that's not the way it worked out. *"I went to a high school specializing in humanities, then I studied law, then I opened the restaurant,"* he tells us. Born in Potenza under the sign of Aries and 40 years old, he hasn't betrayed the stars, which decided he should be a connoisseur. *"I had always loved cooking. I delighted in being in the kitchen at home or among friends."*

When he decided to put himself to the test and he set up the restaurant, he worked alongside a few professional chefs, doing internships in Italy and all over Europe, and began to study hard. His goal was to learn the trade, of course, but above all to dabble in some different concepts of cooking. *"These are experiences which I still continue doing now through reading and comparison with colleagues who are more important than me. I need this to grow and increase my knowledge of food. I actually don't feel like I'm self-taught as that means someone who's really learnt by themselves, whereas I've tried to learn from those who knew more than me."*

Antica Osteria Marconi, which Francesco has been managing for four years with his friend Giuseppe Misuriello, maître d'hôtel and sommelier, opened in 1994, with the aim of offering something different on the city's food scene. It is located in one of the main avenues of the capital of Basilicata, Viale Marconi, in a business area next to the historic center. *"It is an early twentieth-century house and is furnished somewhere in between rustic – with its terracotta flooring and bricks – and elegant, with padded seats and glasses and plates in Riedel crystal."* Two lounges with a total of 30 seats, as well as a garden with a portico, which is used in the summer to add another 20 to 30 seats. *"The ambience is fairly informal. Starting with the name that we chose, our intention was to have an 'old-fashioned inn' in a modern key."* However, the name is misleading. *"Although it's called Antica Osteria Marconi, there wasn't a restaurant here before ours at all. It was a family garage that I decided to renovate."*

The intention was to "*actually start out as an osteria, only offering traditional dishes. Then in 1999 I had enough personal experience that had allowed me to develop to the point at which I wanted to set up the business more as a restaurant, serving more innovative dishes in terms of aesthetic presentation, but also reworking and preparation using more modern cooking techniques.*" In 1999 he actually participated in a course ran by Ferrand Adrià. Through this contact with the creative talent and the avant-garde techniques of the Spanish chef, Francesco began to understand that he could embark on a new path: reworking tradition. From that point on, he set off towards dishes which are not just the toying of a genius, but also an expression of informed and careful thought. Like the majestic architecture of the Ponte Musmeci in Potenza, designed in the 1970's, where the shape isn't purely a work of art, but also a functional optimization of the static system.

For the last eight years, there have been some house specialties that continue to remain on the menu. One of these is *acquasala*, a dish that was made by families in Basilicata using day-old bread, a soup with onion and anything else they had in the pantry. "*There's no such thing as a standard recipe. We've revised it by adding turnip greens as we like the combination, or asparagus when they're in season, or just onions and tomatoes. We make a vegetable stock, using sautéed onion as the base, which we used to add flavor and soften the day-old slices of bread. Then we enrich the acquasala with a poached egg and our traditional Senise cruschi bell peppers, which have been dried and fried.*" They actually use bell peppers from the Valli del Sinni and dell'Agri, "*because when they are dried they don't fall from the stalk and they have a very thin skin that makes them crunchy like a crisp when they're fried.*"

Another of the restaurant's traditional dishes are the *candele* pasta from Gragnano, the historic pasta-making town in nearby Campania, served with sauteed lamb giblets, some tomatoes, and chile pepper, and a few shavings of Caciocavallo Podolico, one of the flagship products of the

renowned dairy industry in Basilicata. Its name derives from the fact that the milk comes from the Podolica breed of cow, reared in the Pollino and Volturino area.

The so-called *arraganato* lamb is a local culinary classic. The lamb is baked in the oven with potatoes, sprinkled with breadcrumbs and served with extra-virgin olive oil, cheese, and diced tomatoes. *"We've updated it. We use leg of lamb, which we cook for 18 hours at a low temperature to keep it tender and pink on the inside. Then we brown it in a pan to give it a crispiness on the outside. We serve it with potatoes and some crispy breadcrumbs. Sometimes I serve it with artichokes, while always respecting the substance of the traditional dish."*

Among the desserts, a millefeuille with coffee-flavored Ricotta mousse is often on offer *"because there's a long tradition of Ricotta in Basilicata."* Making a mousse with a siphon makes this cheese slightly lighter than the original version, but the typicality of the dessert is respected. *"The puff pastry, very thin and crispy, also brings our traditional desserts to mind, such as the cartellate or Carnival crostoli, served with confectioners' sugar or honey. Here in the province of Potenza, there are highly skilled women who make puff pastry that resembles a veil."*

Antica Osteria Marconi always keeps some dishes featuring salt cod on the menu, whether as a starter, pasta or main course. *"It's the only fish that we've always cooked in various ways in our mountain area. There are trattorias that are exclusively dedicated to this fish, which was the only type that reached this far in the past."* The most common recipe is undoubtedly salt cod and *cruschi* bell peppers; the dried Senise bell peppers, which have been pan-fried with a little garlic and chile pepper are placed on top of boiled salt cod fillets. *"We have revised this dish, cooking the salt cod confit in a way that keeps it moist and then serving it with candied lemon and* cruschi *bell peppers."* Among the dishes on offer, there's also fried salt cod with asparagus sauce or a Sarconi bean puree, the famous pulse of the province of Potenza, as well as a pasta dish, *cavatelli* with salt cod, tomato confit, oregano, and Ferrandina olives, typical of a town in the Matera province and dried in the oven.

Typical of the region's gastronomy, Francesco makes the different traditional fresh semolina pasta forms by hand, such as *cavatelli*, which resemble small gnocchi, *strascinati*, whose name comes from the action whereby small pieces of pasta are dragged over a pastry board using fingers, or *manate*, a type of tagliatelle. *"Here women of a certain age still make pasta at home, especially for the traditional Sunday lunch."* On the restaurant's menu, at least two dishes featuring typical pasta forms from Basilicata are offered every day. For example, *"given that we have a long tradition of cheeses: Pecorino di Filiano and Moliterno, Caciocavallo Podolico, Cacioricotta, but also Ricotta, Mozzarella, and Scamorza,"* cavatelli pasta served with fresh cherry tomatoes, onion, sometimes some bell peppers, and Cacioricotta, a fresh goat's cheese that is especially delicious. On the other hand, in the winter, cavatelli are cooked with pulses, another typical product of the land of Basilicata, modernized with the addition of fish, another of the area's ingredients, given that mountainous and densely wooded Basilicata has two short stretches along the Tyrrhenian and Ionian Seas; they are served with garbanzo beans and clams, for example.

"Based on the selection and value placed on the best ingredients, our menu is changed every month in accordance with the seasons and what is found on the market." Both Francesco and his business partner Giuseppe take care of provisioning products. *"We have small-scale suppliers who we trust in the province of Potenza - fishmongers, butchers, fruit and vegetable stores - from whom we order as much as we need and it's then delivered straight to the restaurant."* Using the region's main food resources is the *sine qua non* of his business. *"My cooking aims to revise the traditional cuisine of Basilicata, fundamentally plain, consisting above all of vegetables, whether cultivated or*

wild, fresh homemade semolina pasta and lamb." Like the striking city carved into the tufa of the Sassi of Matera, inhabited from prehistory to the 1950's, once considered to be a national disgrace and now a UNESCO world heritage site, so the humble recipes of Basilicata have been reassessed as an expression of a typically Mediterranean cuisine, simple yet rich in flavor.

"Initially these experimentations with historical dishes were almost a bit of fun, then they became our philosophy." After all, Francesco thinks the world of Basilicata, which is still rather untouched by tourism given the beauty it has to offer, from Maratea on the magnificent Golfo di Policastro to Vulture where the gutsy wine Aglianico comes from, from Metapontino on the Ionian coastline to the small Lucane Dolomites, from the *Parco Nazionale del Pollino*, the largest national park in Italy, to the many villages that recall the numerous peoples who have lived in turn in this region. It's only natural that Francesco wants to celebrate it. *"On the one hand, we are regarded as an innovative restaurant, where you can eat a revised territorial cuisine; on the other hand, we retrieve traditional, now forgotten dishes, such as sautéed lamb giblets or strascinati pasta with baked eggplant and anchovies or with eggplant and Mozzarella."* A concept of cuisine that has revealed itself to be solid in acting as the fortress of traditional flavors like the four-sided mass of the Norman castle in the nearby town of Melfi, which was a particular favorite of Frederick II of Sweden as it was in an ideal position for falconry, his preferred form of relaxation.

The starter that begins the menu for this book is *Acquasala*, made from farm fresh eggs, turnip greens, and *cruschi* bell peppers, and enriched with *Vulture* extra-virgin olive oil. For the pasta course, there's *Candele* pasta with chile-flavored sautéed lamb and shavings of *Caciocavallo Podolico* cheese, followed by salt cod confit with potatoes and bell peppers as the main course. For dessert, Millefeuille of crostoli with fresh *Pecorino di Filiano* foam and acacia honey, a pleasing sweet and savory mix used in many typical cakes and cookies from Lucania. A menu in which the tradition transmigrates from course to course, like the soul did time and time again for Pythagoras, the Greek philosopher whose life drew to a close in Metaponto, the powerful city of the Magna Graecia, which is now a vast archaeological site along the Ionian coast of Basilicata.

ACQUASALE WITH GREENS, BROWN BREAD, AND A POACHED EGG

Ingredients for 4 people
Preparation time: 30'

24 turnip greens (also called Calabrese broccoli), with flowers
3½ oz (100 g) white onions, finely chopped
2 tablespoons vinegar
4 farm-fresh eggs, laid the same day or organic laid no more than 3 days ago
4 slices of brown bread, ¾ inch (2 cm) thick (cooked in a wood-burning stove, day- old)
4 tablespoons Vulture extra-virgin olive oil, or other good-quality olive oil
1 spicy chile pepper, for serving and salt
1 tablespoon flake sea salt, for serving

Method

Clean the turnip greens, separating the small greens (reserving them) from the rest of the foliage. Wilt the leaves with the onion, a little water, and a pinch of salt in a small saucepan over low heat for 5 minutes. Remove from the heat; transfer to a blender and blend at the highest speed setting for 3 minutes. Strain the mixture through a fine-mesh strainer to make a brilliant green sauce. Bring a pot of salted water to a boil in a small saucepan over medium heat. Add the vinegar. Cook the eggs for 2 minutes. Keep warm. In a separate small saucepan, sauté the onion in 4 tablespoons of oil for 1 minute. Add the small leaves of the turnips and cook until lightly browned. Add 1⅔ cups (400 ml) of hot water and a pinch of salt. Cook the *acquasale* for 3 minutes.

Serving

Place a piece of chile pepper in a deep plate, followed by a ladleful of greens sauce. Arrange a slice of day-old bread on top. Spoon a ladleful of *acquasale* on top of the bread, followed by the poached egg with a few flakes of salt.

Wine pairing

"Il repertorio" Aglianico del Vulture DOC, 2005 – Rosso
Azienda agricola: Cantine del Notaio di Gerardo Giuratrabocchetti– Rionero in Vulture (PZ)

CANDELE PASTA WITH SAUTÉED LAMB, SPRINKLED WITH CACIOCAVALLO PODOLICO CHEESE

Ingredients for 4 people
Preparation time: 30'

1 lb (500 g) entire pluck of a lamb (lungs, liver, etc.)
14 oz (400 g) fresh San Marzano tomatoes
1 onion
9¾ oz (280 g) Gragnano candele pasta
1 clove garlic
1 chile pepper
1 bay leaf
Salt to taste
1¼ cups (300 ml) extra-virgin olive oil
3½ oz (100 g) Caciocavallo Podolico cheese, grated

Method

Clean the lamb and cut into ⅛-inch (0.5-cm) pieces. Cut a cross in the bottom of the tomatoes. Blanch the tomatoes in a saucepan over medium heat for a few minutes. Remove the skins and seeds and cut into large pieces. Slice the onion. Sauté the onion and lungs with the tomatoes in a nonstick pan and cook for 20 minutes. Remove from the heat. Transfer to the food processor for 3 minutes, then press through a fine-mesh strainer. Spoon the sauce into a pastry bag. Cook the candele pasta in plenty of salted boiling water until *al dente*. Meanwhile, sauté the chopped onion and some diced tomato in a little olive oil in a crepe pan. Add the garlic, chile, bay leaf, and the remaining diced meat. Sauté quickly in the pan. When you drain the pasta, use the pastry bag to fill one candela pasta shape and leaving the next one empty, alternating them. Toss the pasta quickly in the pan with the vegetables and meat, then serve on a long platter. Sprinkle with the grated Caciocavallo Podolico.

Wine pairing

"Re Manfredi" Basilicata IGT, 2007 – White
Winery: Cantine terre degli Svevi – Venosa (PZ)

SALT COD CONFIT WITH *CRUSCHI* BELL PEPPERS

Ingredients for 4 people
Preparation time: 30'

SALT COD CONFIT
1⅓ oz (600 g) salt cod fillets
1 quart (1 liter) extra-virgin olive oil,
plus additional oil, for frying
3½ oz (100 g) potatoes
3½ oz (100 g) *peperoni secchi di Senise*

(dried bell peppers)

CANDIED LEMON ZEST
3 large oranges or 2 lemons
8 cups (2 liters) of cold water
1½ cups (300 g) of sugar
Chile powder

Method

Cut the salt cod into 4 pieces. Cook at 120°F (50°C) in the oven or in a Roner in a vacuum pack with the extra-virgin olive oil for 12 minutes or in a saucepan full of oil, checking the temperature.
Peel and cut the potatoes into ⅓-inch (1-cm) cubes. Blanch the potatoes in a saucepan of salted boiling water for 2 minutes. Drain well. Pan-fry the potatoes in a little oil in a frying pan over medium heat. Meanwhile, fry the dried bell peppers in the oil heated to 250°F (120°C) for 30 seconds.

CANDIED LEMON ZEST
Peel 3 large oranges or 2 lemons, making sure that you remove the zest from the pith. To remove the bitterness before candying, blanch the zest in boiling water at least 3 times, 10 minutes each time. Drain each batch well, rinsing the zest under cold water and rinsing the saucepan.
Return the zest to the clean pan and add 8 cups (2 liters) of cold water and 1½ cups (300 g) of sugar.
Bring to a boil and simmer, uncovered, for about 1½ hours.
Continue cooking the zest in the syrup (over very low heat) until the syrup has almost completely reduced
The zest should be translucent and thick with syrup.
Transfer the zest to a parchment-lined baking sheet covered in sugar. Roll the zest in the sugar and transfer onto another parchment-lined baking sheet. Let cool, dry and harden for at least 1 hour.

Serving

Cut the salt each cod fillet into 6 pieces. Alternate candied zest and chile powder on each piece of cod. Arrange the bell peppers on one side of the plate and the diced potatoes on the other side.

Wine pairing

"Fiano" Basilicata IGT, 2007 – White
Winery: Bisceglia – Lavello (PZ)

MILLEFEUILLE OF CROSTOLI WITH FRESH PECORINO FOAM AND ACACIA HONEY

Ingredients for 4 people
Preparation time: 2 h – Resting time: 45'

CROSTOLI
1²⁄₃ cups (250 g) durum wheat flour
2 eggs
Scant ½ cup (100 ml) white wine
1 tablespoon sugar
Pinch of salt
2 quarts (2 liters) peanut oil, for frying

PECORINO FOAM
7 oz (200 g) fresh Pecorino di Filiano cheese
²⁄₃ cup (150 g) whole milk
1¼ cups (300 g) cream with 35% fat content
½ cup (125 g) egg whites
Pinch of salt
1 siphon

Generous 3 tablespoons (50 g) honey, for garnish

Method

CROSTOLI
Stir the flour with the eggs, white wine, sugar, salt, and enough water in a bowl to make a very elastic dough. Let rest for 15 minutes in a damp tea cloth. Roll out into a very thin sheet and cut into 1-inch (3-cm) squares. Deep-fry the *crostoli* in peanut oil.

PECORINO FOAM
Finely grate the Pecorino. Bring the milk to a boil in a small saucepan over low heat. Add the Pecorino. Lower the heat and mix until the cheese has melted completely. Remove from the heat. Add the cream and let stand for 10 minutes. Strain the mixture through a fine-mesh sieve and fill the siphon with the mixture. Load with a gas cylinder and let rest in the refrigerator for at least 30 minutes.

Serving

Siphon the Pecorino foam into a Martini glass, adding the *crostoli* and drops of acacia honey.

Wine pairing

"Ambra" 2007 – Dessert wine
Winery: Tenuta Eleano – Rionero in Vulture (PZ)

THE CUISINE OF CALABRIA

"A scene, where, if a god should cast his sight,
A god might gaze, and wander with delight!"
These are the words of Homer of Calabria, in Book V of *The Odyssey.*

Back then as now, this land, which lies right on the heel of the boot of Italy, seduces those who pass through it: kilometer after kilometer of coastline on a sea that varies from emerald to sapphire, flung about by the currents; the propagated plains of vineyards (the Greeks called it *Enotria*, land of vineyards), gardens and orchards, the olive-clad hills, the harsh mountains which have molded the proud character of the citizens over time. Here the Mediterranean sun and breeze ignite the air with the colors and aromas of its citrus plantations, oleander trees, and orange blossoms.

From the mountains of La Sila where untamed nature makes life difficult and customs informal, you drop down to the plain in the province of Reggio Calabria, where the cultivated lands, although scattered, yield first-rate products: citrus plantations, with the specialty of bergamot; all types of vegetables; expanses of olives; flower-growing for the extraction of essences. Calabria is a sort of treasure chest that has protectively guarded its historical and cultural traditions. An intriguing mixture of the worlds that created it: the Magna Graecia, Rome, and the various rulers who followed, from the Arabs to the Normans, from the Spanish to the French. The ancient legacies of the palate have also been kept intact in the gastronomy, faithful to the flavors of the sea and the mountains, and infused with foreign flavors as they sat side by side at the table.

Calabrian cuisine is spicy in flavor as the accompaniment of pepper and chile pepper (another local product) is more or less ubiquitous.

While mostly being a land of sheep farming, the main meat used in food is pork. Many and varied are the pork-based products also known throughout the rest of Italy: the sausage flavored with sweet and spicy peppers, *Soppressata, Capocollo di Calabria PDO* (see box), and *'Nduja*, a salami that combines the fatty parts of the pig with sweet and spicy peppers, typical of Spilinga and the villages of Monte Poro, prosciutto, and an entire range of products associated with pig farming.

The cornerstones of the Calabrian dairy industry are *Abbespata*, a delicious type of Ricotta cheese with a smoked flavor, and *Giuncata*, a fresh, creamy sheep's cheese. Both are produced on the Sila plateau, a granite rock formation that rises up to the north and west on the Crati basin and to the south on the isthmus of Catanzaro, and in the Crotone province, an almost lunar landscape of clay and sandstone which is invigorated by a tapestry of rivers and torrents. We should also mention Caciocavallo Silano PDO, whose flavor varies from sweet to intense, and is aged from fifteen days to four months.

Nowadays various types of bread are also made, often in dimensions that weigh several kilos, and a series of *focaccia* flavored with tomatoes, herbs, bell and chile peppers, fish, etc. which are called *Pitte*. A special type of focaccia, *Morseddu*, is topped with various tripe or giblet-based sauces or stewed salt cod.

In addition to pork, the other main ingredient in Calabrian cooking is undoubtedly fish, which is prepared in many recipes.

Traditional ingredients used in Calabrian baking are almonds, honey, and a whole range of fresh and candied fruit. One of the many desserts is *Mostaccioli*, which is Arab in origin, made from flour, honey, and sweet wine. We should also mention the typical *Torrone di Bagnara*, a type of nougat that is exported all over the world, with its many ingredients and the sweetness given above all by the honey.

To accompany the potent flavors of this cuisine, quality wines with big personalities are served: the intense red Cirò, Greco, Gerace, Montonico, Nicastro, and Squillace.

Unique and already well-known by the end of the eighteenth century, there's also the fresh, digestive *Liquirizia di Rossano*, an elegant Byzantine town with its seven Basilian monasteries and the hermitages of the surrounding valleys. A museum has been set up here, which illustrates its history and characteristics.

A welcoming land in terms of its delicious cuisine and because it preserves the traces of the illuminated culture of the distant past (it isn't by chance that present day Crotone was chosen by Pythagoras as the place to establish his famous school of mathematics) and the beauty of the art that has nourished and praised it over the centuries (just admire the splendid *Bronzi di Riace*, two bronze statues now in the Museo di Reggio Calabria).

CAPOCOLLO DI CALABRIA DOP

IN ADDITION TO PANCETTA, SAUSAGE, AND SOPPRESSATA, IT IS ONE OF THE FOUR SALAMIS WITH PROTECTED DESIGNATION OF ORIGIN IN THE REGION.

THE *CAPOCOLLO DI CALABRIA* IS MADE FROM THE UPPER PART OF THE PORK LOIN. THE MEAT, WHICH HAS BEEN BONED AND SALTED, IS FLAVORED AND SOMETIMES ALSO SMOKED SLIGHTLY. IT IS AGED FOR AT LEAST 100 DAYS. IT IS ALSO SOMETIMES PRESERVED IN OIL.

GAETANO ALIA

RESTAURANT LA LOCANDA DI ALIA - CASTROVILLARI (COSENZA)

HE PRACTISES COOKING LIKE ART, BUT NEVER ASKS HIS DISHES *"WHY DON'T YOU TALK?"*, AS IT IS SAID THAT MICHELANGELO DID WITH HIS SCULPTURES. FOR CHEF GAETANO ALIA, CO-OWNER WITH HIS BROTHER PINUCCIO, MAÎTRE D'HÔTEL, OF THE RESTAURANT *LA LOCANDA DI ALIA* IN CASTROVILLARI, IN THE PROVINCE OF COSENZA, EVERYTHING IS EXPRESSED IN A COMPREHENSIBLE LANGUAGE. *"EVERY MORNING, THE VEGETABLES CALL OUT TO ME ON THE MARKET STALLS, JUST LIKE THE FISH AND MEAT,"* HE ASSERTS. *"JUST BY LISTENING TO THE PRODUCTS YOU CAN CHOOSE THE BEST AND THE IDEAS COME TO ME FOR A DISH."*

A FUSION OF INGREDIENTS – THE CULINARY TALENT KNOWS THEM PERFECTLY, JUDGING BY THE RESTAURANT, WHICH IS ONE OF THE MOST RENOWNED NOT ONLY IN CALABRIA, BUT IN THE SOUTH OF ITALY. SITUATED A FEW MINUTES FROM THE TOWN, IN THE WONDERFUL SCENERY OF THE *PARCO NAZIONALE DEL POLLINO*, THE NATURAL HABITAT OF THE SUPERB AND RARE BOSNIAN PINE (*PINO LORICATO* IN ITALIAN, WHOSE NAME COMES FROM THE BARK, WHICH RESEMBLES THE ARMOR OF THE ROMAN SOLDIERS, THE *LORICA*), THE RESTAURANT *"IS LOCATED IN AN OLD COUNTRY HOUSE OWNED BY OUR FAMILY, WHICH WE'VE RENOVATED OVER TIME AND HAS ALSO BECOME A RELAIS. SINCE 1992, NEXT TO THE RESTAURANT, THERE'S BEEN A SMALL HOTEL WITH 14 ROOMS SET IN A HECTARE OF LUXU-RIANT AND PERFUMED MEDITERRANEAN GARDENS, ABUNDANT IN OLD, LOCAL SPECIES OF FRUIT TREES."* THERE ARE MANY VINEYARDS AROUND THE ESTABLISHMENT, WHICH WERE PRAISED BY THE LATIN WRITER PLINY THE ELDER. IN THE CASTROVILLARI AREA, POLLINO IS PRODUCED, WHICH IS ONE OF THE LEADING DOC WINES IN THE REGION.

THE ENVIRONMENT IS RUSTIC, *"YET ELEGANTLY FURNISHED. THE WALLS IN THE DINING ROOM HAVE BEEN FRESCOED BY AN INTERESTING CALABRIAN ARTIST, LUIGI LE VOCI,"* AND THE SERVICE IS ATTEN-TIVE, *"YET HIGHLY CONFIDENTIAL AND FRIENDLY;"* PERFECT FOR A STOPOVER, AS HAS TAKEN PLACE FOR OVER HALF A CENTURY. ESTABLISHED IN 1952, THE RESTAURANT IS ONE OF THE OLDEST IN CALABRIA. *"THE WAR HAD JUST ENDED AND MY FATHER ANTONIO, A TAILOR, AND MY MOTHER LUCIA, A HOUSEWIFE, DECIDED TO OPEN A MODEST TRATTORIA, WHICH QUICKLY BECAME A STOPPING PLACE FOR LORRY DRIVERS AND TRAVELING BUSINESSMEN. ONE OF THOSE TRATTORIAS, WITH SIMPLE COOK-ING AND FIRST-CLASS INGREDIENTS, WHICH ACTED AS THE BACKBONE FOR ALL THE RESTAURANTS THAT CAME ABOUT AFTERWARDS IN ITALY."*

In 1978, when his father died, Gaetano and his brother were obliged to take over the management of the trattoria – Gaetano in the kitchen alongside his mother and Pinuccio in the dining room – which was gradually transformed into a restaurant. *"We started to understand that the future lay in those true flavors by studying them again, without ever ruining the original philosophy of regional cooking that our mother offered: praising the quality of ingredients, simpler cooking methods, and essential combinations. We try to plate up not only the product, but also the idea."* Success wasn't slow in coming. *"The first food guides started to come out which took an interest in our work, stating that the restaurant was one of the most charming places in the south of Italy."* Meanwhile, the Alia brothers invested in the cellar, *"which now commands deep respect, with all the historic vintages of truly great wines."*

Gaetano thinks along the lines of the Cosenza-born natural scientist Bernardino Telesio, who left behind the theological view of nature in the sixteenth century and smoothed the way towards modern science, even cuisine was regarded with humility, without any abstract and metaphysical conceptual schemes, but analyzing it according to its own principles and specific laws. Great dishes can only be created based on respect and knowledge. Like the food that *La Locanda di Alia* has been offering for 30 years *"and couldn't be altered in any way without risking an uprising of the customers."* For example, Candele pasta with piquant *'nduja di Spilinga* ragù and shavings of cave-aged Pecorino. A traditional type of pasta from southern Italy, broken up, and served with *'nduja*, an exquisitely spicy Calabrian salami. *"The chile pepper burns the palate and I use it very little in my cooking, only if it can't be helped; while the spiciness that has been consumed for a long time and by other ingredients, like in this salami, is a completely different story."*

The ravioli stuffed with herbs and *Ricotta di bufala*, served with wild aniseed from La Sila are a must in the restaurant. *"When I created this dish, I wanted to base it on the typical cookies that contain aniseeds which are eaten in Calabria."* The aniseed produced on the La Sila plateau is therefore renowned. *"It is bought by the teaspoon as it's as precious as black truffle."* Another his-

toric dish of *La Locanda* is pork 'ncantara-
to with a honey and chile pepper sauce. *"A
recipe that I came across by chance by
reading a letter sent by a lady to a friend,
which features pork preserved in an earthenware pot, the* Kantaros, *and the accompanying sauce that comes from one of the
many Albanian communities in our area."* In
this recipe, *"the combination between the
sweet taste of honey and the sharpness of
the chile pepper is extraordinary."*

Gaetano's cuisine is *"genuine and
regional."* Like in the narrow streets of the
town of Diamante, the so-called jewel of
the Tyrrhenian that juts out over a crystal
clear sea and set among citron groves, the

murals created by internationally renowned painters and artists from 1981 onwards make the individual facades of the houses into an original experience, every dish of *La Locanda di Alia* has a personal touch. In Calabria, *"the cooking of the past is still frequented and there's an attachment to
typical dishes; that's why it makes sense to offer a revisited version of the area's cuisine. Nobody
would ever go and eat* lagane e ciciari, *or tagliatelle and garbanzo beans, in a restaurant when
they could eat them at home."* The same tradition *"is repeated innovation. For example, ravioli
filled with red potatoes from La Sila with salt cod. In our area, salt cod is always eaten with potatoes, sun-dried bell peppers, which have been soaked, tomatoes, onion, and black olives. What did
I do? I decided to put the potatoes in a sheet of pasta, cook the salt cod in the tomatoes and onions
as per usual, and the* cruskj *bell peppers as a sauce with the black olives. We re-propose the flavors, which our mother taught us, but we recreate them in a new way."* A salad consisting of tomatoes, Tropea red onion, and tuna bottarga, sweetened with the precious Dottato fig, cultivated in
the Cosenza plain, is also a revamped tradition. *"Imagine the delicious contrast between the sweetness of the tomato, onion, and fig, and the saltiness of the bottarga."*

The quality of the ingredients is obviously fundamental. For example, for the baby octopuses in
peasant sauce, the little baby squid are red when alive and resemble strawberries when they're
caught, served with a sauce into which Gaetano puts whatever ingredient is in season, keeping the
tomatoes as a base – *"a dish without tomatoes is unconceivable in Calabria, although you need to*

know how to use them" – the ingredients are what matters. You should be able to make out the aroma and flavor of the sea. *"My cuisine is a patchwork of moments and inspirations, and therefore of flavor; that's why it's enjoyed so much."* In particular, plain products become noble, as written in the *New York Times, "Here simplicity is the authentic choice for a refined Mediterranean cuisine."* This reminds us of the distinctive sobriety of the monastery of San Bernardino da Siena in Morano Calabro, the striking town at the foot of the Pollino mountain chain, one of the best examples of fifteenth-century Franciscan architecture in Calabria, elegant yet in line with the ideals of poverty of St. Francis of Assisi.

For Gaetano, *"the restaurant must stock up at a maximum of five kilometers from its front gate."* He is lucky to have the sea and mountains at hand: *"In addition to salt cod, which is used all over Calabria, I use the fish from our Ionian Sea: oily fish, shrimp, red mullet, tuna, etc. The meat is reared in our Pollino mountains, as well as the herbs and vegetables, when possible, from our garden right behind the restaurant."* The Pollino also offers excellent cheeses, *"which are mostly combined with traditional preserves from La Madia, where we also produce salami and liqueurs like rosolio according to old Calabrian recipes."* There are many specialties, including Tropea red onion caponata, chile pepper jelly, elderflower preserves, and Christmas dried fruit, which are served with delicacies from the regional dairy industry. A full spectrum of undertones which make you think of the perfections of the rich Greek city state of Sybaris on the Ionian coast, where you can still visit the archaeological park and the superb *Museo Nazionale della Sibaritide* today.

Gitaeno attributes his culinary refinement to the training he received at his mother's knee. *"I went to a hotel institute, but I learned most things from my mother. She had a good hand, gentle* and measured, it was a gift of nature, so much so that many people still remember her dishes today. She never studied, but learned from the school of life." He also learned how to do the shopping from her. "When I go to Castrovillari market in the morning, I always follow the rule that she taught me: I buy the products I like the most, without ever asking how much they cost. Our suppliers have worked with us for a long time and would never offer me something that isn't right or at a price that's over the top as they know that I'd no longer buy from them the following day."

The menu for the book is in the spirit of the area. For starters, Black Calabrese pork cheek, dried and salted tuna roe from Pizzo Calabro, walnuts, and licorice oil. "These three flavors summarize the land of Calabria. In Italy I don't think that there's a region that knows the Calabrese pig better than us. Tuna is one of our fishes and is called the "pig of the sea" as we don't dispose of any of it. The licorice, which grows all over Calabria, is the best in the world."

For the pasta course, there's Candele pasta with a 'nduja ragù, which also features the famous Pecorino di Crotone, followed by Salt cod with fresh green onions marinated in sweet pepper, mint, and wild fennel for the main course. To finish: Chocolate figs, a gluttonous example of a revamped tradition. In Calabria, it is the custom for all families to gather figs, letting them dry in the sun, stuffed with walnuts or almonds and covered in chocolate. "My idea was to take these dried figs, to cut them thinly and cover them with toasted almonds, walnuts, a little cinnamon, cloves, and grated orange zest or candied citron, a typical Calabrian product. Then serving them on top of a white and mint chocolate sauce and sprinkling them with a handful of diavolilli, or colored sugars."

A menu that watches strongly and kindly over the traditions of the land of Calabria; a little like Madonna del Pilerio, the old medieval icon preserved in Cosenza cathedral, whose name derives from the Greek word puleros, or rather guardian, which has protected the city for centuries.

BLACK CALABRESE PORK CHEEK, DRIED AND SALTED TUNA ROE FROM PIZZO CALABRO, WALNUTS, AND LICORICE OIL

Ingredients for 4 people
Preparation time: 15' - Sauce: 2 days

3½ oz (100 g) lamb's lettuce
1½ oz (40 g) dried, salted tuna roe (bottarga) from Pizzo Calabro
4 walnuts, shelled and coarsely chopped
8 slices of black Calabrese pork cheek (bacon)

SAUCE
Generous 1 tablespoon (20 g) extra-virgin olive oil
Licorice stick

Method

Two days before, coat the licorice stick with the extra-virgin olive oil and keep in a dark place. Clean the lamb's lettuce. Thinly shave the tuna roe using a mandolin.
Slice the pork cheek.

Serving

Arrange the lamb's lettuce on a plate. Arrange the dried, salted tuna roe and 2 slices of pork cheek on top.
Dress with the flavored oil and sprinkle with the walnuts.

Wine pairing

"Val di Neto Efeso IGT" 2006 – White
Winery: Cirò Librandi – Cirò Marina (KR)

CANDELE PASTA WITH 'NDUJA

Ingredients for 4 people
Preparation time: 30'

2 small, round green bell peppers
1⅓ lb (600 g) fresh San Marzano tomatoes
1½ oz (40 g) Pecorino di Crotone
1 small bunch of parsley
4 tablespoons extra-virgin olive oil
1 clove garlic
1 basil leaf
Pinch salt
2¾ oz (80 g) 'nduja (typical Calabrese salami)
14 oz (400 g) candele pasta

Method

Wash the bell peppers and cut into little stripes lenghtwise.
Clean the tomatoes and cut a cross into the bottom. Blanch in boiling water for
2 minutes. Let cool in ice water and dice them.
Thinly shave the Pecorino and chop the parsley. Set aside.
To make the sauce, combine the oil, tomatoes, garlic, bell peppers, basil, and salt in an
aluminum frying pan.
Simmer for about 15 minutes. Add the 'nduja and mix well. Cook for another 3 minutes.
Meanwhile, cook the pasta "al dente" in plenty of salted water. Drain and transfer to
the pan with the sauce. Toss well.

Serving

Serve with a sprinkling of Pecorino di Crotone and parsley.

Wine pairing

"Vigna Mortella" 2006 – Red
Winery: Cantine Odoardi – Nocera Tirinese (CZ)

SALT COD WITH FRESH GREEN ONIONS MARINATED IN SWEET PEPPER, MINT, AND WILD FENNEL

Ingredients for 4 people
Preparation time: 25'

1 fillet of Norwegian salt cod, already soaked
4 fairly large fresh green onions, thinly sliced
Scant ⅓ cup (20 g) fennel, fronds only

SAUCE
Generous 3 tablespoons (50 g) extra-virgin olive oil
20 mint leaves and fennel stalks, thinly sliced
2 tablespoons (30 g) sweet chile powder
¼ teaspoon (2 g) wild fennel seeds

Method

Steam the salt cod with the green onions and fennel fronds for 7 minutes.
Break up the fish into pieces.
Mix all the ingredients for the sauce in a bowl. Add the salt cod and set aside for at least 2 hours before serving.

Wine pairing

"Ceraso" 2007 – Cerasuolo Red
Winery: Vignaioli del Pollino – Frascineto (CS)

CHOCOLATE FIGS

Ingredients for 4 people
Preparation time: 25'

Generous 3 tablespoons (50 g) milk
1 sprig of fresh mint
5 oz (150 g) white chocolate
12 almond-stuffed dried figs
1 teaspoon anisette

8 walnuts
10 toasted almonds
Ground cinnamon and cloves
Handful of colored sugar sprinkles
Zest of 1 orange, for serving

Method

Heat the milk with the mint in a small saucepan. Let infuse for 10–15 minutes.
Add the chocolate, broken up into pieces, and mix until it has melted completely.
Cut the figs into slices.

Serving

Cover the plate with the hot chocolate. Arrange the figs on top. Sprinkle with the
cinnamon and cloves. Finish by sprinkling with the sugar sprinkles.
Garnish with a grating of orange zest.

Wine pairing

Rosolio di color d'oro – Sweet liqueur
Winery: La Madia di Alia – Castrovillari (CZ)

THE CUISINE OF SICILY

A multifaceted island of Sicily is at the magical crossroads of the great ancient civilizations, from the Phoenicians to the Greeks, from the Arabs to the Normans, from the Spanish to the French. A land of precious and seductive cultural layers with priceless jewels such as the cathedrals of Monreale and Cefalù, the Valley of the Temples of Agrigento, the delightful Baroque architecture of the town of Noto, and the extraordinary beauty of Taormina. It is a triangle of heavily contrasting climates, with fog and snow inland and an African-like sun along the coasts. There are also contrasts in terms of the people, who are welcoming yet are of few words.

From the restless Mt. Etna, the largest volcano in Europe, to the island of Pantelleria, rugged and windswept, this Sicilian isle is still a wild landscape, although men's creativity has tried to tame it over the centuries. Along the valleys of the rivers and the plains, olive groves extend which give three extra-virgin olive oils PDO (Monti Iblei, Valli Trapanesi, and Val Demone) and perfumed citrus plantation (the red oranges are famous, which were introduced by the Arabs in the Medieval era). The sea, the happy climate, the landscapes, sometimes harsh and sometimes gentle, artistic beauties, the cultivations of olive trees, vineyards, citrus plantations, and almond trees, whose blossoming appeals to many tourists every year, altogether form its wealthy legacy.

Not only are noble vineyards owed to the inland mountainous areas, but also almond, hazelnut, and pistachio trees (the Bronte variety in the Catania province is renowned), pine nut plants, and prickly pears (which are used to make an excellent mustard). On Pantelleria, the island of the *dammusi*, the traditional cubical homes built in lava stone, the production of capers, grown in holes dug into the ground to protect them from the wind, is prized, as is the Zibibbo grape, which is used to make the famous Passito.

Sicilian cuisine, heir of an infinite number of culinary customs that have been sagely reworked and combined, shows strong traces of Arab influence (even though there have been many cultures who have left their mark on the island, from the Carthaginians to Arabs, from the French to Spanish). Some Sicilian dishes have even taken the names from Eastern etymology, for example, *Cuscusu*, from couscous, made like its Middle Eastern cousin from steamed semolina, which is then cooked in fish stock and served with the fish used to make the stock. This is a typical dish in the Trapani province. Additionally, there's *Pane e panelle*, also of Arab origin, a thin sheet of pastry made from garbanzo beans, fried in oil and placed very hot in a bun, made to order in the many permanent or mobile *friggitorie* (fried food stands) in Palermo. In Agrigento on December 8th for the festival of the Virgin, *Pani cca meusa*, the delicious spleen buns, are served. They're sold in Palermo and the rest of Sicily by numerous mobile food stalls and made with pieces of lung, spleen, and flakes of Caciocavallo or slices of Ricotta.

Larger-sized fish, tuna and swordfish, is the traditional catch of the day. It's very important on feast days, which starts with the *Mattanza*, a violent rite that has resonances of a Greek tragedy, to be served in numerous recipes which see them combined with ingredients such as onions, tomatoes, capers, olives, citrus fruit, and so on.

The sea also yields an entire range of catches, of large fish and small, which Sicilian cooking uses to make appetizing meals. This is the case with sardines combined with pasta and served with wild fennel, sultanas, and saffron, and sardines cooked a *beccafico*, a sort of tartlet where whole sardines are mixed with breadcrumbs, cheese, pine nuts, and sultanas. Stockfish, or *stocco*, and cuttlefish are also equally used. The tuna bottarga is also of the highest quality, sun-dried and salted roe, to be grated on meals to garnish with the smell of the sea.

Meat is not widely cooked, beef in particular, and butter isn't much used as a condiment. The few herds are milked mainly to produce exquisitely flavored cheeses: Pecorino Siciliano PDO (see box), one of Sicily's typical products par excellence; Ragusano PDO, a Caciocavallo cheese in a parallelepiped form with a flavor that varies from delicate to piquant with ageing; *Piacintinu*, a mold-ripened sheep's milk cheese, flavored with saffron and/or black pepper, widespread in the Nebrodi mountain chain and the province of Enna; and Ricotta, the basis of the best Sicilian desserts.

Among the salami, the *Salame di Sant'Angelo di Brolo* from the province of Messina should be remembered. It's perhaps the oldest salami in the whole of Italy, with its rather lean meat, cut with a knife, as well as the unique *Salame di Tonno*, made with the king of Sicilian fish (the Atalonga variety is exquisite, recognizable by its long fins).

The shortage of meat-based recipes is widely made up for by the fish or vegetable dishes (including eggplants, tomatoes, and Pachino tomatoes, olives – the Nocellara del Belice ones are special – stuffed in a myriad of ways); while the tradition of pasta founded in Sicily during the Arab domination ended up being moved on to Genoa and then onto Naples. Rice, which although it too arrived in the wake of the Arabs in the region, is only found in one typical dish: *arancini*, rice croquettes filled with meat ragù, dipped in breadcrumbs and fried.

Also in Sicily, as in other regions in the south of Italy, the presence of ingredients such as almonds, pistachios, fruit, honey, and so on provide an excellent basis for desserts: the small fruits made from almond paste, called *Frutta alla Martorana*, after the church in Palermo, reproduced from nature by skilled hands (often those of nuns belonging to convents); traditional cannoli, and cassata, also of Arab origin, with the soft filling of candied fruit and Ricotta cheese.

Homemade ice-cream and sorbets are typical of Sicily, introduced by the Arabs and distributed from 1682 in Paris by the Giarre-born Francesco Procopio dei Coltelli, the founder of the oldest coffee shop in Europe. A land so sun-kissed and rich in aromas can do no other than produce excellent grapes and leading wines. Sicilian wines are famous worldwide. In addition to Marsala – the renowned wine of Roman tradition, refined by the Spanish and then reworked by the English enologist Woodhouse at the end of the eighteenth century – there are also the Malvasia and Moscato from the nearby Aeolian Islands and Pantelleria, as well as Corvo, Partinico, Monreale, Eloro, Pachino, Albanello, Capo Bianco, Milazzo, Barcellona, Val di Lupo, and so on. There's still a pinch of local flavor missing: the salt mines to the south of Trapani, which look towards the islets of Maraone and Formica. They are located in the territory of the ancient salt civilization and provide a fascinating spectacle, especially when the sun's rays light up the pure, tasty, snow-like landscape around midday.

PECORINO SICILIANO PDO

Produced all over the island, but especially in the hilly and mountainous areas of the Messina and Ragusa areas and in the province of Enna from October to June, Pecorino Siciliano PDO is a hard, mold-ripened cheese with an exquisite taste that errs on the piquant (black peppercorns are sometimes added during production). It is also used in non-aged forms; before the salting, the *tuma* is obtained, which be-comes *primusali* (literally 'first salt') after 15 days.

PINO (GIUSEPPE) CUTTAIA

RESTAURANT LA MADIA - LICATA (AGRIGENTO)

YOU DON'T EXPECT TO FIND A RESTAURANT LIKE *LA MADIA* IN LICATA, AN INDUSTRIOUS HARBOR TOWN IN THE PROVINCE OF AGRIGENTO. *"IN A SIMPLE AREA LIKE OURS, FINDING A SIMILAR PROFESSIONALITY SURPRISES OUR CUSTOMERS,"* PINO CUTTAIA ASSERTS, CHEF AND CO-OWNER OF THE RESTAURANT, WITH HIS WIFE LOREDANA, THE MAÎTRE D'HÔTEL. STEPPING INTO THIS ELEGANT AND MODERN RESTAURANT HAS THE SAME EFFECT AS THE FAMOUS GIRLS IN BIKINIS IN THE MOSAIC DECORATION OF ONE OF THE ROOMS OF VILLA ROMANA DEL CASALE CLOSE TO PIAZZA ARMERINA, WHICH THE AVERAGE TOURIST WOULD NEVER DREAM ABOUT STUMBLING ACROSS.

"THE RESTAURANT WAS ESTABLISHED BY ME AND MY WIFE IN 2000. WE HAD A FEW PROBLEMS AT THE BEGINNING AS THE LOCALS WEREN'T USED TO CONCEPTUAL CUISINE. PEOPLE WENT OUT FOR A MEAL TO EAT COZZA SCOPPIATA (STEAMED MUSSELS) OR A MIXED GRILL. IT DOESN'T MEAN THAT THESE DISHES AREN'T GOOD, BUT I WANTED TO OFFER A NEW TAKE ON REGIONAL CUISINE. GIVEN THAT WE STILL DIDN'T HAVE THE RIGHT LEVEL OF VISIBILITY, WE HAD TO 'EDUCATE' OUR CUSTOMERS FOR AT LEAST A COUPLE OF YEARS." EVEN NOW, WHAT PINO OFFERS DOESN'T GET AN IMMEDIATE RESPONSE, *"BUT WE'RE MORE CERTAIN OF OURSELVES AND OUR IDEAS AND WE HAVE A GREATER RESPONSE FROM OUR CUSTOMERS TOO, WHO COME FROM OTHER TOWNS IN SICILY, AS WELL AS THE TOURISTS WHO COME HERE AS THEY FIND THE RESTAURANT LISTED IN THE LEADING FOOD GUIDES."*

THERE ARE SOME DISHES WHICH *LA MADIA* HAS INCLUDED ON THE MENU FOR YEARS: SICILIAN CROQUETTE WITH RED SNAPPER RAGÙ AND WILD FENNEL; BABY PERLINA EGGPLANT CANNOLI WITH RICOTTA WRAPPED IN CRISPY PASTA AND VINE TOMATOES; FINELY DICED KING SHRIMP WITH MANDARIN OIL AND BOTTARGA MAYONNAISE; *OCTOPUS VULGARIS* KEBABS WITH GARBANZO BEAN PUREE AND ROSEMARY SAUCE; OR FLATTENED SWORDFISH WITH SMOKED OIL WITH POTATO MASH AND CRISPS. REFINED CREATIONS, YET CONCRETE AND BALANCED, LIKE THE GREAT DORIC TEMPLES OF AGRIGENTO, WHICH STAND MIGHTY OVER THE CRYSTAL CLEAR SEA, AMONG FIELDS OF WHEAT AND ALMOND TREES. THEY'RE A SOLID AND INCOMMUTABLE TESTIMONY OF A SPLENDID PAST THAT MADE IT INTO "THE MOST BEAUTIFUL CITY OF MORTALS," AS THE GREEK POET PINDAR WROTE.

Pino's cuisine, purely based on fish, *"could be defined as creative and based on the territory – by territory I mean actually this area where I was born 39 years ago. I work really well with what's in my blood, and when I talk about conceptual cuisine, I'm referring precisely to the possibility of expressing my memories in terms of aromas, flavors, and colors."* It's an inevitable choice for his identity. *"Sicily's big and many different cuisines live side by side on the island."* Yes, the island is a land of contrasts, not only geographical ones, from the mountainous inland climate to the mild and sunny weather of the coasts, which is epitomized by the view of snow-capped Etna that drops down to the sea at Taormina, but also cultural contrasts, given that it was the crossroads of many civilizations that have come one after another over the millennia. It follows that today the cuisine of Sicily has many foundations, having treasured all of its gastronomic legacies.

In terms of typical products, his gaze focuses *"on everything that the region has to offer:"* vegetables, from Pachino tomatoes to Perlina eggplants and Spinello artichokes; nuts, from pistachios to almonds; cheeses, from Ragusano Caciocavallo to *Piacintinu* Pecorino from Enna, Ricotta, and the historic *tuma persa*, made from raw milk, Provolone dei Nebrodi and Maiorchino, typical of the Messina province; as well as extra-virgin olive oil and sea salt from Trapani. *"Sicily is very rich from the point of view of food and wine. In addition to its particularly fertile land, it has been dominated by many peoples over the course of its history and each has left something, from spices to a range of ingredients."*

There are some traditional dishes that have been revamped, such as the fish-based couscous, a meal originally from Tunisia and found in the areas of Marsala and Trapani. *"I've served it with a king shrimp broth, adding Raffadali pistachio nuts."* There are also rice croquettes, the typical Sicilian street food, traditionally filled with ground meat in a sauce, peas, and soft cheese cut into cubes. *"I've revamped it, serving it in an elegant way and ennobling it with a filling of fish."* Pino enhances tradition so that it reveals itself at its best. Similar to how Antonello da Messina, the great fifteenth-century painter, gathers the divine light in human nature, choosing, for example, a beautiful and sensual humble woman for the delicate and gentle figure of the *Vergine Annunziata* which hangs in the *Museo Nazionale di Palermo*.

Although Licata, like every seaside town, does not have unique culinary traditions, apart from *pasta con le sarde* (pasta with sardines), which is also typical of the Palermitan coastline, *"in an area where people still cook at home, offering dishes featuring the traditional heritage is a challenge. It's difficult to place a value on the territory, refusing to use globalized products – where's the sense in using Norwegian salmon when we have excellent Sicilian fish? – because we need to offer dishes that the locals perhaps also eat at home, but making and serving them in a creative way."* Offering a cuisine based on research, communication, and promotion of the area's typical products *"should be part of a cultural project supported by the State: it's like a mission."* Also because *"it isn't always easy for those who want to live in a provincial dimension like my own with all its values, far away from the major tourist destinations."* And yet, his attachment to his area has been rewarded. The restaurant, which bears a Michelin star, is one of the cornerstones of the island's gastronomy. Its story recalls the myth of Alpheus and Arethusa, to which the lovely spring of Arethusa is connected, the freshwater source on the island of Ortigia at Syracuse, which flows into the Ionian Sea. Like Alpheus received from Zeus the chance to become reunited with his shy beloved across the sea, who fled to the area of Syracuse and transformed into the spring of Artemis, customers are able to come to Pino, whose restaurant is off the beaten track and enjoy the local cuisine that leads to a sure success.

The chef of *La Madia* started off self-taught. *"Ever since I was a child I was fascinated by catering. I saw the chef as a mysterious being who knew how to transform ingredients."* He found himself doing this job nevertheless by chance. *"I didn't attend a hotel institute. One New Year's Eve, when I was 13 years old, a friend of mine told me that if I went and washed the plates in the restaurant where he worked, at midnight we'd break open some Champagne. As I'd never tried it before, I accepted. From that point on, I've never left the kitchen."* He did internships, the most important being at the restaurant *Il Patio di Pollone* in Biella, in Piedmont. *"This is where the talk about research started, not only in terms of the ingredients, but also the craftsmanship. Given that conceptual catering embraces various types of trade, from bread-making to patisserie and butchery, I began to do short internships within these businesses to make up for lost time."*

Pino is the one who takes care of the shopping for the restaurant. The majority of suppliers are based in the town, with a few in the Ragusa province. *"I've also tried to 'educate' them. For me the most important thing is the quality of the ingredients, not the price. I demand reliable people, not mercenaries. For my type of catering, I'm not bluff or profit-oriented, but I'm aiming for dignity and transparency of what I offer to my customers. Everything that comes out of my kitchen must be done with awareness and a conscience. It's been a battle, but I've overcome it in the end."* Knowing your ingredients is fundamental for a chef. *"The better you know them, the more you can get them to express."* Technology, however, also has a role to play. *"It helps to bring out what you want to get across to the customer: feelings. You can groom the aesthetics of a dish, not only the flavor; thereby creating something beautiful without transforming the ingredient. If the fabric of a fish remains intact also in terms of its cut, it's better visually, as well as maintaining its liquids and aroma."*

Pino lives this trade like a frame of mind. *"I'm interested in the final result. I don't care if I live like a marathon runner, both in a physical and mental sense. After all, ours is a world apart. In the kitchen we talk a language that others find difficult to understand and time no longer exists for us. And yet, it's so fascinating! When there's a heavy dose of passion and the will to show something of ourselves, the work is as creative as the person who's doing it."* It becomes an education in style, *"where we learn a detail every day and our knowledge grows."*

For his work, he would like to complete a study into all the countries that face onto the Mediterranean from east to west. *"Sicily is undoubtedly attached to this sea. For those who offer a conceptual cuisine, a study into the traditions, customs, and costumes of the peoples of the Mediterranean basin would be important. We would have even more things that unite us to talk about at the table, perhaps even aspects that have been forgotten or unheard of. We have a duty; people want to talk about these things when they sit down to eat."* The idea, in short, is to set sail to his talent heading towards a cuisine based on a cultural melting pot, similar to the noted and composite Norman Monreale cathedral, where Arab inspiration and Romanesque taste blend together with Byzantine reminiscence and a Venetian air, a paradise of singularity and harmony.

The menu for this book focuses on the area. The starter of pine-smoked cod with crushed potatoes and *pizzaiola* dressing uses a typically regional fish and sauce. *"It's the review of a classic dish made from leftovers. Roasted meat that tastes of smoke left over from lunch is moistened with some tomatoes, olives, and oregano in the evening."*

For the pasta course, there's eggplant cannoli with Ricotta wrapped in crispy pasta and vine tomatoes. *"This is another dish that's been revamped with a double helping of eggplant from the Messina area. I've turned the ingredients inside out; instead of putting the pasta inside the eggplant, I've wrapped it around the outside, without altering the flavors at all."* For the main course, it's stuffed scabbard fish with Sicilian caponata, *"which features a typically Sicilian recipe and our classic vegetable caponata, flavored with capers, pine nuts, and olives and tossed in a pan with honey and vinegar."* For dessert, cornucopia of cannoli wafers with sheep's Ricotta and orange marmalade. *"This is the classic Sicilian cannoli, but in the form of a cornucopia and served with a preserves that is made from the main citrus fruit cultivated in Sicily."*

A menu that finds in its roots a unifying element and the chance for new culinary combinations, as was the case with the sumptuous buildings of the picturesque town of Noto, known as "the world capital of Baroque," wholly rebuilt after the 1693 earthquake. Each architectural episode recalls a shared cultural soil and lives on a coherent play of stylistic associations

PINE-SMOKED COD WITH CRUSHED POTATOES AND PIZZAIOLA DRESSING

Ingredients for 4 people
Preparation time: 45' - Marinating: 2 h

1 cod fillet, weighing 1 lb (500 g)
Salt
Sugar, as needed
1 pine cone
3 potatoes

Scant ½ cup (100 ml) extra-virgin olive oil
2 tomatoes
Basil (optional)
½ cup (50 g) black olives in brine

Method

Marinate the cod with the salt and sugar for 2 hours. Chop or break up pinecone into small pieces. Put pieces in a frying pan and place over medium heat. Heat well. When the pinecones are very hot, set them on fire and let burn for about 1 minute. Cover the pan to put out the fire. Place the smoking pinecones in the bottom of a roasting pan and arrange the fish on a wire rack placed inside the pan. Do not touch the pinecones.
Cover with another tray of the same size and seal with plastic wrap.
Wash and smoke the cod in the oven at a very low temperature with the smoking pine cone for about 30 minutes.
Boil potatoes a pot of salted water until cooked. Peel and dress them with oil and salt, mashing them with a fork.
Wash the tomatoes. Cut a cross into the bottom and blanch in boiling water for 1 minute. Let cool in ice water and dice them. Dress with oil and basil.

Serving

Make 3 quenelles of the potato mixture and place them on the plate, crushing them slightly. Thinly slice the cod and arrange a slice on top of each quenelle. Top with 2 tablespoons of the seasoned diced tomatoes.

Wine pairing

"Gloria" – White
Winery: Tenuta la Lunia – Campobello di Licata (AG)

EGGPLANT CANNOLI WITH RICOTTA WRAPPED IN CRISPY PASTA AND VINE TOMATOES

Ingredients for 4 people
Preparation time: 2 h

1 round eggplant, cut in half lenghtwise
Cornstarch, as needed, for frying eggplant
2 egg yolks, separated
Generous amount of oil, for frying
½ onion, chopped
¾ oz (20 g) fresh basil
Generous ¾ cup (200 g) cow's Ricotta cheese
Pinch of salt
Pinch of pepper
¾ oz (20 g) grated Ragusano PDO cheese (about 3 tablespoons)
4 *perlina* baby eggplant
7 oz (200 g) capelli d'angelo pasta
1 teaspoon (5 g) ground saffron

TOMATO SAUCE
¼ onion, chopped
7 oz (200 g) vine tomatoes
1¾ oz (50 g) basil
2 cloves garlic, unpeeled
Scant ¼ cup (50 g) garlic honey
Generous 1 tablespoon (20 g) extra-virgin olive oil

BASIL OIL
1 small bunch of fresh basil
Generous ¾ cup (200 ml) extra-virgin olive oil

TO GARNISH
1¾ oz (50 g) Ragusano PDO cheese, in shavings
Fresh basil leaves, for garnish

Method

Thinly slice one eggplant half into 16 rounds. Dip each round in the cornstarch. Wrap them around an aluminum cannoli mold, using a dab of one egg yolk to seal. Fry the eggplant rolls in plenty of oil.

Cook ½ chopped onion, the basil leaves, and remaining eggplant, cut into cubes, in a saucepan until softened. Add the Ricotta (there's no need to strain it) and finish cooking by seasoning with salt and pepper to taste. Blend, adding the remaining egg yolk and grated cheese. Transfer mixture to a pastry bag and pipe filling into eggplant cannolis. Meanwhile, peel and fry the *perlina* eggplant, which have been cut in half and are still attached, making sure to leave the upper part whole. Let cool.

Parcook the *capelli d'angelo* pasta in boiling water with the saffron. Spread out on a work surface to cool. Insert a stuffed eggplant cannoli inside the perlina eggplant. Wrap the *capelli d'angelo* pasta around the eggplant cannoli, already been wrapped in the *perlina* eggplant.

Bake the cannoli in the oven at 400°F (200°C/gas mark 6) until the pasta is crispy and lightly browned (the time depends on the type of oven).

TOMATO SAUCE

In a skillet, sauté the chopped onion and add the diced tomatoes and basil. Cook until the tomatoes soften and break down. Add the unpeeled garlic and honey. Cook over low heat for 20 minutes. Press through a fine-mesh strainer or food mill.

BASIL OIL

In a blender or food processor, blend the basil leaves with the oil. Pass through a strainer to make a green-colored oil.

Serving

Pour a generous spoonful of basil oil on the plate. Top with a crunchy eggplant cannoli; add the tomato sauce, the Ragusano shavings, and a few basil leaves to garnish.

Wine pairing

Maria Costanza" IGT – White
Winery: Cantina Milazzo – Campobello di Licata (AG)

STUFFED SCABBARD FISH WITH SICILIAN CAPONATA

Ingredients for 4 people
Preparation time: 1 h

2 lb (1 kg) scabbard fish

STUFFING
Generous ¾ cup (100 g) breadcrumbs
1 small bunch of parsley, chopped
Juice and zest of ½ lemon

SALMORIGLIO SAUCE
Scant ¼ cup (50 g) extra-virgin olive oil
Scant ¼ cup (50 g) water
2 teaspoons (10 g) lemon juice
Pinch of sea salt

CAPONATA
3½ oz (100 g) eggplant
½ onion
1 vine tomato
2 tablespoons (30 g) pitted green olives
2 teaspoons (10 g) pine nuts and honey
Scant 1 tablespoon (8 g) of capers
Scant ¾ cup (100 g) celery chopped
Scant ¼ cup (50 g) white wine vinegar
2½ tablespoons (35 g) extra-virgin olive oil
Pinch of chile powder

Method

Fillet the scabbard fish and remove the backbone. Scale and cut into 8 rectangles measuring 3–4 inches (8–10 cm) with a pastry cutter.

STUFFING
Make the stuffing by mixing the breadcrumbs, parsley, and the grated lemon zest. Gradually add the lemon juice, mixing constantly.
Fill 2 fillets with the stuffing. Wrap in parchment paper. Steam for about 20 minutes, or until fish is just opaque.
Season with the sea salt.

SALMORIGLIO SAUCE
Pour the oil, the lemon juice and the salt in a terrine. Warm the water separately. Gradually mix the warm water into the oil with a wooden spoon.

CAPONATA
Peel the eggplant, onion, and tomato. Dice all the vegetables, keeping them separate. Chop the olives, pine nuts, and capers. Arrange the vegetables in layers in a saucepan (celery, then eggplant, onion, tomato, capers, and pine nuts). Cook them for about 10 minutes over high heat, then add the honey and finally the vinegar.
Increase heat to high and reduce cooking juices until thickened, then reduce heat and cook over low heat for another 10 minutes. Turn off the heat.

Serving

Arrange the caponata on a plate and place the scabbard fish on top. Drizzle with a little salmoriglio sauce and garnish with a parsley leaf.

Wine pairing

"Vignavella" – White
Winery: Cantina Milazzo – Campobello di Licata (AG)

CORNUCOPIA OF CANNOLI WAFERS WITH SHEEP'S RICOTTA AND ORANGE MARMALADE

Ingredients for 4 people
Preparation time: 40' - Resting time for the pastry: 1 h

FILLING
Scant ½ cup (100 g) sheep's Ricotta cheese
2 tablespoons (30 g) superfine sugar
Generous 1 tablespoon (20 g) candied orange, diced

PASTRY
⅓ cup (50 g) all-purpose flour
2 tablespoons confectioners' sugar

2 tablespoons (10 g) cocoa
Generous 1 tablespoon (20 g) red wine vinegar
1 teaspoon (5 g) sugar
1 teaspoon (5 g) lard
Pinch of cinnamon
Oil, for frying

Confectioner's sugar, for serving
Orange marmalade, for serving

Method

FILLING
Strain ricotta liquid to make cheese creamier. Beat the Ricotta and sugar in a bowl. Add the diced candied orange at the end. Keep the filling in a cool place until ready to use.

PASTRY
Make the wafer mixture by mixing together all the ingredients by hand on a work surface (or using an electric mixer) until a smooth dough is formed. Let rest for about 1 hour at room temperature if you are using it immediately. You can also make it the evening before, keeping it overnight in the refrigerator.
Roll out a fairly thin sheet of pastry (1.5 mm) using a rolling pin or a pasta machine, making sure that you sprinkle it with all-purpose flour if it begins to stick.
Cut the pastry using an oval cutter (about 4 inches in diameter) based on the size of the metal cannoli mold.
Cover the metal cannoli mold with the pastry (it doesn't have to be greased) and seal the edges by brushing it lightly with beaten egg yolk.
Heat the oil in a large pot to 350°F (180°C). Add the cannoli and fry until golden brown. Drain on paper towels and let cool. Carefully remove from the molds.

Serving

Use a pastry bag to stuff the cannoli with the filling just before serving, so that they stay crunchy. Arrange the cannoli on the plate and dust with confectioners' sugar with a quenelle of orange marmalade on the side.

Wine pairing

Passito di Pantelleria "Ben Ryè" – Dessert wine
Winery: Donnafugata – Marsala (TP)

THE CUISINE OF SARDINIA

Legend has it that when God finished creating the world he found that he had a handful of stones leftover. He threw them into the sea and from these Sardinia and her smaller islands were born. Among the splendors hidden in the depths are those of the Maddalena archipelago, a group of harsh, craggy granite rocks, which have been carved by the wind and rain into bizarre shapes.

The southern coast is a series of untamed creeks and silent beaches, a feeling of earthly paradise on land and in the water to which the whole of Sardinia owes the majority of its charm. Things of beauty that are at times stark and essential, ruins of archaeological interest like around ancient Nora. The town of Cagliari, meanwhile, is a blend of monuments and airy urban spaces. Looking at it from the sea, it appears to perch on its hills. And then there's the cobalt color of the sea in wind-blown Gallura, the exclusive *Costa Smeralda*, and the memories of the Nuragic era or the house of Garibaldi on Caprera, the hero of the two worlds and a protagonist in the Italian Risorgimento. Sardinia is an island with an old-fashioned appearance, beaten by the sun and wind, rich in charm and mystery, where colors and aromas mix with the shades of the water and the odors of the Mediterranean shrub, a pastoral land of old beauty.

Farming is widespread in the wild Gennargentu hinterland and in the elevations that form a ring around it, while fishing, with its unique resources provided by the tuna of Carloforte and lobsters at Alghero as well as the sea reserves, completes the food scene.

Sardinia is an island that has known how to preserve its traditions, in terms of culture as well as cuisine.

The predominant vocation of Sardinians to sheep-farming is in fact born from the natural geography consisting of poor vegetation and just enough grass and few bushes; it is not a fixed farming life, but a nomadic one in pursuit of flock, with little else available to live on than the milk of their sheep, the meat of lambs or game, a little cheese and bread brought from home.

There are two types of bread that the women make, with the main purpose being durability. The first kind is called *Chivarzu*; cooked in domestic ovens, it sometimes ends up weighing almost 10 kilos. It is a soft bread that remains such for a long time. The other bread, perhaps more famous, is *Carasau* or *Carta da musica*, thus named as it resembles a sheet of paper music. It's a dry bread that's easy to transport, and must be dampened with water just before eating.

The pastoral tradition has developed an entire set of open-air cooking methods, of which the Sardinians are specialists. In addition to the spit – with which suckling pig, or *porceddu*, is cooked (once wild, now tamed) over an aromatic wood fire that imbues the robust meat with its aromas – there is also the typical *a caraxiu* system, which consists of digging a hole in the ground in which a fire is lit that is left to burn out. A suckling pig or lamb (sometimes even mutton) is wrapped in herbs and then placed in the hole. It's covered with earth and another fire is lit on top, which is kept alight for a long time until the meat is cooked.

Some recipes in particular were originally borne of the Sardinian need to preserve food and to keep it with them; some examples include *Merca*, a sachet of herbs that contains mullet cooked in salted water the salt preserving them for many days), and *Sa tacculas*, the same salt-preserving treatment applied to thrushes and preserved in cloth bags with myrtle leaves. In some villages, cooked hen is also preserved in this way.

Excellent Pecorino cheese is made from sheep's milk to be eaten as is or used as an ingredient in many recipes.

Indeed among the typical products, Fiore Sardo PDO (see box) and Pecorino Sardo PDO are excellent, produced from fresh and full-fat sheep's milk on the island; the young version is sweet, rich, and appetizing, while the aged Pecorino is aromatic and piquant.

In terms of the pasta dishes, in addition to *Culingiones*, the Pecorino-filled ravioli, we find *Malloreddus*, semolina gnocchetti that are often served with a rich sausage-based ragù, *Impanadas*, small timbales of pasta filled with pork or lamb, and *Zuppa gallurese*, or *Suppa cuatta*, made with stock-soaked bread and slices of *Casizzolu*, a fresh cow's milk cheese similar to Caciocavallo. Along the coast, it's easy to find pasta served with lobster and spaghetti and flavored with *bottarga*, a dried and salted mullet roe. The roe is fished in the coastal lagoons of Cabras, west of Oristano, in the first week of September. Extremely delicious with pasta, it is an ideal condiment for many dishes.

Also worth mentioning is the renowned Sardinian artichoke, used to advantage in many different recipes, whether raw or cooked.

Sardinia offers a countless number of desserts, one for each village or festival, from *Gueffus* with almonds and lemon zest to *Seadas* (fried pastry puffs with a cheese filling covered in honey), as well as amaretti cookies, honey-based ladyfingers, almonds, raisins, candied fruits, walnuts, and much more.

Every flavor in Sardinian cuisine meets its match in terms of wine. The region's winemaking, headed up by a great white, Vermentino di Gallura DOCG, covers all food requirements. Equally strong wines accompany a cuisine of vigorous flavors: Malvasia, Cannonau, Girò, and Vernaccia.

Finally, Mirto (available in red and white) is a fragrant liqueur that provides a conclusive note to the symphony of Sardinian flavors. Drunk chilled at the end of the meal, it has excellent invigorating and digestive qualities. Made by infusing alcohol with the bluish berries of the Mirto shrub, it is sweetened with honey or sugar. A white or greenish liquid is made with the Mirto sprouts, using the same procedure.

Sardinia is clearly a special island, filled with nature and a memory that preserves, unchanged, the cultural and culinary traditions.

FIORE SARDO DOP

THIS IS ONE OF THE OLDEST *SARDESCO* CHEESES, MENTIONED IN THE CHRONICLES OF THE EIGHTEENTH CENTURY. NOWADAYS ONLY LIMITED QUANTITIES ARE PRODUCED, ABOVE ALL IN CENTRAL SARDINIA, IN FORMS WEIGHING ABOUT FOUR KILOS WITH A TECHNIQUE THAT HAS REMAINED ALMOST TOTALLY UNALTERED OVER TIME. AS A YOUNG CHEESE, IT HAS A SUSTAINED AND COMPACT TEXTURE THAT IS GOOD FOR CHEESEBOARDS AND ALSO EXQUISITE GRILLED OR TOASTED. WHEN MATURE, IT FLAKES WHEN CUT AND HAS A COARSE-GRAINED STRUCTURE. GRATED, IT'S USED TO ENHANCE THE FLAVOR OF PASTA DISHES AND SOUPS.

LUIGI POMATA

"This land isn't like any other place. Sardinia is something else... Enchanting spaces and distances to travel, nothing finished, nothing definitive. It is like freedom itself," the English novelist D. H. Lawrence wrote in 1921 in his travel journal. A liberty that Luigi Pomata, chef and co-owner with his cousin Raffaele Mameli, the maître d'hôtel, of the restaurant *Luigi Pomata* in Cagliari, intuitively knew how to use to his advantage.

The descendant of an historic family of chefs and restaurateurs from Carloforte, the only inhabited town on the island of San Pietro and founded in the eighteenth century by a colony of Ligurian fishermen coming from Tabarka, a small island off the coast of Tunisia. Luigi didn't remain in his father Nicolo's restaurant. *"My father, following in his father's footsteps as my grandfather Luigi worked as a chef in the restaurant of Hotel Riviera in Carloforte, opened his own restaurant in 1968, which he still manages today,"* Luigi tells us. *"I graduated from the nautical institute and then the hotel institute."* In 1999, he started to work alongside his father in the family restaurant, making the most of the winter months to continue his training in Italy and abroad. *"I spent about 10 years traveling, working for leading restaurants in Milan, London, and New York. I worked as sous chef in restaurants with three Michelin stars, such as Oak Room of Marco Pierre White in London and Le Cirque and Osteria del circo of Sirio Maccioni in New York, and many others. Even though I don't use all the techniques that I've learned, I now have an excellent cultural preparation. This is a job that changes constantly where the training can never stop. The job is never finished. We can even learn from those washing the dishes or from the commis chef who's the last to arrive at the restaurant."*

In July 2006, Luigi decided to set up his own restaurant in Cagliari, the capital that blossoms like a turquoise flower in the south of Sardinia, a magnificent island in the middle of the Mediterranean. The island is ancient and mysterious, enchanting and untamed, with a landscape that alternates between mountainous profiles to scrub and forests, pools and lagoons to impetuous torrents, long sandy beaches to jagged and sheer cliffs. *"I am amazed by the purity of some areas of my region. It's most famous for the* Costa Smeralda, *but the south-western part is beautiful and yet to be discovered."*

Opening his restaurant was a challenge: *"For two months I went around looking at places to see what Cagliari had to offer and I established my restaurant based on this experience."* Situated in the historic center, with the possibility of being able to eat outdoors when the weather allows it, it's furnished in a youthful and minimalist style. *"It's a mix of all my experiences from traveling around the world."* 99 percent of the time, he serves fish. *"Especially raw fish, like an Italian-style carpacceria, or a restaurant serving mainly carpaccios."* Luigi's cuisine emphasizes the local territory by using native ingredients and revisiting typical dishes, then reworking them with new, lighter flavor combinations. In a way his creations are similar to the Basilica della Santissima Trinità di Saccargia in the Nuoro province, the most illustrious example of Pisan Romanesque style on the island, which was built entirely in local stone, black basalt, and white limestone.

A flexible cuisine, *"off the cuff, which comes together based on the products I find and like when I go to the market"*. That explains why the menu changes every two months, *"not only to follow the seasonality of the products, but also as a policy. I like to offer my customers something new."* Managing the cooking for both family restaurants, he cares about the fact that they have two different menus. *"In Carloforte our customers are tourists on vacation. In Cagliari, they are local people, individuals who work and want to go out and eat well, spending the right amount of money."*

In the restaurant that bears his name, he has been able to create a menu with dishes that range from 8 to 15 Euros, with the price including any water and cover and service charges. *"The ingredients are of the highest quality and cooked to order. We do 'fast food' in 38 square meters of kitchen. We have been clever about lowering the food costs involved in preparing vegetables."* All the dishes are also blessed by *"a wide selection of wine by the glass, homemade beers, and a great choice of sparkling wines, both Italian and French."*

Many are the examples of reinvented tradition. The Eggplant millefeuilles with layers of strawberry tomato, herbs, and semi-aged Pecorino cheese is a Sardinian take on Eggplant Parmesan. The spaghetti with sea urchins, bottarga, and carrot juice *"in which the sea urchins give a taste of iodine, the bottarga lends saltiness, and the carrot a sweetish aftertaste,"* instead rework the classic spaghetti with bottarga, the mullet roe preserve that is typical of the regional cuisine. On the other hand, there are *fregola,* the characteristic Sardinian durum wheat pasta that is small in size, a sort of grated pasta, which when made homemade is toasted in a wood-burning oven to give it a taste of wood and make it crisp. The traditional durum wheat pasta is usually cooked in fish or meat stock; Luigi offers it cooked in many ways. *"At the moment, it's on the menu served with king shrimp and Mozzarella puree."* He also unleashes his creativity in using the delicious Carloforte red tuna. *"I changed the way in which it's eaten. I offer it raw, alternating three different cuts on the various menus. With this fish, like with pigs, nothing is wasted and every part works well with a certain cooking method."* At the moment he is serving herb-crusted tuna steak with white onion caramelized in Cannonau balsamic vinegar, the most famous of Sardinia's red wines, and a tuna capocollo, with herbs and spices and roasted juices, fennel, and oranges. Among the dishes that he continues to serve, there's not just red tuna, served in different side dishes and cooked in several ways, but also breaded king shrimp with a Gorgonzola Sardo fondue (a blue-veined cheese made from goat's milk) and a Cannonau balsamic reduction, followed by *cassulli alla carlofortina. "These are the typical gnocchetti of Carloforte – they resemble gnocchetti sardi pasta, the malloreddus, but are smaller – with a sauce from my town of tomatoes, pesto, and Pecorino. Here the basil is pounded with the mint; then the pesto is combined with the tomatoes and pecorino to make it more delicate."*

According to Luigi, who's a member of *Jeunes Restaurateurs d'Europe*, *"nobody invents anything in cooking. Innovation is put to work on traditional recipes or typical products. This is always done intelligently, putting flavors together, playing on the sour, salty, sweet and bitter, setting them aside and picking them up again until you find your own taste, which may or may not be liked, but tries to reflect the customer's taste. The important thing is not to ruin the ingredient and not to use more than two or three ingredients per dish. I'd like the flavors of the individual products to be recognisable. I don't have a Baroque cooking philosophy, but a minimalist one. For me the ingredients aren't fois gras or caviar, but field tomatoes and a simple lettuce. In Sardinia, we are lucky to have natural products. We have organic produce at home."* Therefore it's a cuisine that stands out due to its simplicity. It resembles the Santuario di Nostra Signora di Bonaria in Cagliari, a small Gothic temple with a humble bell-shaped roof, whose essentiality stands out compared to the large eighteenth-century basilica of the same name, to which it is joined on the right side of the nave.

Luigi's working day is intense, also because the restaurant performs a catering service of an international standard. *"At 8:30 a.m., I will already have phoned the suppliers to find out what fish they have available and to order it. Someone will also call me at 6 a.m. to see if I'm interested in a certain product. Although they are people I trust who know what I want, I'll also make a trip to San Benedetto market in Cagliari in the morning to have a look at what's on offer in terms of vegetables, meat, and fish. On the other hand, for some special products, I receive supplies from small-scale producers in the area, which guarantee me home-grown ingredients like those in the past."*

In the evening, Luigi likes to stop and have a chat with his customers. *"I also go into the dining room during dinner or lunchtime to give the customer my recommendations, as well as to listen to his comments. I'm a chef who likes to question himself. Customer relations help me to develop. I accept criticism because it's constructive. If the idea that inspired a dish, which may arise not purely from seasonality or the ingredients, but also from a concept, hasn't been understood, I'll happily explain how it came about."*

Food traditions are still alive in Cagliari and Luigi, to emphasize this, is opening some themed establishments, *"those which have disappeared over the years to make way for new culinary fashions."* He is opening a restaurant *"where we'll serve solely barbecued meat and make a different type of fresh pasta every day, using gizzards and giblets to make the various sauces"* and a classic old trattoria *"where you will be able to eat minestrone and tripe, like in days gone by."* Luigi certainly isn't lacking in entrepreneurial enthusiasm. His business is stepping up, with the same intelligence that was used to found the Nuraghi, the megalithic monuments and symbol of Sardinia prehistory, the first evidence of rational construction skills. As we can see in the Nuraghic site of Su Nuraxi at Barumini, perhaps the most complete of the sites scattered about on the island, the truncated conical shape of the constructions facilitated the dry arrangement of large masses of stone from the bottom to the top.

This menu for this book is completely traditional. The starter, called New *capunadda*, is a new take on the typical tuna *capponata*, a Tabarkin specialty of Carloforte. *"Six or seven galettes soaked in water are arranged in a salad bowl. Some tuna, tomatoes, cut into wedges, and sliced white onion are added. It's dressed with oil, vinegar, salt, and pepper and garnished with basil or marjoram at the end."* For the pasta course, there's fregola cooked like a risotto with clams and lemon, a typical dish of regional cuisine, followed by Lamb with artichokes, saffron, and egg for the main course, which uses a meat that comes from the atavic pastoral traditions of inland Sardinia, a typical and renowned vegetable from the island, with tomatoes, asparagus, eggplant, and wild cardoons, as well as a classic Sardinian spice. In the autumn, it is commonplace to catch a glimpse of entire meadows stained with the brilliant purple of the floral stigmas of crocus among the just ploughed fields of the hills of southern Sardinia. To finish, the dessert is a *pardulas* semifreddo, a typical Easter sweet that is offered to guests in all families, a small cheese or Ricotta-based tartlet, flavored with orange or lemon.

These are dishes which trickle through the entire regional gastronomy, like the karst spring of *Su Gologone* in the Supramonte di Oliena area. The water gushes unstoppably from the rift of an imposing rock formation and its course, with a known depth of over 100 meters, but still partly undiscovered, is embedded in the soil of the whole of Sardinia.

NEW CAPPUNADDA

Ingredients for 4 people
Preparation time: 30'

TUNA
14 oz (400 g) fresh tuna scraps
7 oz (200 g) sea salt
¼ cup (50 g) brown sugar
2 teaspoons (10 g)
Black pepper
1 bunch of mixed herbs
(thyme, mint, marjoram)

GALETTE PASTRY
1 cup (150 g) flour
Generous ¾ cup (200 ml) water
1 tablespoon extra-virgin olive oil
Salt and pepper, to taste

GALE
6 red tomatoes
1 white onion
½ cup (100 ml) water
1 tablespoon vinegar
1 bunch of fresh basil
Salt, pepper, marjoram to taste

Method

TUNA
Wash the tuna scraps and dry them. Make the marinade with salt, brown sugar, flavored pepper and the mixed herb leaves. Place the tuna in the marinade and refrigerate, covered with plastic wrap, for 3 hours.

GALETTE PASTRY
Mix the flour with the water, oil, and salt to make a thick dough. Roll out the dough to ⅛ inch (½ cm) thick and cut into 2¾-inch (7 cm) squares. Prick with a fork and brush with oil. Season with salt. Bake on a baking sheet at 400°F (200°C/gas mark 6) for 7–10 minutes until golden and crisp. Let cool.

TOMATO-ONION SALAD
Cut a cross in the bottom of the tomatoes and blanch in boiling water for 30 seconds. Peel and cut into quarters. Remove the seeds, reserving them. Slice tomato. Finely julienne the onion and soak in a scant ½ cup (100 ml) water and 1 tablespoon of vinegar for about 20 minutes. Remove from the liquid and squeeze them dry. Sweat the onion in the oil in a frying pan for about 5 minutes. Wash the basil leaves and dry them (reserve some leaves for garnish). Puree in a blender with the water and reserved tomato seeds and a few tablespoons of oil to make a thick pesto. Add salt and pepper. Rinse and dry the tuna. Combine in a bowl with the tomatoes, the onion, and marjoram leaves. Add the oil, but no salt as it's already been salted. Mix well.

TUNA CAPPUNADDA
Cappunadda is a cold dish that's usually made in the summer. It's easy to make this specialty from Carloforte. 6 or 7 galettes are left to soak in water, making sure that they don't absorb too much water. They're then broken into different pieces and arranged in a large salad bowl. 6 or 7 tomatoes, cut into wedges, and a white onion, sliced, are added. It's dressed with oil, vinegar, salt and pepper.

Serving

Spread out the basil sauce on the plate. Place a gallette on top of the basil sauce. Arrange some of the tuna-tomato mixture on top; repeat 3 times. Finish with basil.

Wine pairing

"Entemari" Isola dei Nuraghi IGT – White
Winery: Cantine F.lli Pala – Serdiana (CA)

FREGOLA WITH CLAMS AND LEMON

Ingredients for 4 people
Preparation time: 30'

2 lb (1 kg) *arselle* (live clams), or other clams
2 tablespoons (30 ml) extra-virgin olive oil
1 clove garlic
1 bunch of parsley
1 large floury potato

1 cup (150 g) *fregola**
1 quart (1 liter) vegetable stock
Salt
1 red chile pepper, thinly sliced
1 lemon, not too yellow

*Fregola

A typical dish, *fregola* or *frugla* is a small-sized durum wheat pasta (with the appearance of a grated pasta). There are three different types based on size: small, medium, and large.
The real homemade *fregola* involves toasting in a wood-burning oven to give a smoky taste, while drying the pasta out at the same time. It's usually cooked in meat or fish stock.

Method

Wash the clams and place them in a container, covered with salted water, for a couple of hours to help remove any sandy residue.
Put the oil, 1 unpeeled clove of garlic, and a bunch of parsley in a wide pot. Cook the clams, covered, until they open up.
Transfer clams to a plate and strain the remaining cooking water, reserving it.
Remove the clams from their shells.
Boil the potato, remove the peel, and mash with the strained clam liquid.
Cook the fregola like a risotto, adding the stock a little at a time, for about 9–12 minutes.
Add the clams, chopped parsley, the thinly sliced chile pepper, and lemon zest at the end.

Serving

Spoon the creamy cooking liquid in the bottom of the plate and top with the fregola.

Wine pairing

"Villa di Chiesa" – white IGT – White
Winery: Cantina Sociale di Santadi – Santadi (CA)

LAMB WITH ARTICHOKES, SAFFRON, AND EGG

Ingredients for 4 people
Preparation time: 50'

2 lb (1 kg) leg of lamb
1 sprig of mint, chopped
1 sprig of thyme. chopped
1 lemon, zested
1 bunch of parsley
1 onion, chopped
Extra-virgin olive oil, as needed
2 cups (500 ml) dry white wine
1 sachet of saffron
10 oz (300 g) artichokes, dark green outer
leaves removed and purple heart
removed
2 eggs
Salt and pepper to taste

Method

Butterfly the leg of lamb and remove the bones and fat (or ask your butcher to do this for you), tenderizing it. Sprinkle with the chopped mint, thyme, and lemon zest. Roll it up and secure as tightly as possible with kitchen string.
Sauté the parsley and onion in the oil in a large pot. Add the leg of lamb and wine. Add the saffron and cook over high heat for 10 minutes.
Cover the pot and bake in a ventilated oven at 275°F (130°C) for about 40 minutes. After 20 minutes, add the cleaned artichokes (to clean, remove the dark green outer leaves and scoop out the bristly, purple center), cut into wedges. At the end of the cooking time, remove the leg of lamb and let rest on a cloth. Remove the artichokes and keep warm.
Off the stove, add the eggs to the cooking liquid and mix well. Season with salt and pepper to taste.

Serving

Arrange the slices of lamb on the plate with the artichokes and finish with the sauce.

Wine pairing

"Korem" IGT – Red
Winery: Cantina Argiolas – Serdiana (CA)

PARDULAS SEMIFREDDO

Ingredients for 4 people
Preparation time: 40' - Resting: 5 h

PASTRY
1⅓ cups (200 g) flour
1 egg white
2 teaspoons (10 g) lard

SEMIFREDDO
Scant ⅔ cup (130 g) sugar
Generous 2 tablespoons (36 g) water
Scant ½ cup (100 g) egg yolks
Generous ¾ cup (200 g) Ricotta cheese

1 sachet saffron
1 orange
¼ oz (7 g) gelatin (1 sheet)
2 quarts (2 liters) semi-whipped cream
Confectioners' sugar

SAUCE
Mixed berries
1 pinch of sugar

Method

SEMIFREDDO
In a saucepan, cook the sugar in the water, stirring occasionally, to 250°F (121°C).
Beat the egg yolks in a stand mixer. Gradually add the sugar syrup and beat until the mixture cools.
Add the semifreddo, strained Ricotta, saffron, and orange zest to the mixture.
Add the softened (in cold water) gelatin and lighten it all with the cream.
Spoon the mixture into the molds and let cool in a chiller.

PASTRY
Mix the flour with the egg white, lard, and a pinch of salt to make a smooth dough.
Roll it out. Cut into rounds that are about 4 inches (10 cm) in diameter.
Place the pastry rounds into molds. Bake in a ventilated oven at 400°F (200°C/gas mark 6) for 10 minutes.

Serving

Place 1 tablespoon of filling in the center of each round.
Arrange the molds on a baking sheet and freeze for about 5 hours.
Serve with a fruit or chocolate sauce and sprinkle with the confectioners' sugar.

Wine pairing

"Assoluto" Isola dei Nuraghi IGT White dessert wine
Winery: Cantina F.lli Pala – Serdiana (CA)

GLOSSARY

ACHILLEA

An herbaceous plant characterized by jagged-edged leaves and a slightly bitter taste, Achillea is used to flavor salads, soups, and various liqueurs. Thanks to its beneficial effects on the digestive system, is it also used in the preparation of natural medicines.

AGAR AGAR

Better known to the Japanese as kanten, agar-agar is a polysaccharide used as a natural gelatin and is obtained from various genera of red seaweed. Agar agar has a high content of mucilage (65%) and of Carrageenas (a gelatinous substance, known as alginate in Pharmacopoeia). The gelatin produced by agar agar has a mild flavor and is very nutritious because it is rich in minerals. It is used in the preparation of gelatin for desserts and aspic because it has the property of not affecting natural flavors. Preparation is quick and easy and requires little cooking; most of the preparation time is taken up by setting, which takes about an hour at room temperature. It is suitable for light refreshing desserts, particularly in summer.

ALKERMES

This very sweet liqueur has a bright red color, the name of which derives from "qirmiz", meaning scarlet. The Florentine monks of Santa Maria Novella, to whom its origin is attributed, prepared it by marinating cinnamon, cloves, nutmeg, vanilla and aromatic herbs in alcohol together with sugar with rose leaves and jasmine aromas. The characteristic red color was given by cochineal, a food coloring derived from the insect bearing the same name. Subsequently, some variations were introduced, in relation to the type and quantity of the spices used. Today Alkermes, the alcoholic content of which varies between 21 and 32%, is used almost exclusively in cakes and desserts.

BASTARDELLA (bowl with handles)

A semi-spherical metal bowl (copper, tin plated iron or stainless steel) with two handles, the bastardella is used for beating, cooking and reducing sauces directly over a flame or in double boiler fashion, or for beating mayonnaise or other cold sauces.

BAVARESE

Made from tea, milk, and alcohol, bavarese is usually served hot and can have numerous variations, such as the addition of an egg yolk, or the substitution of coffee for tea.

BAVARIAN CREAM

This is the name of an important sweet, with a light and delicate consistency similar to that of a cream or custard, belonging to the group of cold entremets, known as "soft serve dessert". Bavarian cream is easy to make and has a custard and whipped cream base, mixed with isinglass to give the mixture a thicker consistency. Fresh and candied fruit, jam or marmalade, chocolate, vanilla coffee, etc., can be added to this basic mixture. The concoction is then poured into a mold, with a central hole and low sides, which allow the sweet to cool down quickly and uniformly.

BISQUE

An exquisite sauce made from the carapace of crustaceans, bisque can be used to accompany various fish dishes. The shells, once cleaned, are crushed and toasted with a little oil and coarse salt, so that they release the albumin, which "binds" the dish. After twenty minutes, diced carrot, celery, tomato and onion are added with white wine and cognac. Once the alcohol has evaporated, water is added until it covers everything; the liquid is left to simmer for another twenty minutes. It is subsequently puréed at high speed or pressed through a sieve. Parsley, curry, or saffron is often added to taste.

BRAISING

A method of cooking used mainly for meat and poultry and extended, with some differences, to include some preparations of fish and vegetables. The term derives from "embers" and refers to the time when the main cooking instrument was the fireplace; today the same result is obtained by putting the dish into a low-temperature oven. In a professional kitchen, braising is done in a special pot that is dedicated for such purpose, the braising pot; in home kitchens a sealed heavy pot or cast iron casserole dish can be used. Generally red meats and game are braised; the meat, typically a joint of reasonable size, can be marinated in wine and vegetables before flouring according to the recipe and searing in oil, lard or bacon fat. Cooking, which must be very slow, should be done in the oven. As far as poultry is concerned, only duck is suitable for braising: the braising pot or casserole is lined with fresh bacon rind and vegetables that have been softened in butter (in which the duck is also lightly fried before proceeding with the cooking). Fish, unlike meat, must not be fried but simply placed on aromatic vegetables soaked in cooking liquid (wine or fumet). Here also, it is advisable to choose fish of a reasonable size, otherwise the rapidity of the cooking would make the exchange of flavors between the fish and the cooking base ineffective. Before braising, vegetables must be parboiled in salted water and subsequently placed in a greased braising pot and put in the oven. The vegetables that are best suited for this way of cooking are leeks, celery, carrots, cardoons and Belgian endive.

BRUNOISE

A term of French origin which indicates a particular method of cutting vegetables (very finely diced) and also a mixture of vegetables cut in this way. The most common brunoise is onion, celery, carrot, leek, and turnip, to which celeriac and peppers can be added. It can be used raw to add flavor to stews, casseroles and braised dishes or lightly fried in butter to garnish consommé and soups.

BRUSCANDOLI or BRUSCANSI (shoots or sprouts)

A term used in the Veneto region for two types of wild shoots or sprouts: hop shoots in the province of Padova, and Butcher's Broom in the province of Verona. The shoots are used to make a classic risotto in the style of asparagus risotto, preferably using Vialone Nano rice.

CHINA CAP

See chinois.

CHINOISE or CHINOIS

A French word used in international cuisine, it refers to a special steel conical sieve with very fine holes. The Chinois is used to filter sauces, broth, and other cooking liquids. It is different from the mesh strainer because being sturdier it is possible to press the filtered ingredients.

CIAUSCOLO

A type of sausage with a texture that resembles paté in consistency, ciauscolo is eaten spread on bread. Highly flavored parts of meat are used, such as ham, bacon, and shoulder pork with an adequate addition of fat. The flavors are simple, usually garlic, salt, and pepper crushed in a mortar, sometimes with the addition of a drop of wine. The sausage casing is made of the large intestine. The stuffed sausage is smoked for a couple of days over juniper berries and then matured for 2 to 3 months in a cellar. It is produced in an area extending from the Province of Macerata to a few municipalities in the Ascoli area up to the region of Umbria.

CLARIFIED BUTTER

Clarified butter is produced by removing most of the water and the casein from normal butter. Clarified butter can be found in shops under the name of concentrated butter, but it is also possible to make it at home. Clarified butter has a higher fat content than traditional butter: almost 100% instead of 86% because it does not contain water. To make clarified butter, take some butter and cook it in a double boiler for around 15-20 minutes.

COMMIS (chef)

A term used to denote an apprentice or assistant chef of another cook, an assistant reporting to a chef de partie, or a line cook.

COURT BOUILLON

A French term meaning "short boil" or "reduced broth," court bouillon is a flavored liquid used to poach fish and crustaceans. In its simplest form, it is made with salted water that is flavored with onion, celery and carrot, while in professional cooking there are various versions depending on the type and size of fish to cook.

FILO

Filo pastry, from the Greek word phyllo meaning "leaf," refers to tissue-thin layers of puff pastry. Characterized by a very short cooking time, it can be baked or friend in a large variety of dishes, and makes an excellent substitution for the roll casings of different international cuisines. Thanks to its versatility, it has found its way into Italian cooking. Unlike most common puff pastries, it is produced without any fat and thanks to its neutral taste it can be used in the preparation of both sweet as well as savory dishes. Traditionally and historically, it has been used throughout the Middle East for sweet pastries filled with hazelnuts and pistachios and dipped in syrup such as Baklava.

GOOD KING HENRY (Chenopodium bonus-henricus) or POOR-MAN'S ASPARAGUS

An erect, tall, perennial herbaceous plant that grows 11 to 30 inches (30-75 cm) high, Good King Henry has a thick rhizome and a light-colored stem. The numerous wart-like projections give it a slightly floury and sticky appearance. The lower leaves are wedge-shaped and have a long stalk; they are dark green at the top, light and floury at the bottom. The flowers are in the form of a leafless spike at the top of the stem and are formed by small brown-greenish flowers with 5 sepals and stamens. The seeds are black and shiny. This plant is widespread in the hills and mountain areas all over Europe, North America and in Siberia. It flowers from May to August amongst rubble, along fences, and near houses and Alpine huts. The young raw leaves are eaten in salads dressed with oil, pepper, lemon juice and nut kernels. The leaves, lightly boiled in salted water, are cooked like spinach and used in fillings, minestrone, and omelets or cooked in butter. The floral tips can be eaten like asparagus. The plant is rich in iron, mineral salts and vitamins with de-mineralizing, fortifying, anti-anemic, laxative, depurative, skin emollient properties.

ICE-CREAM MAKER

A multi-functional appliance ideal for preparing and serving ice-cream and sorbets made with fresh fruit, fruit juices and champagne, wine or liqueurs.

ISOMALT

Isomalt is a sugar substitute, a type of sugar alcohol, primarily used for its sugar-like physical properties. It has only a small impact on blood sugar levels and does not cause tooth decay. It has 2 kcal/g, half the calories of sugar.

LAVARELLO (Common whitefish)

Also known in Italy by the name of "coregone," lavarello belongs to the Salmonidae. It lives in large lakes. Its flesh is exquisite and it can be cooked in the same was as trout or perch--in the oven or fried in breadcrumbs.

LOMBO (Loin)

Loin of pork or carré (boned).

LOVAGE

An aromatic herbal plant that is also called "mountain celery" in Italy, lovage originated in Asia but can now be found all over central Europe. In Italy it is rare to find in the wild, but it is widely cultivated. Its leaves have an aroma that is similar to that of celery but much stronger.

LYON SHAPED FRYING PAN

A round, shallow metal pan with curved edges and a handle that is generally as long as the pan's diameter. It is still produced today in black metal, a material that is well suited for all types of frying as it is a modest conductor and regulator of heat.

MANTECARE

In general, this Italian term means to stir and render homogeneous a preparation of a buttery consistency such as ice cream. Nowadays the term is also used for pasta and rice; once cooked and strained, the pasta or rice is transferred to a pan together with sauce where it is also simultaneously mixed with grated cheese for binding, sometimes with the addition of butter or cream.

MANTECATO

Type of soft ice cream and also a recipe for baccalà.

MORCHELLA

Also called "sponge mushroom" it is a mushroom family characterized by a very high cap, composed of a network of ridges, and is of varying color from ocher to brown, gray or black. The flesh is white, pleasant-tasting and highly prized and excellent even dried. In classical cooking, the morchella is almost always cooked with cream and used as a pasta sauce and to accompany game; in general, however, it is not widely used in regional Italian cuisine, except for in the Modena area, where it is used to accompany tagliatelle and lasagne.

NAPPARE

An Italian term that means to spoon sauce or cooking juices onto a composed dish.

NEPITELLA (Blue cloud)

An herbal aromatic plant, Nepitella is widespread in the wild in meadows and other uncultivated areas. Although similar in appearance, its leaves are not to be confused with those of Basil Thyme or Mint.

PARFAIT

A French term indicating the classic light ice cream that is as soft as froth. It is prepared directly in the typical conical mold or parfait dish, or in a round cake mold.

PLANETARIA

The trade name of a pastry making machine for producing uniform dough that can be used in industry and at home.

QUENELLE

A very common preparation in French and international cuisine, quenlles consist of a "loaf" mixture of fish or meat, sometimes combined with breadcrumbs, and a light egg or fat binding. The mixture is cooked in boiling water or in a creamy béchamel sauce. "Quenelles" are served as an hors d'oeuvre, in soups, or to garnish important dishes.

RONER

The RONER, which was designed by Joan Roca and Narcís Caner respectively of the "El Celler de Can Roca" and the "La Fonda Caner," two restaurants in the Province of Girona, keeps water in motion and maintains a constant temperature all around the cooking recipient of a double boiler. Thanks to the Roner it is possible to control very accurately the temperature in low-temperature sous-vide cooking in the 41° F to 212° F (5°C to 100°C) temperature range. It can be adapted to any type of recipient depending on the type and quantity of food to be cooked.

ROSTI RING

A stainless steel, ring-shaped bottomless mold of varying diameters, rosti rings are ideal for cutting pastry for ravioli or biscuits, or for plating food in an elegant manner.

ROUX

Made from a mixture of equal quantities of butter and white flour, roux can be easily prepared at home. When the butter has melted, the flour is added and stirred until it is blended completely. It is then cooked for a few minutes to obtain a white roux and the longer it is cooked, the darker (and more deeply flavored) it becomes. Roux is used to thicken sauces such as Spanish cream and demi glace. It is also the thickening agent for béchamel sauce.

SAC À POCHE

A cone-shaped bag made of plastic or other waterproof material that is filled with a soft mixture and used to fill or decorate.

SAUTÉING

The term sauté (literally "jumped" in French, the past participle of "sauter," meaning to fry lightly) indicates a dish prepared mainly by lightly frying the main ingredients (tossing) in a frying pan, over a high flame. Because of the sudden hot temperatures to which the ingredients are subjected, a protective film is formed which seals them and prevents the loss of flavor, aromas and mineral salts. The sautéing technique is most suitable for cooking in a frying pan. It is done over a high flame without the addition of fat or liquid. Using this technique, it is possible to cook fish, vegetables and pasta as well as meat.

SKIMMING

The act of removing the foam that forms on the surface of a cooking liquid, such as a broth, sauce, or jam. The most suitable instrument for this operation is a skimmer or spoon or ladle with holes.

STEWING

A method of cooking meat, vegetables and occasionally fish, in liquid, the word in Italian (stufare) derives from "stufa" meaning stove, presupposing slow cooking, and in this sense, it is applied to meat. For vegetables, on the other hand, the term conveys cooking in a small amount of liquid or fat, over a very low flame. For fish the expressions "braising" or "poaching" are normally used.

TIMBALLO

Also called "dariola," the timaballo is a slightly conical mold, of the same height as the diameter, from ¾ to 9 inches (2 to 20 cm), and made out of tin-plated iron or stainless steel. The dish called "timballo" should be cooked in the mold by the same name, but in reality the name refers to anything made with pasta or rice, sometimes wrapped in shortcrust or short pastry, usually with a bolognese sauce and placed in various pans and cake tins. Dishes that are defined as "timballo" are the various "timpani," the meat and maccheroni bakes and the Neapolitan lasagna, the sartù and the bomba di riso (rice bomb) from Piacenza.

ZEST

A term which derives from the French "zoster," zest refers to thin strips of orange or lemon rind separated from the inside of the fruit and the internal white part.

RESTAURANTS

VECCHIO RISTORO DA ALFIO E KATIA
www.ristorantevecchioristoro.it
info@ristorantevecchioristoro.it
Via Tourneuve, 4 • Aosta

I BOLOGNA
Via Nicola Sardi, 4 • Rocchetta Tanaro (AT)

IL VIGNETO
www.ilvignetodiroddi.com
manolo@ilvignetodiroddi.com
Località Ravinali 19/20 • Roddi (CN)

ARIANNA
www.ristorantearianna.net
jrearianna@libero.it
Via Umberto I, 4 • Cavaglietto (NO)

IL SOLE
www.ilsolediranco.it
info@ilsolediranco.it
P.za Venezia, 5 • Ranco (VA)

LA LUCANDA
www.lalucanda.it
info@lalucanda.it
Largo Kennedy 1 • Cavenago di Brianza (MI)

CAPRICCIO
www.ristorantecapriccio.it
info@ristorantecapriccio.it
P.za S. Bernardo, 6 (Loc. Montinelle)
Manerba del Garda (BS)

MALGA PANNA
www.malgapanna.it
paolo@malgapanna.it
Via Costalunga, 56 • Moena (TN)

ZUR ROSE
www.zur-rose.com
info@zur-rose.com
San Michele - Appiano (BZ)

PERBELLINI
www.perbellini.com
ristorante@perbellini.com
Via Muselle, 130 • Isola Rizza (VR)

AGLI AMICI
www.agliamici.it
info@agliamici.it
Via Liguria, 250 • Godia (UD)

IL DON GIOVANNI
www.ildongiovanni.com
info@ildongiovanni.com
Corso Ercole I D'Este 1 • Ferrara

LE MASCHERE
www.lemaschere.it
info@lemaschere.it
Via Cesio Sabino, 33 • Sarsina (FC)

PARIZZI
www.ristoranteparizzi.it
parizzir@RISTORANTEPARIZZI.191.it
Via della Repubblica, 71 • Parma

BALDIN
www.ristorantebaldin.com
info@ristorantebaldin.com
P.za Tazzoli 20R • Genova Sestri

ARNOLFO
www.arnolforistorante.com
arnolfo@arnolfo.com
Via XX Settembre, 50 • Colle di Val d'Elsa (SI)

ROMANO
www.romanoristorante.it
info@romanoristorante.it
Via Giuseppe Mazzini, 122 • Viareggio (LU)

BRACALI
www.bracaliristorante.it
info@bracaliristorante.it
Via Perolla, 2 • Ghirlanda • Massa Marittima (GR)

ENOTECA LE CASE
www.ristorantelecase.it
info@michelebiagiola.com
Località Mozzavinci 16/17 • Macerata

IL POSTALE
www.ristoranteilpostale.it
info@ristoranteilpostale.it
Via R. De Cesare, 8 • Città di Castello (PG)

AGATA E ROMEO
www.agataeromeo.it
ristorante@agataeromeo.it
Via Carlo Alberto, 45 • Roma

VILLA MAIELLA
www.villamaiella.it
info@villamaiella.it
Località Villa Maiella, 30 • Guardiagrele (CH)

VECCHIA TRATTORIA DA TONINO
C.so Vittorio Emanuele II, 28 • Campobasso

TORRE DEL SARACINO
www.torredelsaracino.it
info@torredelsaracino.it
Via Torretta, 9 • Loc. Marina d'Equa
Vico Equense (NA)

AL FORNELLO DA RICCI
www.jre.it/ristoratori/scheda.aspx?id=19
ricciristor@libero.it
Contrada Montevicoli • Ceglie Messapica (BR)

LA PURITATE
Via Sant'Elia, 18 • Gallipoli (LE)

ANTICA OSTERIA MARCONI
Viale Marconi 233/235 • Potenza

LA LOCANDA DI ALIA
www.alia.it
alia@alia.it
Via Ietticelli, 55 • Castrovillari (CS)

LA MADIA
www.ristorantelamadia.it
info@ristorantelamadia.it
Corso F. Re Capriata, 22 • Licata (AG)

LUIGI POMATA
www.luigipomata.com
info@luigipomata.com
Viale Regina Margherita, 18 • Cagliari

ALPHABETICAL INDEX OF RECIPES

PHOTO CREDITS

All photographs by FOTO RCR, studioparma@fotorcr.it, except:

pages 10-11 courtesy of Max & Douglas
page 16 courtesy of Melanie Dunea
page 19 courtesy of Wynn Las Vegas
pagges 20-21, 22, 23 courtesy of Accademia Barilla
page 25 courtesy of Consorzio Produttori e Tutela della DOP Fontina
page 41 courtesy of Consorzio Tutela Nocciola Piemonte
page 85 top courtesy of Consorzio per la tutela del nome "Bresaola della Valtellina"
page 85 bottom courtesy of Consorzio per la tutela del Formaggio Gorgonzola
page 131 courtesy of Consortium Südtiroler Speck Alto Adige IGP
page 161 courtesy of Consorzio Tutela Formaggio Asiago
page 181 courtesy of Consorzio Per La Tutela del Formaggio Montasio
page 200 courtesy of Consorzio Aceto Balsamico di Modena
page 201 top courtesy of Istituto Valorizzazione Salumi Italiani
page 201 center courtesy of Archivio Fotografico della Provincia di Ferrara
page 201 bottom courtesy of Istituto Valorizzazione Salumi Italiani

page 233 top courtesy of Consorzio del Formaggio Parmigiano-Reggiano
page 233 center courtesy of Consorzio del prosciutto di Parma
page 233 bottom Prima Press/Getty Images
page 249 Nevio Doz/Marka Collection
page 265 courtesy of Consorzio tutela Pecorino Toscano D.O.P.
page 311 courtesy of Fratelli Buccoli Massimo e Giampiero s.n.c, Nocineria e Gastronomia Marchigiana
page 327 courtesy of Servizio Turistico Associato della Valnerina
page 343 courtesy of Caseificio De Juliis
page 359 top courtesy of Accademia della Ventricina
page 359 bottom courtesy of Consorzio di Tutela Formaggio Caciocavallo Silano
page 389 bottom courtesy of Consorzio per la Tutela del Formaggio Mozzarella di Bufala Campana
page 405 Marco Viganò/Marka Collection
page 437 bottom left courtesy of Fagioli di Sarconi IGP
page 437 right Franco Pizzochero/Marka Collection
page 453 Andrea Alborno/Marka Collection
page 467 Nevio Doz/Marka Collection
page 483 courtesy of Consorzio per la Tutela del formaggio Fiore Sardo Dop

THE PUBLISHER, FOR THEIR PRECIOUS CONTRIBUTIONS,
WISHES TO THANK:

Consorzio Produttori e Tutela della DOP Fontina
Consorzio Tutela Nocciola Piemonte
Consorzio per la tutela del nome "Bresaola della Valtellina"
Consorzio per la tutela del Formaggio Gorgonzola
Consortium Südtiroler Speck Alto Adige IGP
Consorzio Tutela Formaggio Asiago
Consorzio Per La Tutela del Formaggio Montasio
Consorzio Zampone Modena Cotechino Modena
Consorzio Aceto Balsamico di Modena
Istituto Valorizzazione Salumi Italiani
Consorzio del Formaggio Parmigiano-Reggiano
Consorzio del prosciutto di Parma
Consorzio del Culatello di Zibello
Consorzio di tutela olio DOP Riviera Ligure
Consorzio tutela Pecorino Toscano D.O.P.
Cooperativa Lenticchia di Castelluccio di Norcia
Consorzio Ricotta Romana DOP
Accademia della Ventricina
Consorzio di Tutela Formaggio Caciocavallo Silano
Consorzio per la Tutela del Formaggio
Mozzarella di Bufala Campana
Consorzio per la tutela Fagioli di Sarconi IGP
Consorzio di tutela dei Peperoni di Senise IGP
Consorzio Volontario per la Tutela del Pecorino Siciliano
Consorzio per la Tutela del formaggio Fiore Sardo Dop

WHITE STAR PUBLISHERS

WS White Star Publishers® is a registered trademark
property of Edizioni White Star s.r.l.

© 2009, 2010 Edizioni White Star s.r.l.
Via Candido Sassone, 24
13100 Vercelli, Italy
www.whitestar.it

Translation by Helen Farrell
Editing by Sarah Huck

ISBN 978-88-544-0451-9
1 2 3 4 5 6   14 13 12 11 10

Printed in China